THE BEST PLAYS OF 1951–1952

THE BEST PLAYS
OF 1951–1952

AND THE
YEAR BOOK OF THE DRAMA
IN AMERICA

EDITED BY
JOHN CHAPMAN

With Illustrations

DODD, MEAD AND COMPANY
NEW YORK - - - TORONTO
1952

INTRODUCTION

THIS volume is the thirty-fifth in the series of New York theatrical records begun by the late Burns Mantle and continued by the present editor. In preparation is a record of the seasons from 1894 to 1899, being done in collaboration with Garrison P. Sherwood, which will close the gap left by the death of Prof. George C. D. Odell of Columbia University. Odell's enormously detailed histories of the New York stage had chronicled its beginnings and were approaching the turn of the century. Mantle and Sherwood began working backward toward this same mark, first doing the Best Plays volume covering the seasons 1909-1919, and later preparing another for the series detailing the records of 1899-1909. Odell's last history brought his monumental labors forward to 1894, which left a five-year blank which presently will be filled.

During this last season, 1951-1952, the American theatre was plagued by the usual ailments and these ills seemed somewhat intensified. As is customary and habitual, complaint was made about the lack of productions, the lack of quality in productions and the lack of public support. The New York theatre fared better, of course, than the theatre in the rest of the United States. Hobe Morrison, keeper of business statistics for *Variety*, reported that, although there were more failures and more money was lost last season than during the season before, the public paid in more money at the box offices. High production costs and high running costs were accountable for financial disappointments, rather than any severe falling-off in public interest.

It was "the road" which suffered most. With disturbing unanimity, the Boston, Chicago, Philadelphia, Los Angeles and San Francisco correspondents for this book complain about the dearth of attractions—and the cities in between and to the South and Southwest were even less fortunate. Frequently a play would set forth on a season's tour, with bookings arranged for in all likely spots between Broadway and the Pacific Coast, and would fold up in discouragement after having got no further West than Chicago. Some attempt was made by the Council of the Living Theatre, in collaboration with the Theatre Guild and the American Theatre Society, to build subscriptions in road cities—subscriptions which would offer a chance of profit to touring companies. The success or failure of these efforts will be determined next season. In the mean time, theatre owners and managers across the country, who had begun the season hopefully with potential bookings of a dozen or more attractions, found themselves able to get only three or four.

But the theatre itself—the theatre as a part of our life and culture —showed heartening resilience. If the touring companies failed to come, local enterprises sought to fill the gap—even though handicapped by being unable to secure performing rights to recent successes. For a single instance, Dallas had eight active theatre groups, including the Municipal Theatre which financed such large musical productions as "Guys and Dolls" and a revival of "Porgy and Bess" —and also including Margo Jones' arena, Theatre '52, which ended its most successful season with a record of having produced twenty-five new plays.

One way or another, as the records of Odell, Mantle, Sherwood and Chapman testify, the stage persists. It is alive, and this book is a report on its present state of health.

JOHN CHAPMAN

Westport, Connecticut, June, 1952

CONTENTS

CONTENTS

ILLUSTRATIONS

THE BEST PLAYS OF 1951–1952

THE BEST PLAYS OF 1951–1952

THE SEASON IN NEW YORK

THE New York theatre season—which means the American theatre season, for all practical and most artistic purposes—was worse
statistically than it was artistically. In the year beginning June 1,
1951, only nine new plays managed to reach or exceed 100 performances. The nine plays were "The Fourposter," "Gigi," "I Am a
Camera," "Remains to Be Seen," "Point of No Return," "The
Shrike," "Mrs. McThing," "Glad Tidings" and "Jane." There were
some plays which deserved longer runs than they got—and others
which deserved only shorter runs than they got.

The city's drama critics, when asked by *Variety* in a poll to express their opinions of the season, replied almost with unanimity in
such terms as "worst ever," "terrible" and "lousay." They had been
forced to report upon such disasters as "Hook 'n' Ladder," which
ran for one performance; "Collector's Item," which garnered three,
and thirteen others which ranged from four to eight showings before
withdrawing from theatres in which they should not have been ex-
hibited in the first place. They had found, officially, that an old
musical, "Pal Joey," was the best that the much-vaunted American
musical stage could offer. They had seen at least one respected manager come forth with a series of ill-chosen clinkers, and they had
wearied of uninspired revivals such as Olivia de Havilland's
"Candida" and Claire Luce's "Much Ado About Nothing." They
were in no good mood in the Spring of 1952.

Among them were one or two—the editor of this book was one—
who were not quite so disheartened. This critic reported to the
Variety pollsters that the season was "not too bad," and he based
this opinion on the quality of the plays he chose as the Ten Best.
Not until Kingdom Come will there be ten perfect new plays, ten
great new works of art, in any one season. All one can do is hope
for the best and make do with what is available. In seasons more
prosperous than this one, the editor—Burns Mantle first and Chapman next—had to dig rather deep in the barrel for the ninth and
tenth best plays, and always he wished that dramatists had provided
something more worthy of preservation in a historical record such as
this volume is.

3

In the season just closed, there were ten plays which measured fairly high and would not have been too deep in the barrel in any given recent season. None was a makeshift or a stopgap. No play of the season approached greatness, but among them were to be found the qualities of craftsmanship, beauty, excitement and entertainment which make for satisfying playgoing. This editor's personal regret is that none of the season's offerings was a fast, solid, haw-haw-haw comedy; it took a revival of "The Male Animal" to remind us that there have been such works.

This editor's personal choice for the best play of the year was, and is, Mary Chase's "Mrs. McThing," a sweet and skillful fantasy. The Critics Circle, however, gave its prize to John Van Druten's "I Am a Camera," a play of delicate atmosphere and mood. The Pulitzer prize went to "The Shrike," a psychological melodrama by a new writer, Joseph Kramm. The very difference in these choices is an indication that the stage season, instead of being impoverished, was fairly rich. And the other works included among the Ten best— "Point of No Return," "Barefoot in Athens," "Gigi," "Jane," "The Fourposter," "Remains to Be Seen" and "Venus Observed"—embrace a wide range of skills and subjects. "Not too bad" is a reasonable summation of the year.

The year began June 13, 1951, with "Courtin' Time," a musical based on Eden Phillpotts' play, "The Farmer's Wife." It was not bad, but was not good enough, even with the affable and expert presence of Joe E. Brown, and it closed soon. The second of the season's offerings, also a musical, achieved a respectable run of 182 performances, thanks to the fresh charm of a youthful cast. The musical was "Seventeen," based on Booth Tarkington's novel. These two attractions took care of June.

Nothing happened until July 19, when a revue, "Two on the Aisle," had a success. The highlights included the clowning of Bert Lahr, the singing of Dolores Gray and the talking of Elliott Reed, and the show ran to mid-March of 1952. This was all for July.

The first offering of the real season, beginning in September, was "Lace on Her Petticoat," a small and sentimental comedy brought over from London by Herman Shumlin. It was too small and sentimental for New York audiences and its career was not a long one. Then came a curio, "Bagels and Yox," described in its program as "an American-Yiddish revue." It was aimed honestly at New York's Jewish theatregoers—and, since these audiences are numerous and show-minded, "Bagels and Yox" had a long run, even though it was no more than a night club floor show. In mid-September the indestructible Mae West came back in the indestructible "Diamond Lil" for a few weeks, and thrived moderately. Next appeared a revue which called itself "English-Yiddish," titled "Borscht Capades." It was about like "Bagels and Yox," but it didn't last as long. Then there was a comedy which might have had something, but didn't—"Out West of Eighth," by Kenyon Nicholson. Mr. Nicholson saw great possibilities for fun in a play about rodeo cowboys quartered in a hotel near Madison Square Garden, but he was unable to get these possibilities out into the open on a stage. It was a four-performance flop. Another September failure was "Twilight Walk," purportedly a thriller about a sex-twisted killer rampaging in Central Park.

Early October brought the first play claiming some style and quality—"Remains to Be Seen," by Howard Lindsay and Russel Crouse. These stage-wise collaborators had confected an affable comedy about a girl singer, a jazz-crazy building superintendent and a murder. They were a little slow in getting the play moving properly, but once it was moving it provided laughter, and it had engaging performances by Janis Paige, Jackie Cooper and Mr. Lindsay. The following evening there followed a handsome Theatre Guild production of Shaw's "Saint Joan," with Uta Hagen in the role once played by Winifred Lenihan and again by Katharine Cornell. It had a run of 142 performances. A revival of the Jerome Kern-Oscar Hammerstein "Music in the Air" had more charm than staying power, but it did serve to bring Charles Winninger and Dennis King back into musical comedy, and Jane Pickens made a very handsome prima donna. There began, in October, an invasion of Hollywood actors which had its victories and defeats all through the season. Melvyn Douglas and Signe Hasso teamed up in "Glad Tidings," a theoretically sophisticated comedy about magazine editing and bastardy. They fared moderately well. Then came a distinct novelty, Christopher Fry's religious verse-play, "A Sleep of Prisoners," which was acted in an Episcopal church on Madison Avenue. It was an allegory about Biblical characters in modern warfare, and had been written by Fry at the behest of a religious group in London, who wanted something suitable for church presentation. This was not a Broadway play, nor did it pretend to be; but it found audiences in New York and in churches, synagogues, auditoriums and theatres on the road. On October 17 there appeared one of the season's curios at the Empire Theatre—a comedy titled "Buy Me Blue Ribbons." It was about a rich, spoiled young man who fancied himself an actor and who produced a play to star himself. What made it a curio was that it was biographical; the rich young man, Jay Robinson, had produced the play and had given himself the leading role.

In the play plot he was so bad he was fired from his own show; in the Empire Theatre he endured for 13 performances.

Before the season ended, Hollywood was to send Broadway some very good and well-appreciated players, but Ginger Rogers was not too happily presented in a comedy, "Love and Let Love," on the evening of October 19, 1951. It was about two men who were in love with her, and she played two women with the help of a wig. Next, on October 24, came a sound success, "The Fourposter," by a Danish-English playwright, Jan de Hartog. This was a two-character play, and so far as the records show the most popular two-character play ever to be presented in New York. It detailed the life of a man and woman from their wedding night to middle age, and was given an expert performance by Jessica Tandy and her husband, Hume Cronyn. In June of 1952 Burgess Meredith and Betty Field were to take over the roles in order that Mr. and Mrs. Cronyn might go on tour. The Cronyns seemed to be about the only actors in Equity who were eager to tour. The final offering of October was Maxwell Anderson's "Barefoot in Athens," a drama about Socrates with modern implications. It was a failure, having only 30 performances, but it was nevertheless a good play and contained some of Anderson's simplest and handsomest writing.

November certainly was time enough for a rousing and rowdy musical to come along—and it did, on the first of the month. It was "Top Banana," concerning a group of old burlesque comedians working in the new medium of television, and it made Phil Silvers an upper-class comedian with a hilariously low-class delivery. The editor of this book was personally distressed when, on the night of November 8, he found himself all alone in approving of a New York waterfront melodrama, "Dinosaur Wharf," by a new writer, Joel Wyman. He thought that this was an absorbing and intelligently written play, but his lonely opinion could gain no more than four performances for "Dinosaur Wharf." Then Herman Shumlin came along with another London importation, "To Dorothy, a Son," which was a swift failure even though it was a hit in the West End. On October 22 there was a single performance at Carnegie Hall of the greatest artistic and box-office success of the year—a performance, or reading, of Shaw's "Don Juan in Hell" (the third and always unproduced act of "Man and Superman") by Charles Boyer, Charles Laughton, Cedric Hardwicke and Agnes Moorehead. Months later, the Critics Circle was in such a delirium of delight that it voted a special award to these players, who called themselves the First Drama Quartette. "Don Juan" played Carnegie Hall only once, then went on to other bookings around the country; it returned to the Century Theatre late in November for 38 performances, then toured some more; finally it came back in April to the Plymouth Theatre and, just before the season ended, rounded out an astonishing run of 105 performances for a "reading" without scenery and without action. It is doubtful that so many New Yorkers had ever before sat still for so long for so much talk. The final two entries in November were "Gigi" and "I Am a Camera." A young English actress, Audrey Hepburn, received such critical praise in the title role of "Gigi" that she was anointed with stardom in special ceremonies conducted by Gilbert Miller; and a young American actress, Julie Harris, received such praise for playing an English nymphomaniac in "I Am a Camera" that she was elevated to stardom during impressive backstage services at the Empire Theatre.

One of the Hollywoodians to venture onto Broadway was Gloria Swanson, who appeared early in December in a French-American comedy, "Nina," set in the locale named Out of Wedlock by the late Ring Lardner. When "Nina" was trying out in Philadelphia Miss Swanson caused a stir by announcing that she wanted to get out of it because it was no good. She did not get out, a contract having barred the way, and came on to Broadway, where critic Chapman agreed with her that the play wasn't very good and added that she wasn't either. One of the great troubles of the stage is that there aren't enough new plays, and nobody has suffered more from this lack than Katharine Cornell. Not having found a new piece suitable to her talent and liking, Miss Cornell agreed in the Summer of 1951 to appear at Central City, Colorado, in a revival of Somerset Maugham's "The Constant Wife." It was a success in the mountain mining town, so in December Miss Cornell brought it to New York and had a satisfying engagement of 138 performances. Elmer Rice, a foremost member of the Playwrights' Company, had no luck with a sentimental romance, "The Grand Tour." Nor did John Patrick with a ghost comedy, "Lo and Behold." But everybody had luck when Leland Hayward brought to the Alvin Theatre Paul Osborn's adaptation of John P. Marquand's novel, "Point of No Return," with Henry Fonda as the star. This play was enthusiastically greeted as expert theatre. The Osborn-Marquand comedy was followed by another of the season's events—the appearance of Laurence Olivier and Vivien Leigh in their much-praised London repertoire of "Antony and Cleopatra" and "Caesar and Cleopatra." Theoretically, this limited engagement—lasting from December 19 to April 12—was almost entirely sold out before the curtain went up; but, somehow, plenty of tickets became available at the box office before the end of the run. A late December presentation was "Legend of

Lovers," an adaptation of Jean Anouilh's French original, "Eurydice." It was a rather baffling version of the legend of Orpheus and Eurydice, notable mostly for a fine setting of a railroad station.

The first success of 1952 was the revival of the 12-year-old "Pal Joey," a musical by Richard Rodgers, the late Lorenz Hart and John O'Hara. It was a greater success than the original production had been, and it so moved the Critics Circle that the members violated their own constitution—which provides that only new works be given prizes—by voting "Pal Joey" the best musical of the year. Which it was. Next came a dreadfully shabby offering of a road company of a fine musical, "Kiss Me, Kate," and it got more than it deserved, which was eight performances. The City Center had an excellent revival of Eugene O'Neill's "Anna Christie," with Celeste Holm as Anna. George S. Kaufman and his actress wife, Leueen MacGrath, tried with unhappy results a fantasy about reincarnation titled "Fancy Meeting You Again." Then the ebullient José Ferrer produced, directed and began acting in Joseph Kramm's "The Shrike," bringing excitement to the mid-January theatre. "The Shrike" could have run much longer than it did; but it closed on May 31 because Ferrer was obligated to make a movie and no other actor had been found who was considered worthy of taking his place. Next came another O'Neill revival, "Desire Under the Elms," well staged by the American National Theatre and Academy. Ever since 1934, *aficionados* of the Clemence Dane-Richard Addinsell musical fantasy, "Come of Age," have been wistfully hoping it would come back and earn the success it should have had in the beginning. So the City Center revived "Come of Age," with Judith Anderson in her original role, but the result was about the same. Thirty-five performances in 1934; thirty in 1952. At the end of January an English movie star, Glynis Johns, could earn only five performances in another of Herman Shumlin's importations of London hits, "Gertie."

Not for some time had S. N. Behrman, American expert on parlor comedy, been represented by a play; but he ushered in the month of February with a bright comedy, "Jane," based on a Somerset Maugham short story. Following the success of "Don Juan in Hell," Emlyn Williams appeared in another sceneryless and actionless "reading"—selections from the works of Charles Dickens. Dickens himself had been a great attraction, in England and in America, reading his own stuff from lecture platforms; and now Williams, made up as Dickens, repeated the success. Four evenings after the refreshing Dickens impersonation there came one of the low points of the season—a baffling and baffled comedy titled "Collector's Item" which had an unearned run of three performances. Then things picked up with Christopher Fry's comedy-in-verse, "Venus Observed," with pleasant performances by Rex Harrison and Lilli Palmer. One week later things were even better when the American National Theatre and Academy presented Mary Chase's "Mrs. McThing." A run of only two weeks was all that was planned or hoped for, for this was a play written for children. Childish grown-ups took a liking to it, however, as they once had embraced "Peter Pan," and the fantasy ran beyond the season's end. It was interrupted so that its company, headed by ANTA President Helen Hayes, could play Central City, Colorado, in August of 1952, and was scheduled to return to Broadway in September.

Another English success, "Women of Twilight," depicted life in a boarding house for unwed mothers and their nameless infants as the first offering of the month of March. It lasted a week. Cornelia Otis Skinner came in with "Paris '90," a sentimental revue of Paris in the 1890s with Miss Skinner playing all roles—mostly characters painted by Toulouse-Lautrec. It was an elaborate production scenically and a successful one artistically, and Miss Skinner planned to take it on tour during 1952-1953. Another ANTA revival, "Golden Boy," had a run of 55 performances with John Garfield again in the title role. It was Garfield's last stage appearance; a few weeks later he died of a heart attack. An interesting actress, Gusti Huber, appeared in a drama about Viennese refugees, "Flight into Egypt." "One Bright Day," a treatise on ethics in a pill factory, failed to find a public but it did reveal some promising writing by a newcomer, Sigmund Miller. A determinedly whimsical musical, "Three Wishes for Jamie," served as a vehicle for Anne Jeffreys and John Raitt, and the month of March finally went out in confusion with Truman Capote's adaptation of his own novel, "The Grass Harp." This fantasy about people escaping from the world by living in a tree house was not well regarded by many reviewers, but the minority in its favor were vociferous, acclaiming its beauty and hailing Capote as a fine new talent in the theatre.

April got off to a practically unnoticeable start with another fantasy, "The Brass Ring," which was followed by a moderately regarded psychological Western, "The Chase," by Horton Foote. This play revealed the movies' John Hodiak as a capable man on a stage. ANTA contributed another public service by reviving the Virgil Thomson-Gertrude Stein opera, "Four Saints in Three Acts." Then Olivia de Havilland absorbed some critical punches for her "Candida," but was comforted by the fact that the production had already done very well on tour and probably made money. Another one-performance nightmare was "Hook 'n' Ladder," but theatregoers cheered up the next night when the City Center revived "The Male Animal." This James Thurber-Elliott Nugent comedy, dating from 1940, was hailed in the press as the best comedy of the season—a rueful commentary on one of the season's shortcomings. Nugent was in his original role, and Robert Preston, from the films, was found to be an excellent comedian.

On May 1 Claire Luce had a four-performance engagement in "Much Ado About Nothing," and on May 5 a handsome revival of "Of Thee I Sing" was presented at the Ziegfeld. The reception of this well-remembered political satire was mixed; Chapman reported that Washington is funnier now than it was in 1931—a circumstance which dated the satire of the show. A hapless new edition of "Shuffle Along" managed to last four performances—just at the time of year when a new musical was needed to liven Broadway's Summer play-bill. On May 16 a good Summer show came along—"New Faces of 1952," a revue, and the season ended with the City Center's revival of "First Lady" and ANTA's new play, "Sunday Breakfast," which wasn't very good.

Holdovers from the previous season which ended long runs included "Kiss Me, Kate," with 1,077 performances, "Call Me Madam," with 644 and "Gentlemen Prefer Blondes," with 740. Continuing strong in public favor were "The Moon Is Blue," "The King and I," "Guys and Dolls" and that well-loved ancient, "South Pacific," which had racked up 1,294 performances at season's end and shown no signs of tiring.

THE SEASON IN BOSTON

By Elliot Norton

Drama Critic of the *Boston Post*

THE theatre managers will remember it with distaste, for their playhouses had altogether too few attractions. Yet the Boston theatre season of 1951-52 presented many good attractions, and the record of its course gives some—if not too many—reasons for cheerfulness.

Some of the best of the year's new productions were presented here in tryout, prior to Broadway: "The Fourposter," for instance, and "Point of No Return"; also, the exhilarating four-man wonderwork "Don Juan in Hell," the rousing musical "Paint Your Wagon," and, for those who liked it—count me not among them—"Top Banana."

There were revivals, too, like "Oklahoma!", which is always pleasant and always welcome, as well as some of the best shows from the post-Broadway season: "Darkness at Noon," presented here with Edward G. Robinson, "The Rose Tattoo" with the brilliant original team of stars, Maureen Stepleton and Eli Wallach, and "The Autumn Garden," with Fredric March and Florence Eldridge.

From happy times on Broadway there also came to Boston, to delight many paying playgoers, the revue "Two on the Aisle," with Bert Lahr and Dolores Gray; the musical comedy "Gentlemen Prefer Blondes," with Carol Channing as its large and hilarious Lorelei Lee, and the elegant revival of "The Constant Wife," with the no less elegant Katharine Cornell.

Two "Fledermice" chased each other into town in a senseless booking competition that nettled the managers but brought some pleasure to playgoers during the Fall. In the Spring, by way of showing that the booking office can destroy the ballet, too, once it makes up its little mind, three major ballet companies followed one another at intervals of two weeks.

Here again, the theatres got a bad deal, because the ballet fans hadn't enough money to support all three companies in such a short period. But the same fans had a wonderful opportunity to select at least one or two good evenings.

11

In the statistics and records, there are further facts that cheer.

The records show, for example, that 46 plays and musicals were presented during the year in the regular downtown playhouses of Boston proper—which you may, if you prefer, call proper Boston.

In the previous year, in the same theatres, there were only 43. In the 1949-1950 season, 39.

According to records compiled and printed by *Variety*, the trade newspaper of Show Biz, the amount of money paid into the legitimate theatre box offices of Boston during the 1951-52 season was the largest amount expended in any city outside New York. The sum runs just under $2,000,000. Note, please, that Boston's population is considerably smaller than that of Chicago, Philadelphia, Los Angeles and San Francisco, whose box-office receipts had always previously exceeded ours.

A further report, which is not exactly a statistic but is nonetheless accurate and impressive, is this: the Boston Summer Theatre, a professional operation in downtown New England Mutual Hall, not only had the most successful season in its history, but apparently made a greater profit than any other house on the entire straw hat wheel.

Since we are dealing with the facts of theatrical life, perhaps it needs to be stressed that the competition with television—if you'll excuse a nasty word—is apparently greater here than anywhere in the country. The survey experts say that there are more TV sets per unit of population (that means people) in Greater Boston than in any urban area of the United States.

Here are one or two more comparative figures:

Number of Musicals Presented in Boston During 1951-52	11
Number of Musicals in Previous Year	15
Number of Tryouts in 1951-52	28
Number of Tryouts in 1950-51	21
Number of Tryouts Which Subsequently Became Hits in New York	6
Number of Tryouts Which Became Hits in Previous Season	7
Longest Run, Season of 1951-52 "Affairs of State"; "The Moon Is Blue"	6 weeks
Longest Run, Previous Season "Mister Roberts"	21 weeks

When the season of 1951-52 officially began, on June 1, 1951, there was one show only available in Boston. Written by Sally Benson from Booth Tarkington's novel, with lyrics by Kim Gannon and music by Walter Kent, the mild musical comedy called "Seventeen" had opened at the Shubert Theatre on May 28 and would continue there until Saturday, June 16. Neither the opening nor the closing created a furore. Although it was financed in part by Milton Berle, nobody hated "Seventeen." On the other hand, nobody fell into the aisle with excitement on watching it. Of it, this could be said, that it was not strong enough to survive in the theatre of the moment.

Except for the lights burning brightly at the Boston Summer Theatre, the playhouses of the city were dark then until September 10.

The Summer Theatre opened on July 2, with a musical version of "Alice in Wonderland," the book and lyrics by Frances Pole, the score by John Sacco. It was not very good, but it appears to have been profitable.

Subsequent shows at this air-cooled Summer theatre in New England Mutual Hall were these: week of July 9, Eve Arden in "Here Today," a box-office bonanza; week of July 16, "Brigadoon," in one of the less effective but most profitable productions which played the summer wheel; week of July 23, "Mirror, Mirror," a new play, and a dreary one, featuring Kay Francis; week of July 30, Julie Haydon in "A Streetcar Named Desire"; week of August 6, Carol Bruce in "Pal Joey"; week of August 13, Melvyn Douglas and Signe Hasso in "Glad Tidings," a pre-Broadway tryout; week of August 20, Arthur Treacher in "Clutterbuck"; week of August 27, Joan Blondell, in "Come Back, Little Sheba"; week of September 3, Joan Bennett (with her daughter, Melinda Markey) in "Susan and God"; week of September 10, Eve Arden in "Here Today," a return engagement, to close the season.

What we call the "regular downtown season" began here at the Colonial Theatre on Monday, September 10, even as Eve Arden started her second cleanup week at the Summer Theatre.

The first of the new attractions was a tryout, "Remains to Be Seen," a thriller-chiller-mellerdrama by Howard Lindsay and Russel Crouse, which generated some laughter, some few melodrama chills when a lady came out of the wall, and some element of fever when Janis Paige emerged from her clothes.

"Remains to Be Seen" remained to be fixed at the Colonial Theatre during three weeks. It remained to be enjoyed in New York for several months, but that is part of another record.

On the 17th of September, two new productions were presented to Boston for the first time. One was Shaw's "Saint Joan," starring Uta Hagen, the other a new musical comedy called "Top Banana." There's a gamut!

On the opening night at the Plymouth Theatre, Miss Hagen was not a great Joan. She suggested the peasant rather notably, but the saint somewhat less. Four days later, she was making some progress in the character, though she still hadn't mastered it.

On the other end of the gamut, at the Shubert Theatre, Phil Silvers in "Top Banana" played to top business and all the local fruit fanciers were enthralled. Here and there a critical curmudgeon frowned and insisted that this banana did not 'peal to him, but the public heeded him not at all.

The only other show of the month was "Kiss Me, Kate," playing a moderately successful engagement at the Opera House, with Robert Wright, who seemed not to be in good voice, and Holly Wright, who did.

October began with another musical revival. For the seventh time "Oklahoma!" came back to town, and those who saw it were well pleased. It wears well, and so far as Bostonians can tell, is continuously well played, though the cast is continually changing.

On the same night of October 1st, while "Oklahoma!" lighted up the Colonial Theatre, the Plymouth received a turkey called "Love and Let Love," in which Ginger Rogers played two sisters, one of whom had a silly baby voice. Everybody who could buy a ticket rushed to see and hear the two sisters and came away dazed by the play, which was pretty silly, and not particularly impressed by Miss Rogers, who is no Duse. The star blamed the author for her trouble, insisting he wouldn't fix the script or do anything about the direction. After a legal hassle of some kind, he agreed that she might import Bretaigne Windust to take over the staging. Mr. Windust was too late.

The first of the Fledermice arrived at the Opera House on October 8. This was the Metropolitan Opera Company version, but its cast was somewhat less gifted than that which had offered "Fledermaus" during the previous Spring as part of the Metropolitan repertory. The music critics, solemn fellows, frowned at the cast change.

"Paint Your Wagon" arrived the next night, at the Shubert, starring James Barton. With a roaring chorus of bearded he-singers and with Mr. Barton singing inaudibly part of the time, it was stimulating but imperfect. Mr. Barton recovered some of his voice during four weeks at the Shubert Theatre and used it rather well in a pretty song which Composer Frederick Loewe and librettist Alan Jay Lerner wrote for him during the engagement here. It was called "I Followed a Wand'rin' Star."

"The Fourposter" followed on the 15th of the month at the Plymouth. Before most of the playgoing public could be convinced that any play with only two characters could really be fun, it was gone, and the skeptics have been kicking themselves ever since. One week was not enough.

"Darkness at Noon" came to Boston with Edward G. Robinson as the Communist captive Rubashov. It was well played and well received at the Colonial Theatre during a three weeks' stand.

The month ended theatrically with the first presentation at the Wilbur, on the 31st, of a British comedy. Called officially "To Dorothy, a Son," it was called other names by critics who found its humor singularly strained. Ronald Howard, son of Leslie, played pleasantly in it, however, and looked rather eerily like his late father in some scenes and attitudes. Two thin weeks for "Dorothy" and her son.

November began brilliantly and proved the busiest month of the season, with ten attractions, some good, some bad, yet all interesting.

On Thursday, the 1st, Concert Manager Aaron Richmond escorted "Don Juan in Hell" into Symphony Hall for two performances only. Both performances had been sold out in advance to audiences who keenly appreciated the brilliant reading by the First Drama Quartette. Set that down as something really memorable, with credit to Charles Laughton, a lounging and sardonic Lucifer; to Agnes Moorehead, a charming Dona Ana, Cedric Hardwicke as Ana's perplexed father, and Charles Boyer, a fabulous Don Juan.

On Saturday of that same week, a comedy called "Never Say Never" arrived at the Plymouth. Nobody paid much attention. It wasn't worth much attention.

They were opening thick and fast now. Gloria Swanson got to the Shubert on Monday, November 5, in a comedy adapted by Samuel Taylor from the French of Andre Roussin. Called "Nina," this had run for many months in France, but apparently a great deal of the dialogue which had convulsed Parisians would have provoked the gendarmes here—or even in New York! In eliminating the blues, Mr. Taylor was unable to find enough substitute jokes. The essentially British performances of David Niven and Alan Webb were curiously out of key against a setting which kept Notre Dame incongruously in the background. Some repair work was done here, but not enough.

The night after "Nina," the Colonial Theatre got "Point of No Return," Paul Osborn's adroit adaptation of John P. Marquand's novel. It was just about perfect at the opening, less perfect a few nights later, when everybody began tinkering. Sometimes they have to fix plays here; sometimes they would do better by leaving them alone. Perfect or otherwise, Bostonians liked "Point of No Return" and Henry Fonda in it during a three weeks' run.

A company of Irish players, most of them young people, turned up now at John Hancock Hall with a repertory of three plays, which they presented without very much success during the next two weeks. They opened with Michael MacLiammoir's fantasy "Where Stars Walk," on Monday the 12th. On Thursday evening they offered "Drama at Inish" for the remainder of the week. Beginning Tuesday, November 20, they presented Paul Vincent Carroll's "Shadow and Substance"; this proved somewhat better in the playing and also more popular than their other production. It was offered on Tuesday, Thursday and Saturday.

In the meantime Clare Boothe Luce's drama, "Child of the Morning," arrived at the Shubert Theatre on Monday the 19th. Two weeks later it closed down for good, with future bookings canceled.

This play is unusual, a religious drama, some of it curiously compelling, some of it almost incredibly corny. It tells the story of a 16-year-old girl who lives in a Brooklyn tenement section, a sweet and pleasant child who is actually a mystic: at prayers alone, she sees and talks to a Heavenly Guide.

Like Maria Goretti, the 11-year-old Italian child who died in 1902 defending her honor from an attacker, this girl is shot to death by a vicious young reefer addict who makes his way into her bedroom.

Clumsily contrived, full of dreadful old clichés of melodrama, "Child of the Morning" had nevertheless some moments of high dramatic insight. As the child, the movie actress Margaret O'Brien demonstrated great power, suggesting with complete conviction the perfect sanctity and serenity of the mystic.

The play was closed down here and withdrawn from production. Presumably it was to be rewritten in large part, then re-staged in the event that the O'Brien girl was still available.

Another kind of theatrical exhibit, the Jose Greco Ballet, spent two pleasant weeks at the Boston Opera House, beginning Monday, November 26, the same night that "The Moon Is Blue" returned to town at the Plymouth. The original "Moon Is Blue" company had started here during the previous year and had gone on to vast success in New York. Company No. Three brought it back, to play it pleasantly for six weeks.

The major event of December was the first production in Boston of Tennessee Williams' "The Rose Tattoo." Although some of the New York players had quit, Maureen Stapleton was on hand here to act brilliantly and Eli Wallach was too. "Tattoo" stayed at the Colonial for two weeks beginning December 3, closed down during the week before Christmas, reopened for eight more performances on Christmas Eve.

Following the Tennessee Williams drama, on December 4, the comedy "Fancy Meeting You Again" by George S. Kaufman and Leueen MacGrath arrived, this at the Wilbur Theatre. This comedy of reincarnation had many very funny moments, and it was played slickly by Miss MacGrath, by Glenn Langan and the others. A try-out, it was revised somewhat here and some more later in Philadelphia. The record shows, however, that improvements were insufficient.

On the 13th, the second "Fledermaus," with Irina Pettina starred, appeared at the Opera House for four performances only. Four seemed to be enough.

The only other events of December, 1951, in Boston, were a return engagement at the Opera House of "The Student Prince," which has been there so often now that everyone has lost count and not a few no longer care, and the arrival of a new musical called "Month of Sundays."

One of the year's lesser events, "A Month of Sundays," derived from Victor Wolfson's drama "Excursion," which recounted what happened when a New York harbor excursion boat skipper decided on his last run to take his passengers to a Caribbean island instead of back to port.

With a book by Burt Shevelove and music by Albert Selden, this one had Nancy Walker as a swaggering passenger and Gene Lockhart as a troubled old skipper.

Clumsily written and dubiously staged, it never really got away from the dock. Margaret Webster arrived to help with the direction, but the Philadelphia record will show that "A Month of Sundays" was closed in drydock there.

With the new calendar year, the openings began to be spaced more widely apart.

The new ones included "Gertie," an English comedy which was obviously not long for this world. The pert English comedienne, Glynis Johns, who was later to be made a Dame by the British government, was this drama's only ornament. There is nothing like a Dame.

"Gertie" opened at the Plymouth Theatre, on January 14, the evening Cornelia Otis Skinner chose to make her first appearance at the Shubert in "Paris '90," her virtuosic one-woman panorama of Paris in the age of Toulouse-Lautrec.

The booking office being more confused than usual, there were no openings between the 14th of January, which had brought the two just named, and the 28th, when three others arrived simultaneously: Emlyn Williams in his Dickens readings, at the Plymouth, "The Autumn Garden," with Fredric March and Florence Eldridge, at the Colonial, and, at the Shubert, what was identified in advance as a modern version of "The Merry Widow."

Beautifully played, "The Autumn Garden" attracted only modest business to the Colonial Theatre. Beautifully read, the Dickens evenings of Emlyn Williams attracted little advance interest but won a big following by the end of the single week. "The Merry Widow" was not a vast success.

The booking office policy of opening attractions in pairs by way of making life more difficult for everyone, continued into February. On Monday the 11th of that month, the shows which opened simultaneously were the musical "Three Wishes for Jamie" and a new prose play by Alexander Greendale with Henry Hull as star and the provocative title, "A Little Evil." Headquarters for "Jamie" was the Shubert, for the other, the Plymouth.

As the New York record will show, "Jamie" was derived from a novel called "The Three Wishes of Jamie McRuin," a lilting Irish romance. Its lilt was only imperfectly reproduced for the stage by Abe Burrows. He McRuined it.

As regards "A Little Evil," it appears to be true—judging by those who had to see it—that the title was an understatement of this drama's quality.

The only other attraction of February, 1952, was called "The Long Watch." It was a melodrama about WAVES on a Pacific island, written in part by Morrie Ryskind, who supplied the jokes, and in part by Capt. Harvey Haislip, U.S.N., who furnished the story. Both jokes and story were in short supply on the opening night, which was Monday the 18th.

There were two ballet companies here in February, as the booking office made a wonderfully impressive effort to wreck the dance business entirely—and a third in March!

The Monte Carlo company, a bedraggled troupe, arrived at the Opera House February 4 for a week. Very few people went to see them.

On February 18, along came the Ballet Theatre, an excellent organization. Not enough people went.

On March 17, the Sadler's Wells Theatre Ballet appeared to very good business, also for one week, and also at the Opera House.

There were other plays in the meantime, some of them good and some of them not.

"Flight into Egypt" was at the Colonial beginning on March 3, for one week only—not long enough to iron out all the script problems. This melodrama by George Tabori had Paul Lukas and the gifted Gusti Huber as principal players. It was directed by Elia Kazan and produced by Irena Mayer Selznick. In advance, it looked most imposing. On the stage, it seemed less than entirely convincing, yet exciting in many ways.

Here it was altered. A troublesome final scene was rewritten three times—then finally discarded for New York, which saw another. If some of the discarding and rewriting had been done before it had first been put into production "Flight into Egypt" might well have been a success.

About this time, Boston was visited by the Yiddish-American revue, "Bagels and Yox," which had its first public performance here at the Shubert Theatre and flourished for two weeks. Its audiences were mostly special theatre parties.

"Affairs of State" came into the Plymouth for six weeks on the 10th, with June Havoc starred. It was terrible, but the audiences didn't catch on. It prospered.

On Thursday, March 13, Truman Capote's "The Grass Harp" had its "world première" at the Colonial Theatre and stayed there for nine days. Opinions of its quality were mixed, ranging from lyrical praise to outright calumny. Business was bad; backstage there was friction as some elements of the management strove to eliminate symbols and solemn significance and to substitute simplicity. They lost, and a tender play was swamped by pretentious nonsense.

The only other entries of March were a slender and unsuccessful comedy called "Salt of the Earth" and the revue "Two on the Aisle," with the Broadway stars Bert Lahr and Dolores Gray.

Written by Mary Drayton, "Salt of the Earth" was a comedy about the Mormons in the days when multiple marriages were permissible. It brought Teresa Wright back to the stage from the movies, to give a pleasant performance, supported by Kent Smith. It was withdrawn from production after one week at the Wilbur Theatre and rests now in the limbo of those dramas which will be restaged, one is told, "next season." Don't believe it.

April brought five productions, a mixed bag. First there was the new comedy called "To Be Continued," which Guthrie McClintic directed and which was not worthy of his trouble. It opened at the Wilbur Theatre on the 8th for two weeks of poor business. Then, on the 14th, "The Cocktail Party" opened at the Colonial. With Dennis King, Neva Patterson and Harry Ellerbe, this T. S. Eliot drama was booked for three weeks, which was one too many.

Carol Channing got here a week later, to fill the Shubert with roaring excitement. "Gentlemen Prefer Blondes" is not the best musical comedy ever, but Carol is a commedienne worth her weight in those baubles which are a girl's best friend.

On the same night that "Blondes" bowed, a quickie called "For Crying Out Loud" tried to slip past the doorman at the Wilbur. It lasted a whole week and was then put quietly away. Note that the only kind of euthanasia which is legal in Massachusetts is the dramatic form.

Maurice Schwartz, who had not acted previously in this city except in Yiddish, began presenting in English a drama called "Conscience," in which he was the only actor. There was nothing wrong with the cast of "Conscience," but the script was less than effectively dramatic. The public was not impressed.

There was one opening only in May, but it happened to be a good one. Katharine Cornell came here on the 5th in her revival of the Somerset Maugham period piece—for such it is now—"The Constant Wife" and acted it with distinction and with increasing popular response during three weeks.

On the same evening, Saturday, May 24, both "The Constant Wife" and "Gentlemen Prefer Blondes" ended their engagements here, and all the legitimate theatres of Boston were dark.

The Brattle Theatre company began the season of 1951-52 with a 19th-century version of "Love's Labour's Lost" on the stage of its Cambridge playhouse. This production had opened on May 23 and would play for five weeks. Succeeding attractions of the Brattle year were as follows: "The Devil's Disciple," Shaw, opened June 27, for three weeks; "The Critic," by Sheridan, and "A Phoenix Too Frequent," by Christopher Fry, opened July 11, for two weeks; "He and She," by LeNormand, opened July 25, for two weeks; "Billy Budd" opened August 7 for eight weeks (*Note:* This was one of the most successful productions at the Brattle.); "A Midsummer Night's Dream" opened October 3, for four weeks; "Macbeth," with William Devlin and Ruth Ford, opened October 30, for three weeks; "King Lear," also with Devlin and Miss Ford, opened November 21, for one week, followed by "Macbeth" and "Lear" in repertory, for three additional weeks; on December 18 "A Phoenix Too Frequent" was revived for two weeks, paired this time with Thornton Wilder's "The Long Christmas Dinner."

Getting into 1952, the Brattle actors presented for what would seem to be the first time in English in this part of the country Chekov's "Ivanov," with John Beal. An unsuccessful production of a lesser Chekov work, it was hastily withdrawn after ten days.

The next attraction, opening January 17 for four weeks, was "Captain Brassbound's Conversion," with Anne Revere.

A new play by Edward Caulfield, "The Idea," about a ruthless South American dictator hiding in this country opened February 12, with the Greek actor Alexis Minotis playing the lead. It wasn't strong enough to last. Two weeks.

On February 26 the Brattle offered Sheridan's "The School for Scandal" for four weeks and then brought in Eric Bentley's new version of Pirandello's "Right You Are," with Philip Bourneuf, Mildred Dunnock and Martin Gabel, the last two giving extraordinary performances in a production which lacked popular appeal. It ran for two weeks.

A revival of "Billy Budd," beginning April 8, continued for three weeks, to be followed then by 'Heartbreak House." As principals, the Brattle management brought in two pairs of husbands and wives, Philip Bourneuf and Frances Reid and Peter Cookson and Beatrice Straight. All four played with high spirit and enough success to make plans for subsequent Summer theatre productions seem feasible. Broadway even loomed. Three weeks at the Brattle.

The final production of the season at the Brattle Theatre was the first anywhere in Greater Boston of Eugene O'Neill's "Desire Under the Elms." When this stark drama was first produced in New York, thought was taken about a possible visit to Boston, but city officials here indicated the script would have to be altered so extensively that the Theatre Guild decided it wouldn't be worth the trouble. The Brattle players notified the authorities of Cambridge, who were perturbed enough to send two policewomen to the opening performance, but on the recommendation of these ladies in blue only minor deletions were made. Opening May 20, "Desire" ran profitably for three weeks.

Opera is considered separately in this record. During the season of 1951-52, Boston got very little opera, the figures show.

The Metropolitan Company came in from New York with its battalion of high-salaried stars for seven days, Monday through Sunday, April 21-27, and for the first time in memory sold out every seat in advance. Music critics complained that almost every opera performed was an old chestnut. H. Wendell Endicott, president of the Boston Opera Association, whose members cautiously guarantee the season against loss, pointed to the empty ticket racks and shushed them down somewhat.

Our only local opera enterprise is the New England Opera Theatre, whose director is Boris Goldovsky. The works offered by this company during the year—all in English and each for one performance only, at the Boston Opera House—were the following: Puccini's "La Bohème," November 11; Tchaikovsky's "The Queen of Spades" ("Pique Dame"), December 9; Britten's "Albert Herring," January 13, and Bizet's "Carmen," March 2.

Dance programs of the season, in addition to those by the three ballet companies previously reported, were these: Talley Beatty and Co. in "Tropicana" at John Hancock Hall, January 14-15; and Jean Leon Destine in "Fiesta in Haiti" at John Hancock Hall, April 18.

For one week beginning October 7, the Salzburg Marionette Theatre performed for the first time in Boston at John Hancock Hall.

At the Esquire Theatre on Huntington Avenue, once active as the Civic Repertory Theatre, but long since committed to the movies, there came on May 1 a hypnotist, The Great Morton. Mr. Morton put on a two-hour show which was pretty good fun, but not enough people wanted to be put to sleep or watch others being put to sleep. One week for Mort.

One other event of the season should be placed in the record. At meetings held April 4-5 at the Gershwin Theatre Workshop of Boston University, an organization called The New England Theatre Conference was founded. Affiliated with ANTA (The American National Theatre and Academy) yet actively independent, this conference is dedicated to stimulating the theatre in all its branches throughout New England.

THE SEASON IN PHILADELPHIA

By Arthur B. Waters

Drama Critic of the Philadelphia *Gazette-Democrat*

APPROXIMATELY one year ago, on this very typewriter, in reporting on the Philadelphia legitimate theatre season of 1950-51, the phrase was used describing it as the "year of the big musicals."

The season of 1951-52, which, to all intents and purposes, called it a day with the closing on Saturday night, May 10, of Leonard Sillman's revue, "New Faces," very decidedly did not have even this restricted distinction. In fact the season just past will have to be characterized as one of the dreariest and least productive of any within recent memory.

Perhaps it might also be described as the Season of Returning Hollywood Stars, for no less than thirteen footlight offerings boasted the presence of cinema celebrities and even a couple of others had film performers in their casts. Unfortunately most of these evenings in the theatre proved to be most disappointing though not, to be sure, in most cases because of any shortcomings on the parts of the celluloid artists but rather the ineptness of their material. Notable exceptions were "Point of No Return" in which Henry Fonda repeated his triumph of "Mister Roberts," and John van Druten's "Bell, Book and Candle," which, when seen here, had Rosalind Russell as its bright feminine luminary.

There were, to be sure, plenty of musical shows (possibly as many as in 1950-51) but their caliber was considerably inferior and there was certainly no outstanding quintet comparable to "Guys and Dolls," "A Tree Grows in Brooklyn," "Out of This World," "Make a Wish" and "Flahooley" of the preceding winter. Best of this season's crop were "Paint Your Wagon" and "Top Banana," which tried out at the Shubert in September and October; "Three Wishes for Jamie," which arrived here in March, and the aforementioned "New Faces" which wound up local stage business in May. Of these, "Paint Your Wagon" and "New Faces" were "world premières."

Another point worth noticing is that, for once, it was not the musicals that ran away with the best attendance records. In fact, local

23

box-office records for a number of the new musicals were far from commensurate with their merits. "Top Banana" and "Gentlemen Prefer Blondes" probably did as well as any and "Three Wishes for Jamie" wound up with capacity figures after a slow start; but the excellent "New Faces" never got going and other tune pieces that lagged lamentably were "Of Thee I Sing," "Month of Sundays," "Seventeen," "Shuffle Along" and "Curtain Going Up." It should be added, to be sure, that the last-named quintet left much to be desired in quality, as displayed here.

Statistically, the 1951-52 season was closely comparable to its two immediate predecessors. There were 44 bookings, not including the two revivals of "Fledermaus" at the Academy and the First Drama Quartette ("Don Juan in Hell") at the same historic house, but including a week of the Mask and Wig at the Shubert and engagements of the Greco Ballet and the two "one-man" shows—Cornelia Otis Skinner's "Paris '90" and Maurice Schwartz' "Conscience." 1950-51 had 41 shows. All of the 44 bookings were in the Forrest, Walnut, Shubert and Locust, except the return engagement of "Gentlemen Prefer Blondes," which played at the independent Erlanger.

However, while there was a slight upward trend in the number of bookings, there was a drop in the number of busy weeks in local houses—100 down to 90.

There were 29 stage offerings that were pausing here on their way to Broadway although several of them never got that far. As was the case the previous year, there were notably few Broadway hits that came to visit us—nine, all told, not including a couple of perennials such as "The Student Prince" and "The Merry Widow" and such return engagements as "Kiss Me, Kate," "Member of the Wedding" and the aforementioned "Gentlemen Prefer Blondes."

The 1951-52 season got off to an early but not-too-promising start Labor Day night with "Love and Let Love," first of the many offerings starring or featuring Hollywood notables. In this case it was Ginger Rogers who, of course, was quite a favorite behind the footlights. "Love and Let Love" did two fairly good weeks at the Forrest but then nothing else arrived until the week of the 17th, when "Paint Your Wagon" had its première at the Shubert. It received divided and somewhat reserved notices but most observers thought it had enough merit to warrant revision and it played several subsequent tryout weeks in Boston after its local run of three weeks which, financially speaking, was only fairly successful.

There followed another inactive week and then, on October 1, "Faithfully Yours," which teamed Ann Sothern and Robert Cummings of the "fillums," arrived at the Forrest, where it was gingerly received. The first conflict occurred the week of October 8 when "Top Banana" came to the Shubert for a three weeks' tryout, and a melodrama, "The Number," re-lighted the Walnut for what was expected to be a two weeks' run but became three. "Top Banana" was generally liked and its ultimate Broadway success was anticipated; "The Number" was thought to be a creditable thriller. First attraction with a New York success trademark, "The Moon Is Blue," began a four weeks' run at the Forrest October 15, but the first-string critics covered Maxwell Anderson's "Barefoot in Athens" with a divided verdict.

"Black Velvet" slipped into the Locust on October 29 and slipped out again after just one week. "Gigi" had its American première at the Walnut on Thursday, November 8, and was generally acclaimed here, although it was the star, Audrey Hepburn, who received most of the attention. Despite the good notices business was only fair during its week and a half stay. There was another conflict on November 12 with the first-string critics choosing "I Am a Camera" at the Forrest as opposed to the New York success, "Rose Tattoo," at the Locust, although here the decision was somewhat harder to make. The Philadelphia reviewers were more reserved in their estimations of the van Druten play than were Broadway's later on.

"Kiss Me, Kate" (third engagement) played the week of November 19 at the Shubert after the big house had been dark three weeks. For the critics, however, the evening of the 19th was notable for the arrival of the much-heralded "Nina" after its break-in elsewhere. Despite the presence of cinema stars Gloria Swanson and David Niven, there were few kind words found here for this French importation.

However, "Point of No Return," arriving on November 26 at the Forrest, was something else again. Critics and first-nighters both applauded and the Marquand-Osborn play had a very profitable two weeks' stay despite the illness—for several performances—of the star. The single week's engagement of the Mask and Wig (University of Pennsylvania) show at the Shubert and a two weeks' stint of the Greco Ballet at the Forrest starting December was all the pre-holiday activity the city had and it looked, right up until the week before Christmas, as if the traditionally busy holiday period would also be without bookings. Finally, however, three attractions were secured—"Bell, Book and Candle" (Forrest) and "Fancy Meeting You Again" (Locust) both on Christmas night, and the musical, "Seventeen," on Christmas Eve at the Shubert. Notices for the last-named were lukewarm here, but two-thirds of the first-string critics thought well of the Kaufman play, "Fancy Meeting You Again," and it did quite well here, adding an extra week. "Bell, Book and Candle" fared admirably indeed in its three weeks at the Forrest.

The almost-fabulous José Ferrer scored once again with his psychiatric play, "The Shrike," which had its world première January 7 at the Walnut, with "The Student Prince" (umpty-umpth local visit) at the Shubert, where attendance was phenomenal. "Jane" began a tryout run at the Walnut on January 14 and "Month of Sundays," musical that had been poorly received up in Boston, tried it again here but folded, for good and all, after two dismal weeks at the Forrest.

"Venus Observed" after several delays finally opened on January 28 at the Shubert and had two sensational weeks there. Cornelia Otis Skinner opened her "Paris '90" at the Locust on the same date and did well for a week. "Dear Barbarians," a tryout, was well regarded here and built to excellent business during its fortnight's stay at the Walnut and local playgoers were surprised at its reception in New York.

"Curtain Going Up," a revue, had its première at the Forrest February 15 and closed—for keeps—ten days later. Except for a return of "The Merry Widow" at the Shubert for two miserable weeks starting February 18, there was no more real activity until the week of March 3 when—for the first time all season—there were four legitimate openings. Three of these were on Monday night with the critics choosing the tryout, "One Bright Day" at the Walnut in preference to the musical, "Three Wishes for Jamie" at the Shubert and Olivia de Havilland's "Candida" at the Locust. "One Bright Day" was generally liked and when they got around to seeing it several of the local reviewers raved about "Three Wishes for Jamie." On Tuesday (4th) "The Long Watch" opened at the Forrest and got a general panning. Business was, at best, fitful for all this quartet of shows.

On March 17 another Broadway hit, "The Cocktail Party," opened two weeks on subscription at the Walnut and the critics clapped hands. "Bagels and Yox" came to the Locust the same night for a fortnight. Three stage offerings, one a return, arrived on March 31 with the "first-stringers" choosing "The Chase," starring John Hodiak, at the Locust, over "The Brass Ring" at the Walnut. Neither did much at the box office here but "Member of the Wedding," back after a year's absence, scored nicely at the Forrest.

"Gentlemen Prefer Blondes," which originally opened here at the Forrest two seasons ago, elected to play its return visit at the independent Erlanger and it was a near-capacity engagement. One instance of the reviewers not choosing the new play, or tryout, was to be observed on April 14 when all the first-string aisle-sitters preferred Katharine Cornell in her revival of "The Constant Wife" at the Forrest to "Hook 'n' Ladder," a farce, at the Locust, and "Of Thee I Sing," new version, at the Shubert. Miss Cornell did nice if not sellout business for two weeks but the other two "died." "Hook 'n' Ladder" deserved its demise.

"Shuffle Along" (new edition) came to the Shubert April 28, got fair notices but folded after a week. Then "New Faces of 1952" made its bow on Friday, May 2, at the Forrest and was welcomed by one and all first-nighters, but thereafter, despite the raves, attendance was inexplicably light. Mr. Schwartz brought his one-man "Conscience" to the Locust for the single week of May 5.

One feature of the 1951-52 season to which attention should be called is that the American Theatre Society added a supplementary three-play subscription series, making nine plays in all. This coming year there will be twelve subscription plays. Apparently that's what Philadelphia is coming to as, during the season just past, with a few notable exceptions, such as "Point of No Return," no nonmusical NOT on subscription fared very well financially.

Incidentally, two of the special attractions mentioned which were seen at the Academy and mentioned at the beginning of this article—namely, the Met's restaged "Fledermaus" and the First Drama Quartette—did very well indeed. The last-named was on the Forum list and next season that same Forum (sponsored here by the Philadelphia *Inquirer*) will offer a return of the First Drama Quartette, Emlyn Williams in his Dickens readings, Tyrone Power and other players in readings of Benét's "John Brown's Body" and Eddie Dowling's Dublin Players in Irish one-acters. This may be seen as some kind of new trend.

Artistically as well as monetarily, the season of 1951-52 must be classed as one of the most disappointing of the last decade in Philadelphia.

THE SEASON IN CHICAGO

By Claudia Cassidy

Drama Critic of the *Chicago Tribune*

THIS contumelious chronicle crops up season after season for all the world like a bleeding heart in the theatrical garden, but facts are facts, and Chicago's devotion to theatre remains unrequited. We had even fewer shows in 1951-52, a scant 20 by generous count, but they ran 35 weeks longer than last season's 25, flouting the lures of television for 187 weeks in all.

This was mighty skimpy fare. Theatres brooded in the unbooked dusk, insatiable playgoers could have cued any actor in any decent show in town, the Palace went opulently legitimate with "Gentlemen Prefer Blondes," only to lapse into movies when it couldn't get another show, yet "Guys and Dolls" toured itself blue in the face while waiting for "South Pacific" to quit the Shubert.

That same Shubert is the town's theatrical talisman on the unbeatable theory that shows are hits there, so it gets hit shows. It had another jackpot season, losing just half a week while brooms and dusters flew in the wake of 67 weeks of enchanted evenings so that spick-and-span premises might honor the newcomers' marker with a courtly, "Brother Abernathy, your dice."

Only the Harris could snub such a record, for it had no hiatus at all. A year ago this space was noting that "The Moon Is Blue" might have struck bonanza by duplicating itself delightfully within two months of the New York triumph. It did. It ran fleetly and gaily through 1951-52, piling up 57 juicy weeks, surviving the loss of Murray Hamilton and hoping it could survive another Summer even shorn of Maggie McNamara and Leon Ames, who had become old and cherished settlers. Among other things, this was the town's first show to try an early curtain—7:30 on Tuesday nights—and it boosted business.

When it came to wine of choice, the Erlanger had the most bottles, not all of them well corked. Ethel Waters and Brandon de Wilde kept much of the magic of "The Member of the Wedding," Kermit Bloomgarden did a remarkable job in retaining the quality of "The Autumn Garden," and Edward G. Robinson was a weary man with

28

flashes of humor in "Darkness at Noon," though it had lost more in transit than an actor with a glint of Caesar, Claude Rains. But Olivia de Havilland's "Candida" was a pallid comic strip, and "The Cocktail Party" had turned into preposterous fraud, with even the scene of libation misrepresented as a champagne toast. "Remains to Be Seen" was the house's last entry, gags and jive in a corn popper with Janis Paige and Jackie Cooper to keep it warm.

Witchcraft smiled on the Great Northern. When Rex Harrison and Lilli Palmer quit "Bell, Book and Candle" and Irene Selznick couldn't replace them, we seemed to be out of luck. But Shepard Traube took over the production, got Rosalind Russell, Dennis Price and Dorothy Sands to act in it, and John van Druten to direct it, and the first thing he knew he had a hit. The engagement was extended until Miss Russell was paged by Hollywood and Mr. Price by London; then Joan Bennett and Zachary Scott stepped in, the play moved to the smaller Selwyn, and the Great Northern went briefly musical with Bert Lahr, Dolores Gray and "Two on the Aisle." Its only other tenant was a woebegone error, a one-week return of "Peter Pan," with Veronica Lake shorn of her moonstruck mane as Peter and Lawrence Tibbett shorn of his song as Captain Hook.

"The Happy Time" was not universally regarded as such by the time it reached the Blackstone, where the Greco Ballet had its innings. "The Student Prince" paid what it swore was its last visit, and there was a May basket called "Bagels and Yox." "Season in the Sun" expired with its ragtag cast at the Selwyn, and although the returning "Fledermaus" had a skimpy two weeks in the Opera House, 7,000 customers packed the two performances of the Boyer-Laughton-Hardwicke-Moorehead "Don Juan in Hell." "A Sleep of Prisoners" played several churches and synagogues around town, but it had lost the simple living of the play that grew out of the ancient dusk of St. Thomas' in London.

So it was, this 1951-52 season, when Irene Bordoni's Bloody Mary turned out to be a woman with a core of primitive pride, the only one of the lot who did not seem a procuress for her own daughter, and when the Kungsholm restaurant opened an enchanting puppet theatre, where they play not Kukla, Fran and Ollie, but opera.

Otherwise, for the record, the 1951-52 listing, compiled as of May 31:

Harris: 52 weeks—"The Moon Is Blue," 57 to date.

Shubert: 51½ weeks—"South Pacific," 38 weeks' holdover, 67 in all; "Guys and Dolls," 13½ to date.

Erlanger: 27 weeks—"The Autumn Garden," 3; "Candida," 3;

"The Cocktail Party," 4; "Darkness at Noon," 5; "The Member of the Wedding," 8; "Remains to Be Seen," 4.

Blackstone: 17 weeks—"The Happy Time," 8; Jose Greco Spanish Ballet, 2; "The Student Prince," 4; "Bagels and Yox," 3 to date.

Great Northern: 13 weeks—"Peter Pan," 1; "Bell, Book and Candle," 10; "Two on the Aisle," 2.

Selwyn: 11 weeks—"Season in the Sun," 3; Jose Greco Spanish Ballet, 4; "Bell, Book and Candle," 4 to date.

Palace: 13½ weeks—"Gentlemen Prefer Blondes."

Opera House: 2 weeks—"Fledermaus," 2; "Don Juan in Hell," 2 performances.

THE SEASON IN SAN FRANCISCO

By Fred Johnson

Drama Critic of the *Call-Bulletin*

EACH succeeding year this report has seemed to mark San Francisco's lowest possible tide in affairs theatrical. But as of now there has not been, as in the affairs of men, a likely turn of the tide with its promise of relief from this western outpost's famine in entertainment. In the fewer and sadder words which showmen and playgoers have come to employ, things have been getting worse. The road show score—eight plays, seven musicals.

Not that the Coast Defenders haven't been active in their efforts to fill the void as fewer touring companies ventured westward. But in spite of this the professional theatre continued to suffer.

ANTA heard the wilderness cries in this quarter and supported the first regional drama festival in historic Monterey, 100 miles distant from San Francisco. The results were of minor concrete value, but freshened the spirit of community zealots of the theatre.

Robert T. Eley brought down the final curtain on his Repertory Theatre, which had struggled for more than a year in the tiny Bush Street playhouse with a series of off-beat plays. The Municipal Theatre, conducted for several years under the Board of Education's sponsorship, found the caliber of its plays and available talent unable to win adequate public support.

The pioneer Theatre Arts Colony, most enduring and worth while of the little theatre groups, aspired to taking over the legendary Alcazar, for years a link in the former Henry Duffy chain. But the renamed United Nations, dedicated to motion pictures in the year of U.N.'s San Francisco Conference, was found too deeply entrenched to be available for the legitimate, though long dark.

But since the Curran and Geary, sole important stage houses, also had been unlighted for weeks on end during the past season, there seemed small reason for adding another unless it were to supply top-grade attractions. Theatre Arts, however, has contributed the town's best semi-professional entertainment, though limited in its repertoire to such plays as "The Curious Savage," "Dark of the Moon" and Clifford Odets' "The Big Knife," staged within a week of the demise

31

of John Garfield, its original Broadway star.

As the season ended, the newly organized Alcazar Theatre Associates leased the United Nations for a subscription series of plays to open in July with "The Moon Is Blue," following a brief run at La Jolla (Cal.) Playhouse. Its cast was headed by David Niven, Diana Lynn and Scott Brady. It was to be followed by Edward Everett Horton in "Nina," with the hope of returning the theatre permanently to its former popularity.

The Stanford University Players took on larger regional importance with their productions of "The Madwoman of Chaillot," with Aileen MacMahon, and "The Merchant of Venice," starring Clarence Derwent as Shylock.

So modest is the inventory of road company attractions for the season that their listing appears almost an afterthought. The plays totaled eight, the musicals seven, as previously noted, within the season ending June 1. In its negative way this is the city's record for the former; for the music shows it was an over-supply to the point of satiety.

Due to the hunger for dramatic and comedy entertainment, most of these offerings had fair runs. "The Cocktail Party" did well for four weeks, with a cast headed by Vincent Price, Marsha Hunt, Estelle Winwood, Harry Ellerbe, Rose Hobart and Reginald Denny. It was an excellent production from the Hollywood-powered LaJolla Playhouse. Olivia de Havilland brought "Candida" to her girlhood homeland, for mixed notices which contrasted with New York's later and unanimous panning. But her play was good for one month's run.

"Mister Roberts," first with Henry Fonda as the previous season ended and then with Tod Andrews within a six months' period, was well received, the former engagement for a seasonal record of eight weeks. "The Member of the Wedding," with Ethel Waters, had a profitable stay of three stanzas, as did "The Rose Tattoo," co-starring Maureen Stapleton and Eli Wallach. Edward G. Robinson in "Darkness at Noon" won heavy patronage for the same period. But Lewis and Young's production of "The Happy Time," scheduled for four weeks, lasted but one. Heading the cast were Reginald Gardiner, Irene Hervey, Maria Palmer and Lloyd Corrigan. Carl Ebert's production of Gian-Carlo Menotti's "The Consul" played its scheduled one week. The surfeit of musicals was due to competition with the San Francisco Civic Light Opera Association by Gene Mann's productions from the Los Angeles Greek Theatre, a first-year venture that failed miserably, with heavy loss to the backers.

Following "Where's Charley?" and a revival of "The Merry Widow" in the Spring, the Civic season's June attraction was "Guys and Dolls," with Allan Jones, Jan Clayton, Pamela Britton and Julie Oshins. It did capacity business for four weeks. "Three Wishes for Jamie" had its world première, with John Raitt, Marion Bell and Cecil Kellaway in leading roles, with its rewriting and revisions under way from the start and destined to continue in a lay-off period before going to New York. The première notices were generally good.

The Gene Mann productions numbered five to the Civic Light Opera's four, beginning with an unfortunate revival of "Girl Crazy," starring Mickey Rooney. The others were "Bloomer Girl," with Dick Haymes and Frances McCann; "Bitter Sweet," teaming Anne Jeffreys and Lawrence Brooks; "Finian's Rainbow," with Ella Logan and Albert Sharpe, and "Annie Get Your Gun," with Martha Raye and Ray Middleton.

The Civic Light Opera's 1952 regular season was preceded by Judy Garland's International Variety Show, opening in May, which played to capacity houses for four weeks. It was to be followed through the Summer by a revival of "Song of Norway," with Helena Bliss and John Tyers; "South Pacific," with Janet Blair, Webb Tilton and Irene Bordoni, and "Jollyanna," the revised "Flahooley," teaming Bobby Clark and Mitzi Gaynor.

The Monterey Drama Festival's one-week inaugural had promise of ANTA support for future annual programs and benefit to the San Francisco area's theatre as well. Six major productions were given by groups of the Theatre Council of Northern California and Nevada. Discussions in their interest were a part of the agenda, with Clarence Derwent, vice chairman of ANTA, and Christian Westphalian, administrator, as principal speakers. A special performance was the reading of Robinson Jeffers' narrative poem, "The Roan Stallion," by Rollo Peters, the Festival president.

THE SEASON IN SOUTHERN CALIFORNIA

By Edwin Schallert

Drama Critic of the *Los Angeles Times*

WHETHER the 1951-52 season in the theatre in Southern California represented rock bottom in activity became anew the familiar topic for discussion. Each year, with few exceptions, devotees of the stage and its bigger and better entertainment gather around the wailing wall, and it becomes only a question of whether their cries over the state of the show business will become more or less intense. They are nearly all willing to concede that the theatre, as once known, is in a situation of horrible decline today.

Only the new generation, to whom the footlight world of the past is nothing more than a legend, seem to go on viewing the future brightly and hopefully. They are willing to settle for play-giving as best they can. They do rather well, too, as exemplified by the continued progress of theatres-in-the-round in Hollywood. Admittedly this is the economical way of presenting shows, but as long as it enables the production of shows at all, it seems highly deserving of encouragement.

To the Circle and Ring Theatres, already established, was added during the past season the Gallery Stage, related to the Ring. At this triangular-shaped arena affair on Santa Monica Boulevard "On the Town," the Adolph Green-Betty Comden musical, was offered for the first time on the West Coast. A group of young people really put their hearts into the presentation, without scenery or props, and won amazing acclaim.

The absence of settings was naturally a strange anomaly in "On the Town," because the New York backgrounds meant so much to the Broadway production. But somehow the Gallery Stage people were able to override this handicap and supply a delightful entertainment.

Both Circle and Ring Theatres pursued their way with special emphasis on new attractions. Circle offered notably "The Girl on the Via Flaminia," by Alfred Hayes, and "The Devil in Boston," by Lion Feuchtwanger, doing very well also with the comedy "Susan"

34

by Steve Fisher and Alex Gottlieb, even though this was not a very noteworthy play.

The Ring, after exploiting the tried-and-true in "Dark of the Moon" and "Merrily We Roll Along," became more venturesome with "Penelope" by Leonard Bercovici. For the beginning and end of its season this group offered revues, the first being "Ring Around the Ring," the other, exceptionally good, being "Strictly Informal."

For the first time in half a decade light opera suffered a setback, due to the financially unsuccessful Greek Theatre season. Estimates are that the losses on five shows, all revivals, totaled more than $300,000. More than $200,000 of this was attributed to the failure of presentations to appeal in San Francisco. The Greek Theatre management experimented with the staging of its attractions in the northern city, as well as Los Angeles. This custom has been followed now for some years, of course, by the Los Angeles Civic Light Opera Association, with much mutual benefit.

"Girl Crazy," with Mickey Rooney, seemed to get the Greek Theatre season off to a bad start, and other events like "Bitter Sweet," "Bloomer Girl" and "Finian's Rainbow" did not help to lift the pall sufficiently. Only that old reliable "Annie Get Your Gun," with Martha Raye in a lusty starring performance, seemed to endow the season with the right *esprit*, but it could not compensate, particularly in San Francisco, for the other deficiencies.

Light opera again supplied a banner run for major attractions. It was Edwin Lester and the Civic Light Opera Association which scored this coup with "Guys and Dolls." Top-flight among the 1951 season's offerings of the organization, this spirited show played nine and a half weeks at Philharmonic Auditorium, thus closely rivaling the 1950 10-week record of "South Pacific." Allan Jones, Pamela Britton, Jan Clayton and Maxie Rosenbloom were in the company, which, with some changes, subsequently went touring nationally.

Important on the Civic Light Opera schedule was the tryout of "Three Wishes for Jamie," with John Raitt, Marion Bell, Cecil Kellaway and others. This show, which achieved a rather confused result at its Los Angeles première, was subsequently rewritten to advantage for New York.

Judy Garland, accompanied by vaudeville similar in practically all respects to the Palace in New York, supplied a preliminary program for the 1952 Civic Light Opera season. This was a complete sellout, and Miss Garland was welcomed at a première that compared with the most spectacular for which Hollywood has become famous. After her four-week engagement the strictly light opera season began with a revival of "Song of Norway," which had been subjected to some revisions. It could not be said to possess all its old zest, especially with Irra Petina absent. John Tyers and Helena Bliss in the Petina role, Jean Kent in the former Bliss part as Grieg's Norwegian love, and Sig Arno, still excellent, as well as the fine-singing Robert Rounseville headed the company in this production.

Touring attractions playing the Biltmore included "The Cocktail Party," which originated in La Jolla, "The Rose Tattoo" from New York, "Darkness at Noon" with Edward G. Robinson, and "Member of the Wedding" with Ethel Waters, Brandon De Wilde and Betty Lou Holland. De Wilde had to leave the cast just before the end of the engagement, because of a motion picture commitment.

Southern California, which helped to cradle the First Drama Quartette in its presentation of "Don Juan in Hell" the previous season, saw Judith Anderson engaging in a similar program at Ojai Festival late in May, 1952, with Henry Brandon assisting. She gave scenes from "The Tower Beyond Tragedy" and "Medea." And while this idea did not carry the metropolitan significanec of the rare Bernard Shaw interlude from "Man and Superman," Miss Anderson's enactments, with special material written by Robinson Jeffers, it was believed, could well serve for a planned tour managed by Russell Lewis and Howard Young.

"The Cocktail Party," staged at the Biltmore Theatre and on tour, made its La Jolla Playhouse debut in the Summer of 1951. It was offered there with Vincent Price, Patricia Neal, Harry Ellerbe, Rose Hobart, Lillian Bronson and William Schallert as its principals. There were many changes in this personnel as the tour went forward under Lewis and Young management. For the West Coast road engagements Marsha Hunt took over the feminine lead, while Estelle Winwood very advantageously replaced Miss Bronson.

Major launchings on the Pacific shores apart from these amounted to almost nil during the 1951-52 season, though a number of attractions, locally confined, had their birth in the Southern California area. Creditable indeed were the renditions of "Ring Round the Moon" with Diana Lynn and Mel Ferrer and "Second Threshold" with Raymond Massey at La Jolla. Eddie Bracken shone brilliantly in a revival of "Room Service," presented by Preston Sturges at The Players for a long run. Bracken, oddly enough, made a starring part of the play author in this old riotous comedy.

Harold J. Kennedy, who managed to help keep the theatre rolling in Los Angeles during 1950-51, fought it out bitterly to the end during 1951-52. He proffered "For Love or Money" with Wanda Hendrix and a revival of the antique "Peg o' My Heart" with Joan

Evans and John Agar. However, he found he could not win out against a seemingly fading interest in play-giving on the part of audiences, and differences that arose between him and Herman D. Hover. So the Ivar Theatre went dark during the season, except for a few sporadic ventures like the fantastic "Assembly Call," dealing with the hereafter for service men.

An oddity during the season was the 12-week run of "The Beaustone Affair," exemplifying that type of sensationalism which often manifests itself in shows in Los Angeles. This was presented by Wallace R. Parnell at Las Palmas Theatre, and attributed to him in the writing.

Among other oddities were Myron Fagan's attempts to introduce "Red Rainbow" and revive "Thieves' Paradise," both anti-Communist plays, at the Beaux Arts Theatre.

The Pasadena Playhouse maintained its all-year-round status, beginning with the George M. Cohan Summer festival in 1951. Included in the regular season as a world première was "Once upon an Earthquake," by Dan Totheroh, built somewhat shakily around the 1906 San Francsico disaster for comedy. It did have hilarious results during its Pasadena run, though the question was raised how far the play might proceed in the long range. The cast included both Carol and Dorothy Stone, with Byron Foulger, Marion Kerby, Madge Blake and others.

"David Copperfield" in the Ingram D'Abbes adaptation was cited as the first American presentation, while Coast firsts included "Curious Savage," by John Patrick, and "Golden State," by Sam Spewack. Other items of the Playhouse repertoire were "Detective Story," "Goodbye, My Fancy," with Author Fay Kanin in the lead; "The Madwoman of Chaillot," "Southern Exposure," "Come Back, Little Sheba," "Old Acquaintance," "Nothing but the Truth," "Legend of Sarah," Shakespeare's "Macbeth," "Berkeley Square," "Gramercy Ghost," and "Life with Mother."

In the adjunct theatres of the Playhouse there were such unique offerings as "The People Win Through" by Thakin Nu, prime minister of Burma, which had sociological purpose, and "The Great Highway," by Strindberg, in its American première.

Very early in the season Zoë Akins was represented by "The Swallow's Nest," with Billie Burke appearing, which missed the desired impact at its première. Miss Akins also figured in a dramatization of Claude André Puget's "Happy Days," at the Coronet, which had charm and delicacy.

Summer theatres were briefly augmented when an effort was made to install an arena playhouse at the Del Mar and Deauville Clubs in

Santa Monica. "The Post Road" with Zasu Pitts inaugurated the series of three plays, which included "The Importance of Being Earnest" and "Rain," with Gladys George. The Laguna Beach Summer theatre had such events as "Old Acquaintance," "The Royal Family," "Guest in the House," "Portrait in Black" and others. La Jolla Playhouse today is the major goal for Hollywoodians, and one of the most promising of Southern California enterprises.

Drawing on Southern California talent is the Sombrero Playhouse, which has flourished during recent Winter seasons in Phoenix, Ariz. Out of this resort capital came "The Happy Time" to play San Francisco, though it did not reach Los Angeles as scheduled.

Various groups still function with more or less success in and around Los Angeles, notably the Call Board. The Footlighters, which performed "Present Laughter" during the year, Sartu, Ben Bard Players, Bliss-Hayden and others provided activities.

Newly organized before the season's ending about June 1, the Hollywood Guild Productions staged "Born Yesterday," with Jean Parker and Robert Lowery, at the Geller Theatre.

Continuing as before were "The Drunkard," which culminated its 18th season; the Turnabout revue and puppet show, "The Pilgrimage Play," Ramona Pageant, and the Padua Hills Theatre, with its unique Latin-American entertainment. Turnabout missed Elsa Lanchester for a good part of the season, not too happily either, though Joseph Marais and Miranda proved an especially compensating attraction, with Elizabeth Talbot Martin also aiding.

So while it was a slow year, it wasn't an entirely dead one in the theatre in Southern California.

MRS. McTHING *

A Play in Two Acts

By Mary Chase

IT might be said of this fantastical comedy that never was so little expected of so much. In 1945, when her "Harvey" was in the first few months of its great and prolonged success, author Mary Chase confided to the late Antoinette Perry, director of "Harvey," that she would like to write a play for the entertainment of children in the living theatre. Mrs. Chase had noted the joy of English children over the pantomimes in London, and felt that the stage could offer certain enticements to the young which could not be found in the regular diet of movies. (Television had not yet made its great impact on the infant mind.) Miss Perry offered words of caution and other words of encouragement. Said she—as Mrs. Chase recalled the interview in a piece she wrote for the *New York Times*—"Will you bring children to the theatre by writing down to them? Isn't the problem rather to convince the parents that children raised on a diet of movies would adore the theatre if they had a chance to see it?"

Mary Chase began her work, and her one aim was to write a full-length play for the professional theatre which would hold the attention of children between the ages of 7 and 14. As the work progressed in the city of Denver, numberless tryouts and auditions were held—not the usual tryouts and auditions Broadway holds for possible financial backers, but readings held to test the ultimate backer: the audience. In five years of writing, rewriting and experimentation, Mrs. Chase took advantage of a mother's rights and conducted her auditions, or readings, before her three sons and their various friends. "I had to bribe the audience with food, more elaborate each time because word of the trap had spread and, with it, a resistance to it," she wrote for the *Times*. She recalled a session in the Summer of 1950, when five boys of 12 and 13 entered the Chase yard at the

* Copyright, 1949, under the title "Mr. Thing," by Mary Coyle Chase; revised version copyright, 1952, by Mary Coyle Chase. Published as an illustrated children's book by the Oxford University Press. Author's agent, Harold Freedman, 101 Park Avenue, New York City.

behest of her youngest son.   From her library she heard one of them say, alluding to her son, "Chase's old lady wants to read us some kind of a play."   Groans went up, but spirits rose when incidental hot dogs and ice cream were mentioned.

Five years before this time Mrs. Chase had tried out her first version of the play on an audience which then was age 8.   The audience got bored half-way through and began wrestling on the floor, but one lad with nice manners complimented the author on having written "a nice long play."   Something was wrong about this project for bringing the living theatre to children.   About a week later Mrs. Chase discovered one of her mistakes.   There had been a sensational jail-break at the State penitentiary, fully covered by newspapers and radio, and now the potential theatre audience was busy in the yard playing its own melodrama about Escaped Convicts—and there had been no gangsters in the children's comedy tentatively known as "Mr. Thing."

America hath no industry like a mother aroused.   Mrs. Chase was determined to lick her neighborhood audience—to bring it to terms; but she was not going to truckle to it by writing plain melodrama like a Grade B movie.   She tried a version which was pure comedy, and this was the greatest failure of all.   "Comedy," she wrote, "pure comedy, is an adult approach.   Children like slapstick, but insist on facing the fact that there is sadness in the world—separation and loneliness along with melodrama and slapstick."

So another version was written and tried out.   The audience reported, "It's an okay play—okay for children—but not for us."   The patient author was ready to give up and burn all her scripts, but a few days later she heard some of the audience talking in the lingo of one of the play's characters and was somewhat encouraged.   Perhaps she *did* have a play—but now where would she find a theatre for it, full of children and with professional actors on the stage? "I put the play away with indescribable sadness," Mrs. Chase recalls.

Robert Whitehead, the new managing director of the American National Theatre and Academy, heard of the work, read it, visited Mrs. Chase in Denver and told her that the trouble with the piece was that it did not recognize the existence of adults, too.   So yet another version was made, admitting the world of the adult into the comedy.   This version first was called "Mrs. Thing," instead of "Mr.," and finally "Mrs. McThing."   Whitehead and ANTA decided to present it as a high-minded enterprise—the kind of production with certain merits which no commercial management would or could afford to attempt.   Helen Hayes, the president of ANTA,

agreed to play the leading role, and Whitehead assembled a supporting cast which included Jules Munshin and young Brandon de Wilde
and engaged Joseph Buloff as director.

"Mrs. McThing" opened February 20, 1952, and was expected to
run two weeks—a nice and normal little engagement in the ANTA
play series. Nobody anticipated the chance that adults—including
drama critics—might find unusual charm in this play which had had
such a grueling and prolonged workout in a Denver yard. But
adults, including critics, *did* discover unusual charm, and a fortnight's engagement was indefinitely extended. The comedy was
still playing at season's end. It was scheduled to spend the month
of August, 1952, as the festival play at Central City, Colorado, and
to resume its Broadway run in September. The author of "Harvey"
had patiently evolved another hit without ever expecting that it
would be one in the Broadway commercial sense.

The curtain rises on an imposing setting and an imposing woman.
The setting is the morning room of Larue Towers, palatial country
estate of the no less palatial Mrs. Howard V. Larue III. French
period furniture is tastefully arranged, a large window offers exit to
a well-kept terrace, and on one wall hangs a large portrait of a small
boy—Howay Larue. Mrs. Larue is standing by the window, holding
a toy train coach and contemplating it, when a maid, Carrie, comes
in with a portable telephone and plugs it in for her mistress. A
Dr. Hyslop, a dentist, is returning Mrs. Larue's call. "Doctor," says
Mrs. Larue in a tone of cool command, "would you be good enough
to come out here tomorrow to Larue Towers on VanTyne Road and
bring your dentist chair and look at his teeth? . . . And, Doctor,
please, bring your credentials with you. Otherwise the guards might
not let you in at the gate."

The dentist seems willing enough to come—and with chair. With
this matter settled to her satisfaction, Mrs. Larue now returns her
attention to the toy car she is holding and asks Carrie about it. Is
this the only car left out of Howay's trains? The maid reports that
it is—only one car left from eighteen, and the engine has been missing for more than a week, too. This disappearance of practically
an entire railroad is most puzzling, for how could a thief get over
the high walls and past the watchman and Howay's bodyguard?
Certainly it couldn't be an inside job by any of the other servants
like Sybil or Nelson or the cook. Who would want a boy's toy
train? Howay's deprivation seems serious, for all he has left is his
pony and cart and the little swan boat on the lake. Mrs. Larue
makes plans to hire another watchman for night patrol, and muses,
"Since only toys are missing, the thief must be a child.

"Where is Howay now?"

Carrie consults her watch and reports, "He finished studying his arithmetic and he's gone for a half-hour walk around the grounds with his bodyguard." This news seems startling to the boy's mother, who exclaims, "But that's just what I *told* him to do! Have you noticed that lately he does exactly what I tell him to do at exactly the time I tell him to do it?" Quite bitterly, Carrie admits that she has noticed this. Carrie would prefer Howay to be the way he used to be.

Sybil, the nursemaid, steps into the morning room to announce callers—the "Lewis girls," Maude, Grace and Evva. These ladies, not too stylish and not too young, are sisters, and Evva is boss of the three. They are full of chatter and are ready to be filled with tea, but when Belle Larue suggests that her son might join them the Lewises are less than enthusiastic. They remember the last time they had tea here: Howay had thrown cookies at Evva, had made Grace sick with a rubber mouse and had squirted all three with a water gun. Nevertheless, the boy is brought in by a bodyguard who wears two guns.

The boy looks as neat as a department-store dummy and is at least as formal as he greets his mother politely and hands his beret and gloves to the maid. He greets each of the astonished Lewises with elegant *politesse,* and when his mother and the visitors prepare to have tea on the terrace he announces he would like to join them. "But first," he says, looking critically at his fingernails, "I must make myself a little more presentable." After the boy has gone upstairs, Evva Lewis exclaims, "That boy is the most adorable little gentleman I have ever seen!"

His mother accepts this compliment with vague uneasiness, asking, "You don't feel that he has suddenly become *too* grown-up, do you?"

Evva—My dear, he is perfect.

Grace—You should be so grateful.

Evva—Whatever method you used—write an article about it for a parents' magazine. You owe it to them.

Larue—Have any of you ever happened to hear of a person named Mrs. McThing? (All Three *turn toward* Larue.)

Evva—Mrs. McThing—Mrs. McThing— Does she belong to the club?

Grace—Have we ever met her socially, girls?

Maude—We'd remember if we did—such an odd name— Who is she?

Larue—I don't really know. I think she must be new in the

neighborhood. I understand she has a place up in the Blue Blue Mountains— (*Goes closer to window.*) Can you see a house up there?

Evva—Nothing but snowy peaks—does she live up there?

Larue—I have never laid eyes on her—but about three weeks ago—one afternoon—just about this time of day—

Evva—Yes—

Larue—Her child—a ragged little girl—climbed over the wall and I found her playing with Howay down by the lake. I knew nothing about the child, and—well, I simply cannot allow every child off the road who takes a notion to come in these grounds and play with Howay—

Evva—You never have.

Larue—And what's the sense of my hiring a bodyguard for him and having a high wall around these grounds if any ragged dirty girl off the road can climb in here and play with him?

Grace—You're right—

Maude—She might have been full of germs—

Larue—Do you know what this youngster had the audacity to say to me? She told me her mother was Mrs. McThing—a witch—

Grace—A witch— Oh, don't children say the rudest things about their parents these days?

Larue—And she told me—that if I sent her home—her mother would do something to me.

Grace—As if she could do anything to you, Belle!

Evva—You didn't let her bluff you, I'll bet.

Larue—I did not. I sent her home anyway. Oh, Howay was screaming and kicking—he wanted to play with her—but I was firm. And then I had a little talk with Howay about his responsibilities and what he owed me and this home of ours. (*She stops and looks at them.*) It was the most amazing thing. Apparently what I said to him that afternoon made a big impression on him. Sometimes children will listen to you—and the very next morning he was a different boy. He began to mind—his manners improved after all this time,— and—well—you just saw him.

Tea has been served on the terrace and the four ladies leave the room—the Lewis "girls" amazed at and admiring the change in Howay, but the boy's mother vaguely uneasy. For an instant the morning room is vacant, and then Mimi, an ill-clad little waif, tiptoes in, snatches the toy railroad car, and vanishes. Another maid, Carrie, comes in to straighten up the room, and from the stairway leading up Howay asks where his geography book is. Carrie doesn't know—hasn't seen it; the boy pulls a bell cord which summons Sybil, and Sybil doesn't know where the book is, either. Coolly, the lad asks his nursemaid to try to find it, and then joins the ladies at tea on the terrace.

Left alone, the two servants discuss Howay. Sybil states flatly that he gives her the creeps. Nelson, the bodyguard, appears and announces that the pony is now ready to take Howay for his ride. Nelson has the creeps, too. Carrie offers a flat pronouncement: Howay isn't the same boy he used to be—is not, indeed, the same boy. Carrie knows what happened; "I knew it right away when she stole the real boy and left this stick."

Nelson, confused, asks, "Who stole what?" Carrie answers, "Mrs. McThing—she did it—she stole the boy away."

"You mean the dame that lives up in the Blue Mountains everybody calls a witch?"

Carrie nods emphatically and explains, "The night she got angry at Mrs. Larue, when Mrs. Larue sent her child home. Mrs. McThing played her music and she stole the boy away and put in his place a stick—a creature who looked just like him—that kid out there is the stick she left." Carrie is so positive that Sybil and Nelson almost believe her, and Sybil wonders aloud where the real boy might be now.

The Lewis girls are stayers; having had tea, they now look as though they might remain for dinner, and Mrs. Larue comes in from the terrace to ask Carrie to tell the cook about extra guests. The telephone rings and Mrs. Larue picks it up. "Howay?" she says. "Darling, what are you doing on the telephone? I just left you on the terrace with the girls. Are you on the garage telephone? You're what—you're working in a pool hall?" The mystified mother tries to make sense out of what she is hearing—phrases like down by the railroad tracks, under the viaduct, lower Seventh Street. . . . But now the boy comes in from the terrace, and, seeing him, Mrs. Larue hangs up the phone. Carrie dashes to pick up the instrument, clicks it futilely and exclaims, "You hung up on him! What did he say? . . . So *that's* what she did with him. She stole him away and she put him out to earn his bread among strangers!"

The boy who has come in from tea on the terrace steps quietly toward Carrie, orders her to calm down and says he will get her some hot tea. When he has returned to the terrace, the maid cries to Mrs. Larue, "That stick is not your son! You mean to tell me you haven't felt the difference?"

Mrs. Larue cannot bring herself to confess such a feeling, but she does feel strangely upset and she begs off having the Lewis girls for dinner. When her callers have taken the hint and departed, she asks for an album of snapshots that were taken of Howay at the beach last Summer. The boy has reappeared, and now he asks, chidingly, "Mother—aren't you going to the door with your friends?" She looks at him with growing disbelief, and when he asks if it isn't time to change for dinner she weakly says she doesn't feel hungry. "The cook," she tells him, "will bring your dinner to your room. . . . Good night, dear. Sleep well."

"Like a log, Mother," he replies—a commonplace phrase which now strikes her as fearsome. When he has gone upstairs she snatches the phone, dials the operator and asks if a call she got five minutes ago can be traced. It can't, of course. Sybil brings in the album of snapshots, and after a quick look Mrs. Larue snaps the book shut. "I—I believe I'll go into town tonight," she falters. "I want you to go with me. And we'll take Howay along. Tell Nelson to order the car. . . ."

The curtain falls.

SCENE II

Both the interior and exterior of the Shantyland Pool Hall Lunchroom can be seen. An alley and a shabby street skirt the place, which is in the worst part of town. Inside, near the kitchen, are a table, a couple of chairs and some empty beer cases; swinging doors at the back lead to the lunchroom proper. The kitchen is behind a cutout in the wall, and there is a sliding panel which the chef can raise or lower to open or close the kitchen. A door leading off to the left bears the legend, OFFICE, E. SCHELLENBACH, PROP. The door on the other side of the room leads to the street. Ellsworth, the chef, has his kitchen open and is playing the piano soulfully. Since he has no piano he uses the kitchen counter for an instrument and seems to be deriving great pleasure from his soundless music. Virgil, the young waiter, comes in from the lunchroom and orders a bowl of chili. The burly Ellsworth stops playing and demands who wants it. Virgil, having forgotten to get the customer's name, returns to the lunchroom to get it and the chef resumes his concert. Outside, on the street, Mrs. Larue appears with Nelson, Sybil and the boy—or Stick, as the case may be. They have been searching for a long time and the boy complains that it's 20 minutes past his bedtime. Mrs. Larue leads her party around a corner.

Virgil returns with the customer's name, Lancelot E. Mehaffey of Green River, Wyoming; this sounds nice to the chef and he pushes out a bowl of chili, then resumes his music. The waiter pauses to listen, begins to dance and then asks where the boys are. "They went off on a bank job and the boss is off on his own," he is told.

As the Larue search party finds its way down the alley, "the boys," Joe and Stinker, come into the lunchroom from the street. Joe is a wiry little fellow and Stinker is a gangling youth without much appearance of brains. They report to Ellsworth that the bank job was a failure—the bank was closed and they couldn't get in. Virgil comes back with an order for a sandwich, but the customer's name doesn't suit the chef and no sandwich is forthcoming.

CHEF—Joe, what's the matter with the Stinker? He seems low tonight.

JOE—The Stinker is losin' his nerve.

STINKER (*rising menacingly from beer case R*)—Say that again!

JOE—The Stinker is losin' his nerve.

STINKER—That's twice you said that—I'm keepin' count. (*Sits.*)

JOE—You know how the Stinker's always goin' around town lookin' for an old, old lady to push under a street car—

CHEF—It's all he talks about—he's a bore on the subject.

STINKER (*aflame with a vision*)—Clang, clang, clang—here comes the car! Push her under— I dream about it— It's music— It's rhythm—

CHEF—You talk about it, sure—all talk—but have you done it yet?

STINKER—I'm tryin', ain't I?

JOE—He's tryin'. But when he catches a street car there's no old ladies—and when he catches an old lady, there's no street car. He needs a break.

CHEF—What I can't figger is WHY you want to push some old lady under a street car!

STINKER—Why—for a laugh, you dope! (*The coughing of* SCHELLENBACH *is now heard offstage UL.*)

CHEF—Jiggers, boys— (*He listens, more coughing is heard.*) It's the boss. His cough has personality. (*The* BOYS *assume a tough, nonchalant pose.* EDDIE *enters, crosses to his office silently, kicks the door open and goes in—as:*)

STINKER—*Hello,* Boss.

JOE—Hiya—Boss.

CHEF (*as* Boss *disappears*)—Don't the boss look swell, boys?

EDDIE (*instantly comes back in*)—How wah-yah—boys? Don't answer! (*Walks back and forth, lost in thought—wheels around a couple of times to look at them and puts hand on his gun inside of coat.*) The cops are out like flies. I'm hotter than a firecracker but they can't prove a thing. There's ice in this town, but it's all behind plate glass. I've cased this burg from end to end and all I bring home is alibis. What's on the agenda? (*Sits in chair.*) Call a meeting— (*Glares at* STINKER.) Call a meeting!

STINKER—That's what I'm gonna do—I'm gonna call a meeting!

EDDIE—Well, call it then and don't just stand there saying you're gonna call it— Call it!

STINKER—I'm not gonna just stand here sayin' I'm gonna call it— I'm gonna call it. (*Whistles.*) I called it! (*They grab beer cases quickly and sit facing* EDDIE's *table.*)

The purpose of the meeting, Eddie announces, is to decide whether to take the boy they call the Squirt out of the dishwashing department and promote him to the mobster department. Joe is dubious; they've only known the boy three weeks—since the time he ran in here with a cop chasing him and they hid him. It seems he broke a street lamp and Joe doesn't think this is enough of a crime. Stinker finally summons enough decision to vote that the lad is a cream puff. The balloting is still going on when a wiry little woman bursts in the door and roars, "Edward Arthur Schellenbach!" She is Eddie's mother and he cowers as she cuffs, slaps and kicks him. She also boots Stinker and then bustles out with a warning to her son to be in early tonight—"and don't bring any of these bums home with you!"

Eddie, dazed, is about to resume the voting when they hear a knock at the street door and Stinker fearfully opens it on Mrs. Larue, who timidly asks if he knows of a place called the Shantyland Pool Hall. Stinker admits he knows but refuses to tell where it is. The boy with Mrs. Larue—the Stick—chides Stinker for his rudeness, so Stinker socks him and slams the door. Outraged, Mrs. Larue orders the bodyguard to do something about it while she takes the boy down to the Salvation Army to let him rest a bit. Nelson timidly enters the lunchroom, says to Eddie, "You sock that kid?"—and gives Eddie two dollars before retreating hastily. Eddie pockets the bills and flips Joe and Stinker a dime. "Here's your cut," he snarls. After more debate about the Squirt's qualifications as a mobster, Eddie orders the chef to send the boy out.

The boy emerges from the kitchen, carrying a tray and protesting that he'd been promised he could eat after he'd finished the dishes. He is, of course, the real Howay—Howard V. Larue IV himself, but now quite soiled. He asks the chef if anybody has been around asking for him, but vaguely answers "Oh, nobody" when Ellsworth asks whom he's expecting. The three gangsters now are hiding beneath the chef's window, observing the boy's conduct. They approve of his close-mouthed attitude toward the chef, and when the boy goes to the lunchroom and returns with an order their approbation rises— for, all on his own, he has told a customer named DeWitt T. Ferdestaller of Keokuk, Iowa, that he can't have a roast beef sandwich. Howay had figured correctly that Ellsworth wouldn't like a name like that.

Soon Howay is back with another order—roast chicken for a Duane B. Wilson of Alamosa, Colorado. Immediately the chef produces a roast chicken, but Howay drops it off his tray onto the floor. Cautiously he picks the fowl up, spits on it, wipes it on his pants and starts off with it. The mobsters pop up from their hiding place and congratulate the boy on his conduct. Eddie pronounces him one of the mob—but instead of being grateful the boy is hesitant. He wishes he could, but he can't; he explains that he was finally able to get his mother on the phone and she should be along any minute to get him. Outraged, Eddie snarls, "I've got a notion to rub you out right now." Howay pleads that he's all his mother has got— at least, that's what she always says. Eddie orders the boy back to work.

Joe and Stinker have been banished to the street, and suddenly they take off after a pretty girl. For a moment Eddie is alone in the lunchroom, and then in comes the same waif who had appeared so mysteriously at the Larue mansion. She is carrying the toy railroad car. Eddie demands who she is and the lass answers, "Me. They hung the big round moon up there for me to look at. When birds sing in the trees they sing for me and no one else. The grass grows just for me to walk on. I am a dear little white rose—the loveliest child in the whole wide world." She knows so because her mother has told her—but Eddie growls disparagingly about mothers. Look at him—Poison Eddie Schellenbach—and *his* mother used to call him her little apple dumpling. The child persists, "I am Mimi—a dear little white rose. My mother is Mrs. McThing." She is explaining to Eddie that her mother lives up there in the Blue Mountains in a big dark woods when Howay, coming in from the kitchen, greets her by name.

Eddie is surprised that the children know each other, and does not approve of kids running in with toys—it gives the place a sissy name. He starts to ease Mimi out, but Howay stops him and whispers some information. "So she says her old lady is a witch? So what?" Eddie is not impressed, nor is he taken aback by Mimi's announcement, "I will turn you into a cuspidor if you send me home."

"She likes me," Howay explains, and Eddie comments, "Well, kid, I have been in the same situation myself with bigger dames, and there is no cure for it but death." He allows Mimi to remain and goes into his office. The girl reports to the boy what she's been doing. She got into his home, but not close enough to talk to his mother. "A boy was riding your pony," she adds. "The boy looks just like you. My mother made him—she put him in your bed the night you ran away. She has magic—my mother—she put this stick there."

Howay announces, "Your mother is a jerk," and Mimi threatens to turn *him* into a cuspidor. Howay can't understand his mother letting that stick ride his pony, but Mimi explains that Mrs. Larue likes him because he is so clean and obedient and polite—he even kissed the Lewis girls. Howay, infuriated, shouts, "This drippy boy! Wait till I get home and I'll clean him!" Mimi reminds him that he can't go home—the place is guarded and they don't let anybody in. Howay begins to feel sorry for himself and the little girl comforts him as Mrs. Larue and Sybil reappear in the street for a moment, still searching.

Soon Joe and Stinker come in from the street on the run, shouting for Eddie, who pops out of his office. The mobsters report that there's a car at the corner with a dame and a chauffeur. Howay joyfully runs out, crying, "My mother! She's coming for me." Stinker and Joe haven't finished telling about what they saw—this dame with long gold hair blowing in the wind, smiling and throwing red roses. The boys got one each and one for Eddie. Now it's Mimi's turn to run out, crying, "It's my mother—she's come for me."

Eddie takes a look down the street and can see no one, no car. Howay returns without finding anybody. When Stinker describes the lady as looking like a movie queen—a glamorous witch—Howay realizes that the woman they saw was Mimi's old lady. "And my old lady," he adds angrily, "she can take a long jump for herself into a lake—for all I care." He runs into the kitchen, sobbing, and the mobsters follow him. Suddenly Howay announces, "Mr. Schellenbach, I changed my mind. I want to join the mob." There is general handshaking as the curtain falls.

Scene III

A few minutes have passed. The chef is playing his "piano" again, alone, until Mrs. Larue comes in from the lunchroom looking for a telephone, which she finds on a wall. As she dials a number she is followed in from the lunchroom by the Stick and the bodyguard.

Mrs. Larue has called Evva Lewis, but the line is busy, and the three sit down to wait a moment. Mrs. Larue wants to ask Evva the name of a friend who is a social worker and might know of the place they are looking for. Virgil, the waiter, comes in with an order for hot roast beef from ex-convict 89999999. The chef, recognizing the number as an old friend named Maloney, dishes up the food, and Nelson looks longingly at it. Howay's mother suggests that he have some food, and asks the boy what he'd like. "You decide, Mother," he says. "You know best." He keeps insisting he only wants whatever she wants him to have, and she becomes exasperated, snapping, "I wanted you to grow up—I wanted you to get some sense—but I didn't expect you to go so far."

When the waiter comes in Mrs. Larue orders roast beef for the bodyguard and milk for the boy, and Virgil insists on having her name. He calls to the chef, "Hot roast beef san and one glass of milk for Mrs. Howard V. Larue—three." The chef slams the window in disgust, and Virgil explains that everything is all out—everything. She demands an audience with the manager and Virgil says he will see if Mr. Schellenbach is busy. Nelson wonders if it's Poison Eddie Schellenbach, the mobster. In a moment Eddie comes in, followed by Joe and Stinker, who spot the dandified boy, snatch his hat off his head and tussle with it as Eddie tries to explain to Mrs. Larue that the chef is a musician and therefore temperamental. Soon the boy is reduced to tears and Mrs. Larue orders Nelson to take him home; then she turns in fury upon the mobsters and says she hopes they are thoroughly ashamed of themselves. She is about to stalk out when she sees Mimi coming from the kitchen. "You!" she exclaims. "What are you doing here? Are you following me?" Mimi sweetly explains, "I want to play with your boy." Mrs. Larue is horrified at the thought of her boy playing with a child from such a neighborhood, but Eddie disowns her. "And where, may I ask, is your mother if you have one?" Mrs. Larue coldly inquires. Soft music is heard as Mimi points upward and says, "Where the trees are tall there is a hush, hush, hush. My mother is walking through the woods. And her dress is long and green and silk, and it goes swish—swish—swish—through the hush—hush—hush—"

At all this swishing and hushing Joe and Stinker begin a hepcat dance which ends in a scuffle. Mrs. Larue snorts, "This child is very odd and I thought so from the first. She is obviously trash." Mimi happily agrees—she *is* trash. That was where her mother found her when she was three days old—so Mrs. McThing took her up to the Blue Mountains and raised her. Mrs. Larue suggests that Mimi go back to her mountains, but the girl insists she wants to play with

Howay. "Well, you can't," says Mrs. Larue flatly, and she leaves. Eddie, too, tries to get Mimi to go home, but she won't; so he gives her a broom and puts her to work in the kitchen. Then he and the boys go into his office for another meeting, and the chef raises his window.

Mrs. Larue returns, having forgotten her handbag and gloves in her hurry to get away. Out of the kitchen comes Howay, dressed in a striped gangster suit and derby just like Poison Eddie's. He and his mother see each other at the same instant and walk slowly toward each other. She grips his shoulders and shakes him, chiding, "How dare you! How could you!"

"You know me?" Howay inquires.

Of course she does, and she continues shaking him in maternal hysteria. Gradually her fierceness changes to self-pity, and Howay pleads with her to let him go, but she clings tightly to him. Suddenly she looks toward the door where Nelson and the boy have gone and asks, frightened, "Who is—*he?*" Her son explains about Mrs. McThing and the trick she played. Howay, now sorry for himself, tortures his mother by accusing her of liking the Stick better than him because he is such a perfect boy. Soon they are in each other's arms. "Let's go home—right away," she cries—but Howay says he can't go because he has joined the mob.

Mimi appears and Mrs. Larue cries, "You—you get away! This all started the day you climbed over our wall. . . . You get away from him and stay away from him. Get out—"

Quietly, menacingly, Mimi announces, "That was your last chance. You get no more chances. Never—no more. No more chances." And she goes out.

Howay's mother announces she will call the house and have the car sent. She is furious at Mimi and mutters about building higher walls and hiring a night bodyguard. She dials her home and says, "Nelson? This is Mrs. Larue speaking. No, I don't want to speak to Mrs. Larue—this *is* Mrs. Larue speaking." Howay begins to realize what has happened as his mother is put on to someone else— someone who says she is Mrs. Larue. She puts the receiver to Howay's ear and asks, "Is that me?" The boy nods yes. Staring unbelievingly at the receiver, she lets it drop and staggers.

"Don't you see, Mom," says Howay, "Mrs. McThing has skunked you again. She put a stick in *your* place this time." His mother utters a terrified cry as the curtain falls.

ACT II

A few days have passed and the Shantyland has acquired a new employee—Mrs. Howard V. Larue III, who now is clad in scrub-woman clothes and is sweeping the floor. The chef is playing his piano. On the floor she spies a nickel, furtively snatches it, rushes to the phone and begins dialing. Virgil comes in with an order from a man who wouldn't give his name but gave his social security number. He tries to remember it—1253—no, 1462—no, 42578. . . . He keeps on trying numbers, which is very confusing to Mrs. Larue, who is trying to dial Evva Lewis. Finally she does get Evva and pleads with her, "That woman you see in my home is not I. She's a stick. I am Belle Larue—" But it's no use; Evva has hung up.

Howay comes in from outside. He may be a mobster in a loud suit and a hard hat, but motherhood is hard to conquer; Mrs. Larue chides him for his dirty ears and forces him to submit to being scrubbed. Surprisingly, the chef sides with her and advises the boy to listen to his mother. Howay goes into the lunchroom to comb his hair in the washroom, and Mrs. Larue exclaims indignantly, "Does he want to grow up to be a bum—end on Skid Row— Oh! I forgot where I am." She thanks Ellsworth for his help, and he allows that Howay is a pretty good kid.

Eddie enters and demands what's going on, and Mrs. Larue scurries to the kitchen. When Howay comes back, Eddie bids him sit down for a serious talk—about his mother. He didn't dream he'd be having her on the payroll, but now she is . . . and she isn't working out very well. Her attitude may be okay, but she doesn't wash dishes and she can't sweep. "Her work don't satisfy me," says Eddie, "and I'm not what you'd call a particularly clean mobster, am I?" He wants Howay to have a private talk with his mother and warn her she may lose her job if she doesn't improve. Howay promises, just as Stinker and Joe run in from the street. They've found out something and they want a meeting, so all but Howay go to the office. The boy asks Ellsworth to send in his mother, but when she appears he doesn't know how to begin. He offers her a doughnut; the help aren't supposed to take doughnuts, but he's one of the mob. His mother shudders—but hungrily takes the food. He begins by observing what a swell place this is, but she says if they don't stop nagging her she will resign.

"Where would you go?"

"Why—I don't really know . . ."

Ellsworth calls for Belle to get back in the suds in the kitchen, and she obeys. Eddie and the boys come out of the office filled with excitement; they're going on a job and Howay is to be the key man. The job is no less than cracking Howay's own home; the boys have cased it, pony and swan boat and all, and they will blast through the gate with rods. Howay says he doesn't want to go; he isn't yellow— he just doesn't like it back there, being in his bedroom at night and hearing other kids playing down the road. Eddie sympathizes, but after all Howay is in the mob and they're going to blast their way in. He is threatening to belt Howay for not wanting to work with them when Mrs. Schellenbach appears in the doorway. Eddie cries out a terrified "Mama!" and everybody runs for cover. The old lady pursues her son into the office and there are crashes and yells; then she stomps out, snorting, "These bums!" Mrs. Larue has witnessed the invasion from the kitchen and observes to the chef that the old lady has a worse problem than she has because her boy's habit pattern is pretty well set. She goes back to her work, and into the restaurant come the three Lewis girls, looking for the woman who has been making such a pest of herself on the phone claiming she is Belle Larue. Belle comes out, broom in hand, and with great joy encounters her friends. But the friends aren't so friendly; Evva demands, "Who are you?" They won't believe the story about Mrs. McThing and suspect that some cunning scheme is afoot. In vain Mrs. Larue tells intimate details of past events to prove her identity, and she gets Evva into hot water by a veiled reference to some interesting occurrence in Phoenix one time. The trio prepare to leave, deaf to Mrs. Larue's pleas, and in parting Evva declares, "A scrubwoman in a place like this—to mention a thing like that to me. Girls, this is not Belle Larue." And, to Howay's mother, "Even if you were Belle Larue—I would never admit it."

The infuriated woman shoos the girls out with her broom, shouting after them, "If I ever get home, you'll run faster than that!"

Howay comes in from the lunchroom and tells his mother of the mob's plan and at once she is excited, exclaiming, "Oh, what I'd give to go home right now!" She will change into her good clothes immediately. As Howay hangs back she urges, "Don't stand there, dear, you've got to get out of those awful clothes. Oh, I hate that hat!" She takes the derby off his head and throws it on the floor.

HOWAY (*jams hat back on his head*)—I like it here. I've got friends here. Why do we have to go home?

LARUE—Friends, yes, but not your type, dear. Good people, but not quite right for you. (*She is by his side now.*) There is nobody like you and that's not just because you're my child. I know—I've observed other children, and they don't have that certain something you have. You are very, very special. (*He draws away sullenly and sits in chair. She is worried.*) I'll buy you an Alaskan husky—right away. We'll get that chemical company to come out and freeze the lake and you can go dog-sledding even in Summer.

HOWAY—Could—could—Mr. Schellenbach and the mob come home with us?

LARUE (*gets angry*)—Those people at home with us? Oh, Howay —you are incorrigible—I'm losing my patience— Don't you care anything about me— Do you like to see your mother washing dishes! (*She is on her knees to him.*) I want to be in my own home—my own bed—look at my own garden—I've been so unhappy. Doesn't that mean anything to you— Don't you love me at all?

HOWAY (*now beaten—pats her head*)—Okay—

LARUE (*instantly jubilant again*)—Get your own clothes—get ready—get ready— (*She exits into lunchroom; he turns chair facing lunchroom and sits dejectedly. Enter* MIMI *from street.*)

JOE (*grabs her*)—Hey, where you goin'?

MIMI—I'm going to play with the boy.

JOE—He can't play with you tonight.

STINKER—He's goin' on a job. Leave him alone.

JOE—You can play with us if you want to play.

STINKER—What if she wants to play fair?

MIMI—I came down from the Blue Mountains to play with the boy.

JOE—You and your fairy stories—

MIMI—I will tell you a story—a sad, sad story, and you've got to cry. Some day my mother will take me to the edge of the woods and she will kiss me good-by. Because I am people and some day I must go to live with people. It will break her heart to kiss me good-by but she must do it and it will break my heart to kiss her good-by but I must do it—because your heart has to break—yours and yours—and everybody's heart has to break. Now cry!

Obediently the boys weep until the little girl tells them they've had enough; after all, it hasn't happened yet.

Howay gets up to leave the room and is seized by Joe, who thinks he may be taking a runout. The boy tells Mimi of the plan to blast into the Larue home. "My mother says no," the girl announces. Guns won't make any difference; they can't get rid of sticks. But how, Howay pleads, and Mimi, self-assured, says *she* knows how. She overheard her mother once. If she gets rid of the sticks, will Howay's mother let her play with him? He vows his mother will— he'll make her.

"MRS. MC THING"

Mrs. Howard V. Larue III, in considerably reduced circumstances, discovers that her son, Howay, has become a mobster and is working in a pool hall lunchroom. He likes it better than she does.

(*Helen Hayes, Brandon de Wilde*)

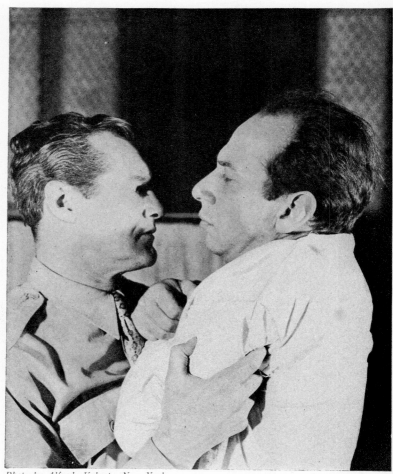

"THE SHRIKE"

Jim Downs, a would-be suicide under observation in the psycho ward of a hospital, has had an emotional outburst and is being warned by an attendant that he must get hold of himself and keep hold of himself if he hopes to get out.

(*Philip Huston, José Ferrer*)

"I AM A CAMERA"

Sally Bowles, late of England, fancies herself as quite a decadent young woman in pre-war Berlin. Prairie oysters are her regular breakfast dish.

(*Julie Harris*)

Photo by Alfredo Valente, New York.

"THE FOURPOSTER"

Being a dutiful husband even on the first night, Michael demonstrates to his bride, Agnes, that he hasn't any alcohol on his breath. Not much except for some champagne, at any rate.

(*Jessica Tandy, Hume Cronyn*)

Photo by John Swope.

"POINT OF NO RETURN"

Banker Charles Gray does not like what has been written about his home town in a book, so he throws the volume into a wastebasket while his wife, Nancy, looks on.

(Henry Fonda, Leora Dana)

"BAREFOOT IN ATHENS"

Says Socrates to Xantippe: "I was in love with you when we were married. I'm an old codger now, but I'm still in love with you as much as any ancient party can be."

(*Lotte Lenya, Barry Jones*)

"VENUS OBSERVED"

The house has burned, but the Temple of the Ancient Virtues still stands and in it amateur astrologist Hereward resumes his wooing of the lovely young Perpetua.

(Lilli Palmer, Rex Harrison)

"JANE"

Millicent Tower has long been divorced from William Tower, the novelist, but she is more or less glad to see him whenever he returns from one of his world jaunts.

(*Irene Browne, Basil Rathbone*)

"GIGI"

Worldly old Aunt Alicia decides that it is time for young Gigi to have more appropriate clothes if she is to begin a campaign to get a man.

(Cathleen Nesbitt, Audrey Hepburn)

"REMAINS TO BE SEEN"

Jody Revere is somewhat indignant when she discovers that Benjamin Goodman, whom she has come all the way to New York to see, is only a lawyer and not Benny Goodman, the band leader.

(*Jackie Cooper, Janis Paige, Howard Lindsay*)

Mrs. Larue flutters in, dressed and ready to go. She can't be bothered with Mimi now. "But, Mother," Howay expostulates, "Mimi says—" She drags her son into the office and shuts the door in the little girl's face. There is a loud, repeated knocking at the door and Mimi, hiding under the table, whispers to the chef, "It's my mother. Don't tell her I'm here." The chef puts his hands on his imaginary piano and is frightened when there is a sound of music. Mrs. Larue and the mobsters, including Howay, come from the office and hear it, too. "The kid said it was her mother," the chef whispers, and Mrs. Larue is frightened. Howay seizes his opportunity and urges, "Look, Mother. Mimi can do it. She can get us back home." Mimi assures them Howay is right—she can do it, and she *will* do it because she wants to go with Howay. Mrs. Larue gives in and Mimi leads off on tiptoes, saying, "Don't be afraid—follow me." They all tiptoe after her, in step.

The curtain falls.

SCENE II

It is later that night, in the morning room at Larue Towers. The Stick boy is in the center of a sofa, reading a book on psychology to the three Lewis girls and his Stick mother. ". . . Therefore, the problem facing each and every one of us . . ." Maude Lewis asks for candy in a loud whisper and the boy shushes her. When Evva says something to one of her sisters the boy firmly stops her; but in a moment Evva starts again and he slams the book shut in annoyance. His mother meekly asks if it is all right for the women to chat now, and he grants permission.

The gabfest is interrupted by the appearance of Nelson, who reports that the lodgekeeper at the gate has seen a gang of hoodlums climbing over the wall. The stick Mrs. Larue orders him to call the police. Sybil runs downstairs into the room to report that the wires are cut and there are screams of fright. The mob appears at the head of the stairs, and all flee out of the room except the two Sticks, who freeze where they sit. Joe, Eddie and Stinker look in awe at the luxury around them—like the lobby of the Bijou Movie Theatre, Stinker ventures. With his hand in his pocket, Eddie commands the Sticks, "Reach!" They don't move, and they ignore repeated commands. Eddie seizes the woman's head and it turns as if on a swivel; he exclaims, "They ain't breathin'—they're stiffs!"

Outside there is a sound of sirens, bells and police whistles. They all make a dash to escape, but Joe calls, "We're surrounded!" They miss Belle and Howay. Eddie urges his pals to make for the roof, but suddenly Mimi appears and they flatten against a wall. "Where's Howay?" she asks.

Eddie, remembering Mimi's promise, urges, "Kid, whatever you do, do it now!" Mimi murmurs, "I am a dear little white rose." Walking toward the Sticks, she has a firecracker in her hand. The Sticks raise their hands in fear and watch her as she chants,

> "Knives and stones won't cut your bones
> And guns will never hurt you—
> So burn—sticks—burn—
> Fire—fire—fire—"

Mimi throws the firecracker and there is a blinding flash, then a blackout. Nelson and police are heard running, and they enter at the head of the stairs with flashlights. Nelson gloats, "Poison Eddie Schellenbach and his mob." Joe wants to know where Belle and Howay are, and Stinker says they went to the basement to turn off the police alarm—too late.

Nelson switches on the room lights, and where the Sticks sat are now two burnt pieces of wood. Nelson orders the mob to drop their guns on the floor, but nothing drops. While he covers, a policeman frisks the trio—and finds no guns. All he gets is Superman comics, hair vaseline, Hopalong Cassidy comics and six cereal box tops.

Nelson picks up the two burnt sticks, looking at them curiously, and a policeman suspects the mob of arson; but Mimi speaks up, saying she did it. At the head of the stair Howay and his mother appear and Mrs. Larue demands, "Nelson, what's the meaning of this?" The bodyguard explains, "I found three bums and two sticks in here."

Coolly Mrs. Larue orders, "Well, throw out the sticks and leave the bums—these men are my guests." Howay puts in, "This is my mob." His mother continues, "Nelson, send the police away at once. Somebody has played a joke on you." The baffled bodyguard obeys. The three baffled Lewises creep in from the terrace.

Evva—You're letting them go—but, Belle—they are robbers.

Larue—Girls—how could you—they are my friends. Home— home—I could kiss every piece of furniture in this room and every person and you—(*Crosses to* Mimi.)—especially you—oh, you wonderful little girl—you adorable darling. (*She moves* Mimi *to join* Howay *sitting on the steps.*) Oh, girls—I have dates for you. (Gangsters *smile shyly.* Lewises *are indignant at first.*) I want you to meet Mr. Schellenbach. And Mr. McGinnis. And Mr. St—er—Steinway. I have been visiting them. They have a fascinating place. Oh, I will never forget how kind you were to me—

when I was out in the cold, cold world—how you took me in and were so dear to me and would have kept me forever. There isn't anything I wouldn't do for you—have a piece of candy— (*She offers candy from compote on coffee table.*)

EDDIE (*takes some—*OTHERS *reach over his shoulder*)—Well, I tell you, Belle—I could use a few bucks, too.

LARUE—As many as you want. Just name the figure. I'll write you a check.

EDDIE—Well—I've had a little trouble with checks, lately— What about the silver? (*Indicating whatnot SL.*)

LARUE (*sits in chair R,* LEWISES *sit in their places*)—Take it—all of it—it's yours— (*They fill burlap bags they have been carrying.*)

EVVA—Do you collect silver, Mr. Schellenbach?

EDDIE (*sits DS of* EVVA *on chaise longue*)—Yes—I do—

EVVA—Do you favor any particular period? We have Queen Anne and Georgian.

EDDIE—That so—where are you located?

Howay reminds his mother that Mimi has done everything, and Mrs. Larue asks the girl what she can do for her. Mimi replies, "I want to stay with Howay." The boy gets out a toy train and the children begin to play as the Lewises move to go home. Eddie gallantly offers to see them home. "We have our own car," says Evva. "We'll be glad to give you a lift." Eddie accepts a ride as far as their house and orders Stinker to get another bag—for gumdrops. To Mrs. Larue he calls, "So long, Belle—been swell—"

Belle Larue is indeed grateful to Mimi for her impish miracle— but she also is terrified of reprisals from Mrs. McThing, who might resent her taking the girl. The best plan, she tells the children, is to ship Mimi off to a girls' school in La Jolla. She'll have plenty of money and a bicycle and a pony like Howay's. Mimi wants none of this and is heartbroken; there is only one person who can help her now, and she calls out desperately, "Mother!" Now Mrs. Larue is frightened and begins issuing orders that nobody is to be allowed in; then she gives a panicked screech as a hideous old crone appears at the head of the stairs, in a black hat and cape and carrying a stick; she demands, "Where is my child?"

Mimi speaks up and her mother scolds her for siding with humans. "Come back where you belong," she orders, grabbing the girl. This is too much for Belle Larue; she pulls Mimi back, snatches the hag's stick and begins beating her, crying, "Get out—get out." Mrs. McThing vanishes and Mrs. Larue, flushed with victory, says, "If you think I could let that horrid old hag have a lovely child like this—never! Never you mind, Mimi—you'll stay here with us and be our little daughter and our little sister." Howay is overjoyed, but Mimi flings herself on the stairs and weeps, "You beat my mother—she isn't ugly—she's beautiful—and she didn't kiss me good-by. Mother—Mother—"

The lights dim to a soft, rosy glow and Mrs. McThing reappears. Her cape and hat fall from her; she is dressed like a fairy and she is very beautiful. She runs down the stair and gives her daughter a kiss, saying, "My little girl—you've left me forever."

MIMI—I want to play with this boy.

MOTHER—I know.

MIMI—Will you ever come again?

MOTHER—No.

MIMI—Won't I ever see you or hear you or touch you again?

MOTHER—No. But when you are happy I will be there.

MIMI—Mother, my heart is breaking.

MOTHER—Yes.

MIMI—Is your heart breaking too?

MOTHER—Yes.

MIMI—Let us press our broken hearts together and maybe they will heal. (*They press themselves together.*)

MOTHER—Better now?

MIMI—Yes, is yours?

MOTHER—Yes—and now— (*She stands.*)

MIMI—Don't say it, Mother—don't say good-by—

MOTHER—No—only good night— (*As she starts to move she sort of limps.*)

MIMI—She did hurt you, Mother—she did—

MOTHER—No—that's only my broken heart—good night. (*Lights slowly come back up as she goes.*)

MIMI—Wave to me, Mother—wave to me—

LARUE (*at sofa with* HOWAY)—Mimi! Mimi—Mimi—

HOWAY—Mimi—who was the ugly one? Who was she?

MIMI—My mother.

HOWAY—I don't understand.

MIMI—Sometimes when my mother is helping me she has to look ugly.

LARUE—I never thought of that.

The children resume play with the train on the floor. Mrs. Larue goes up the stair and, turning back, calls softly, "Good night—children—"

THE CURTAIN FALLS

THE SHRIKE *

A Play in Three Acts

By Joseph Kramm

THERE was more than one reason for critical cheering at the advent of "The Shrike." It was a holding melodrama, it had an excellent production by José Ferrer, it was well acted by Ferrer, Judith Evelyn and their supporting players—and it was by a new playwright. No one complained when, in the Spring of 1952, Mr. Kramm won the Pulitzer prize for his drama—for new talent in the theatre is to be encouraged. Kramm, however, is not exactly a *débutant* in the theatre; he is 44 and is another alumnus of Eva Le Gallienne's Civic Repertory Theatre. "The Shrike" was his first produced play, but he had eight others in his trunk. His tenth work, "The Gypsies Wore High Hats," was scheduled for production during the 1952-1953 season. Kramm wrote his first nine plays while laying off from various jobs as actor, director and teacher at the American Theatre Wing. When "The Shrike" opened he was directing commercials for a daytime television show.

When "The Shrike" begins, one sees Ward MN 3 of City Hospital—any city hospital in any sizable city. It is a drab place—no ornamentation and no flowers; just beds, and metal cabinets next to each bed for patients' belongings. The ward differs from other sections of the hospital in that there are heavy wire screens in front of the windows—not outside them. Near a door—a locked door— are two desks, two chairs, lamps, papers, patients' charts and telephones. The door is the only one into this ward, and nurses, attendants and doctors use their own keys getting in and out. It is 11:30 on a Tuesday morning. Patients are in their beds—one reading, one asleep, one just staring into space, a fourth talking to a student nurse, Miss Cardell, who is at his bedside. The nurse in charge, who has been soured rather than mellowed by her years of contact with illness, is at the first desk, closest to the ward door, making notes on some charts. Near the other desk is a tall, good-looking man, Dr. Kramer, who is reading a chart.

The student nurse accuses the patient she is standing beside of having been smoking, and with his heart condition he shouldn't. He tries to deny it, but the girl bulldozes him into fetching a pack of cigarettes from beneath his mattress and giving up a paper of matches from his pajama pocket. The nurse in charge, Miss Hansen, answers a ring on her desk phone and after a moment of listening says, "Emergency suicide coming up, Dr. Kramer."

Kramer is efficient. Another bed will have to be provided. Dr. Barrow should be summoned on the hospital intercom. Two hospital orderlies, Perkins and Grosberg, wheel in a bed. Says Grosberg to Perkins, "Dr. Barrow's nice. You know her? She's a psychiatrist." The attendants make up the new bed, but are interrupted when the patient who has been forced to give up his cigarettes hisses at Grosberg, hands him a dollar bill and says, "Chesterfields." Grosberg goes back to help Perkins with the bed linen and muses, "Now what would a man want to do that for? Some woman, I guess." He isn't talking about the smoke-hungry patient, but about the would-be suicide whose reception is being arranged. A bell sounds, Miss Hansen unlocks the ward door with her key, and a patient is wheeled in on a high carriage. Beside the carriage walks a handsome, intelligent-looking blonde who, when she is challenged by the nurse, identifies herself as Ann Downs, the patient's wife.

Dr. Kramer goes to the high carriage, wraps a sphygmomanometer around the man's arm, takes his blood pressure, reports "110 over 60" to Dr. Barrow, who has just come in, and begins slapping the patient's face, commanding, "Wake up! Wake up!" After a particularly hard slap Jim Downs emits a low grunt. Dr. Barrow asks gently, "What did you take?" Another grunt. The wife, Ann, supplies the information: "Phenobarbital," and Dr. Kramer interjects sharply, "Let *him* answer." Kramer shakes Jim and demands, "What did you take?" Thickly, hazily, Jim answers "Phen . . . o . . . bar . . . bital." "How many did you take?" "A hun . . . dred and fif . . . ty-six." Dr. Barrow doubts that this number would be possible, but the dazed Jim repeats the number 156. Dr. Barrow puts her hands on Jim's face and remarks that he seems very cold.

"He was lying on the floor. It was an unheated apartment," Ann volunteers.

The patient is moved onto his bed and Dr. Kramer quietly orders a stomach pump, a screen for the bed and a saline solution with high vitamin content for intravenous injection. He says the man will be on the critical list for a while and he wants special nurses for at least 48 hours; the wife can stay here if she likes. With the machinery of life-saving in motion, Kramer now turns to the wife to find out just how it happened.

"I don't really know," says Ann. "I got a phone call from his brother about 9:30 this morning . . ."

"Wait a minute—weren't you there? I thought you were his wife."

"I am. We were separated. He was living in this cold-water flat." Ann fills in: Jim's brother is a business man in a small town near Pittsburgh, and he'd got a letter from Jim saying that Jim was going to take pills, so he had telephoned and Ann had immediately called the police. By now she is weeping gently but still is in emotional control of herself. "I gave them the address," she continues, "and thank God they were there by the time I arrived."

Kramer wants to fix the time Jim took the pills and Ann tries to figure it out. This is Tuesday. She had talked with her husband about 12:30 Sunday night, and had made a date to see him at her apartment at 4 o'clock Monday afternoon—and he hadn't appeared. That's all she knew until the brother phoned from Pennsylvania this morning.

Dr. Barrow has been by the patient's bedside, and now she emerges from behind the screen with a question for Ann: "Excuse me—are you Charlotte?" Kramer introduces Ann and Dr. Barrow explains, "I wanted to identify the name Charlotte."

Ann answers, "She's just someone he knew."

"I see." Dr. Barrow gives Ann a brief look and returns to Jim. Kramer pursues his business—asking, for instance, what Jim's religion is and explaining that he should have the last rites of his faith. Ann is now fighting for control of herself, and Kramer eases her by saying, "You have no idea how many men have walked out of here after last rites have been said over them." He gives Ann permission to see her husband for a moment, and she goes behind the screen, saying quietly, "Jim! Jim!"

The lights fade quickly.

SCENE II

It is about 2 A.M. the next day, Wednesday, and the only light in the ward comes from the desk lamps and a dim light in the corridor. Ann, sitting in the chair at the doctor's desk, is trying hard to keep awake; the student nurse comes from Jim's bed with a thermometer and goes to the nurses' desk to record the temperature on the chart.

Then Miss Cardell, noting Ann's weariness, goes down the corridor to fetch her some coffee. Dr. Barrow drops in, checks on her patient, then asks Ann, "Has he spoken yet?"

ANN—A few things.

DR. BARROW—What?

ANN—Why didn't you let me die, he said—why didn't you let me die. He repeated it several times. I wanted to question him, but I didn't think I should.

DR. BARROW—Oh, by all means—that's most important. When he starts talking again, you must try to keep him awake.

ANN—I'm afraid to do something wrong.

DR. BARROW—Not at all. You must question him, talk to him— get all the information you can. The things he says now are the most important. That's what he really thinks and feels. As he regains consciousness, he will begin to build the walls again. You understand?

ANN—Hm-hmm.

DR. BARROW—Cigarette?

ANN—No, thank you.

DR. BARROW—Self-deception. His defenses will come back to protect him. (*Lights cigarette.*)

ANN—I understand.

DR. BARROW—You spoke to his brother this morning?

ANN—Yes.

DR. BARROW—Was there anything in the letter—any reason for taking his life?

ANN—I don't think so. His brother read the letter to me on the phone. I don't remember anything.

DR. BARROW—Have you any idea why Jim didn't leave a letter for *you*, Mrs. Downs?

ANN—No—unless he felt . . . I don't know. (MISS CARDELL *enters with coffee.*) Oh, thank you, Miss Cardell, you're very kind.

MISS CARDELL—Not at all.

DR. BARROW—Coffee! I'd love some. (*A questioning look at* MISS CARDELL.) Would it be too much trouble?

MISS CARDELL (*doesn't like to run errands for doctors*)—Not at all. (*Exits.*)

DR. BARROW—What does your husband do, Mrs. Downs?

ANN—He's in the theatre.

DR. BARROW—Singing—dancing?

ANN—No—it's what they call the legitimate theatre—he's a director.

DR. BARROW—Has he worked recently?

ANN—No. Several years ago he directed a show that got good notices. . . .

DR. BARROW—On Broadway?

ANN—Yes. The critics said he was a fine, new talent.

DR. BARROW—Then I don't understand. . . .

ANN—Well, that's the theatre. It ended right there. He expected to be flooded with offers from other producers, the movies, what not —but nothing came of it. Time went by—several years now, in fact—the show was forgotten. He never got another job.

DR. BARROW—I see. Well, that's only part of the reason. Is there anything more?

ANN—He had to start all over again—anything at all, just to make a living. It made him very unhappy. (JIM *moans.*) That's Jim—he's trying to move. Oh, yes, once he said—why did they tie my hands and feet?

DR. BARROW—You understand—we *had* to tie him—the intravenous needle in his arm. (*Another moan.*) Maybe he's awake. (*They go to* JIM's *bed.* BARROW *turns on bed lamp.*) What's the matter, Jim?

JIM (*still indistinct—in everything he says there is a sense of struggle*)—Why don't you let me die?

Jim's voice has acquired strength enough to disturb other patients as he cries that he is no good, that he had his chance and didn't make it, and now he'll have to do it all over again.

"There's still time, dear," Ann urges—but Jim has the hopeless feeling that he is an old man . . . and he is only 42.

"I love you," Ann pleads. "Do you hear me, Jim?"

Bitterly he answers, "It's too late, Ann. I don't want you to love me." And in a different voice he muses, "A hundred and fifty-six pills. . . ." Dr. Barrow can't bring herself to believe so large a number—or why the number should remain so exact in the patient's mind.

Dr. Barrow asks Ann, "Are you in the theatre, too?"

"I was. I was doing very well in the theatre when I met Jim. When we married I felt one career in the family was enough, so I gave it up."

"Do you regret it?"

Ann pauses briefly, smiles bitterly and answers, "We all have our vanity, Doctor."

"Of course. Do you have any children?"

"No."

"How long have you been married?"

"Nine years." Then, in a sudden burst of tears, Ann cries, "I love him, Dr. Barrow. I know he loves me." The doctor murmurs that this will help.

The lights fade quickly.

Scene III

A bright sun makes the ward look almost cheerful. It's about noon, two days later—Friday. The attendant Grosberg is serving "dinner"—trays of a soft diet. Jim Downs is sitting up in bed, and from his attitude there is no awareness that anything unusual has taken place; now that he is alive, the only thing that matters to him is to get out of the hospital as soon as possible. Jim calls Grosberg over and asks if he'll do something for him—mail a letter which he takes from beneath his pillow. Grosberg asks Jim why he doesn't have his wife mail it—she'll be here soon—but Jim stammers that he'd rather have Grosberg do it. Grosberg extracts the promise of a pack of cigarettes and pockets the note just as Ann rings the bell from outside. The attendant lets her in. Fleming, the patient with the bad heart who likes to smoke, gives her a cheery greeting which she returns as she goes to her husband's bedside. Grosberg begins to feed another patient—the man who is always staring into space.

Ann has some wonderful news for Jim: The Joe Williams office called and wants to see him about a job on Monday afternoon. Jim is excited; now he must really try to get up—try to walk. Ann reminds him he is in the care of doctors, and he seems to remember a Dr. Kramer and a Dr. Barrow. Just now Dr. Barrow enters and the enthusiastic Jim, after telling her she is very attractive, says he wants to start walking around because he has an appointment for a job on Monday. Dr. Barrow, professionally cautious, counters with a question, "Isn't it more important that you get well?" Anyhow, she explains, she is only the psychiatrist; Dr. Kramer is the medical doctor and he is the one to pass on Jim physically. And then there is Dr. Schlesinger, the chief psychiatrist on this floor, who has the final say. Dr. Barrow starts out to see if she can find Dr. Schlesinger, and Ann forces Jim to take a spoonful of his baby-food diet. She is happy to see him in good spirits again and says, "When you come home, I'll make everything you like."

Jim stops eating and becomes suddenly fearful. "Ann," he says, "I'm not going to come home."

They would talk more about this contretemps, but Dr. Kramer has let himself in. Jim tells him about his Monday appointment and asks if he can make it. Says Kramer, "Today's Friday. From the medical point of view it's quite likely you can leave by Monday. You've come along pretty well with your wife's help. You ought to be very grateful."

Dr. Barrow returns with Dr. Schlesinger, and the three medics and Ann move down the corridor away from Jim's bed for a consultation. The patient, Fleming, comments to Jim, "The star chamber is in session." Schlesinger, after having introduced himself, asks Ann, "Have you any way of knowing whether this is a legitimate appointment or not?" Ann assures him it is legitimate—the call came to her. Schlesinger asks Kramer's opinion, and Kramer says it's medically possible for Jim to keep the appointment; Dr. Barrow thinks it is psychiatrically possible, for Jim has been thinking himself a failure and this job would be healthy for him psychologically. Schlesinger turns to Ann:

"Mrs. Downs, what do you think?"

"Of course, I'd like to see Jim get the job, but do you think it's possible?"

DR. SCHLESINGER—Why not?

ANN—Well, you would know more about these things than I. . . .

DR. SCHLESINGER—What's troubling you, Mrs. Downs?

ANN—Well, his eyes . . . They don't always seem to focus. . . . *(The doctors look at each other.)*

DR. BARROW—He sounds rational most of the time, doesn't he?

ANN—Yes, it's only once in a while he'll say something wild and incoherent.

DR. SCHLESINGER—Like what?

ANN—I don't remember at the moment. Doctor, what would happen if he kept the appointment and didn't get the job?

DR. SCHLESINGER—Of course, it would be another failure and that would be worse.

DR. BARROW—Yes, that's true. But, somehow, if it's important . . .

DR. SCHLESINGER—And I see the chart indicates he said many times he would do it again.

DR. KRAMER—Isn't that a normal reaction? I mean, it isn't at all unusual for a man to say such a thing unconsciously, so soon after making the attempt.

DR. SCHLESINGER—Yes, I know, but . . .

DR. KRAMER *(to* DR. BARROW*)*—He hasn't said it since the first day, has he?

DR. BARROW—No.

ANN (*reluctantly*)—No.

DR. SCHLESINGER—It would still be a great risk.

DR. KRAMER—We have until Monday.

DR. BARROW—Suppose we see what happens. Dr. Kramer, you see what *you* can do about Mr. Downs, and we'll take it from there.

DR. SCHLESINGER (*looks briefly at* DR. KRAMER; *takes the charts*) —I'll have a talk with him on Monday. (*To* ANN.) I'd like to speak to you first, if possible, Mrs. Downs. Can you be in my office at eleven on Monday?

ANN—Certainly.

DR. SCHLESINGER—Good. (*He and* DR. BARROW *start to leave.*) Oh, one more thing, Mrs. Downs. (*He returns to* ANN.) I've been getting several phone calls a day from a Charlotte—somebody or other. She wants permission to see your husband. (*A pause.*)

DR. BARROW—If this girl is an emotional complication for your husband . . .

ANN—I—I don't know what to say. The whole thing is so humiliating to me.

DR. SCHLESINGER—I must tell you, Mrs. Downs, as his wife, the law is entirely on your side. (*Another pause.* ANN *finally looks to* DR. BARROW.)

ANN—I think it would be very bad for Jim to see her—don't you, Doctor?

DR. BARROW (*to* DR. SCHLESINGER)—It would be a great strain.

DR. SCHLESINGER—I quite agree. I'll leave word downstairs she's not to be admitted at any time. (DOCTORS SCHLESINGER *and* BARROW *go.*)

Dr. Kramer returns with Ann to Jim's bedside and cheerfully orders, "O.K., Jim. Let's see you go." Jim can't believe he's to be allowed up, but Kramer, with a wink to Ann, assures him he is serious. They help him out of bed and the patient, Fleming, shouts, "Oh, no! What are they trying to do to that guy? Kill him?" Jim clutches Ann's arm, takes two or three steps and with a beaming face exults, "I'm walking!" Then his legs give way and he slumps. Kramer and Ann put Jim back into bed, where he falls asleep. Fleming comments, "Those crazy bastards. I've never seen a hospital like this."

The lights fade quickly.

SCENE IV

Three days later—Monday—at 11 A.M., Ann is keeping her appointment in Dr. Schlesinger's office. "Do you think we should keep him in the hospital for a while?" To this question Ann replies, "It would help Jim immensely, I think, to get over this slowly. . . . If he could be in the hospital's care for a while, I'm sure he'll realize our separation was a mistake."

This reminds Schlesinger of the girl, Charlotte, whom Jim has referred to and about whom Ann seems reluctant to talk. What about her? "Well," says Ann, "I can't help but feel that in some way she was responsible for this action."

Jim is due any moment, and the doctor would like to see him alone. Ann is sent into another room to wait, and soon Jim appears—by himself, walking. He takes a chair facing Schlesinger and says he feels fine.

"I suppose you know you did a very serious thing."

Jim shrugs and smiles, and the doctor pursues, "You don't think it was serious? . . . Why did you do this thing, Mr. Downs?"

JIM—Well, it's a complicated business. It wasn't just one thing. It was a lot of things. This was the week-end before Thanksgiving. I was having a friend to dinner—it was Saturday night—and I had spent practically my last cent—I was doing the cooking. When my friend arrived, she asked me what was for dessert. I didn't have any dessert. I couldn't afford it—and I started to cry.

DR. SCHLESINGER—Do you cry easily? I mean, at other times?

JIM—No, not often.

DR. SCHLESINGER—Well, not having dessert is hardly a reason to take your life.

JIM—I didn't mean to give that impression. It was simply an indication of how I stood. I had sixty cents left to last me eight days.

DR. SCHLESINGER (*always looking for the holes in a story*)—I understood you weren't working.

JIM—Not at my profession. I was teaching English privately and there was a check due in another week.

DR. SCHLESINGER—All right. Any other reasons?

JIM—A couple of years had passed since I did my last show. It didn't look as though I was ever going to get another one.

DR. SCHLESINGER—I understand you have an appointment for a job—this afternoon, as a matter of fact.

JIM—Yes. It could be an important break.

DR. SCHLESINGER—Hm-hmm—anything else?

JIM—I tried writing. Many years ago, while I was still in college, I was a newspaperman. And since I had the time, in the past few years, I mean—I thought I'd write. But nothing sold. I was working on a play, and I had finished the first act about a week before this happened. That Sunday night I re-read what I'd written. I don't know what made me do it—but I did. And I thought the whole thing was terrible. Everything just seemed hopeless.

DR. SCHLESINGER—Why do you feel you're an old man?

JIM (*startled*)—When did I say that?

DR. SCHLESINGER—In the unconscious state.

JIM—Really? (*Pause.*) Well, I guess I began to think about it when I was in the Army. I was too old to become an officer. I forced myself to try and keep up with the younger men. It wasn't easy. I was made painfully aware of the difference.

DR. SCHLESINGER—Were you overseas?

JIM—Yes—the whole European war—straight into Germany.

DR. SCHLESINGER—I see. And when you came out of the Army?

JIM—I found young men in the profession I didn't know. They didn't know me.

The doctor doesn't seem to think that these are enough—or all of—the reasons for suicide. How about Ann, for instance? Jim remembers that she called him Sunday afternoon and they made a date for Monday afternoon.

"And when did you take the pills?"

"Monday morning, at about 11:30."

"Didn't you want to see your wife?"

Jim shrugs. No, he saw her several times after they separated. He knew she needed money, and he thought of his G.I. insurance policy for ten thousand dollars. "I guess that clinched it. This was about twelve-thirty, that Sunday night. I wrote the first letter to my brother that night."

Since only one suicide letter has been mentioned up to now, Schlesinger is interested and Jim explains: Jim had written his first letter, and then he'd remembered he hadn't paid the November premium on his insurance; so he figured he'd have to wait until next morning to check with the Veterans Administration to see if his policy was in force. Which is just what he did—he went to bed, slept like a baby, got up and went out for the papers, had coffee, phoned the Veterans Administration—and learned that his policy would be in force for thirty-one days after the last payment. So he tore up the first letter to his brother and wrote a new one, telling about the insurance and enclosing the key to his apartment.

"Did you give any reasons for taking your life?"

"No. Does a man ever really give reasons?" Jim says the only hesitation he had was whether to mail the letter before or after taking the pills. He decided he'd leave the letter on the kitchen table and leave his apartment unlocked, and then he got a glass of water, went back to the bed, and took all the pills.

As if the question had never been asked before, Dr. Schlesinger queries, "How many pills did you take?"

"A hundred and fifty-six." The doctor's look implies that he knows Jim is lying, but Jim explains that he counted the pills in groups of ten, because he had once read of somebody who tried suicide with thirty-three pills and all it did was make him sick. "I wanted to be sure I had enough." After taking the pills nothing happened, so Jim decided to go out and mail the letter to his brother; he got quite a kick out of greeting people he knew and thinking, "They don't know it, but I'm a dying man." Back in the apartment he lay down on the bed—it seemed the most comfortable bed he'd ever known—and it must have been ten minutes later that he passed out.

Now the doctor asks a question which frightens Jim—what would he do if he got out? Would he go home to his wife? Her devotion at the hospital shows she must love him very much.

Jim struggles with his answer, saying, "Doctor, this may make me out an awful heel. But you don't know my wife. She makes a terrific impression on everyone. Not only in the hospital. It's been that way for years. Everybody thinks she's wonderful. I'm not trying to discount what she did for me here—but twenty-four hours a day living together over a period of years is a completely different story." Jim's theory is that his wife wants him back, not so much out of love, but from a fear of loneliness.

"Then you don't think going back to your wife would mean a more stable life for you?"

Jim replies honestly, "There was no stability before. Why should there be now?" Reflectively, he adds, "My wife is a very possessive woman. It took me a long time to get out of her clutches."

The doctor jars Jim with the next question—"Who is Charlotte?"

"A—a friend."

DR. SCHLESINGER—The friend who came to dinner that Saturday night?

JIM—Yes.

DR. SCHLESINGER (*toying with his pen*)—You tried to have a letter mailed to her. Didn't you know that was against the rules?

JIM—How did you know about the letter? Did Grosberg . . .

DR. SCHLESINGER—Yes, Mr. Grosberg gave me your letter. That's part of his job—keeping an eye on the patients. You must understand that when you are brought here for suicide you give up certain rights to privacy.

JIM—There was no harm in the letter. I just asked her to visit me, that's all. I can't understand why she hasn't been here.

DR. SCHLESINGER—Oh, she's been here all right, and she's been pestering me with phone calls. We haven't thought it wise for you to see her.

JIM—Who's we? My wife?

DR. SCHLESINGER—No, Dr. Barrow and myself. Are you involved with this girl?

JIM—How do you mean—involved?

DR. SCHLESINGER—Are you in love with her?

JIM—I don't know what you're getting at.

DR. SCHLESINGER—Do you *think* you're in love with her?

JIM—Well . . .

DR. SCHLESINGER—Aren't my questions clear?

JIM—Yes, they are—but it seems like an awful lot of prying. If —if I'm well—I'd like to go home.

DR. SCHLESINGER—Why don't you want to answer my questions?

JIM—I'll co-operate in any way I can, Doctor, but I fail to see why Charlotte has to be brought into this.

DR. SCHLESINGER (*making a note*)—Hm-hmmmm.

JIM (*while the doctor is writing*)—May I go home, Doctor? May I keep my appointment?

DR. SCHLESINGER—I'm afraid it may have to be postponed, Mr. Downs.

JIM—Why? For God's sake. This is the most vital appointment of my life.

DR. SCHLESINGER—I'm going to transfer you to another ward for a few days. Now, if you don't mind, look at my finger, please. (*He holds his index finger before* JIM's *eyes and moves it from left to right several times. Then, as he writes:*) It's a convalescent ward, on the first floor. You'll like it. You can wear your own clothes there, instead of these hospital things. They play games down there—all sorts of interesting things. It's only for a few days.

JIM (*dazed, still sitting*)—I see.

DR. SCHLESINGER—That will be all, Mr. Downs. (*Slowly* JIM *rises and goes.* DR. SCHLESINGER *goes on writing.*)

The lights fade quickly.

SCENE V

In the ward, Grosberg is filing the nails of the man who stares into space; Fleming is in bed, and Miss Hansen is at her table. Jim returns dejectedly from Schlesinger's office and reports to his fellow patients that he is being transferred to the first floor for a few days. "A few days my foot," says Fleming. "That's the observation ward. . . . You're in the psycho building, Downs. Didn't you know that?"

This information strikes Jim like a blow. Grosberg tries to tell Jim the new ward won't be so bad—it's the nicest one, and lots of people go home from there.

"And if they don't go home?"

"State hospital."

"Can you go home right from *this* ward?"

Grosberg concedes that it has happened, so Jim reasons, "Then it isn't hospital procedure that a suicide is automatically sent to observation."

"No."

A bell rings and Ann is admitted; her husband runs to her, terror-stricken, and cries, "Ann, they're putting me away. They think I'm insane."

Soothingly she says, "It's only for a few days"—and he draws away from her. A chill runs through him as he looks at her. "You knew about this!" he gasps.

The curtain falls.

ACT II

Essentially, Ward MN 1 on the first floor is the same as the one upstairs, but down here all the beds are made up, except for one with a bare mattress. Some patients are wearing their own clothes; others are in hospital pajamas. No one wears a necktie or a belt; to hold his trousers up a patient is given a length of white gauze bandage. It is the next day—Tuesday—and Sam Tager, a Jewish boy about 27, is sitting on the edge of his bed in pajamas. Small, thin George O'Brien, who has a pronounced Spanish accent, is standing near him. Reading a newspaper on his bed is a swarthy Greek, John Ankoritis, and Joe Major, a powerfully built, graceful Negro in his early thirties, is quietly drumming with his hands on the metal cabinet next to his bed. Sam Tager is admiring a painting O'Brien has made, and O'Brien says, "When I get out, I'm going to school, I get thousand dollar a picture when I learn." O'Brien got his Irish name from a father who deserted George's mother in Havana before he was born—and his mother had died in bearing him.

The ward door is unlocked and Jim enters, followed by Don Gregory, a tall, slender man of 24 dressed in army suntans—the improvised uniform of a ward attendant. Jim is in a hospital night shirt;

Gregory is carrying Jim's charts. Gregory goes to get some bed linen and pajamas for Jim, and the other patients in the ward introduce themselves. They all seem pleasant, and particularly so is the Greek, John Ankoritis, a courtly fellow who speaks in grammatical flourishes.

The Negro, Major, and Ankoritis have just lighted cigarettes when young Gregory returns with the linen and begins making Jim's bed with Jim's help. "Now you fellows know you're not to smoke in the ward—go to the john or the day room, and give me the matches," Gregory chides gently. Ankoritis tosses him a pack of matches with the cheerful information, "I have more."

"Don't let me see them," says Gregory. "You can always ask me for a light. You know I'm supposed to report this. Why do you do it? If someone else catches you, you'll wind up on 'seven.' "

An old Negro, past 60 and the gentlest man in the world, shuffles in from the corridor. He tells anybody who will listen that the student nurses want to play cards all the time, and he, Carlisle, doesn't want to play cards. The Greek explains that it's the student nurses' job. "They want to engage you in conversation, my dear Mr. Carlisle. They wish to extract information which they in turn pass on to the esteemed physicians."

From the talk and byplay in the ward Jim is getting a picture of just the kind of place he is in—an observation ward indeed, where everything a man does and says has a meaning and is reported. Young O'Brien comments, "Just because you act a little crazy is no reason to say that you are." He, for instance, came here by himself. He felt run down and a friend told him to ask any policeman and the policeman would take him to the hospital.

"Anybody walks in here by himself ought to go straight to 'seven,' " says Carlisle. Jim summons the courage to ask what this "seven" is.

"The seventh floor. It's the violent ward," Tager informs him. "I was in a straitjacket up there. I tried to throw myself in front of a subway train. Some cops grabbed me and I put up a fight—which I know now was a stupid thing to do." His recollection of "seven" is grim—like the movie, "The Snake Pit." A man up there dancing on one foot and playing an imaginary fiddle; another one pretending to be waving at people through windows.

From down the hall comes a medium-sized man, Schloss, whose accent brands him as a "Greenpernt" Brooklynite. "Where is the new guy?" he asks in a hurry, and Jim is pointed out. From the cabinet by his bed Schloss takes some papers and announces that he's writin' a novel. He has heard by hospital grapevine that Jim is in the theayter, and therefore must be interested in literature. "I want you should hear this here chapter," he says to Jim, and begins to read: "So Captain Redbeard faces his bunch of cutthroats—the most villainous scoundrels that sailed the seven seas . . ."

Jim tells the pitifully eager Schloss that it's good and he should keep on with it. "That's what the doctor tells me," Schloss agrees. "He says I got ideas—I just gotta learn some grammar, that's all. Would you believe it, I never did no writin' before?" Schloss isn't too happy here, though; he'd rather be in jail, like when he gave Uncle Sam two years of his time in Leavenworth and eighteen months in Atlanta for defraudin' the govament. He happened to get in *here* because he slugged the wife and kids and the cops trun him in.

"You should be ashamed to admit it, Mr. Schloss," says O'Brien.

"You shut your mouth, you spic bastard."

O'Brien flies into a tearful rage which grows more intense as Schloss taunts him, "Your mother was a spic whore." Schloss grabs the boy's shoulders and pushes him to the floor; Ankoritis pulls the man off, and Carlisle helps O'Brien to his feet. Tager and Major have edged in. Major stays clear of the fight, but he cries furiously, "There ain't one of us here who wouldn't like to break Mr. Schloss's neck. But we're the ones who'd wind up in 'seven'—not him."

Quietly but venomously the Greek says, "It makes me sick to my stomach to look at you, Mr. Schloss." The men fall silent as Gregory enters, and the attendant senses something wrong. "A few words," Tager explains, and Gregory counsels, "Just keep it to words, boys—and no one will get hurt." He has come to tell them it's time for lunch and is about to lead them off when Jim stops him with a question: "How soon can I see a doctor?"

"It may be a few days before you're even assigned to a doctor. You'd better learn to be patient, Mr. Downs, if you want to get out of here. You start being anxious and you'll beat your head against the wall." Jim is not in a patient mood; in a pitch of fury he demands, "Why was I sent here in the first place?"

Gregory says soothingly, "There isn't a patient in this building who doesn't feel as you do."

Jim almost shouts an expostulation, "But I'm not—" Then, in full realization, he stops suddenly and says quietly, "I see—no one else thinks he is, either."

Gregory moves on toward the dining room, calling, "Are you all here?" As the men move out the Greek says to Jim with uncon-

scious humor, "You see, Mr. Downs, we are all *here*, but the ques‑
tion is, are we all *there?*"

The lights fade quickly.

SCENE II

On the next afternoon, Wednesday, the pajama-clad Jim is inter‑
viewed by another doctor—a young fellow named Bellman—in his
office. Bellman wants to know everything and Jim expostulates,
"Isn't it down in the chart? I gave all the details to Dr. Schles‑
inger." Nevertheless, Dr. Bellman wants it all over again, so Jim
tells of being out of work, his wife wanting money, his insurance,
the pills. He can't understand why everybody makes so much
about his knowing the exact number of pills—156.

Bellman asks if Jim frequently gets periods of deep depression
and great elation, and Jim startles the doctor by answering, "I'm
no manic-depressive—if that's what these questions are intended to
elicit." As the interview continues, Bellman asks Jim if he knows
he has a reputation for being belligerent and nasty, and Jim won't
believe it; he knows his friends think him easy to get along with.
"May I ask—who told you I had such a reputation?"

"People who know you well."

"But who can they be?"

"Your wife knows you well, doesn't she?"

Next, the doctor tries to draw Jim out about Charlotte, but the
patient is very reluctant to speak of her. He does admit that he
has tried to give up Charlotte a dozen times, not wanting to hurt
Ann. But he was miserable with Charlotte and miserable at home,
so he took his own apartment and began living alone. Jim is anxious
to get away and says, "I've answered your questions, Doctor. May
I go home? I don't belong here—you can see that."

But Bellman has more questions—who is the mayor of New York,
the President, what is the capital of France, when did Roosevelt die?
What does a rolling stone gathers no moss mean? Subtract by
sevens from a hundred. Jim's intelligence is affronted and he can't
help saying something he shouldn't. "Four years ago," he begins,
"I knew a doctor—a young psychiatrist in exactly your position. He
wanted me to write a play with him based on some of his case his‑
tories. One day, while he was making the rounds, he stopped in this
screened-in porch and he asked one of the patients—what day is
today? The girl didn't answer and he said—do you know who I
am? She still didn't answer, but I could see the disgust on her face.
Then one of the other patients answered. She turned around and

said, 'Who's the mayor of New York? Who's the governor of the State? Who's the President of the United States?' "

Bellman confusedly asks what this proves. It proves, says Jim, that institutional practice and honesty are not compatible. "We should be treated as individuals," he urges, "but we're handled in categories—the same routine for everyone. What is it, Doctor—inexperience? Lack of time?" Bellman refuses to discuss the matter and orders Jim to stand up, close his eyes for a moment, then look at the doctor's moving finger. "All right," he says finally, "that's all for now."

Jim asks, "When do I go home?"

"You don't, Mr. Downs. Not for a while."

The lights fade quickly.

SCENE III

It's nearly 9 P.M. in the ward—bedtime—and a nurse, Miss Wingate, comes in. Tall, heavy, middle-aged, unintelligent, she has the broadest possible Southern accent as she orders, "Bedtime, boys." She has broken up a conversation centered mostly around Jim, for the patients have been asking him about his experiences in the theatre. The Cuban boy, O'Brien, has been particularly eager, wanting to know if Jim ever met any stars. At the nurse's order most of them get into bed, but the boy follows Jim. "O'Brien," says Miss Wingate, "your bed's not over there." He scurries back to his own bed and says "Good night, Miss Wingate"—which seems to irritate her. The Greek takes it up, saying "Good night, Miss Wingate."

"Who was that—Ankoritis?" She pronounces it Ankoreyetis.

"Yes, Miss Wingate—and it's pronounced Ankoreetis. It is a name, not a disease."

Furiously she threatens, "You'd just better be careful how you talk to me, Ankoreyetis, or you'll wind up in 'seven.' " She puts out the ward lights with a key in a switch panel near the door, and leaves. O'Brien calls softly from his bed, "Mr. Downs—what movie stars do you know? Do you know Betty Grable?"

Schloss whispers tensely, "Shut up, for Christ's sake. You ever got near Betty Grable you'd wet your pants." O'Brien whispers just as angrily, "Is that so"—and in a moment Schloss is again taunting the boy about his mother being a whore. "I'll break your neck!" O'Brien cries.

Schloss, jumping out of bed, cries loudly for Miss Wingate, and the others can't quiet him. When the nurse appears he accuses O'Brien of threatening to break his neck. The nurse is all grim action. She orders Schloss to get the attendants. In vain other patients try to tell her that Schloss was responsible for the outbreak. When two attendants appear, she points out the boy and says, "Take him up." The boy is led away, screaming repeatedly, "Please don't take me to 'seven'!" She orders the others back to bed and sits at her desk to do some work. She notices a telegram addressed to Jim and calls him over to read it. Jim is so shocked by what he has just seen that he vaguely holds the message without opening it, until the nurse reminds him to read it. He will, of course, have to let her see it afterward.

When Jim has read the telegram he passes it over and Miss Wingate reads, "Darling, you must tell the doctors you want to see me— otherwise am not permitted—I love you—Charlotte." This intrigues the nurse—a wife and a girl friend. "You'll never get out of here," she tells Jim. She advises him to write to Charlotte tonight and tell her to stop trying to see him. "I'm trying to help you," she insists. "The law recognizes only the wife—so get used to it."

Jim still can't see what Charlotte has to do with the case. "Your wife," says the nurse, "can get you out of here if she wants to." This is news to Jim. She continues, "We can't hold you, Mr. Downs, if she wants to take you home. That's the law. It happens all the time."

Jim writes a note to Charlotte telling her not to try to see him and that he will explain when he gets out. He gives it to the nurse, then harks back to the O'Brien boy—he really didn't do anything. Brusquely she orders Jim to keep his nose clean, and he goes back to bed. In a moment the old Negro, Carlisle, gets out of bed and goes from one patient to another, quietly telling them to get up and get out because his daughter is coming home. With unexpected gentleness Miss Wingate leads the old man back to his bed and assures him she will take care of his daughter when she comes.

The lights fade quickly.

Scene IV

After lunch on Thursday, the next day. Ann is admitted by Gregory on a special pass—for these aren't visiting hours—and the attendant inspects and okays a package of fruit and candy she has brought. She gives it to Jim and he says he is glad to get it, for most of the fellows share whatever they get here and the others will be glad to have some. Jim tells his wife the new doctor has said he'll have to stay a while. "You can get me out on your say-so," he declares. "You can do it, Ann—if you want to."

"Of course I want to," she assures him. "But it isn't as simple as all that."

As he pleads, Jim becomes more agitated. He tells her of "seven," the violent ward, and the green slip, which means commitment to a state hospital. Is she trying to get him committed?

"That's not going to happen to you," she assures him.

"It can. I've seen it happen on the flimsiest pretext. You've got to hold on tight to keep your balance here, Ann. Everything you say and do is reported. You can't have normal feelings here, Ann. Only continuous calm. Is that normal—for anyone?"

Ann raises Jim's hopes by saying she has been to their own physician, Dr. Davidson—but his hopes are dashed when she says Davidson has some influence with the Veterans Administration and thinks he may be able to get Jim into a Veterans Hospital. Jim almost shouts that he wants to go home. He demands why Ann told Dr. Bellman that he was belligerent and nasty. Why isn't she trying to get him out, instead of into another hospital? He begs her to tell Davidson to come down here and see Dr. Bellman, and to get Dr. Walker, too—the one who wanted Jim to write a play with him. Tomorrow, he insists.

Ann promises to call them. As Dr. Bellman enters, Ann asks Jim if it's true that he tried to reach Charlotte. She reminds him of all she has done for him since he came here. And, by the way, would he please endorse this check for his teaching so she can cash it and pay his special nurses and other expenses? Helplessly Jim endorses the check, and she dismisses him by saying she'd better talk with Dr. Bellman now. "I'll see you Saturday. Take care, dear." She promises to bring some of his clothes with her on Saturday, and Jim goes off down the corridor.

When they are alone Dr. Bellman asks, "What do you think?"

"About Jim? He frightens me—the things he says. He is afraid of being committed." Bellman says it is possible that he could be committed—but that he can also be discharged in her custody—if she wants to assume the responsibility.

"I'd gladly assume that responsibility, Doctor. But if he isn't well enough . . ."

"He may be committed to a State Hospital."

"I see. He wanted me to reach several doctor friends on the outside. What do you think?"

"I wouldn't suggest it."

"You know best, Doctor. Thank you."

The lights fade quickly.

Scene V

Jim still is in the ward five days later—Tuesday. Joe Major is drumming on a table and singing a calypso song, and Ankoritis and Tager are singing with him. Miss Wingate comes in to wake old Carlisle up and give him some medicine. Above the noise Jim tries to ask the indifferent nurse if he can have an appointment with Dr. Bellman. She takes old Carlisle out without bothering to answer. The jam session continues. When the attendant, Gregory, comes through, Jim again begins asking about an appointment with Dr. Bellman. At the breaking point, he cries to the noise-makers, "For God's sake, fellows, you're not the only ones in this ward!"

Gregory counsels, "Take it easy, Jim." But Jim is beyond taking it easy; he snarls at Gregory and kicks over the table Major is drumming on. Gregory pins his arms, finally manages to get Jim to a bed, with Jim almost weeping, "Why are they keeping me?" His rage subsides. Patiently, almost with sweetness, Gregory says, "Listen to me, Jim. The doctors take most cases of suicide to be an inverted homicidal tendency. Do you know what that means? . . . You're a potential murderer in their eyes. . . ."

The attendant leaves. The calypso song begins again. The curtain falls.

ACT III

The scene is the ward dining room, two days later—Thursday, visiting day, but early—about 1:30 P.M. Gregory brings in Ann and Jim's brother, Harry Downs, who looks what he is—a small-town business man. He is nervous and fearful in such a place. "Why was he sent here?" he asks.

"You know what he did," says Ann, disturbed.

"I know—but hundreds of people have tried the same thing. They don't wind up in a—in a . . ."

Jim comes in; he hasn't slept, and shows it. He is strangely embarrassed at seeing his brother, but he says "Hello, Harry," quietly. He asks his brother why it took two weeks for him to get here and Harry talks vaguely of things to do. The brother goes off to find Dr. Bellman and have a talk with him.

Ann tells her husband that some of his students had heard he was sick and called.

"How did they know to call you?"

Hesitantly, Ann explains, "I had your phone disconnected and the calls switched to me." Seeming so sympathetic, Ann reveals other horrors. Jim couldn't go back to his flat—the doctors have said it would be too depressing. And she has had to tell his pupils to find another teacher, because he might be ill some time. . . . Yes, she really did call Davidson and Walker, but Walker wouldn't take the responsibility, and Jim already knows Davidson's attitude about the Veterans Hospital.

Harry returns from his interview with Bellman, and is disturbed. He wants to speak to Jim alone, but Ann is reluctant to leave. Finally she goes and Jim demands, "What did you want to tell me?"

Harry lays it on the line, earnestly. First, Jim has got to stop shooting off his mouth. Second, Harry has consulted lawyers and they can't do a thing; Jim is in the hands of the authorities and if he wants to get out he must play ball. So far as the hospital is concerned, he must become a model patient.

"What else?"

HARRY—With Ann it will be harder. I don't know how things were with you in the past few years. You seldom wrote. But you were separated. Is that right?

JIM—Yes.

HARRY—I went down to that address you gave me in the letter. Your apartment's been rented to somebody else.

JIM (*stunned*)—And all my things?

HARRY—Everything's been moved back to Ann's place. The landlady told me.

JIM—She's got rid of my students. I have no place to go. . . .

HARRY—She's made you completely dependent on her, Jim. That's what she set out to do, and that's what she's achieved.

JIM—Why, for God's sake? What does she want of me?

HARRY—She loves you, Jim. She wants you back. She told the doctor that. I won't try to explain it. I think there's something distorted in taking advantage of your being here to get you back this way. But I don't question that she loves you—and my advice to you is to be in love with her. That's the only way you'll get out of here quickly.

JIM (*quickly*)—I can't do it, Harry.

HARRY—You lived with her for nine years. It can't be that difficult.

JIM—You don't know.

HARRY—Ann is the only one who can help you, Jim.

JIM—I can't keep walking out on myself like that.

HARRY—Well, any other way will mean months—not in this

place, because they can't keep you here. There's some kind of law, I was told, about a city hospital. You can be sent away to a state hospital, if that's what she wants.

After a long pause, Jim muses, "I don't know if she'll believe me now."

Harry warns his brother that life outside will not be easy. Jim won't be a free man—he'll be in his wife's custody. He is trapped, and now if he wants to get out he must play ball. Jim nods slowly. The lights fade quickly.

SCENE II

Four days have gone by; it's Monday and Jim is in for another test at the hands of Dr. Bellman and Dr. Barrow, with Miss Wingate and Don Gregory assisting. The four of them have been talking over Jim's case—quite an improvement. He's played ping-pong and has eaten better and gone to the movie—has become quite adjusted to the hospital routine. And sometimes he speaks of his wife.

Gregory goes and gets Jim. "How do you like it down here?" asks Dr. Barrow.

"All right."

Dr. Barrow plunges into a word-association test, with Dr. Bellman observing. She is to say a word, and Jim is to say the first other word that pops into his mind. "Black," she says. "White," says Jim. He goes along without apparent hesitation, but when she says "Suicide" there is a catch before he says "Death."

"Wife." Jim is wrestling with himself and the doctor repeats, "Wife."

"Sweetheart." But Dr. Bellman thinks he detects a calculated response, not an instinctive one. "If Dr. Barrow had said 'Charlotte' we might have expected such an answer."

Jim is fighting for his life now. He assures Bellman that this isn't true any more—that he has realized he has made a mistake. He explains desperately, "I was in love with my wife when I married her."

Bellman remains suspicious of Jim's sudden change, but Jim angrily argues that he's been in the hospital for two weeks, away from both Ann *and* Charlotte, and he has a new perspective.

"And what do you think now?"

"I think of the good things I have had with Ann."

"And Charlotte?"

"I—I indulged myself, I guess—I . . ."

Jim is dismissed, and when he has gone Dr. Barrow declares, "I am inclined to believe him."

"We'll wait and see," says Dr. Bellman.

The lights fade quickly.

SCENE III

It is visiting day again—Thursday, three days later. Some visitors have already arrived, and patients like old Carlisle who don't have any visitors get pleasure from standing around and watching others embrace and laugh and cry. Ann comes in with her package of fruit and candy—and with her brother, Tom. Jim comes up, greeting his wife with "Ann! I've been waiting." He shakes hands with Tom. Jim is in a fine mood. To Tom he says, "You have no idea what her being here every visiting day has meant to me." Ann smiles. "She's been wonderful, Tom—simply wonderful." Jim pours it on, and his act is good—they will soon be making up for lost time, for they're in love. All he wants is to settle down to a good job, and he'll even give up the theatre if Ann wants him to.

Tom breaks in, and it is an attack. He fumbles for words as he tells Jim that Ann's friends and her doctor don't think it would be smart of her to take him back. Jim is in a desperate panic. "After all," Tom points out, "you left her—you've been carrying on with another girl—you even tried to reach her here in the hospital."

Jim insists, "But that's all over. I don't want to see this girl again."

That's all Tom wanted to find out. If Jim is on the level, he can write this girl and tell her very plainly—or if he wants to see her and tell her, Tom will go with him. Jim, in a trap, agrees, "Sure." To Ann he says, "I said I was finished with—with Charlotte. I meant it. If—you'll have me back—I want to go back. I'm sure things will be better between us than they were."

"They will, darling," Ann agrees.

Dr. Bellman comes in, and Jim, tired, excuses himself.

"There's a tremendous improvement in Jim," Ann tells the doctor.

He asks, "How do you feel about taking him back?"

"I love him, Doctor."

"It may be only another day," says Bellman.

The lights fade quickly.

Scene IV

The next day—Friday. Dr. Bellman and Jim are having an interview. Jim is making one last fight for liberty, telling the psychiatrist that he is sure he is cured and that all he wants to do is find work and support his wife. "When do you think you should leave?" Bellman asks—but Jim, ready for this question, says agreeably, "That's up to you, Doctor."

DR. BELLMAN (*a brief pause*)—That's all for now.

JIM (*gets up, starts off, turns*)—Is it unreasonable to ask how long it will be?

DR. BELLMAN (*slowly*)—No.

JIM (*his throat is dry*)—Then may I know?

DR. BELLMAN (*looks at* JIM—*a long "Hmmmmm"*)—Call your wife.

JIM (*unable to believe*)—What?

DR. BELLMAN—Call your wife. You may go home today.

JIM (*simply*)—Thank you, Doctor. (*A few steps back.*) May I call from here?

DR. BELLMAN—Yes.

JIM—Thank you.

DR. BELLMAN—You may use that phone. (*Indicates phone on table.* JIM *goes to the phone.* DR. BELLMAN *rises—to* JIM:) You'll be in her custody, you understand.

JIM (*nods;* DR. BELLMAN *leaves*)—Yes. (*He dials a number, and waits. The lights fade on all but* JIM.) Ann? I'm discharged. I can leave today. Dr. Bellman just said so. Ann, would you bring a tie and my overcoat? Thank you, dear. You won't be long— will you? (*He hangs up. The tears have started. He knows he is trapped. He turns and slowly walks across the stage, convulsed with sobs.*)

THE CURTAIN FALLS

I AM A CAMERA *

A Play in Three Acts

By John van Druten

NOT long ago John van Druten startled a newspaper interviewer by saying that he was not—at the moment, anyhow—interested in the well-made play. Here was a stage craftsman who had turned out such well-made works as "Young Woodley," "There's Always Juliet," "The Voice of the Turtle," "I Remember Mama" and "Bell, Book and Candle" trying to tell an interviewer that dramatic structure, for structure's sake, was not as important to him as it might be. It was people and not plot and structure who interested him as a dramatist. Some months before this interview, van Druten had written about his newest play, "I Am a Camera," and had sketched its background—not its immediate origin and how it had come to the stage, but its psychological background within van Druten himself. This play began, in a manner of speaking, long before Christopher Isherwood wrote "Sally Bowles" and his other Berlin Stories; it began in 1911, when van Druten was 10 years old. His mother had seen, in London, Chekhov's "The Cherry Orchard" and had reported to the family that the play was either completely insane, or the audience was. This play, says van Druten, was to many playwrights a new door to freedom, and he counts himself as one of these playwrights. He confessed, in writing about "I Am a Camera," "I have never been any good at plot. I simply cannot think of one. And I have never been a man for messages, either. All I really know about is people. If people can make a play, that is fine." The people in the Berlin Stories interested him and he began a play about them. "These people were not my own, not of my own invention, but in any case, when one is writing well, the people never seem to remain one's own for long. They have been invented, and now they have taken control. The best one can do is sit and listen, and attempt to transcribe what one has heard, and the mood it has evoked." The best that van Druten could do was good enough for the New York Drama Critics Circle; this body of one woman and many men of various sizes, shapes and intellectual persuasions voted "I Am a Camera" the best play of the season of 1951-1952.

The time is around 1930 and the scene throughout is a room in Fräulein Schneider's flat in Berlin. The room is excessively German and middle-class. A bed is partly hidden behind curtains; there is a best chair like a bishop's throne, and a washstand, and a tall, tiled stove. Antlers make a hatrack by the door. There is a small table for tea and a big one for books and papers. The furnishings also include a backless sofa and an ottoman. The occupant of the room is Christopher Isherwood, an untidy English writer in his twenties. He is writing and smoking at the big table and now he reads some of his own stuff to himself: "In the last few days, there has been a lot of Nazi rioting in the streets, here in Berlin. They are getting bolder, more arrogant." Chris stops, crumples the page and throws it aside and says to himself, "No, that's all wrong. I must explain who it is who is telling all this—a typical beachcomber of the big city. He comes to Berlin for the weekend, stays on, runs out of money, starts giving English lessons. Now he sits in a rented room, waiting for something to happen—something that will help him understand what his life is all about."

Chris goads himself into writing something, and reads the result: "I am a camera, with its shutter open, quite passive. Some day all of this will have to be developed, printed, fixed." Here his creative burst ends, for his landlady is knocking at the door and saying "It is I, Herr Issyvoo." She is a large, bosomy woman who is bringing a lace tea cloth for the small table. If Herr Issyvoo is having a lady guest, he must have things elegant. "This young lady you are expecting—she is very attractive?"

Just one of his pupils, Chris explains; in fact, the only pupil he has left. Which reminds him that he must talk with Fräulein Schneider and now is as good a time as any. "I don't think I can go on living here," he announces. He just can't afford it. "Oh, that can wait," says the cheerful landlady; but Chris reminds her that he is already two months behind in his rent. He has the rent now, but must cut expenses. Perhaps that little room just across the passage . . . ? The fräulein doesn't relish the idea of her big room going unlet with the Summer coming on, but she agrees to rent the little one to Isherwood for a reasonable sum. "Soon," she encourages him, "you make a great deal of money with your stories

that you are always writing, and you take this room again, and
everybody is happy once more."

Chris promises, "I'll buy you a fur coat."

The bell rings. That would be Isherwood's young lady, and the
fräulein departs to bring coffee. Isherwood asks her not to mention to his guest that he is leaving this room.

But it isn't the young lady who rang. It is Fritz, a dark, young
German friend, come to call, so Chris asks the landlady to make coffee for three. Fritz's mood seems low. Business, he admits, is terrible. "Lousy and terrible. Or I pull off a new deal in the next month,
or I go as a gigolo. . . . I am speaking a lousy English just now.
Sally says maybe she will give me a few lessons."

"Who is Sally?"

"She is a friend of mine. Eventually she is coming around here
this afternoon. I want that you should know each other." Fritz
further explains that Sally is an actress—she sings at the Lady
Windermere. Her mother was French and she is hot stuff. Chris
wonders what Natalia Landauer, his pupil, will think of anybody
like Sally. Fritz pricks up his ears: "Landauer? Of the big department store? But they must be enormously rich." Stinking,
Chris admits.

"And are you going to marry her?"

"Me? No, of course not," Chris laughs.

"Then if I should meet her and perhaps make a pass after her,
you would not mind?" Fritz, confident of his charms, visions his
conquest—perhaps a partnership in Natalia's father's business. "I
suppose she is a Jewess?"

"Oh, yes."

"Well, there is always something. And you know, Chris, I am
very broad-minded."

The bell sounds again; *this* should be Natalia, the pupil, but it
isn't. It is Fritz's night club singer, Sally, who pushes past the
landlady. Sally is young, attractive, and clad in slinky black silk
with a page boy's cap stuck jauntily on one side of her head. Her
fingernails are painted emerald green. Fritz introduces Chris to
her and Chris orders another coffee from the fräulein. "Oh, not
for me," interposes Sally. "I'm allergic to coffee. I come out in
the most sinister spots if I drink it before dinner." She chatters
on, in a curious mixture of naïveté and toughness, "I always have
prairie oysters for breakfast. . . . Eggs with Worcester sauce all
sort of wooshed up together. I simply live on them." Right now,
Sally would settle for a whiskey and soda. Chris ruefully admits
he hasn't any whiskey.

"I thought you were English."

"I am. But I'm also poor."

Sally shrugs this off; she's poor, too. Chris thinks he can manage some gin, and while he's rummaging in a cupboard for it Sally tells Fritz she has just had a row with her landlady and has walked out—swept out, as she puts it. Chris brings some gin in a tooth glass. Sally samples it, notes a peppermint taste from toothpaste and offers a sip to the men. She continues with her story about the landlady: "You should have heard the things she called me. I mean—well, I suppose in a way I may be a bit of a tart. . . . I mean, in a nice way—but one doesn't like to be called that. Just because I brought a man home with me last night. And anyway, I'm terribly in love with him." The man was Klaus, her accompanist—and now Sally must find another room.

Chris offers this one, explaining that he can't afford it and is moving across the hall. It's fifty marks a month, breakfast included, which sounds reasonable to Sally. She decides to take it. Will the landlady make trouble about an occasional man visitor? Chris doesn't think so, so long as the room is rented.

"I say," says Sally, "am I shocking you, talking like this?"

Chris, amused, replies, "No one ever shocks me when they try to." Fritz agrees that Chris is quite unshockable—which reminds Isherwood that a lady who is coming *is* shockable, so would Sally mind being careful? The young woman promises to be terribly ladylike. "And," warns Chris, "don't let her know I'm going to move out of here. She'd probably start cutting down on my terms."

Again the bell, and this time it is Natalia Landauer. She shakes hands with Sally and doesn't miss the green fingernails. Natalia is a proper young woman and she speaks proper, but quite labored, English. In response to Sally's "How do you do" she says she is well; she has just had a cold but it is better now. It was a cold in the chest. "All the plegm was here," she says, pointing to her chest. Chris gently advises her that the word is phlegm, with the "h" pronounced, and the thorough Natalia now can't understand why phthisis should be pronounced without the "h." Chris can't put up an answer to this problem.

"All stories about illness make me want to throw up," Sally offers cheerfully. "I saw a movie about syphilis the other night that was too awful. I couldn't let a man touch me for almost a week." Natalia is beginning to freeze, but the tension eases when Sally excuses herself to go have a talk with the landlady.

Natalia wants to know more about this Fräulein Bowles, who seems a remarkable girl. Fritz explains that she sings at a club called the Lady Windermere, and, boldly pushing the opportunity, asks if he may take Natalia there one night. Chris tries to convey that he doesn't think it would be quite the right place, being a bit Bohemian. "Then I must see it," Natalia decides. She asks Fritz, "When shall we go?"

"We could go tonight, if you are free."

"I can be free. You will come and fetch me at a quarter to nine."

"Oh, but it doesn't start until after midnight."

"Then you fetch me please at a quarter to midnight. I will give you my address. You will come, too, Christopher, and we will be a party to hear your girl friend sing." This brings on another lesson in English as Chris explains the meaning of "girl friend" as opposed to "friend."

Sally comes bouncing back in with everything fixed with the landlady, and cheerfully declares she is moving in here. Chris, hurrying to change the subject, tells her they're all coming to hear her sing tonight. "Don't let the proprietor bother you," Sally warns. "He's quite a darling, really, but he takes dope quite a lot, and sometimes it doesn't agree with him. He pinches people. It doesn't mean anything." Natalia, stiffening again, says she must go and declines Fritz's offer to accompany her—but he goes along with her anyway. "Good-by, Christopher," says Natalia. "I think I will talk to your landlady on my way out. I do not like these rooms, and she is charging you too much." Somehow, Sally seems to have acquired the idea that the German girl doesn't like her very much. Also, Sally can't understand Fritz capering around Natalia, but Chris explains that Natalia is rich and Fritz is very broke. The direct Sally observes, "I should think his best way with a girl of that kind would be to make a pounce."

Looking at a paper on the table, Miss Bowles reads, "Chapter One. Are you writing a novel?"

CHRIS—Starting one.

SALLY (*reading*)—"I am a camera, with its shutter open, quite passive." Do you mean this is a story written by a camera?

CHRIS (*laughing*)—No, it's written by me. I'm the camera.

SALLY—How do you mean?

CHRIS—I'm the one who sees it all. I don't take part. I don't really even think. I just sort of photograph it. Ask questions, maybe. How long have you been in Germany?

SALLY—About two months.

CHRIS—And your mother is French. (*She looks blank.*) Fritz told me she was.

SALLY (*irritated*)—Fritz is an idiot. He's always inventing things. Mother's a bit County, but she's an absolute darling. I simply worship her. I'm afraid Daddy's side of the family comes out in me. You'd love Daddy. He doesn't care a damn for anyone. It was he who said I could go to London and learn acting. You see, I couldn't bear school, so I got myself expelled.

CHRIS—How did you do that?

SALLY—I told the headmistress I was going to have a baby.

CHRIS—Oh, rot, Sally, you didn't.

SALLY—Yes, I did. So they got a doctor to examine me, and then when they found out there was nothing the matter they were most frightfully disappointed. And the headmistress said that a girl who could even think of anything so disgusting couldn't possibly be let stay on. So I went to London. And that's where things started happening.

CHRIS—What sort of things?

SALLY—Oh—things. I had a wonderful, voluptuous little room —with no chairs—that's how I used to seduce men. One of them told me I'd do better in Berlin. What do you think, Chris?

CHRIS—I think you're doing fine. I think you're wonderful, Sally.

SALLY—Do you, Chris dear? I think you're wonderful, too. We're going to be real good friends, aren't we?

CHRIS (*rather slowly*)—Do you know, I believe we are. Real good friends.

SALLY—You know, Chris, you were quite right about my wanting to shock people. I do, and I don't know why. I do think you were clever to notice it. And, Chris, there's one thing more. I'm not sure if you'll understand or not. I did tell Fritz my mother was French. I suppose I wanted to impress him.

CHRIS—What's so impressive about a French mother?

SALLY—I suppose it's like whores calling themselves French names to excite men. I'm a bit mad like that sometimes, Chris. You must be patient with me.

CHRIS—I will, Sally.

SALLY—And you'll swear on your honor not to tell Fritz? And if you do, I can cut your throat? (*Stands over him, mock-bullying him with a paper knife.*)

CHRIS—From ear to ear. Sally, was that all true just now, what you told me about your family?

SALLY—Yes, of course it was. Well, most of it. (*Puts paper knife down.*) Only, Chris, you mustn't ever ask me questions. If I want to tell you anything, I will. But I've got to be free.

Chris, amused, acquiesces. Impulsively she embraces him, then goes to get her things. Alone, Chris begins packing for his own move, talking to himself about Sally. It strikes him that he'd better put something down on paper about her right away. "How would you describe her? Her face is young, but her hands look terribly old. And they were dirty, too. Dirty as a little girl's hands." He writes, "Sally's hands were like the old hands of a dirty little girl."

Scene II

Three months go by, and there are a few new feminine touches in the room—a doll or two and some bottles and jars; the Medici prints are missing and in their places are a couple of very sentimental pictures. Fräulein Schneider is tidying up the room when Chris comes in, looking for his thermometer; he thinks he is ill. The landlady locates the thermometer—Sally has been stirring prairie oysters with it. The fräulein chatters about Sally and that friend Klaus of hers, who has been away in England six weeks and has written only one letter.

Fritz comes calling and he and Chris chat about Natalia, who has become a problem. Fritz, the woman-conqueror, can do nothing with this one. Chris remembers Sally's theory that Fritz should pounce, and suggests that the young man simply ravish Natalia. "She is away now," says Fritz. "I write to her every day. Now I will write no more. I wait for her to come home, and then I will pounce, and I will ravish, and I will snarl."

Sally comes home, looking a bit smarter now, but her new hat is rather unsuitable. She carries several packages and looks tired. "You are very dressy today," Chris observes.

"I am? Oh, this hat. Yes, it's new. Clive bought it for me. I don't like it much, but it cost so much money. Let's have a prairie oyster." Chris declines, but Fritz is willing to try one and Sally mixes a couple in tooth glasses. Fritz wants to know who this Clive is who gives away hats, and Sally explains that he's an American whom Chris and she met a week ago at a bar—and ever since then they've hardly been apart. "He's so rich," Chris chuckles, "we daren't let him out of our sight." The packages Sally has brought are, indeed, from Clive—a dozen pairs of silk stockings, a great quantity of perfume and some loud silk shirts for Chris.

Sally has tossed off her prairie oyster but Fritz is struggling with his. Chris asks the girl if she's feeling well and she admits she isn't, so Fritz makes polite adieux and departs.

"Chris," says Sally, "I went to the doctor this afternoon and— I'm going to have a baby." It is Klaus's child, but Klaus doesn't know, she adds.

CHRIS—Well, you're going to tell him, aren't you?

SALLY—I don't know. Chris, I haven't heard from him for weeks and weeks. I wrote to him last week, the nicest letter I could, and he hasn't answered. Not a word. You didn't like him, did you?

CHRIS—I didn't really know him. I didn't think he was good enough for you.

SALLY—That's sweet of you.

CHRIS—But you're going to tell him this, now?

SALLY—No. Not if he doesn't write to me. It's awful, Chris. I do want to marry him, and have a family. But I can't beg him. And that's what it would be like. I mean, I mayn't be up to much, but I do have some pride.

CHRIS—Well, what then—if he doesn't write?

SALLY—I don't know. That's what scares me. It's silly, Chris . . . it happens to other girls. Almost all other girls. But I am scared. Do you suppose they all are, too? (*A knock at the door.*)

FRÄULEIN SCHNEIDER'S VOICE—It is I, Fräulein Sally. The post is here.

CHRIS (*sotto voce*)—She's been keeping an eye out for it.

SALLY—Come in.

FRÄULEIN SCHNEIDER (*entering*)—There is a letter for you. The one you want. From England.

SALLY—Oh, thank you.

FRÄULEIN SCHNEIDER—Ja, Fräulein. (*She hands it to her, and waits. SALLY starts to undo her packages. FRÄULEIN SCHNEIDER gives up and goes out. SALLY waits for her to leave. Then she rips the letter open. CHRIS stands by. She reads it. Her face changes.*)

CHRIS—What's the matter?

SALLY—It's what I thought. He's throwing me over.

CHRIS—Oh, no.

SALLY—Right over. With a whole lot of stuff about how badly he's behaved to me. (*She hands CHRIS the first page. He reads it. She goes on with the second.*) Apparently there's someone else. An English girl. A Lady Gore-Eckersley. He says she is wonderful. She's a virgin. A Communist Virgin. (*She lays the letter down.*) Well, those are two things no one could ever say of *me*.

CHRIS (*going to her, putting his arms around her*)—Oh, Sally, I'm sorry.

SALLY (*leaning against him*)—It's silly, isn't it?

CHRIS—It is a kind of bloody letter.

SALLY—I'm afraid he's rather a bloody person, really. Oh, Chris, I am a lousy picker. Always the duds who'll do me in.

CHRIS—I won't, Sally.

SALLY—I know. I suppose that's why I haven't been interested in you that way.

Sally wants the baby—if she's married and can look after it; but she knows that Klaus would run away. Chris volunteers, "I'll marry you, Sally." The girl has begun to weep now as she says this would do no good. She must get rid of the child—find someone—and Chris suggests the landlady, who knows just about everything. It turns out he is right, for when the fräulein is summoned and affairs are explained to her, she knows the name of a doctor. It will be rather expensive—250 or 300 marks—but after two or three days in a nursing home and a few days' rest here, it will all be forgotten. The good fräulein goes to phone the doctor. Sally is worried about the money, but Chris says he has started making a little more and will be glad to lend her some.

"I think," says the girl, "maybe you had better come with the fräulein and me. We'll say you're the father. I think it looks better to have him along." Chris agrees, and Sally clings gratefully to him. But there is an interruption: Clive has come calling. Clive is in his late thirties, large, American, blond and drunkish. He has never been to the room before and now he brings an enormous box of expensive flowers. He is not much impressed by the room as he noses about, and he even tries to investigate Chris's tiny room and is dissuaded only when Chris hints that a lady is resting there. A good-time boy, he says he has heard of a fine place out on the Wannsee and suggests that the three of them drive out for dinner. They agree, and Clive is all ready to start now—but Sally says she can't leave yet. The fräulein reports that she has telephoned "the man" and he will see Sally right away. Clive, the curious, wants to know what man, and the girl explains it's about a job—a sort of audition. Clive is all for driving her there, but Sally says it wouldn't look right, arriving for this job in a Duesenberg. Finally they get rid of their fun-loving visitor by agreeing that he can send his car back for them at six.

"He's awfully sweet, really," the girl says of the departing visitor. "Perhaps when this is over, I can devote myself to him. I've always thought I'd like to have a really rich man for a lover. . . . Or maybe I could marry him, and then I might reform him."

Chris grins, "Sally, do you really think you could reform anyone?"

"Oh, Chris, don't. Don't pull me down again. I feel awful."

They get ready to go with the landlady to the doctor. "Thank you for offering to marry me," she murmurs. Chris muses about what is happening—the "facts of life," and then having an expensive dinner and drinking too much, and soon they won't believe or remember a thing about it—either of them. Then he stops and says to himself, "Or will we?"

The curtain falls.

ACT II

About a week has passed. Chris is sitting on the ottoman pasting photographs in an album and chiding himself for his obscene laziness. Sally, pale and ill, comes in from the bathroom clad in a robe. She wishes she could have some champagne—but there isn't any and they are desperately broke. Clive, the old provider, should have provided some champagne along with everything else—along with, for instance, promising to put up all the money for a show for Sally . . . when she finds the show.

SALLY—You know, Chris, in some ways now I wish I had had that kid. The last day or two, I've been sort of feeling what it would be like to be a mother. Do you know, last night I sat here for a long time by myself, and held this teddy-bear in my arms, and imagined it was my baby? I felt a most marvelous sort of shut-off feeling from all the rest of the world. I imagined how it would grow up, and how after I'd put it to bed at nights, I'd go out and make love to filthy old men to get money to pay for its clothes and food.

CHRIS—You mean, a baby would be your purpose in life?

SALLY—Yes, I wouldn't think of myself at all. Just it. It must be rather wonderful never to think of yourself, just of someone else. I suppose that's what people mean by religion. Do you think I could be a nun, Chris? I really rather think I could. All pale and pious, singing sort of faint and lovely hymns all day long.

CHRIS—I think you'd get tired of it. You'd better just marry and have a child.

SALLY—I feel as if I'd lost faith in men. Even you, Christopher, if you were to go out into the street now and be run over by a taxi . . . I should be sorry in a way, of course, but I shouldn't really care a damn.

CHRIS (*laughing*)—Thank you, Sally.

SALLY (*moving to him*)—I didn't mean that, of course, darling—at least, not personally. You mustn't mind what I say when I'm like this. I can see now why people say operations like that are wrong. They are. You know, the whole business of having children is all wrong. It's a most wonderful thing, and it ought to be the result of something very rare and special and sort of privileged, instead of just *that!* What are you grinning about?

CHRIS—Well, that's what it's supposed to be. The result of something rare and special. That's what *that's* supposed to be.

SALLY—Oh, goodness, is it? Yes, I suppose it *is* supposed to be. Oh, is *that* why people say it's wrong to do it when you're not married, or terribly deeply in love?

CHRIS—Yes, of course it is.

SALLY—Well, why didn't anyone ever *tell* me?

CHRIS—I expect they did, and you didn't believe them.

SALLY—Did *you* believe them when they told you?

CHRIS—No, Sally.

SALLY—But you think they're right?

CHRIS—I suppose I do.

SALLY—Then why can't we do things that we know are right?

CHRIS—I don't know, Sally. But it seems we can't. Do you really think you're going to stop having sex just because of this? Forever?

SALLY—No, I don't suppose I do.

CHRIS—I don't think we'll ever quite trust things, in the long run.

SALLY—I trust you, Chris. I'm terribly fond of you.

CHRIS—I'm fond of you too, Sally.

SALLY—And you're not in love with me, are you?

CHRIS—No, I'm not in love with you.

SALLY—I'm awfully glad. I wanted you to like me from the first minute we met. But I'm glad you're not in love with me. Somehow or other, I couldn't possibly be in love with you. . . . So, if you had been, everything would have spoiled. Hold my hand, Chris, and let's swear eternal friendship.

Joining hands, they solemnly pledge eternal friendship.
Natalia Landauer, having returned from her trip and having learned that Sally has been ill, comes to pay a call and bring some flowers. What is it, please, that has been the matter with Sally? Chris and the girl say something vague about an operation, and the literal-minded Natalia tries unsuccessfully to get every last detail.

She even offers to send one of her uncles, all of whom are doctors, to make sure Sally is all right.

Sally asks Chris to make their visitor some coffee, and Natalia asks him to stay away for a while, for she has something private to say to Fräulein Bowles. It's about Fritz Wendel; Natalia wants some advice. Forthrightly she declares that, when Fritz made love to her, she did not take him seriously because it was all too formal and discreet—but, two nights ago, it is all changed. "He throws aside his formality, and it is quite different. I have never known a man like that. And it has disturbed me. I cannot sleep for it. And that is not like me."

Natalia wants to know if she should marry Fritz. Her parents, wanting her to marry a Jewish man, oppose it—but Natalia doesn't care about this. She wants to know if there has been anything in Herr Wendel's life that would make it inadvisable for her to become his wife.

"Yes, I . . . I think perhaps there is," Sally falters. But she is vague about it; he just isn't Natalia's kind. "I don't think you ought to marry him."

"I do not think so, too. But I think if I do not, that perhaps I will kill myself." Natalia begins to cry. She sobs, "I did not know that love was like this. It is not what the poets have said. It is awful, and it is degrading." Sally, sympathetic, agrees—and decides to tell Natalia what has been wrong with herself. "I was going to have a baby, and the chap let me down, and I had to get rid of it."

Now it is Natalia's turn to feel compassion. She will give up Fritz, she determines—but what will she do with her life? Sally suggests she could become a nun, if they have Jewish nuns. Chris returns and Natalia, recovered, announces that she will resume her lessons with Chris and that she will take two every day. "I need an awful lot to do," she explains—and hurries out.

Soon there is another caller who has heard of Sally's illness—Clive, and he brings a basket of champagne. He's all for having a dinner party tonight and seems unable to realize that Sally is not well enough to go out. When he is finally persuaded of this, he announces they will have dinner here, and they can start now with some champagne. Chris goes out to get glasses. Clive, examining Sally, says, "We'll have to pack you off some place to perk you up a bit. Where would you like to go?" When she objects that she wants to stay here because of her career he overrides her with, "You leave that all to me. Leave that all to Uncle Clive."

As Chris returns with glasses—tooth glasses again—and starts to open the champagne, Clive observes that this Berlin is a funny city. Driving here just now he ran into a bit of shooting; he doesn't know what—just some shooting and a fellow lying in the street and a lot of people running away, right in front of one of the department stores, Birnbaum's. Chris allows that this is a Jewish store and the shooting would be Nazi rioting. Clive asks innocently, "Are the Nazis the same as the Jews?" The champagne poured, the playboy drinks to "two real good playmates." Then, "You know, kids, this is a pretty dreary sort of town. . . . What do you say we *all* go? All three of us."

"But where?" asks Chris.

"Where would you like to go?" Clive queries simply. As if in a game, Chris says he'd like to go to India, but Sally holds out for Egypt. Clive suggests both—Orient Express to Athens, fly to Egypt, back to Marseille, by boat to South America, then Tahiti, Singapore and Japan. "I'd get kind of a kick out of showing them to you two kids. And then we can end up in California." They can't believe he means it, but he does. Sally is all for it, but Chris is hesitant; what about her career—and his, for that matter? Before Chris quite realizes it, Sally and Clive have set a week from today as the departure date. And now, Clive must dash out and order their at-home dinner—some caviar, and green turtle soup, and a partridge, and a few little things, and a half dozen bottles of brandy so it will be a real picnic.

Chris, stunned, asks Sally, "But what will become of us?"

SALLY—We shall have a wonderful time.

CHRIS—And then?

SALLY—I don't know. Oh, stop bothering with it, Chris. You always spoil things so.

CHRIS—We shall never come back.

SALLY—I don't want to come back.

CHRIS—I suppose you'll marry him.

SALLY—Of course I will.

CHRIS—And I? What will I be?

SALLY—You'll be a sort of private secretary, or something.

CHRIS—Without any duties. You know, Sally, I can suddenly see myself ten years from now—in flannels and black-and-white shoes, pouring out drinks in the lounge of a Californian hotel. I'll be a bit glassy in the eyes, and a lot heavier round the jowls.

SALLY—You'll have to take a lot of exercise, that's all.

CHRIS (*going to the window*)—You were both quite right. We've got nothing to do with these Germans down there—or the shooting, or the funeral, with the dead man in his coffin, or the words on the banners. You know, in a few days, we shall have forfeited all kinship with about ninety-nine per cent of the world's population. The men and women who earn their livings, and insure their lives, and are anxious about the future of their children.

SALLY—It's the only way to live. Isn't there something in the Bible about "Take no thought for the morrow"? That's exactly what it means.

CHRIS—I think in the Middle Ages people must have felt like this when they believed they had sold themselves to the devil.

SALLY—Well, you needn't come, if you don't want to.

CHRIS—Oh, no, I shall come. It's a funny feeling. Sort of exhilarating. Not really unpleasant. And yet, I'm sort of scared, too. If I do this, I'm lost. And yet I'm going to do it.

Sally gaily pours more champagne and asks, "Chris, what is it they say in German when you're going on a journey, and they want to wish you luck?"

" 'Hals und Beinbruch.' "

"What does that mean?"

"Neck and leg-break. It's supposed to stop you having them."

So they toast, neck and leg-break.

The curtain falls.

SCENE II

It is five days later, Chris is at the table finishing some coffee, and the room has dress boxes and an open suitcase lying around. The landlady brings a box to "Herr Issyvoo" from the Landauer store. She explains she brought the box here because the repairs to the ceiling of his own room have not been finished. The man didn't come; perhaps it was the news that stopped him.

"What news?"

"They have closed the National Bank. . . . There will be thousands ruined, I shouldn't wonder. . . . It is the Jews. I know it is the Jews." He tells his landlady she doesn't know what she is saying, but she insists that the Jews are too clever—and here is Chris, buying things at a Jewish store. What did he buy? "A suit—a tropical suit," he says, opening the parcel; and, this being as good an opening as any, he breaks the news: Fräulein, Sally and I are going away—right round the world. We're leaving on Thursday."

The landlady is distraught—both going away and her other rooms empty and the banks closing—what shall she do? Her anger rises and Chris tries to pacify her by saying she can have all the new china and glassware they've got. The fräulein weeps from self-pity. Sally, wearing a new, light suit and carrying a dress box, comes home gaily and is brought up short by the woman's weeping. Chris explains that he has just broken the news about their leaving. Angrily, Fräulein Schneider says she is, indeed, upset—and as for their glass and china, she will throw that from the windows at their taxi as they go away. She flees from the room.

Sally is too happy to be downed by such an outburst. From the box she takes a fluffy pink negligee which she has bought for the trip to lie around in. "I expect we'll do lots of lying around."

The landlady, frozen and grim, reappears to announce Herr Wendel. Sally and Chris tell Fritz about their marvelous plans for going away on Thursday, but Fritz has little enthusiasm. "I am not good," he says, and this is why he has come to see them. He has had a note from Natalia saying it is all over, and when he goes to see her Natalia shows him a note her father has received. The note, unsigned, has read, "Herr Landauer, beware. We are going to settle the score with all you dirty Jews. We give you twenty-four hours to leave Germany. If not, you are dead men." This note came last night, and last night Natalia told Fritz she could think of nothing else, and he must go away and never come back.

"What is Herr Landauer going to do?" asks Chris.

"He will not go away. And Natalia will not. I think her mother will go to Paris, but Natalia will stay by her father."

Sally has poured champagne and still is trying to be gay; but Fritz, throwing his glass away melodramatically, utters a curse in German and buries his head in his hands. In a moment he says he has something else to tell:

"It is something I have never told anyone in my life before. But now I must make confession. I am a Jew."

This means nothing to Sally. She confesses she always had an idea he was because he made so much fuss about not being one—but so what? She thinks Fritz is taking it all too seriously. The bell sounds below; that'll be Clive's car, to take them to lunch. But it isn't; it's a messenger with a note which the now-unfriendly landlady brings up to Sally. The girl opens it, reads it, and can do no more than gasp, "But . . . but . . ."

Chris, seeming shocked, asks what it is, but Sally rallies enough to say that it is nothing—and then, to Fritz, "Look, we've got to go out to lunch." Fritz would like to remain and share more of his misery with his friends, but he takes the hint and leaves. "Come tomorrow," the girl invites.

"Good-by, Sally. Good-by, Chris," Fritz intones mournfully. "I think maybe now I go pray a little. But in what church? I do not know."

The girl hands over the note to Chris, who reads, "Dear Sally and Chris, I can't stick this damned town any longer. I'm off to the States. Hoping to see you some time. Clive. These are in case I forgot anything." Chris looks in the envelope and finds 300 marks. After a long pause he comments, "Well!"

The bottom has been cut from under the two young people. Perhaps Clive hasn't left the hotel yet. Perhaps . . . But neither wants to call him. They summon Fräulein Schneider and ask her to call the Adlon and simply find out if he is there, and without a word the landlady goes to do what they ask.

CHRIS—You know he's gone, don't you?

SALLY—I suppose I do, really. But we've got to be sure. Do you think he did it on purpose? Just to get us all steamed up, and then let us down like this?

CHRIS—I think he just got fed up.

SALLY—And what about us?

CHRIS—I don't imagine he even remembered us—or not for more than a minute. I think that's the way he lives. And that he leaves every town and every set of acquaintances just that way.

SALLY—Easy come, easy go.

CHRIS—Yes.

SALLY—We were easy come, all right. But, Chris, don't you think it was outrageous? I mean, really outrageous?

CHRIS—Sally, I don't think we've got too much right to have an opinion anyway, about the whole thing.

SALLY—And what have we got out of it?

CHRIS—Not much. But it didn't last very long.

SALLY—I don't think we're much good as gold-diggers, are we, darling? (*They begin to laugh.* FRÄULEIN SCHNEIDER *returns.*)

FRÄULEIN SCHNEIDER—Herr Mortimer has left, Fräulein. He has gone back to the United States.

SALLY—I see. Thank you.

CHRIS—And, Fräulein Schneider, we won't be going away—after all.

FRÄULEIN SCHNEIDER (*overjoyed*)—Ah, Herr Issyvoo, you mean that?

CHRIS—Yes, I do.

FRÄULEIN SCHNEIDER—Oh, but that is good. That is wonderful. Neither of you? Not Fräulein Sally, either?

SALLY—No, neither of us.

FRÄULEIN SCHNEIDER—Then, that is a miracle. Oh, but I am happy. I am happy. (*She seizes* SALLY *by the waist, and starts to dance.*)

SALLY (*releasing herself*)—Yes, I'm sure you're happy, Fräulein. But not now, please. I'd like you to leave us alone.

In an instant life for the two young people has changed from gay to grim. They divide the 300 marks, then take stock of the future. They must find work immediately. Sally remembers a horrible old man in Frankfurt who offered her a job. Chris will again advertise "English lessons given" in the papers. Chris feels relieved, somehow—as if they'd been delivered from the Devil. Sally admits that it couldn't have gone on forever—that Clive would have ditched them somewhere. "You're right," she agrees. "He *was* the Devil."

Chris shakes his head. "The Devil was in *us*. Sally, how about our trying to reform, and change our ways of life a bit?"

They contemplate reform with enthusiasm, as if it were a new pastime. Sally vows never to look at another man with money. Chris is going to start work tomorrow morning. They will behave well and sleep well and wake up without coughing or feeling the least little bit sick. They'll get up at half past seven and have cold baths. They will study something—Chris laughingly suggests weaving and making small, hand-painted boxes. And while he is writing his novel she will practice interpretive dancing.

CHRIS—Sally, joking aside. You are serious about all this, aren't you?

SALLY—Of course I am. Terribly serious. (*She gets the address book.*) I'm going to start calling up everyone I know.

CHRIS—What for?

SALLY—To see what's going on. And then, one decent piece of luck . . .

CHRIS (*urgently*)—Oh, no, Sally. That isn't what we need. A piece of good luck today—a piece of bad luck tomorrow—always at the mercy of *things* again . . .

SALLY—One *is*. That's life. It's all accident.

CHRIS (*as before*)—Accidents are only the result of things one's done. Things that one is.

SALLY—Why, I could go to a party tonight, and I could meet the most wonderful man, who'd make all the difference to my whole life and my career . . . (*She breaks off, looking at him.*) What's the matter? Why do you look like that?

CHRIS (*slowly*)—Sally, you weren't serious. You didn't mean a word of it.

SALLY—Yes, I did. I meant every word. I'm going to be quite different. But there's no reason why I shouldn't go out. I don't have to shut myself up in prison. That isn't what you want, is it?

CHRIS—No, Sally, of course not. But . . .

SALLY (*angrily*)—Well, then, stop looking so disapproving. You're almost as bad as Mother. She never stopped nagging at me. That's why I had to lie to her. I always lie to people, or run away from them, if they won't accept me as I am.

CHRIS—I know you do, Sally.

SALLY (*putting on an act*)—I think I'm really rather a strange and extraordinary person, Chris. (*Pause.*) What's the matter? You laughed at me the first time I told you that. Can't you laugh now? Come on. (*She starts to laugh, not too brightly. He starts a moment later, still more feebly. The laughter dies. She tries again—it fails. They move slowly away from each other.*)

The curtain falls.

ACT III

It is two days later. Chris has written a magazine article which Sally has said she can sell to an editor she has met, and now he comes to ask about it. The room is untidy, for Fräulein Schneider has just begun work. Old coffee and a glass of brandy sit on a tray. Chris seems surprised that Sally is not there, and the landlady informs him she did not come back until almost six this morning, and maybe she drank a little too much. Sally, in a robe, comes in from the bathroom—a tired and hung-over girl. They chase the landlady out, and Chris demands, "What were you doing last night?"

"I was out with some people. I've been out both nights. I've been an awful fool, Chris. But don't scold me, please."

They never stopped going around, she relates. And the first night she got drunk and sentimental and telephoned Mother in London, but the connection was bad. Sally is glad to be back here; she puts her arms around Chris and declares earnestly, "I do think we belong together. Much more than if we'd ever had an affair."

Chris asks about his article. Sally, at first vague, now says too brightly that it won't do—not snappy enough. But it's all right, because she has got someone else to do it—Kurt Rosenthal, the scenario writer. Kurt is doing the article as a favor to her, and is dictating it while shaving. He's so busy he can only dictate while he's having a bath, and he's writing a novel in his spare time.

Chris observes bitterly, "I bet that makes it wonderful"—and from this sour comment there builds a first-class quarrel. Sally makes slanted remarks about authors with one book feeling authorized to talk largely on art and imagination. The furious Chris says he shouldn't have expected Sally to like his article—not with that snappy little bird-brain of hers; and the friends she goes with are the same. She retorts that these friends are saying she should leave Chris—that he is devouring her like a vampire and she is losing all her sparkle. "I've gone beyond you," she proclaims. "I'd better move away from here." The sooner the better is fine with Chris. Sally dresses swiftly and leaves the room haughtily and angrily.

But she isn't gone long, and she looks shattered when she comes back. "Chris, something awful's happened. Guess who I met in the street, right outside. I met Mother." Apparently the girl's drunken phone call upset Mother, and Mother has taken a plane, and now Sally is in a spot. She explains to Chris, "I've never had the nerve to tell you, but I sort of gave her to understand—when I first moved in here—that we were engaged." The girl defends her fib; she needed someone who sounded like a good, steady influence, and Chris was the best she could think of. Now, she has warned Mother the place is untidy, but nevertheless Mother is coming up in a moment. Chris is appalled.

SALLY—Well, I needed someone who sounded like a good, steady influence—and you were the best I could think of. She's in the sitting-room. I told her this place was all untidy, but she'll be in in a minute. Oh, and her name isn't Mrs. Bowles. It's Mrs. Watson-Courtneidge. That's my real name. Only you can't imagine the Germans pronouncing it.

CHRIS—And I'm supposed to stand by and pretend? Oh, no, Sally.

SALLY—Chris, you've got to. You owe it to me.

CHRIS—For what? For letting me eat you up? I'm sorry. And I'm going to my room.

SALLY (*getting in his way*)—If you don't, I'll tell her the most awful things about you.

CHRIS—I'm afraid I don't care. Tell her what you like.

SALLY (*pleading*)—Chris, you can't do this to me.

CHRIS—After the things you just said to me? That I made you sick.

SALLY—That was just an expression.

CHRIS—No, Sally. We're through. Quite through.

SALLY—Well, we still can be, after she goes home. Only, help me keep her happy. Don't believe everything I said at first about Mother. She isn't easy. Please, darling. Please! (*Her arms are around his neck. He struggles to disengage himself. Then* MRS. WATSON-COURTNEIDGE *comes in. She is a middle-aged English lady, in tweeds. She carries a coat.*)

MRS. WATSON-COURTNEIDGE (*catching sight of the embrace*)—Excuse me.

SALLY (*extricating herself*)—Oh . . .

MRS. WATSON-COURTNEIDGE—I hope this is Mr. Isherwood.

SALLY—Yes. Christopher.

MRS. WATSON-COURTNEIDGE—I'm Mother.

CHRIS—I imagined that.

MRS. WATSON-COURTNEIDGE—Well—don't I deserve a kiss, too?

CHRIS (*as* SALLY *looks pleadingly at him*)—Oh—yes, of course. (*A kiss is performed.*)

MRS. WATSON-COURTNEIDGE—You're not a bit like I imagined you.

CHRIS—Oh, really. How did you imagine me?

MRS. WATSON-COURTNEIDGE—Oh, quite different. So this is your room, Sally. Yes, I can see why you said it was untidy.

SALLY—I got up very late this morning. Fräulein Schneider hasn't really had time to do it.

MRS. WATSON-COURTNEIDGE—I don't imagine she does it very well at the best of times. I've just been having a little talk with her. I can't say I like her very much. And why does she sleep in the sitting-room?

CHRIS—So that she can watch the corner.

MRS. WATSON-COURTNEIDGE—And what happens on the corner?

CHRIS—Oh—*that!*

SALLY—Chris!

MRS. WATSON-COURTNEIDGE—I beg your pardon?

CHRIS (*vaguely*)—This and that.

MRS. WATSON-COURTNEIDGE—I should think she'd be much better occupied, looking after . . . (*Dusting the table with her fingers.*) that and this! (*She picks up the brandy glass.*) Sally, you haven't been drinking brandy, I hope.

SALLY—That's Chris's glass.

Mrs. Watson-Courtneidge—On *your* breakfast tray?   Where do *you* live, Mr. Isherwood?

Chris answers, "Just across the hall" and Mother is drily cynical. She is now in full charge, announcing that if a wedding date hasn't been set, this must be—shall we say—tidied up.   Does Christopher live on the proceeds of his one odd book?   Well, then, what *does* he live on?   Is teaching English sufficient for two to get by on?   Chris, edgy from this grilling, tries to get away, but Mother insists that he have luncheon with her and her daughter and he departs to don his one ragged, dirty blue suit.

Alone with her daughter, Mother decides, "Well, in any case, I think you two have been together quite enough for the moment." She cannot believe Sally's protestations that she and Chris are not living together and is being grimly broad-minded.   "You had better move into the hotel with me," she orders.

Sally gives in, "Well, all right, but don't rush him.   Don't try and force him, or anything."

"Trust Mother!"

The curtain falls.

SCENE II

Three days have passed.   Chris isn't home, but Fräulein Schneider is setting a tray of coffee—and the coffee is for Fritz, who has come calling.   Since Sally's departure, Chris has moved back into the big room.   He can afford it, for he has more pupils; true, says the landlady, they are almost all Jews.   "Is it true, Herr Wendel," she asks, "that they will take the money away from the Jews, and drive them out?"   The uneasy Fritz says he has no idea.

Outside the room Chris is heard calling, "Go right in there, Natalia.   Are you sure you're all right?   And then come to my room. It's the old room."   Chris, even messier than usual, comes in and greets Fritz.   Then he pours water into a basin to wash his hands. "There was a bit of trouble," he explains; "I was walking with Natalia after her lesson.   We ran into a bunch of toughs.   Nazis, of course.   They were holding a street meeting.   And Natalia insisted on joining in."

Indeed, according to Chris's narrative, Natalia was quite fierce—almost like Joan of Arc.   And then she was hit in the face with a stone, and Chris got mixed up in it, and now they are both here—Natalia to wash her face and Chris to wash his fists.   Chris, a hypochondriac, begins putting Band-aids on his knuckles.

Natalia, coming from the bathroom with a small cut on her face, is surprised to see Fritz there, and even more surprised at Fritz's tenderness as he examines her wound and suggests that he put a little bandage on it. This done, Natalia announces, "And now I think I go home." Chris, worrying about his own wounds, has torn off his bandages and now is painting his fists with iodine.

"I would like that you let me take you," says Fritz to Natalia.

"And if we run into another of these street riots?"

"I would still like to take you." Chris raises his head, exchanges glances with Fritz, and Fritz, nodding very gently, says, "I tell it now." They leave.

The landlady, coming in for the coffee tray, sees Chris painting his knuckles, and the young writer explains that he was in a street riot. Yes, an anti-Jewish riot—but he was defending the Jews. Fräulein Schneider splutters that the Jews are at the bottom of all the trouble, and Chris brings her up sharply and angrily. "I'm ashamed of you. And everything you say is horrible and dangerous and abominable. And now please go away."

Chris is alone with his cherished wounds for a few moments, until Sally comes in, wearing the coat her mother was carrying when Mother first arrived. Sally is closely followed by Mother. "I'm taking Sally home," says Mother. She wants Christopher to come, too, and meet Sally's father, and perhaps be given a job of some sort, and then they can be married at the end of next month.

It is time for Chris to assert himself. Sally senses what he is going to do, but she can't stop him with looks and gestures. "Sally and I," he says, "are no longer engaged. She sent me a note this morning to break it off." This suits Mother, who says to her daughter, "Now you'll come back and settle down again, and quite soon all of this will be forgotten." A subdued Sally says, "Yes, Mother."

With this advantage, Mrs. Watson-Courtneidge gives Chris a chill, formal but thorough dressing-down. Unprincipled drifters calling themselves authors . . . Heading for socialism . . . She is taken aback when her daughter speaks up spiritedly for Chris, saying, "He's a very fine person. He's been wonderful to me. And he's an artist. Well—potentially. All artists need time. He's going to write a wonderful book one day—or a lot of short stories about Germany or something—and then you'll feel very silly for the things you've said." Staggered, Mother says good-by to Chris and leads her obedient daughter out.

The curtain falls.

Scene III

Three evenings later, Chris is packing a large trunk and talking to himself about all the things he has accumulated without knowing it. Sally bursts in, crying "Chris!"

"I thought you'd gone home."

"No. Mother left this morning. I did something awful." Sally giggles. "I got a friend in London to send her an anonymous telegram telling her Daddy was having an affair."

Noticing the packing, Sally asks, "Where are you off to?"

"I *am* going home. Tomorrow night. I'm going to Fritz and Natalia's wedding in the afternoon. Fritz told Natalia about himself, and that did it. Come with me, Sally."

"Oh, I'd like to, but I won't be here. . . . I'm leaving for the Riviera tonight."

"Who's the man, Sally?"

"Man?"

"Oh, come off it."

Well, Sally admits, there *is* a man. Wonderful. He saw her and Mother in the street just as they left here, two days ago, and he sort of followed them to a tea shop. A movie agent with a long, black beard. A Yugoslavian, and he wants Sally for a picture. And now Sally must run.

CHRIS—Oh, Sally, *must* you? Must you go on like this? Why don't you go home, too? Come back with me. I mean it, Sally. My family'll give me some money if I'm home. Or I'll get a job. I'll see that you're all right.

SALLY—It wouldn't be any good, Chris. I'd run away from you, too. The moment anything attractive came along. It's all right for you. You're a writer. You really are. I'm not even an actress, really. I'd love to see my name in lights, but even if I had a first-night tomorrow, if something exciting turned up, I'd go after it. I can't help it. That's me. I'm sentimental enough to hope that one day I'll meet the perfect man, and marry him and have an enormous family and be happy, but until then—well, that's how I am. You know that really, don't you?

CHRIS—Yes, Sally, I'm afraid I do.

SALLY—Afraid? Oh, Chris, am I too awful—for *me*, I mean?

CHRIS—No, Sally. I'm very fond of you.

SALLY—I do hope you are. Because I am of you. Was it true about eternal friendship that we swore?

CHRIS—Yes, of course it was. Really true. Tell me, do you have an address?

SALLY—No, I don't. But I'll write. I really will. Postcards and everything. And you write to me. Of course, you'll be writing all sorts of things—books and things—that I can read. Will you dedicate one to me?

CHRIS—The very first one.

SALLY—Oh, good. Perhaps that'll be my only claim to fame. Well—good-by for now, Chris. Neck and leg-break.

CHRIS—Neck and leg-break. (*They go into each other's arms.*)

SALLY (*starts to go, then turns to* CHRIS)—I do love you. (*She goes, swiftly.*)

CHRIS (*stares after her, for a moment*)—I love you, too, Sally. And it's so damned stupid that that's not enough to keep two people together. (*He starts to move toward the window. The lights begin to dim.*) The camera's taken all its pictures, and now it's going away to develop them. I wonder how Sally will look when I've developed her? I haven't got an end for her yet, but there probably isn't one. She'll just go on and on, as she always has—somewhere. (*He looks out of the window.*) There she goes now. Into the photograph. She's just going around the corner. (*He watches as the curtain starts to fall.*) Don't forget those postcards, Sally.

THE CURTAIN FALLS

THE FOURPOSTER *

A Play in Three Acts

By Jan de Hartog

JAN DE HARTOG, a Dutchman who became a naturalized Englishman, has had two plays produced in New York and both have been Best Plays. The first was "Skipper Next to God," in which the late John Garfield played a high-minded and tough-minded ship captain. This was an anti-Nazi war drama, produced in the season of 1947-1948. In "The Fourposter" de Hartog made about as abrupt a change as a dramatist can make; he wrote, in 1947, a very simple little comedy for two characters—a man and his wife. During ensuing years he put more work on "The Fourposter" until he arrived at the version which was presented by the Playwrights' Company in New York during the season of 1951-1952.

The economic ideal of a play in years of high production costs is a piece with one set and as few characters as possible. Very few dramatists have dared cut themselves down to two characters, and fewer still have succeeded with this reduction. In recent times, the only two-character piece which had success on Broadway was Louis Verneuil's sexy melodrama, "Jealousy." Once in a while the theatre gets a worthwhile three-character piece. The best and most successful of these is John van Druten's "The Voice of the Turtle," which was a Best Play of the season of 1943-1944.

De Hartog, in writing "The Fourposter," essayed a simple and homey comedy about a husband and wife—a miniature, so to speak, of "Life with Father" and "Life with Mother." His sex problems are slight and his dramatic situations are even slighter. His attention is devoted to the everyday problems, few of them important, which a young man and a young woman are bound to encounter after they have said "I do" at a marriage ceremony. When we first meet Michael and Agnes (whom the author simply calls He and She in his script) it is not long after they have said "I do." Michael is bringing his bride home, and as befits tradition is carrying her over

* Copyright as an unpublished dramatic composition, 1947, by Jan de Hartog. Author's agent, Leah Salisbury, 234 West 44th Street, New York City.

the threshold into their bedroom—a bedroom which will become a witness to their lives together for very many years. This bedroom is not particularly elegant, even for the year 1890. It has a door leading into it and another door leading to another room, and windows, and a bed. A rather imposing fourposter bed placed on a dais. This bedroom is obviously on the second floor of a house which might be found in any city. Night has fallen and gas lamps shimmer when He carries She in through the door rather clumsily. She is in her bridal gown, and He is dressed as a bridegroom should be, in frock coat and striped pants and with a silk hat uneasily perched on the back of his head. As the bridegroom transports his burden, She gasps, "Oh, Micky, whoo! Hold me. Hold me tight! Whoo! Whoo! I'm falling. I can't . . ."

Micky, the determined husband, throws his new wife on the bed and tries to kiss her, but she, a proper young lady, struggles up, straightens her hat and dress and warns her new man that the door is still open. He closes it, peels off his white gloves and puts one in each pocket, and kneels before her—an astonishing performance, she thinks. "I'm worshiping you," he explains, and she orders him, "Get up immediately!" He doesn't seem to be able to get up rather immediately and it is possible that he is a bit tipsy, so she hauls him up and demands, "Are you out of your senses? If our Lord should see you . . ." "If I'm drunk," says Micky virtuously as he teeters on one knee, "I'm drunk only with happiness." "Michael," she reproaches him, "that hat!" He still is wearing it, so now he takes it off, holds it a moment and then absent-mindedly returns it to its perch on the back of his head.

"I suddenly feel like saying all sorts of shocking things," the bride announces. "Listen—no, in your ear." He comes to her and she starts to whisper; then she stops, examines both his ears and exclaims, "You pig! Don't you ever wash?" He counters by suggesting she might like to kiss him and she answers, "I would like to go over you from top to bottom, with hot water and soap; that's what I would like to do." Suddenly she cries, "Ouch!" Her shoes are hurting her, and he gallantly kneels to remove them. He pauses to kiss her foot before taking one shoe off, so, impatient for relief, she bends over to remove the other herself and is startled to see him looking at her rather creepily—and amazed, too, that he is still wearing his hat.

"Please get undr—take your hat off!" she orders.

He puts down her shoe, leans against her knee, and exults once again that he is happy. "*Must* you make me cry?" she whimpers.

"You should, you know," Michael observes. "This is a very sad occasion, really. Your youth is over."

Now she wails, "I want to go home! I should never have married you! My youth over! That's what you would like! Undressing me, the whole night long, with your hat on and unwashed ears and . . . oh!" She flings her arms around his neck and weeps. This being Michael's first experience of comforting a sobbing spouse, he is rather clumsy at it; he urges, "You cry, my dearest; that's the spirit."

The storm passes and the two young lovers are happy again. Agnes inquires if Michael has written a poem for tonight; he claims he hasn't but she doesn't believe him. From a pocket he takes a poem he says he *has* been working on—a rather modern thing. He tries a sample on her: "Hissing shoots the slender shower; out of shining, slimy stone swaying shivers sparkling flower; rainbow shimmers in the foam. Flashing, dashing, splashing, crashing . . ."

Agnes has been edging toward the door and now, snatching her suitcase as she goes, she opens the door, takes the key from the lock, calls "Back in a minute"—and locks the door from the other side. He has a moment of panic, thinking she has left him, until he sees her shoes on the floor; then he gets the idea. He puts his own suitcase on the arms of a chair, opens it, takes out a nightcap and puts it on his head. Off come coat, vest, tie and shirt; furtively he removes his trousers, keeping an eye on the door. Next he removes his shoes—and then puts them back on. He dives into a nightshirt, then pulls his trousers on over it; finally he puts on his coat again. He stows his vest, shirt and tie in the suitcase, closes it and puts it in the wardrobe. Moving to the washstand, he dampens a corner of a towel and begins washing an ear as Agnes clicks the key in the lock. Swiftly he dives for a chair and sits with arms folded as his bride enters; her dress has changed, somehow, and she has taken off her wedding hat.

"What on earth is that?" she demands, pointing to the nightcap.

HE—What?

SHE—On your head?

HE—Oh . . . why . . .

SHE—Do you wear a nightcap?

HE—Oh, no. Just now when there's a draft. (*Rises, takes cap off and puts it in his pocket.*)

SHE—Is that a nightshirt?

HE—What have you got on?

SHE—My father has been wearing pajamas for ages.

HE—Oh, has he really? Well, I don't.

SHE—Why have you . . . changed?

HE—Why have you?

SHE—I? Oh . . . I'm sleepy.

HE—So am I.

SHE—Well, then, shall we . . . ?

HE—Why, yes . . . let's.

SHE—All right. Which side do you want?

HE—I? Oh, well. . . . I don't care, really. Any side that suits you is all right with me.

SHE—I think I would like the far side. Because of the door.

HE—The door?

SHE (*turns back quilt*)—Because of breakfast, and in case somebody should knock. You could answer it.

HE—I see.

SHE (*picks up "God Is Love" pillow from bed*)—What's this?

HE—What?

SHE—This little pillow? Did you put that there?

HE—Of course not! (*Steps up onto dais.*) What's it got written on it?

SHE—"God Is Love." Oh, how sweet! Mother must have done that. Wasn't that lovely of her? (*Puts pillow back on bed.*)

HE—Yes, charming. (SHE *turns away and starts undressing.* HE *takes off his coat.* SHE *turns. After an embarrassing moment in which neither of them can think of anything to say:*)

SHE—Michael, please turn 'round.

HE—Oh, I'm so sorry . . . I just didn't realize. (HE *sits down on the edge of the chest, putting his coat beside him, and takes off his shoes and socks.* SHE *steps from dais, steps out of dress and hangs it in wardrobe.*)

SHE—It's rather a pretty bed, isn't it?

HE (*picks up her shoes and places them next to his*)—Yes, it is, isn't it? It was my father's, you know.

SHE—Not your mother's?

HE—Yes, of course, my parents. I was born in it, you know.

SHE (*taking a step toward him*)—Michael . . .

HE (*turning toward her*)—Yes, darling?

SHE (*backing up*)—No, don't look! Michael?

HE (*turning away*)—Yes?

SHE—Tell me how much you love me, once more.

HE—I can't any more.

SHE—What?

HE—I can't love you any more than I'm doing. I wor— I'm the hap— I'm mad about you.

SHE—That's what I am about you. Honestly.

HE—That is nice, dear.

SHE—I am so happy, I couldn't be happier.

HE—That is lovely, darling.

SHE—And I wouldn't want to be, either.

HE—What?

SHE—Happier.

HE—I see.

SHE—I wish that everything could stay as it was—before today.
I couldn't stand any more—happiness. Could you?

HE—God, no.

SHE—How coldly you say that.

HE—But what the blazing hell do you expect me to say then?

SHE—Michael! Is that language for the wedding ni— before
going to sleep? You ought to be ashamed of yourself!

Michael complains, with a sneeze, that he has a headache and is
dying of cold feet, and Agnes suggests that he get into bed, as she
is doing now. He turns his back to her, begins removing his trousers,
and realizes that the room is brightly lit. He turns off one gas
bracket and is about to turn off the other when Agnes asks if the
lamp could leak. He laughs at her fears, turns out the light, takes
off his trousers and puts them on a chair, gropes his way to the bed,
stubs his toe on the dais and finally eases himself into the bed.

They make conversation for quite a while, until Agnes sits up and
declares in alarm, "Now I'm sure that I smell gas!" He reassures
her, saying she must be smelling the drinks he has had. Agnes
demands to smell his breath, but he is reluctant. She insists, "I want
to smell it. If it is the gas, we may be dead tomorrow, both of us."
Unwillingly he breathes at her as she lies down—ho, ho, ho.
"Again," she says softly. Ho, ho. "Again." Michael raises his arm
to embrace her.

The curtain falls.

SCENE II

It is a late afternoon in 1891. The bedroom is the same, except
that a cradle has been added. Michael is lying in the fourposter with a
towel wrapped around his head. It is obvious from the clutter of
books and things on and around the bed that he has been having a
siege of invalidism. He picks up an oversize dinner bell, rings it
insistently and calls, "Agnes! Agnes!"

His wife, quite obviously pregnant, comes into the room carrying
a pile of clean laundry. Michael complains that the pain has shifted

from his head to his back. "Here?" she asks, putting her hand on his back. "But what sort of pain? Does it come in—in waves? First almost nothing and then growing until you could scream?"

"That's right. How do you know—"

"Micky, that's impossible."

"What's impossible? Do you think I'm shamming?"

She cries laughingly, "You're having labor pains!"

Then she begins to sob, feeling sorry for herself; all this time she's been putting up a brave front and taking care of her husband because she thought he was really ill. Michael flings himself out of bed, gets his clothes from the wardrobe and announces, "If I drop dead on the pavement, I'm going to get that doctor. I'm not going to leave you in this condition a minute longer. He said so himself, the moment you got those pains."

She reminds him, "When *I* got them! Not when you got them!" She hasn't any pains. She coaxes him back into bed and puts the "God Is Love" pillow behind his head—which he immediately throws to the floor. Now Michael begins to fret and worry about the baby: he has lost his wife, for, being the male animal that has done its duty, he now can be dismissed. He jumps from bed and begins to pace, exclaiming that he is nothing but a drone. "I wish I was lying in that cradle," he moans miserably. Tenderly Agnes embraces him and calls him a fool; she has tried every day to prove how much she loves him.

HE (*steps up onto dais*)—Listen! Before that cuckoo pushes me out of the nest, I want to tell you once more that I love you. Love you, just as you are. . . . (*Sits on bed and puts on slippers.*) I thought I loved you when I married you, but that wasn't you at all. That was a romantic illusion. I loved a sort of fairy princess with a doll's smile and a . . . well, anyway not a princess with hiccoughs and cold feet, scratching her stomach in her sleep. . . . (*Takes her hand.*) I thought I was marrying a princess and I woke up to find a friend, a wife. . . . You know, sometimes when I lay awake longer than you, with my arm around your shoulder and your head on my chest, I thought with pity of all those lonely men staring at the ceiling or writing poems . . . pity, and such happiness that I knew at that very moment it wouldn't last. I was right, that's all. (*Rises, goes around to foot of bed; picks up robe.*)

SHE—Well, if you thought about a princess, I thought about a poet.

HE (*fixes sleeve in robe right side out*)—Oh?

SHE—You didn't know that I had cold feet and every now and

again I get an attack of hiccoughs.

HE (*putting on robe*)—You don't do anything else the whole night long.

SHE—What?

HE—Scratch your stomach and sniff and snort and smack your lips, but go on, go on.

SHE—And you lie listening to all this without waking me up?

HE—Yes. Because I don't know anything in the world I'd rather listen to. (*Kisses her.*) Got anything to say to that?

SHE—Yes, but I won't say it.

HE—Why not?

SHE—Never mind, darling, you stay just as you are.

HE—Miserable, deserted, alone? You do nothing else all day and night but fuss over that child—eight months now! First it was knitting panties, then sewing dresses, fitting out the layette, rigging the cradle. . . . (*Ties robe.*)

SHE—And all this time you sat quietly in your corner, didn't you?

HE—I retired into the background as becomes a man who recognizes that he is one too many.

SHE (*rises, goes to him*)—Oh, angel! (*Puts her arms around his neck and kisses him.*) Do you still not understand why I love you so much?

HE—You . . . you noticed how I blotted myself out?

SHE—Did I!

HE—I didn't think you did.

SHE—You helped me more than all model husbands put together. Without you I would have been frightened to death for eight whole months. But I simply had no time.

Suddenly Agnes gasps and grasps at her back, and her husband stares at her in horror. He picks up his clothes and frantically unties his robe, crying, "The doctor! For God's sake, the doctor!"

"Stay here," she begs him. Convulsed by pain, she grasps a post of the bed and begins singing "Yankee Doodle"—the doctor had said singing would help the pain. The spasm passes, and she tells Michael he mustn't go yet—not until the pains become regular. Nevertheless, he begins to dress—but is calmer now. He talks of the fun he will have with his child, fishing if it's a son and taking nature rambles if it's a girl. She bravely starts for the door to take down the rest of the laundry from the roof, but he stops her and gently seats her on a chest. He will read to her—the start of a book he has begun. He reads from a scratch pad: "When she entered the attic with the double bed, she bent her head, partly out of reverence for the temple where she had worshiped and sacrificed, partly because the ceiling was so low. . . ."

Another pain seizes her. He kneels before her and she buries her head in his shoulder. "Now," she breathes, "now I think you'd better go and call him."

"I will, my darling," he says, putting on his coat and going to the door. Then he returns to her, comforting, "Now you just sit tight." Once again he makes for the door, then comes back to kiss her. Another start, and this time he notices the bassinette. He runs to it, pulls it over close to his wife, and dashes out.

The curtain falls.

ACT II

It is a night in 1901—ten years later. The fourposter still is in the room, but the rest of the room has changed. The washstand is gone, for now there is a bathroom adjoining; paintings hang on the walls and expensive furniture crowds the room. Everything is elegant and expensive and new. Only one side of the bed has been made, with one pillow, and on top of this is the "God Is Love" pillow. Agnes, in elegant evening dress, comes in and slams the door behind her. There is a knock at the door and she ignores it; again a knock, and she says, coldly, "Come in."

Michael enters, resplendent in full dress, top hat and cane, mutters a polite "excuse me" and goes to the new dressing room to get his night clothes. Returning, he opens the door and says "Good night."

She chides, "You were the life and soul of the party this evening, with your interminable little stories."

"My dear," he replies, "if you don't enjoy playing second fiddle, I suggest that you either quit the orchestra or form one of your own." He goes out and shuts the door. She flings the door open and bellows for him to come back, demanding what on earth is the matter with him.

HE—Now, let me tell you one thing, calmly. My greatest mistake has been to play up to you, plying you with presents. . . .

SHE—I like that!

HE—Calmly! Do you know what I should have done? I should have packed you off to boarding school, big as you are, to learn deportment.

SHE (*turns to him*)—Deportment for what?

HE—To be worthy of me.

SHE—The pompous ass whose book sold three hundred thousand copies!

He—That is entirely beside the point.

She—It is right to the point! Before you had written that cursed novel, the rest of the world helped me to keep you sane. Every time you had finished a book or a play or God knows what, and considered yourself to be the greatest genius since Shakespeare . . . (He says, "Now really!" He puts cape, hat, gloves on chair.) . . . I was frightened to death that it might turn out to be a success. But, thank Heaven, it turned out to be such a thorough failure every time, that I won the battle with your megalomania. But now, now this book, the only book you ever confessed to be trash until you read the papers . . . Oh, what's the use!

He—My dear woman, I may be vain, but you are making a tragic mistake.

She (laughs)—Now listen! (Laughs.) Just listen to him! To be married to a man for eleven years, and then to be addressed like a public meeting. Tragic mistake! (He sits. She crosses to him.) Can't you hear yourself, you poor darling idiot, that you've sold your soul to a sentimental novel?

He—Agnes, are you going on like this, or must I . . .

She—Yes, yes, you must! You shall hear it. (He pounds floor with evening cane.) And don't interrupt me! There is only one person in this world who loves you in spite of what you are, and let me tell you . . .

He—You are mistaken. There is a person in this world who loves me—because of what I am.

She—And what are you, my darling?

He—Ask her.

She—Her . . .

Agnes tries to take this implication calmly, but she is shaken nevertheless. She pretends that the news is not so shocking or important—not to a woman with two children. She knows now why he has been sleeping in the study lately.

Michael had expected a different reaction, and now it is he who becomes upset. "For three weeks I have lived through hell," he exclaims. "I must have that woman or I'll go mad!" It's encouraging news to Agnes that he hasn't had her yet. Michael rants on in self-defense: He has begged for warmth and understanding and got nothing; his book, which was written for her, is regarded by her as a rival. She hated that book even when it brought a carriage, servants, money, paintings . . . everything; so now she has driven him into somebody else's arms.

"What does she do?" Agnes inquires.

"She listens. She encourages me—with a look, a touch. . . . When I cheer she cheers with me, when I meditate, she meditates with me." Then, with great nobility, he announces, "I'm sorry it was necessary for me to hurt you. . . . I'm at the mercy of a feeling stronger than I."

Agnes' sympathy and understanding is uncanny—and disturbing. How could she know how he feels?

She hands him a jolt: "I'm a human being, aren't I? I might have my experience too, mightn't I?" Coolly she goes toward the bed and bids her husband good night, but he demands to hear a little more about this. She fends off his questions with collected calm, and when he demands, "Aren't you going to be alone, if I leave you?" she counters mysteriously, "Alone? I've got the children, haven't I?" She opens the door for him and again bids him good night. When he refuses to move she announces, "Then there's only one thing left to be done." She takes her evening wrap to the dressing room and returns with another wrap and a suitcase. "Would you mind calling a cab for me?" She begins to pack—and now he is on the defensive. When she has finished packing her overnight things and goes to the door, he blocks her way. Another attempt to leave, and he picks his kicking, fighting wife up and drops her on the bed. She wounds him with a kick on the shin. He takes off his coat and roars, "Where's my pillow! Make up that bed properly!"

Agnes, in a complete fury, denounces him as a vile swine and a silly hack writer. She strikes him with the "God Is Love" pillow; he orders her off the bed, throws a comforter at her and commands her to fold it; she throws it back and goes for him, trying to pound and scratch. He slips, recovers, pinions her arms behind her. She tries to bite him, and he exults, "If you could see your eyes now, you'd close them. They're blinding."

"With hatred," she snarls.

"With love." He gives her a quick kiss; she breaks free and he is on guard—but unexpectedly she sits on the bed and begins to sob and wish she were dead.

Michael suggests, "Before you die, look in my eyes, just once. Look!" She looks. "What do you see there?"

"Wrinkles!"

"What else?" He sits on the bed beside her. She knows what he means, and asks, "But . . . what about her?"

"I was lonely."

Standing, she suggests, "You'd better go now. Please go." He moves toward the archway of the dressing room and offers a piece of news—he has started a new book.

"And you haven't read me anything yet? Impossible!"

"I read it to her."

"Oh . . . and?"

"She liked it all right. But she thought it a little . . . well, coarse."

Agnes cries indignantly, "You, coarse? What kind of sheep is she?"

"Shall I go get the manuscript?"

Agnes picks up her husband's pillow, which fell to the floor during the scuffle. "Tomorrow," she suggests. "No, now," he says, making for the door and his study. Agnes, going to the bed and putting Michael's pillow on it, pleads, "tomorrow . . . tomorrow." He throws his coat on a bench, ascends the dais of the fourposter and embraces his wife.

The curtain falls.

SCENE II

It is before dawn, and the year is 1908. Agnes is asleep in the fourposter, but is awakened when Michael comes in, wearing an overcoat over his pajamas and carrying a bourbon bottle and a riding crop. "Look at this," he demands, showing her the bottle. "In his drawer, behind a pile of junk—this!" He is in a fatherly fury—a son 17—18—and it's four o'clock in the morning, and now this bottle. Darkly he threatens, "It's time I took over his education."

Agnes doesn't seem to be alarmed. After all, the boy had got permission to go to that dance, and had said he would be late. . . . Michael, in the bathroom, hunts for his old shaving strop and roars, "You think it's perfectly natural that a child boozes in his bedroom and paints the town until four o'clock in the morning?" He heads for the door, saying he is going back downstairs, where he has been waiting since one o'clock. And when the boy comes home, he'll—

Agnes clambers from bed, dons a robe and declares firmly, "If you are going to beat that child, you will have to do so over my dead body. Even if he has taken to opium, I will not let you beat that child!"

He gives in angrily, throwing down the riding crop, ripping off the overcoat, flinging himself into bed and pulling the covers over him. Then he sits up and shouts, "I hope you enjoy being a drunkard's mother!"

Agnes is amused at his tantrum and chuckles, "I can't help thinking what your attitude would be if it were not Robert, but Lizzie, who stayed out late." "Exactly the same," he insists. "With this difference, that Lizzie would never do such a thing."

"Ha! . . . I could tell you something about her that would . . . No, I'd better not." She sits on a sofa and again tells him he is going a little too far. She hears something outside and goes to the window; he leaps from bed and grabs his coat. From the door he calls, "Robert!" There is no answer; it was a false alarm. Agnes urges Michael to go back to bed, but he is too worried to do so. Her thoughts return to the whiskey bottle—what drawer was it in?

"The one where he keeps all his junk."

"I can't believe it. It can't be true."

Michael explains how he found it: he'd gone to his son's room, thinking maybe the boy had come in through a window, and had seen the bottle lying in an open drawer. Agnes insists it isn't possible; a child can't drink on the sly without his mother knowing it.

Suddenly he demands what his wife was hinting about Lizzie, and she replies, "She is in love. She's secretly engaged."

"To whom?"

"To the boy next door."

Michael's astonishment and indignation are great as he splutters, "To that—ape? To that pie face?" He babbles that Lizzie is only a child, and if the boy ever asks him for his daughter's hand, he'll shoot him.

Agnes tries to get her husband to go back to bed, but he is determined to wait up for Robert. She offers to make him a cup of tea, but he declines it. Then, picking up the bottle, he regards it speculatively, then uncorks it. "I think what we both need is a swig of this." He takes a swig and an expression of horror suffuses his countenance. Thrusting bottle and cork into his wife's hands, he dashes to the bathroom. She smells the bottle and grimaces. Looking nauseated, Michael emerges and asks, "What is that?"

"Cod liver oil!" With a moan he runs back into the bathroom. When he's feeling better he again comes out, muttering that the little monster must have set a trap for him. Agnes, in a burst of inspiration, solves the mystery. She recalls that, three years ago, her son had to take a spoonful of oil every night, but didn't want to do it in his mother's presence. So she left the cod liver oil bottle with him and measured it every morning. Obviously, instead of taking the stuff, Robert had poured it into the whiskey bottle and hidden it.

There is a sound downstairs: it's Robert. Michael picks up the riding crop and goes menacingly to the door, ignoring his wife's protests and grumbling, "Three-year-old cod liver oil!" He whips the air with the riding crop. Agnes fearfully sits on the bench at the foot of the bed, muttering to herself and listening. Soon Michael reappears, dejectedly holding the riding crop.

"Well," she asks breathlessly, "what did you say?"

"I beg your pardon?" he asks, distractedly, as he closes the bedroom door.

"What did you *say* to him?"

"Oh—er—'Good morning.'"

"Well, I must say! To go through all this rigmarole and then to end up with— I honestly think you could have said something more."

"I couldn't," Michael explains helplessly. "He was wearing a top hat."

The curtain falls.

ACT III

Late in the afternoon of the year 1913. The bed is the same, but again the décor has been changed; now it is in more conservative taste. Agnes is bemusedly sitting at a dressing table, holding a wedding bouquet that matches her gown and hat. In the dressing room Michael is humming the Wedding March. In a moment he jauntily comes in, wearing a smoking jacket. "Your hat still on?" he inquires. "Agnes!" She starts and smiles absently. "Come on, darling," he urges. "The only thing to think is, little children grow up. Let's be glad she ended up so well." The whole day long she's been acting so . . . so strange. She isn't ill, is she?

"No," says Agnes, putting down her bouquet. Then, "Today is the first day of Lizzie's marriage. . . . And the last day of ours."

"Beg pardon?"

SHE (*takes off gloves*)—I waited to tell you, perhaps too long. I didn't want to spoil your fun.

HE—My *fun?*

SHE—Yes. I haven't seen you so cheerful for ages.

HE—Well . . . I'm . . . For your sake I have made a fool of myself. For your sake I have walked around all these days with the face of a professional comedian, with a flower in my buttonhole and death in my heart! Do you know what I would have liked to do? To hurl my glass in the pie face of that bore, take my child under my arm—and as for that couple of parents-in-law . . . (*Looks heavenward.*) And now you start telling me that you didn't want to spoil my fun. (*Searches pockets for match to light his pipe.*)

SHE—With the information that I am going away.

HE—You are what . . . ?

SHE—I'm going away.

HE (*feeling pockets for match*)—Huh?

SHE—Away.

HE—How do you mean?

SHE—Can't you help me just a little by understanding quickly what I mean?

HE—But, darling . . .

SHE—Michael, I'll say it to you plainly once, and please try to listen quietly. If you don't understand me after having heard it once, I'll . . . I'll have to write it to you.

HE—But, darling, we needn't make such a fuss about it. (*Sits on sofa.*) You want to have a holiday now the children have left the house; what could be more sensible? No need to announce it to me like an undertaker.

SHE—Not for a holiday, Michael—forever.

HE—You want to move into another house?

SHE—I want to go away from *you.*

HE—From me?

SHE—Yes.

HE—You want to . . . visit friends, or something?

SHE—Please, darling, stop it. You knew ages ago what I meant; please don't try and play for time, it makes it all so . . . so difficult.

HE—I don't know a damn thing. What have I done?

SHE—Nothing, nothing. You are an angel. But I am . . . not.

HE (*rises, backs up a step*)—Agnes, what is the matter with you?

SHE—I would appreciate it if you would stop asking me what is the matter with me. There never has been anything the matter with me, and there couldn't be less the matter with me now. The only thing is, I can't . . .

HE—Can't what?

SHE—Die behind the stove, like a domestic animal.

HE—Good Heavens . . .

SHE—You wouldn't understand. You are a man. You'll be able to do what you like until you are seventy.

HE—But, my dear good woman . . .

SHE—I won't! Today I stopped being a mother; in a few years' time, perhaps next year even, I'll stop being a woman.

HE—And that's what you don't want?

SHE—I can't help it. That happens to be the way a benevolent Providence arranged things.

HE—But, darling, then it's madness.

She—I want to be a woman just once, before . . . before I become a grandmother. Is that so unreasonable?

Agnes is in a frenzy of self-pity and imagined frustration. There is nothing between them any more, she feels; they are dead as door-nails, doing the same things like puppets. For once in his life, Michael is completely baffled, and Agnes finally falls onto the bed, weeping. He puts his pipe in his pocket and goes to comfort her, but she cries, "Don't touch me!" After a while she gets up and goes to the sofa and continues, "I don't think— I'm sure I don't love you any more. I don't say this to hurt you, darling, honestly I don't. I only want you to understand. Do you? Do you a little?"

He dazedly replies, "Yes. I think so."

She remembers when it was she realized she didn't love him. It was about a month ago. He was in the bathroom rubbing lotion on his scalp and she brought him his coffee. "I said something about that boy's poems that you had given me to read, and then you said, 'I could tell him where to put them.' And then . . . then it was suddenly as if I were seeing you for the first time."

Michael agrees that she has something. If *he'd* come into the bathroom with *his* head full of love lyrics, and if he'd found her rubbing her face with skin food or shaving her armpits, he might not be overcome by any wave of tenderness. Then a thought strikes him: Whose poems is she talking about?

"That boy, who keeps asking you what you think about his work."

Pointedly he asks, "You liked what he wrote, didn't you?" Now he knows what is wrong with Agnes: She thinks she is in love with a juvenile poet. He remembers the book the boy gave her, with an inscription on the title page stating, "Dedicated in reverent admiration to the woman who inspired my master."

"Well," says Michael, "I have been his master only insofar that I wrote him a letter: 'Dear sir, I have read your poems twice. I would advise you to do the same.' I should like to read those poems again. Have you got them here?"

Agnes retrieves the book of poems from a drawer in the bedside table, hesitantly hands them over and pleads, "You aren't going to make fun of them, are you?"

He assures her he is not; this is a serious business, and they both ought to find out exactly what they are talking about. He reads the title—"Flashing Foam—Jetsam on the Beach of Youth." Agnes still is fearful as he begins to read the first sonnet, titled "Nocturnal Embrace." He makes small criticisms, such as why should the boy have called a tree an acorn tree instead of an oak tree. He muses over a couplet,

> "From a church tower far unseen,
> A solemn bell strikes twelve."

"Well, now, that rhyme could be definitely improved," he observes. After a moment's thought he recites,

> "From a church tower far unseen,
> A solemn bell strikes thirteen."

Agnes tries to suppress her amusement, but the effort grows greater as her husband good-humoredly dissects the youth's poetry.

He—That's not what he was after in any case, but let's see how it ends. (He *reads.*)

> "For a foot has stopped behind the door.
> Silence. Thumping. It's our hearts
> Waiting with our breath—"

Wondering where the other foot's got to, I suppose. . . .

She—Michael, please stop it!

He—Why? Am I his master or am I not? And has he got the cheek to dedicate this bad pornography to my Agnes or has he not?

She—He meant it for the best.

He—Oh, now, did he really? (*Throws poems on sofa.*) Do you call that for the best, to turn the head of a woman, the best wife any man could wish himself, at the moment when she's standing empty-handed because she imagines her job is over? To catch her at a time when she can't think of anything better to do than to become young again and wants to start for a second time fashioning the first damn fool at hand into a writer like me?

She—But you don't need me anymore.

He—Oh, no? Well, let me tell you something. People may buy my books by the thousands, they may write me letters and tell me how I broke their hearts and made them bawl their damn heads off, but I know the truth all right. It's *you* who makes me sing . . . and if I sing like a frog in a pond, it's not my fault. (*Sits on sofa; takes off glasses.* She *is so amused and relieved that she cries and laughs at the same time. The laughter gets the upper hand.*)

She—Oh, Michael!

He—What are you laughing at?

She (*going to him and sitting on sofa beside him*)—Oh, Michael

. . . I'm not laughing. . . . I'm not laughing. (SHE *embraces him and sobs on his shoulder.*)

HE (*comforts her like a man who suddenly feels very tired*)— I'll be damned if I understand that. (*Rests his head on her shoulder.*)

The curtain falls.

SCENE II

The years have sped on to 1925; it's 7:30 A.M. and the bedroom is not the same—not the same at all, for it is obvious that the occupants are moving out. The pictures are off the walls and their discolored outlines show; all the furniture has been taken away—except the fourposter, which still has its canopy and spread. Several large suitcases are on the floor. Michael comes humming from the bathroom, carrying toilet articles, which he dumps on the bed. He opens a suitcase, finds it full, and shuts it. Noticing that he has left a small piece of cloth hanging out of the suitcase, he does not bother to reopen the piece of luggage and stuff the cloth in—he simply tears off the cloth. He drags out and opens another suitcase and manages to make room for the toilet articles. Going to the bed, he picks up his things, but drops them on the floor and has to kneel to pick them up. Kneeling that way, he is out of sight when Agnes comes in the door, carrying the little "God Is Love" pillow. The moment she realizes her husband is in the room she hides the pillow behind her back. She urges Michael to hurry, because the car is coming at eight.

"Hey! Hey! Hey!" he cries, spotting the little pillow which has now been tucked under his wife's arm. "We don't have to take that little horror with us, do we?" "No," she admits. He begins packing his toilet things and she begins to work on the bed, stripping the pillow cases and sheets and leaving the spread. They are having to leave the bed here, because it is too large for the place they are moving to. Michael looks up from his suitcase and again notices the pillow under her arm. "Just what are you planning to do with it?" he demands. She wants to leave it as a surprise for the new tenants —such a nice young couple. Grimly he inquires, "Have you visualized that surprise, may I ask? Two young people entering the bedroom on the first night of their marriage, uncovering the bed and finding a pillow a foot across with 'God Is Love' written on it?" He snatches the pillow from her and tosses it on a trunk.

But Agnes is resourceful; she suggests that Michael go down in the cellar and have a look—perhaps they've left something in the wine cellar. He brightens at this suggestion and disappears; swiftly she retrieves the little pillow, puts it on top of the regular bed pillows and smooths the spread over all. Michael returns exultantly with a dusty bottle of champagne and proposes that they drink it; it must have been left over from Robert's wedding.

Agnes protests that it's too early to drink, and anyway it wouldn't be a nice first impression to make on the new landlady. "I'd be delighted," he chuckles. "I'd go up to that female sergeant major and say, 'Hiya! Hah! Hah!'" He blows his breath in Agnes' face . . . and the memory of their first night here strikes both of them motionless for a moment. She pats his cheek lovingly and then goes to the bathroom to get the tooth glasses for the champagne. He puts the bottle on the floor and goes back to the bed to make sure he has packed all his toilet articles. He pulls back the spread—and there is the little pillow again! When his wife returns, carrying two glasses and a towel, he holds it up and demands, "Did you put this back in the bed?" Self-consciously she stammers that she wanted to leave something friendly for that young couple . . . a sort of message.

He—What message?

She—I'd like to tell them how happy we'd been—and that it was a very good bed . . . I mean, it's had a very nice history, and that . . . marriage was a good thing.

He—Well, believe me, that's not the message they'll read from this pillow. Agnes, we'll do anything you like, we'll write them a letter, or carve our initials in the bed, but I won't let you do this to that boy—

She—Why not? (She *puts glasses and towel on floor beside knitting bag, takes little pillow from him and goes up to bed.*) When I found this very same little pillow in this very same bed on the first night of our marriage, I nearly burst into tears!

He—Oh, you did, did you? Well, so did I! And it's time you heard about it! When, on that night, at that moment, I first saw that pillow, I suddenly felt as if I'd been caught in a world of women. Yes, women! I suddenly saw loom up behind you the biggest trade union in existence, and if I hadn't been a coward in long woolen underwear with my shoes off, I would have made a dive for freedom.

She—That's a fine thing to say! After all these years . . .

He—Now, we'll have none of that. You can burst into tears, you can stand on your head, you can divorce me, but I'm not going to let you paralyze that boy at a crucial moment.

She—But it isn't a crucial moment!

He—It is *the* crucial moment!

SHE—It is not! She would find it before, when she made the bed. That's why I put it there. It is meant for her, not for him, not for you, for her from me! (*Puts little pillow on bed as before.*)

Michael is unswerving; "Whomever it's for, the answer is NO!" he declares—and he takes the little pillow, puts it on the trunk again, and finishes stowing his toilet articles. They close the suitcase by sitting on it, and now he is ready for the champagne. But Agnes is angry and in no mood to celebrate, so he puts the bottle on the floor and they stand around, at a loss for what to do. He asks about the new young couple—what does he do?

"He's a salesman."

"Well, why not? So was I. Only I realized it too late. The nights that I lay awake in that bed thinking how I'd beat Shakespeare at the game . . ."

Agnes, with some bite in her voice, comforts him, "Never mind, darling, you've given a lot of invalids a very nice time." Before he can reply to this jab the doorbell rings. The car is ready. He carries two suitcases and a knitting bag out, and she picks up her purse and gloves from the trunk. Then, quickly, she grabs the little pillow and is about to return it to the bed when he returns—so she hides the object under her coat. Next he takes the trunk, but before he drags it out he notices that the pillow isn't on it. As soon as he is out of sight, she puts the pillow back into the bed and covers it and stands waiting.

When Michael returns he is wearing his hat. Purposefully he walks to the champagne bottle and picks it up; then he walks to the bed, flings back the covers, picks up the pillow and throws it to Agnes' side of the bed. On the pillow on *his* side of the bed he places the champagne, then smooths the spread back in place. Walking over to his wife, smiling, he leans down, picks her up, kisses her and carries her out of the room. "Michael!" she cries.

THE CURTAIN FALLS

POINT OF NO RETURN *

A Play in Three Acts

BY PAUL OSBORN

NOVELIST John P. Marquand's faculty for being amused at or
by people makes his work valuable to the stage—but putting it on a
stage is no simple task. Nor is the adaptation of any book for the
stage a simple task—unless, like Steinbeck's "Of Mice and Men,"
the novel is deliberately and originally written in stage terms. The
writer of book fiction has all the room and all the time he needs,
whereas the writer of stage fiction is rigidly limited to a space confined by three walls and to a very brief part of an evening or matinee.
An earlier Marquand novel, "The Late George Apley," was made
into a very successful comedy by the author in collaboration
with George S. Kaufman, and it was reasonable to suppose that
"Point of No Return" would one day find its way into a theatre.
The transference was performed by Paul Osborn, a skilled dramatist
in his own right ("The Vinegar Tree," "On Borrowed Time") and
an adept adapter ("A High Wind in Jamaica"). Marquand and
Osborn do not name real places in "Point of No Return," but this
comedy of climbing in banking and social circles certainly concerns
places *like* the white-tie and white-collar commuting communities
of, say, Greenwich and Darien, Connecticut—and a bank not unlike
the Fifth Avenue Bank, 44th Street and Fifth Avenue, New York
City, before this institution had itself all done over in modern style.

Nancy and Charles Gray have a suburban-style house in a suburb;
this suburb could be in Westchester County, of course, but the editor
of this volume likes to think that the town is Darien. The Grays'
living room is conventional; on a wall is a painting of a three-master
in full sail, and among the furnishings on the floor is a card table
set up with breakfast things. In one of the chairs is Evelyn Gray,
age 11, who has her head buried in a geography book. Evelyn's
mother, Nancy Gray, hurries in with a bowl of cereal, calling "Bill—

Evelyn—" Then she sees that her daughter is already down and says good morning. Looking at the card table, Evie inquires why they are eating in here, and her mother answers, "Change. Variation. Besides, the man is coming to wax the dining room floor. . . . Bill!" From somewhere in the house Bill yells, "Coming!" Bill is a man of his word; he *does* come. He is 13, he is carrying a magazine and he is operating a yo-yo. Bill, too, has to be told why they are eating in here, and why Mary isn't serving. Mary went to spend the night with her sister in Brooklyn and won't be back until tomorrow afternoon. At their mother's urging, the children dawdle with the cereal; the head of the house, Charles Gray, is still in the bathroom.

Bill asks, "Is Dad really going away tomorrow?"

"He's going to Massachusetts," his mother confirms. "Dear old Clyde, Massachusetts—the scene of his childhood. . . . Just business of some kind."

Charles appears, newspaper in hand, and asks, "What are we eating in here for?" He gets the same explanation. Also the same patient explanation about Mary. He decides he will have boiled eggs. He has a slight headache because they stayed out so late last night at the Cliffords'. The children are fuller of talk than of breakfast, but when the horn of the school car sounds outside they gulp their food and hasten away. The car, Charles remarks to his son and daughter, should be a bus; they ought to be going to a public school. Nancy gets the children off, then returns to her husband and says they're smart getting up twenty minutes earlier, because now they don't have to rush any more before going to the station. She notices that Charles has forgotten his handkerchief and he says never mind it; "I'm not running for any office."

"Oh, yes you are, darling! And don't you keep forgetting it! You're right in there polishing apples." Charles doesn't like this, but he admits his wife is right: he's spent most of his life polishing one apple or another—but he doesn't like to be reminded of it.

Nancy speculates, if her husband goes to Clyde tomorrow he'll be back Thursday or Friday morning, and how about asking the Burtons for dinner Friday night?

CHARLES—Nancy! You know we can't ask the Burtons!

NANCY—I don't see why not.

CHARLES—Because it would be too obvious.

NANCY—The Blakesleys are going to ask them. Molly told me.

CHARLES—If the Blakesleys want to creep to Anthony Burton, let them. I'm damned if I will.

NANCY—Well, if Burton gives that job to Roger Blakesley rather than to you . . .

CHARLES—Oh, Roger's a good man. Don't underestimate Roger.

NANCY—You'd never for a minute be worried about Roger Blakesley if you hadn't taken time out to go to the war—when Roger used that time to dig himself in solid—because you're twice the man that Roger Blakesley is.

CHARLES—You think so?

NANCY—You know you are, darling. Charley, why don't you ask Burton today how it stands? Tell him you can't sleep . . . Oh, I heard you tossing around last night. Tell him that if Roger Blakesley is going to get the job—well, at least you want to *know*. You might even tell him how they're making bets in the washroom as to whether you or Roger—all the clerks standing around in there . . .

CHARLES—I don't want to tell him that. It's embarrassing.

NANCY—Burton's the president of the bank. He doesn't know everything that goes on. He hates anything that makes the bank look undignified. After all, he's the one who is always saying banking is an "art."

CHARLES—Just how do you think I should open my remarks?

NANCY—You could say, "Look, Tony, everybody knows that you're considering either Blakesley or me for this vice-president vacancy. Now I've been around here long enough. Of course, I was out during the war and Roger wasn't . . ."

CHARLES—Nancy! That's the most unscrupulous . . .

NANCY—Yes—yes—all right—you don't have to mention that Roger wasn't. He knows that anyway.

CHARLES—Look, Nancy, I'm not going to mention anything. Have you any conception of what would happen if I said all that to Tony?

NANCY—Well, you'd know where you stood.

CHARLES—I certainly would.

NANCY—Well, maybe I got carried away a little?

CHARLES—You got carried away a lot.

NANCY—All right. But if you want to be an assistant vice-president all your life and sit at that desk that's not even on the carpet . . .

CHARLES—I don't. I'd like to be a big *vice*-president and sit at one of those big desks right up there solidly *on* the carpet, but I'm damned if I'm going to creep to it.

In a moment he is sorry for what he has said; he advises his wife not to set her heart on his getting the job, because after all he may not get it. He says he'll be getting the 5:30 tonight and she reminds him of something he had forgotten—the dinner dance at the club tonight.

"Why is it you're going to Clyde, exactly?" asks Nancy. Charles doesn't know the details—some securities Tony wants him to look into. He had once told Burton he'd been born and brought up in Clyde, and Tony remembered this.

"I suppose you'll come back all—funny," says Nancy. "You always act funny even when you only *think* of Clyde." He denies it; says she's the one who gets edgy.

"I suppose you'll run into a lot of people you used to know." Charles doubts it—not after being away twenty years. But she suggests Jackie Mason, the boy who used to live next door—and perhaps that Lovell girl, the one he wanted to marry. He says he doesn't want to see her. Nancy shudders, "I'd hate to go back to the place where I was brought up! All those memories . . . Don't let it get you down, will you, darling?" He has no intention of being got down; as a matter of fact, he's looking forward to the visit. He'd like to see the old house on Spruce Street, and wonders if he'll feel the same way he did when his father was alive there. He muses, "I still can't help but feel my father was a highly intelligent man. He must have known what the odds were against him. . . . He was so damn erratic. He scared me."

Suddenly it is time to go. He kisses his wife here so he won't have to at the station, then hurries for hat, coat and brief case. She makes another stab at getting the Burtons for dinner and he laughs, "The little woman kissing her husband good-by. Everything depends on this moment. Get the job or Junior can't go to boarding school. And what about the next payment on the house? Good-by, darling, don't come back without being the vice-president of the trust company." Nancy is hurt, perhaps angry.

The lights black out.

Charles is in a telephone booth at Grand Central and Nancy is at the phone at home. Charles has called to say he's sorry and didn't mean to start the day off that way. He says maybe he can ask the Burtons for dinner, but his wife says skip it. Nancy is worried about this trip to Clyde, she says; Tony will pass out that job any minute, and "out of sight is out of mind." Charles admits he has thought of this, too—and they're both sure Roger Blakesley will make the most of it.

The lights black out.

Scene II

The main floor of the Stuyvesant Bank doesn't look like a bank; it looks more like the enormous drawing room of an old Fifth Avenue mansion—which it probably once was. Joe, the doorman, lets in one of the tellers; it's before opening time in the morning. The teller and a clerk gossip about the contest between Blakesley and Gray, which everybody seems to know about. The clerk thinks Blakesley has the edge because Mr. Burton had a long talk with Blakesley yesterday, and Blakesley acted in pretty good spirits when he left. Another clerk says he also is betting on Blakesley. They stop talking when the subject of their conversation appears—a confident, good-looking bank type who goes to his desk and says good morning to his waiting secretary, Miss Marble. Miss Marble already has waiting for Roger the first problem of the day—the papers on "that Catlin thing" that Mr. Burton wanted him to look into.

On Roger's heels Charles arrives with good mornings for everybody. "Missed you on the train," says Blakesley, and Charles explains that he just made the train and didn't bother to come up to "the car." Roger inquires what Charles thinks of the Catlin business that Tony wanted them to look into. Charles thinks they should stay out of it, and suggests that he and Blakesley have lunch together and talk it over; Roger is sorry, but he has a date with Tony at the University Club. "Oh," says Charles in a dry voice, "there's a lot more to banking than you think, isn't there?" To which Roger replies, "Banking is an art, isn't it?"

Charles Gray now takes the first phone call of the day from a client, one Mrs. Whitaker. Mrs. Whitaker seems to ramble on the phone quite a bit about her health and her new dog, and then comes to the point: she would like to consult with Charles at her home at six-thirty this evening. Always the pleasant and well-trained banker, Charles says this won't be inconvenient at all—he's looking forward to it.

Tony Burton himself makes his entrance into the bank, with companionable words for everybody. He is, as he has a right to be, well satisfied with himself and with the world. He pauses at Roger's desk and asks if the Catlin matter has been looked into, and Roger offers his firm opinion that the bank shouldn't have any part of it. "Very sound judgment, Roger," says Burton. At Charles' desk Tony makes the same inquiry and gets the same answer. "That's exactly what Roger and I feel," says the bank president. Oh, yes, and would Charley come over to his desk and see him? Charley

would, and Burton summons Roger, too. After a few personal pleas-
antries, Burton gets down to business—the business of Charles Gray's
trip to Clyde. It seems the bank has a new depositor, one Godfrey
W. Eaton, who wants a six months' loan of $300,000. Roger brought
him in the other day. Smugly, Blakesley takes a dig at Charles;
he had met Eaton golfing at the Seneca Club, and he implies that
Charles should have changed from the Oak Knoll to the Seneca,
too, just to meet some new people. Anyhow, Burton says, consulting
a sheaf of papers, this man Eaton manufactures tile, owns several
small factories in the Middle West, and has offered collateral that
is part in government bonds and part in stocks.

"Of course, it's none of my business," Charles offers, "but I wonder
why he didn't go to his own bank." Roger explains that he had
done a job of selling Eaton on the personal services of a small bank
like the Stuyvesant. "He likes us. He likes you, too, very much,
Tony."

Charles drily interjects, "I'd love Tony if he'd lend me three hundred thousand dollars." Burton smiles a moment, then returns to
business: Eaton's security is sufficient, but Tony questions one item—
a block of 5,000 shares at $20 a share in an unlisted company in
Clyde, Mass. He wants Charley to look into it.

CHARLES—Is there any reason I should go tomorrow? Would
a week or so from now make any difference?

ROGER (*quickly*)—Well, it's certainly not too good to keep a man
like Godfrey Eaton waiting. (CHARLES *turns and faces him. They
eye each other.*)

CHARLES—Why not? I imagine to a man like Eaton a few days
wouldn't matter.

ROGER—I sort of had the feeling—well, that this ought to be
finalized right now. Don't you think so, Tony?

BURTON—Have you any especial objections to going tomorrow,
Charles? (*A moment's pause.* ROGER *watches him.* CHARLES
throws it off.)

CHARLES—No. Of course not. It *would* be better now. (ROGER
is obviously relieved.)

BURTON—Stay as long as you like and see if you can get some
figures. As a matter of fact, I envy you getting away for a while.
You're looking a little tired, Charles.

ROGER (*putting his hand on* CHARLES' *shoulder*)—I noticed that
myself. You are looking a little tired, feller.

CHARLES (*laughing*)—Wouldn't you like to come along with me,
Roger? Why don't you all come?

BURTON (*rising*)—I wish I could, for one. But I'm the representative daddy. Well, I see we're open.

CHARLES—Roger . . . (CHARLES *and* ROGER *cross to their desks.*)

BURTON—Miss Dingle! (BURTON *turns back to his desk. Waiting for* CHARLES *is* MALCOLM BRYANT, *a man of about fifty-two, whom we have previously seen enter the bank.*)

MALCOLM—Well, if it isn't Charley Gray.

CHARLES (*puzzled*)—Good morning . . .

MALCOLM—Charley, don't you remember me?

CHARLES (*groping*)—Why, yes, of course—I—

MALCOLM—Come on, I could tell you anywhere, Charley. The child is father of the man.

CHARLES—I just can't . . . Was it in the war?

MALCOLM—Longer ago than that. Over twenty years. My God, Charley, I'm Malcolm Bryant.

CHARLES (*staring at him*)—Good Lord—Malcolm Bryant. I should have known you right away. Sit down, Malcolm. Good Lord, isn't that odd—we were just talking about Clyde. How are you, Malcolm?

MALCOLM—I dropped in to cash a government check and the cashier asked me if I knew anyone in the bank who could identify me, and I came in here to look around and there, by God, was you.

CHARLES (*takes the check, initials it, and hands it to* JOE)—Joe, cash it, will you please? (JOE *takes the check and goes out.*)

MALCOLM (*looking around*)—So here's where you've ended up! What are you, Charley, a vice-president?

CHARLES (*uncomfortable*)—Well, no, I'm an assistant vice-president at the moment.

MALCOLM—How's Jessica?

CHARLES—Jessica? Oh—I don't know. I haven't seen her for a long time.

MALCOLM—What? Didn't you marry Jessica Lovell?

CHARLES—No.

MALCOLM—You didn't? Why didn't you? What happened?

CHARLES—Well, it's a long story, Malcolm . . .

This Malcolm Bryant is an interesting man, and an inquisitive one. He's not exactly shabby, but shaggy, rather; his eyes are alert behind spectacles, and whatever he says or does bespeaks a forceful mind. He is not a Clyde man; he was there just one year, and he wrote a book about the town. He gives the uneasy Charles a copy of it; its title is "Yankee Persepolis." Persepolis, Malcolm explains, was where the Persians worshiped memories. Starting to leave at last, he says, "I wish I knew everything that has happened to you since I used to know you. . . . I'm an anthropologist. . Besides, I always liked you, Charley." Standing over Charles' chair, he extracts personal history from an unwilling subject. Charles says he left Clyde shortly after his father died, met a man in Boston who asked him to look him up in New York, did so, got a job here at the Stuyvesant, married a girl who worked in a law office, has two children and a house in the suburbs not far from Greenwich, and now is bucking for a vice-presidency in opposition to the guy who is sitting at the desk just behind him.

Now Malcolm must be off. He's going to New Guinea for the Pacific Investigation Institute. The only part of the trip that really interests him is the circumcision rite.

"My God," Charles asks, "do they let strangers see things like that?"

"It all depends on how you handle the head man. And head men are all about alike. You must have one here." As Malcolm leaves, he notices Tony Burton and surreptitiously points at him; Charles grins and nods. Roger has been watching. Suddenly Charles reaches a decision to confront Tony, the head man; so he goes to the president's desk and asks point-blank if it was Burton's idea that Charles go up to Clyde. Tony admits it was Roger's idea; Roger had said Charley was looking a little tired and it wouldn't hurt for him to get away from the bank for a day or two.

"I see. Thank you. . . . Er—one other thing—er—Nancy suggested asking you whether—whether you and Mrs. Burton would like to come and have dinner with us Friday night." Tony would be delighted.

The lights black out.

Charles is in a telephone booth, calling home, and is in a hurry. His son, Bill, who is in no hurry, has answered the phone because his mother is taking a bath. Charles instructs the lad to tell her he has some business to attend to and can't get home; he'll have to go straight to the club, and he won't be dressed. Charles now would like to get off the wire, but Bill confuses him with a strange question: "Dad, you believe there's a God, don't you? Then if there's a God there must be an after-life, too." Thinking that this may be an important moment in the formation of a young mind, Charles forces himself to be patient and listen to Bill. But Bill, far from being at some spiritual crossroads, is merely using an ingenious, roundabout method of reminding his father that his father once promised him a boat. Once Charles' father had promised Charles a boat, but the vessel never materialized, and now Bill imagines that Charles' father, in his after-life, must be feeling terrible right now. Moreover, Bill has found a beauty in a magazine ad, second hand, only $850. He will leave the ad propped on the table so his father may look at it when he comes home from the club tonight. Charles wearily agrees, "All right, Bill, all right." The lights black out.

SCENE III

Bill and Evelyn Gray are supposed to be in bed but they aren't. In their night clothes, they are in the living room watching an old horror movie on television. Except for the picture tube, the room is dark. Lights from an automobile make a swing outside and in haste the children switch off the set and scramble out of the room. Nancy and Charles come home from the party at the club, tired, but not unpleasantly so. Charles explains he was late because he had to go wet-nurse the Whitakers, who want to buy a ranch in Arizona for $100,000, but they haven't anything to sell that shows a loss. Then, with elaborate casualness, he says, "Oh, by the way, the Burtons are coming to dinner Friday night." Nancy straigthens up as though jerked by wires; now he must tell her *everything* and not leave anything out.

"Well, Tony and Roger and I were talking about this Clyde business. Roger was pressing it all sort of hard—and well, then another fellow came in to see me—Malcolm Bryant . . ."

"Never mind about Malcolm Bryant."

"Well, it was something he said got me thinking—something about knowing how to handle the head man. He's going to New Guinea and . . ."

"Never mind about New *Guinea*."

"Anyway, it suddenly occurred to me—why was *I* being sent to Clyde? So I asked Tony whose idea it was for me to go . . ."

Nancy is intensely indignant at Roger Blakesley's maneuver to get her husband out of the way, and she is furious at something Roger had said at the club tonight. He had said, "Charley, I hope we can all be friends no matter what happens." Anyhow, Charles has asked the Burtons for dinner, and Nancy begins to plan the menu aloud. Then, cuddled against her husband on the sofa, she asks, "Charley, what will you do if he takes Roger?" He answers, "If they don't like you well enough to move you up, it's time to get out." She clutches him, sobbing softly, "Oh, Charley, we didn't used to be afraid!" He comforts her, and she goes to the kitchen to get them glasses of milk. Charles rises, stretches, then notices the book Malcolm gave him, on a table. He begins to read it, and exclaims in a moment, "Why, the dirty . . . Why, the *dirty!*"

Nancy, returning with the milk, asks, "What is it?"

CHARLES—Well—it's a study he made of Clyde—calls it a typical New England town—and—(*He turns to the front of the book and reads.*)—he's written it all out—hasn't even bothered to disguise it so you won't know who he's talking about. Listen to this:

"It will be well to define the very definite social strata of this town, as follows:

"There are three distinct social groups, the upper class, the middle class and the lower class—but each of these will be divided into thirds—so we have the upper-upper, the middle-upper, and the lower-upper; the same way with the middle class—the upper-middle, the middle-middle, and the lower-middle; and the same way with the lower class . . ."

NANCY (*laughing*)—"The upper-lower, the middle-lower and the lower-lower."

CHARLES—Now just get this. "Typical of a lower-upper family are the Henry Smiths—father, mother, son and daughter. (*He looks up at* NANCY.) The ancestral motif is as marked in this group as it is in the *upper*-upper. The same importance is attached to the preservation of the heirloom and the decoration of the grave. Thus on a wall in the Smith home, hanging over the patriarchal chair is a jealously guarded primitive oil painting of a three-masted sailing vessel captained by the Smiths' ancestor, Jacob Smith." (*He looks at* NANCY *and they both regard the painting on the wall.* NANCY *lets out an explosion of laughter.*)

NANCY—Good Lord, it's you! The Smith family is your family, Charley!

CHARLES (*angrily*)—I know damn well it is! And I remember the exact time when Malcolm asked about that picture and I remember my mother's taking the pains to explain it to him.

NANCY—What else does he say about you? Let's see—what are you—a *middle*-upper?

CHARLES (*grimly*)—A *lower*-upper. "Like other lower-upper families, they dwell on a side street, yet are received on Mason Street." He says Mason Street—that's Johnson Street, of course.

NANCY—That's where Jessica Lovell lived, isn't it?

CHARLES—That's right. "Mr. Smith"—that's my father, of course—"is a member of the Sibley Club, but is not a member of the Fortnightly Reading Club. An intellectual man, whose financial status varies with the stock market, he is free to indulge his whims because he is not bound by the rigidity of the upper-upper class. Therefore, he is able to enjoy his position as captain of the Volunteer Fire Department, a pastime which seems to afford him great amusement." It did, too. "His wife, Mrs. Smith, was Miss Jones, a physician's daughter (middle-upper). She runs their house in a lower-upper manner—(CHARLES *winces*.)—with the aid of one maid (middle-lower) coming in daily from outside. The son Tom, a likable—" (*He begins to mumble something unintelligible.*) Ah, nuts! (*He stops, disgusted.*)

NANCY—Don't mumble! I didn't get that. What about the son Tom? That's you!

CHARLES—It's just too damn silly!

NANCY (*grabbing the book*)—It's fascinating. Let me have it.

CHARLES—Now, Nancy—Now cut it out, Nancy!

NANCY (*getting the book*)—"The son, Tom, a likable young graduate of Dartmouth." (*She laughs.*) My likable young graduate from Dartmouth.

CHARLES—All right, all right.

NANCY—"—is received by the upper-upper but is not a member of the committee for the Winter Assembly—" (*Sympathetically.*) Ohh!—"He is, however, in a position to move by marriage to middle-upper, or possibly even *upper*-upper status!"

CHARLES—Come on, Nancy. Give it to me. (NANCY *has sobered down and seems suddenly very serious.*)

NANCY—No, I want to read it. "He is on friendly terms with the daughter of Mr. Johnson (upper-upper), though there is little prospect of more than friendship." (NANCY *pauses a moment.*) That would be Jessica Lovell.

CHARLES—Nancy, don't—

NANCY (*she doesn't look at* CHARLES)—"An upper-upper-class family may be typified by the Johnsons, who live on Mason Street in one of those fine, Federalist houses. The drawing room was consciously built to house its greatest treasure, a magnificent wallpaper from France. They call it, with modest humor, 'The Wallpaper Room.' This is all a fitting frame for the ritual of Clyde's upper-upper class. Mr. Johnson, the father of the daughter that Tom (lower-upper) is on friendly terms with, is a widower, descendant of shipowners in the late eighteenth century. Judith, his lovely only daughter, is eminently suited to give the family ritual an added charm. It would be a matter of marked interest if Tom (lower-upper) should ever be able to bridge the gap between himself and—"

(*She stops reading.*) She must have been very beautiful, Jessica
Lovell. You did love her a lot, didn't you, Charley?
CHARLES—Yes, I did. But that was twenty years ago.

Nancy urges him to find out what happened to him those years
ago; Jessica Lovell must have done something, and tomorrow is his
chance to get her and Clyde out of his system once and for all. She
asks, "Charley, are you sorry you married me?"
"Listen, Nancy, I love you, I love the children, now stop it." Re-
assured, she starts for bed. He picks up the book again, grumbles,
"That son of a bitch. . . . He might at least have made me a
middle-upper." He drops the book into a wastebasket and goes up
with his wife.
The curtain falls.

ACT II

Charles is in an antiquated day coach nearing his destination. It
is a chilly late afternoon and he has his hat and topcoat on as he
gazes pensively out at old scenes. A man comes from the smoker
and takes the seat ahead of him; Charles looks at the back of the
man's head and frowns in concentration. As if he felt the gaze, the
newcomer turns around. It is Jackie Mason; recognizing each other
instantly, they leap up and shake hands excitedly. They turn
Jackie's seat back, so he can sit facing Charles. "Charley Gray!"
Jackie exclaims, slapping Charles' knee. "You don't look a day
older, Charley! . . . I was just saying to Mother the other day—
it still seems funny not to be able to go out in the back yard and yell
for Charley to come over." Jackie's naive friendliness and enthusiasm are almost embarrassing as he pumps Charles about his family
and business life. "You've got success written all over you," he exclaims admiringly. Somehow this depresses Charles, and he switches
the subject to Jackie. Jackie is still in the accounting department
at Wright-Sherwin—head of it, as a matter of fact. No—he's not
married.
Charles tells his old friend he'll be in Clyde a day or two—looking
into the Nickerson Cordage Company. "Pretty sound, as far as I
know," says Jackie. Charles, looking out the window, surmises,
"Won't be long before we're in the tunnel now."
Jackie uneasily starts to say something and finally brings himself
to it. It's about Jessica Lovell. Charles politely inquires how she
is, and Jackie answers that she is very well and very busy. She
never married, though. Jackie thinks she always hoped that—and

he points wordlessly at Charles. She still talks about him a lot. "I wish you never had left, Charley," Mason bursts out. "Of course I suppose you had to—with your father and all—it was pretty awful, the whole damn thing. . . . I think you ought to call on Jessica while you're here, Charley."

"Oh, no, I couldn't, Jackie.—Here comes the tunnel."

The lights black out; the conductor can be heard calling "Clyde! Clyde!" Jackie can be heard still urging Charles to see Jessica, and Charles can be heard expostulating that it's all over and done with and he doesn't want to think about it any more. That damned wallpaper room—he'll never forget the first time he saw it. He and Jessica had to sneak into the house so they wouldn't wake the old man. . . .

SCENE II

The lights come up—on the Wallpaper Room. In semi-darkness Charles is bumping into furniture and Jessica whispers for him to stand still until she turns on the lights. When the lights are switched on they reveal Charles, at the age of 24, rather stiff and embarrassed, and Jessica, about 21, pretty but perhaps a bit too fancily dressed.

"It's really queer that you've never been in this house before," Jessica laughs. "In fact, it's rather queer we've hardly seen each other before. . . . I've been away so much. Father's taken me to Maine for the Summers. And then at school and then Vassar. Were you ever at Vassar, Charley?"

"No, I went to Dartmouth."

But now Jessica is home, for good, and is glad. But she wishes she hadn't worn this damn dress tonight; why didn't he tell her it wasn't right for the movies?

These young people are in love, but oddly uneasy—even when they finally manage an embrace and a kiss. "If we had only—" Jessica sighs, and Charles completes her thought: "If we had only—met somewhere else, you mean, instead of in Clyde? . . . I suppose if I lived here on Johnson Street everything would be all right. . . . And your father—he won't like it at all, will he?"

JESSICA—He won't mind so much—honestly he won't—if he gets to know about it—gradually—and not all at once. (*She sees* CHARLES *frown and goes on hurriedly.*) I mean—if he could just see something of you—for a while—without knowing that . . .

CHARLES—That his daughter's in love with a boy from Spruce Street?

JESSICA—Charley! Nothing in the world matters but you! Nothing! (*She clings to him.* CHARLES *kisses her. After a moment we hear:*)

LOVELL'S VOICE (*offstage*)—Jessica! Is that you? (JESSICA *starts away, nervously.*)

JESSICA—Oh! Yes, Father.

LOVELL—Ah, good! We'll be right in.

JESSICA (*nervously*)—I thought he would be in bed. (MR. LOVELL *and* MALCOLM BRYANT, *now about thirty-four, enter.*)

LOVELL—And this is the wallpaper I was telling you about. (*To* JESSICA.) I didn't hear you come in. I saw the light and . . . (*He sees* CHARLES.) Oh! Well, well, I didn't know we had company.

JESSICA—You know Charles Gray, don't you, Father?

LOVELL—Of course I know Charles Gray, Jessica—or *of* Charles Gray. Where on earth did you find him? Not that I'm not very glad that you *did* find him. (*He shakes hands with* CHARLES.) How do you do, Charles?

CHARLES—How do you do, sir?

LOVELL—Jessie, this is Mr. Malcolm Bryant. (*To* MALCOLM.) My daughter, Jessica.

JESSICA—How do you do?

MALCOLM—I've been wanting to meet you, Miss Lovell. I've seen you around town a couple of times.

LOVELL—Mr. Bryant has just returned from studying the head hunters in Borneo and now he is making a social survey of Clyde.

JESSICA—I imagine you'll find some remarkable specimens in Clyde. This is Mr. Gray, Mr. Bryant.

MALCOLM—I'm glad to meet you, Mr. Gray. Do you live here in Clyde?

CHARLES—Yes, I live here. On Spruce Street.

LOVELL—That was not a happy remark of mine when I asked where Jessica found you. I'm delighted to have a Gray in the house.

MALCOLM—I'm still trying to orient myself. It's a little hard to get the general structure here, but, my God, it's a wonderful town— a beautiful, static, organized community. Let's see, your first name is Charles, isn't it?

CHARLES—That's right.

MALCOLM—Why don't we get on a first-name basis? I'm Malcolm, you're Charley, you're Jessie. Now let me get this straight. You're a college man, aren't you, Charley?

CHARLES—How did you know?

MALCOLM—Because it's my business to know social groups. Look at Jessica. She has Smith written all over her.

JESSICA—Vassar, please.

MALCOLM—Same pattern. Is your father a college man, Charley?

LOVELL—Charles' father was at Harvard with me for a short time—until he left us after Freshman midyears. Let's see, you went to Dartmouth, if I remember, Charles.

CHARLES—Yes, that's right, sir.

MALCOLM—Now why was that?

CHARLES—My aunt put me through college. She preferred Dartmouth.

LOVELL—I was extremely sorry to hear about your Aunt Jane, Charles.

CHARLES—Thank you, sir.

MALCOLM—Why, what did she do?

CHARLES (*flatly*)—She died.

MALCOLM—Oh, I beg your pardon.

CHARLES—A few weeks ago.

LOVELL—Heart, wasn't it, Charles?

CHARLES—Yes, sir.

LOVELL—Yes, everyone has always known about the Grays. "The Gray Heart," we speak of. I'm very sorry. Well . . . (*He turns to* JESSICA.) Mr. Bryant is very anxious to see the rest of the house. (*He turns to* CHARLES.) So, Charles, in case I don't see you again I'll say good-by. Give your father my regards. Turn out the lights when Charles goes, Jessica.

Lovell, slender, impeccable and cold, leads Malcolm off on a continued tour of the house. Jessica says, not too hopefully, that she thinks her father likes Charles. Everything's got to be all right, she insists, for she feels so terribly lonely. She loves her father—but he wants her to be so perfect—and her father has brought her up from the age of six, when her mother died. And now, when she has found Charles, all the rest of her life is just as though she'd been asleep. They kiss again.

And Jessica's father comes back again, with Malcolm Bryant still in tow and listening to the history of the house and the family. "Why, Charles," he exclaims, "still here? Fine! Jessie, Mr. Bryant is leaving." Charles takes the hint and leaves with Malcolm, but promises he will take Jessica to another movie tomorrow night.

When father and daughter are alone, the girl exclaims rapturously, "Oh, Father, isn't he very nice?"

Lovell agrees. The lights have dimmed out but he can be heard counseling, "But I wouldn't get too interested."

When the lights come up they reveal a part of Johnson Street, and

Malcolm and Charles are walking along it. Malcolm is lecturing:
Laurence Lovell is a typical, desiccated stuffed shirt; Jessica is a
perfect tribal type—and the father is in love with the daughter.
Basically, the daughter is in love with the father—a standard pattern
of behavior, "as old as the first decadent civilization." Charles,
edgy, suggests that Malcolm mind his own business, but Malcolm
remains unruffled. "You interest me," he confesses. "You're an
integrated, contented part of a group. You understand your taboos
and rituals, you're working happily under an almost immobile system.
But don't try to break out of your group, Charley. . . . Don't try to
marry the head man's daughter."

Charles has been made uneasy and he is glad to turn off at his
street, Spruce Street, and be rid of this man. Malcolm would like to
come with him, but Charles offers no encouragement. They part,
but not before Bryant has offered some more advice for Charles to
stay in his class. In Borneo, for instance, to break out one needs
more shrunken heads. In Clyde, one needs wampum. Not just any
wampum. "It's got to be old wampum that your grandfather made
or stole or however he got it. Still, wampum mellows faster now
than it used to."

The lights fade as Charles says to himself, "Wampum."

Scene III

The lights come up again on the living room of the Gray house.
Charles' father, John Gray, looks up from his desk as his son comes
in. John Gray is lanky, easy and intelligent. At his desk he has
been writing a paper for the Sibley Club about Clyde history, but
Charles seems uninterested in his father's account of how many tug-
boats there were in Clyde in 1902, tied up between the Nickerson
Cordage Company and the old coal packet. "Father," Charles bursts
out, "I want to make some money. I was thinking of getting a job
in Boston. I don't believe I'm going to get anywhere if I stay at
Wright-Sherwin." Mr. Gray seems delighted and surmises that his
son is thinking of a brokerage office or a bond house.

CHARLES—I don't want anything for nothing. If I make money,
I want to earn it.

JOHN GRAY—Yes, yes, of course you do—and that's very esti-
mable. But do you remember what Jonathan Swift said about ambition?

CHARLES—I'm afraid not, Father.

JOHN GRAY—Oh, I wish you cared more for the polite adornments

of the mind, Charles. He said: "Ambition often puts men upon doing the meanest offices: so climbing is performed in the same posture
with *creeping*." I've never liked creeping.

CHARLES—And it would be creeping to want to get ahead?

JOHN GRAY—I think I can safely say that no one enjoys the comforts and pleasures to be derived from having money more than I—
and yet I've never been able to creep for them. It has always been
all or nothing with me. (*As* CHARLES *starts to speak, he holds up
his hand.*) Now, no lecture, please. I know you think *my* way of
getting ahead was—unfortunate. But because of the handicaps of
never having enough capital—I was unable to beat the system. The
system is not fluid and it's very hard to beat.

CHARLES—What system?

JOHN GRAY—Why, the system under which we live. The order.
There's always some sort of order. There's always the bundle of
hay out ahead, for any ass who wants to get on, and They make it
look like a very pleasant bundle.

CHARLES—Who are They?

JOHN GRAY—They are the people who own the hay. They are
the people who run the system. And They have to toss out a little
hay now and then to make the system work. They'll tell you there's
plenty of hay for anyone who can get it. But the main thing is
They don't want you to get it. It might be some of Their hay.
You can get so far by effort, Charles. You will find that you can
obtain a little hay but if you reach for more you'll get a sharp rap
on the muzzle.

CHARLES—It seems to me that you've had a lot more hay than
most people—at different times.

JOHN GRAY—Before I tried to get more of it, you mean? Now
don't be so hard on me. I'm not going to do it again. That's all
over.

CHARLES—What are you going to do with the seventy-five thousand dollars Aunt Jane left you?

JOHN GRAY—How very blunt! I suppose I might ask you what
you are going to do with the five thousand dollars Aunt Jane left you,
but I won't.

CHARLES—I'm going to put it in government bonds. But are you
going to play the market with yours? I don't like to talk this
way . . .

JOHN GRAY—I know you don't. That's all right.

CHARLES—I don't care about myself—but what about Mother and
Dorothea? Why don't you set up a trust fund for them?

JOHN GRAY—An excellent idea. I'll have to think about it. Let's leave it that way. You can watch me, and I'll think about it. (*He stirs uneasily.*) But however did we get switched onto me? We were talking about you. How did this idea of your getting a job in Boston ever get into your head?

The father knows very well how the idea got into his son's head—he's in love with Jessica Lovell. John Gray never did like Laurence Lovell, but he's on his son's side. On Monday they will go up to Boston. And from now on his son will want to do all the right things. "But remember," he warns, "beware of too much ambition. Don't dull yourself to the refinements of life. Don't—creep—to your goal."

Jessica Lovell telephones and her voice can be heard as she says she wants to say good night to Charles properly. Informed of Charles' intention of finding a job in Boston, she at first is disheartened, then becomes excited as she realizes that she can see him there; she can visit her aunt and they can dine and go to the theatre . . . alone, without her father knowing. She hangs up. John Gray has left the room. Charles, alone, talks to himself—rehearsing various approaches to the favor of the formidable Mr. Lovell. The direct, blunt approach, the unctuous one . . . or perhaps one in which, with financial genius, he has increased his aunt's little bequest to a small fortune.

The lights black out.

Scene IV

When the lights come up again, on the Wallpaper Room, it is the real scene of Charles actually asking Mr. Lovell for Jessica's hand. Charles is doing well in Boston, is in line for a promotion, and is making sixty dollars a week. "I want to marry Jessica," he says. Lovell seems stunned; in a moment he asks his daughter to pour him a glass of water. Then, frigidly, he brings up the customary parental objection to Charles' modest income—and he ignores his daughter's protestations that she doesn't care how much Charles makes. Charles plays a trump card: He also has $35,000 in government bonds—money he made in the market on his aunt's bequest. Mr. Lovell remains unimpressed. "It is not," he says, "the same as inherited money."

At last, Jessica's father agrees to an engagement—but on terms that make it no engagement at all. It must not be announced, and there will be no engagement teas or other jubilation until matters are more definitely resolved. Stiffly, he leaves the Wallpaper Room.

Jessica cries, "I just can't *bear* to see him hurt. Oh, Charley, if you could only just—well, just do what he says for a little while until . . . Just for now—until he gets more used to it."

Charles looks at her oddly, then says, "All right, if that's the way you want it."

The lights black out. In the darkness a telephone rings. The lights go up on Charles' suburban home and his wife, Nancy, answers. In a moment lights show a phone booth in Clyde, and Charles is in it. He is excited. "You were right, Nancy," he says. "She did something to me way back there." Nancy can't focus on what he means, and asks if he has been drinking. Charles explains that he is talking about Jessica Lovell. No—he hasn't seen her. He hasn't done anything much; after he registered at the hotel it was too late to see anyone, so he has been walking and looking at the houses. His old house on Spruce Street looks smaller. Then he says, "There's too many ghosts up here, Nancy."

SCENE V

The lights fade on the telephone conversation and go up on more ghosts—John Gray, looking very opulent, standing in his living room talking to Charles' mother while a tailor measures him. Charles comes home and his mother senses that something is disturbing the young man. "I'm engaged to Jessica," he explains, "but I'm only to tell you and you're to tell no one. It isn't to be announced yet." Esther Gray gives her son a warm kiss of congratulation; John Gray is more reserved. "I have the feeling," he says, "that Laurence Lovell was mildly insulting. . . . I think I'd better go and see Laurence Lovell tomorrow."

When his mother has left the room, Charles says he hopes his father is being careful, and John Gray assures him that he is as careful as a banker and as sound as Electric Bond and Share. He has had, with his sister's bequest, enough working capital to beat the system, and with great satisfaction he tells his son, "As of today— October 6, 1929—there is in the kitty six hundred and fifty thousand dollars." Charles confesses that he is afraid of money and urges his father to get some of it off paper and set up a trust fund for Mother and his sister Dorothea. John Gray blandly agrees; he has set a limit and he intends to cash in as soon as he has made a million.

The lights black out. In a moment a single light fingers its way to the body of John Gray, stretched on the sofa, one leg and arm hanging down. On the floor are a newspaper, an empty glass and a pill bottle. Charles, dazed, is kneeling there. He puts the limp arm

across the body, kisses his father's forehead, picks up the bottle and
pockets it. The light fades out.

Charles is walking along Johnson Street and he runs into Malcolm,
who is very sympathetic about Charles' father. "What are you
going to do?" he asks.

"Well, right at this moment I'm on my way to . . . Mr. Lovell
sent for me."

"Sent for you?"

"He wants to have a little talk with me. About wampum, maybe,
or lack of it."

Malcolm urges Charles to leave Clyde right now—to go with him
to Afghanistan tomorrow. "There's nothing more for you to get out
of Clyde—and there's nothing more for you to get out of Boston,
either." But Charles isn't interested, and the friends part as the
lights fade.

Scene VI

Again the scene is the Wallpaper Room, and Laurence Lovell has
been waiting for Charles. Jessica is in the library. Lovell offers
conventional expressions of sympathy, then says, "I understand there
was practically nothing left and you have put all your savings in
trust for your mother and sister." Charles admits this. Continuing,
Lovell implies that there has been a change in the whole situation—
and he isn't referring to finance. He says, "Now I don't say there's
anything verging on real scandal, Charles, but we must all face the
implications of your father's sudden death at this especial time. . . ."

"My father," Charles says grimly, "died of heart failure brought
on by the strain of the last few days. . . . I'd like to see Jessica,
please."

"The whole thing is too impossible," Lovell pronounces. "We
must end it." He calls through a door, "Jessica, will you come in,
please?" And to Charles he adds, "It's only fair that she should tell
you herself."

The girl is in tears and she has been weeping a long time. She
sobs, "I'm not fit to marry anyone. . . . It doesn't mean I don't love
you. I do. I do."

Charles hurries from the room. The old man has won. The lights
black out on Jessica's cry of "Charley! Charley!"

Scene VII

The lights again reveal the antiquated day coach. Charles is on
his way from Clyde to Boston to make his New York connection;
he has finished checking up on the Nickerson Cordage Company for

the Stuyvesant Bank and is now on his way back to his job and his home in the suburb. Jackie Mason finds him and sits with him again. "I'm sorry you didn't get to see Jessica," says Jackie.

"I just couldn't make it."

"She knew you were here." Then, self-deprecatingly, Jackie confesses, "I've been seeing a lot of Jessica. I guess Mr. Lovell thought I was pretty harmless. . . . Jessica and I are engaged and are going to be married in June."

The dumbfounded Charles asks, "How did—Mr. Lovell take it?"

Mr. Lovell, says Jackie, didn't seem to mind, but when they had their talk the old man kept calling him Charles. Of course, his mind isn't what it used to be, but he's really a grand old gentleman—and they'll all be living in the Lovell house together. Charles draws a deep breath and shudders a little as Jackie continues with his big news: He and Jessica are to be married in June, but it's not going to be announced right away.

Charles demands, "Did Mr. Lovell ask for a glass of water?"

"Why, yes," says Jackie, "as a matter of fact, he did."

Grimly, Charles advises, "Listen, Jackie! You and Jessica get married in June! Don't let anything stop you, will you?" Then, in an odd mood of jubilation, Charles suggests that when they get to Boston he and Jackie celebrate and take the town apart.

The curtain falls.

ACT III

Charles Gray has come home. It is Friday night, and Charles and Nancy are having cocktails with Tony and Mrs. Burton. The women are in long dresses and the men are in dinner jackets—but Charles' shirt is soft and Tony's is starched. Tony is sounding off about the great art of banking—for banking, for a good banker, is an art, isn't it?

In a dry voice Charles answers, "Well, I suppose it depends on your definition of art."

The bank president looks at his underling coolly and comments, "You know, sometimes you have a very cryptic quality, Charley. I never seem to know whether you're laughing at me or not." Mrs. Burton contributes her opinion that it's good for Tony to have someone an enigma—everybody licks his boots so. Burton now launches into a dull account of a trip he and his wife took to Bagdad in 1933, but at last it is cut short by the sound of the telephone bell. Both Burtons jump up; this must be their long distance call to their daughter, Barbara, who has recently entered Sarah Lawrence College. They hasten together to the telephone, and Nancy has a few tense words alone with her husband. "Why," she demands, "do you have to disagree with *everything* he says? And you wore a soft shirt after all instead of the stiff one I laid out for you!"

Charles, his back up, declares, "I'm not going to wear a stiff shirt just because Tony Burton does!"

"Oh, I hate it when you act this way! It's all because you went up there to Clyde! You've acted differently ever since you came back."

"Maybe I have. I had a lot of time to think." Charles turns away from his wife, then cries, "Oh, it's all so damned contrived! So superficial!"

Nancy and Charles admit to each other that they're licked, and probably Nancy would weep—but the Burtons come back from the telephone. They didn't get Barbara, but they talked with one of the teachers who promised to have Barbara call back as soon as the girl returns from the village. Nancy seems relieved when Burton suggests another cocktail, and then resumes his account of that dull journey across the world years ago. With the cocktail, Tony brightens and compliments Nancy on her good looks. "Why don't you come to work some morning instead of Charles?" he asks with heavy jocularity. "I'm getting pretty sick of seeing Charley around." Nancy catches her breath.

CHARLES (*smiling*)—Perhaps I'd better start looking for a job somewhere else.

BURTON (*after a moment, puzzled*)—You know, Charles, I wish there weren't so many words, or it may be because I'm getting old that they confuse me more than they used to. Somehow they keep having more shades of meaning. Now even with Charles and me it's difficult. I say a word and he says a word and we can look it up in the dictionary, but it doesn't mean the same thing to either of us and it would mean something a little different to you, Nancy, and it would be something a little different to Althea. I don't suppose this is a very new thought of mine, but it's a thought.

MRS. BURTON—I'm not even sure it's a thought. Tony, I haven't the faintest idea of what you're talking about.

BURTON—But Charley knows, don't you, Charley? We both may be worrying about the same thing but we worry about it in different ways.

CHARLES (*slowly*)—Yes, I think I know what you mean. If we are both worried about the same thing—naturally your worry approaches it from one angle—and mine from quite a different one. (NANCY *looks frightened.*)

BURTON—Exactly. I wish we could all get together, we might do something with the world, but of course we never can get together. That's the exasperating part of it.

MRS. BURTON—Really, Tony, I think you've had enough of that cocktail. (*To* NANCY.) Have you the slightest idea of what he's getting at?

NANCY—I'm not sure.

BURTON—Perhaps *I'm* being cryptic now, but all I'm saying is that I wish we might all be friends. I really hope we can be, no matter what may happen in the future, and the future isn't as clear as it used to be. That's all I'm trying to say. I just want us all to be friends, no matter what happens. (*A moment's pause.* NANCY *is stricken,* CHARLES *turns away for a moment, then back.* TONY *is looking at* CHARLES.)

The telephone rings again, and again the Burtons leave to answer it. Nancy begins to weep softly. "Well, I guess that's that," says Charles. "Anyway," he adds, "thank God it's over." He tries to buck up his grieving wife; they will, he assures her, get enough to educate the children—sell the house and take a smaller one, and stop trying to make the Hawthorn Hill Club. Anyhow, he never *did* want to be in the Hawthorn Hill Club. Earnestly, almost fiercely, he says, "From the time I first kissed Jessica Lovell in that damned wallpaper room—that's where it all started. That's where I started to creep." He grins at his wife. "You know, I feel good, I mean really good—I mean strong, independent, like being able to tell somebody to go to hell." He kneels beside his wife's chair and says earnestly, "We *have* got each other—*and* the children—*and* we're alive . . ." Nancy bucks up somewhat and he kisses her.

The Burtons return; they have talked with their daughter. Charles, with nothing to lose, suggests another cocktail.

BURTON—Well—I don't mind if I do. (*He rubs his hands together as* CHARLES *mixes the cocktail.*) You know, it's really cozy here. I like it. (*He hesitates.*) Charley, there's something I want to ask you. I guess it's all right, here in the bosom of the family. What do you think of Roger Blakesley? (*There is a sudden dead pause.* NANCY *looks up at him, quickly.* CHARLES *turns slowly.*)

CHARLES (*casually*)—Why, Roger's okay.

BURTON—No, now, we're all alone here. You can speak frankly. The women won't say anything. Do you like him or don't you?

CHARLES (*after a moment*)—I think Roger is conscientious, ener-

getic, and well trained, but I can't say I like him much. Why
should I?

BURTON—I rather like him. He's been on my conscience lately.
He's so anxious, so much on his toes. He's always in there trying.

CHARLES—I don't know what else you could expect. I've been
trying pretty hard myself.

BURTON—Not in the same way, Charley. You're subtler. You're
developed, you've matured. Of course, I'm out of touch with things,
being where I am, but I've been getting an idea—and maybe I'm
entirely wrong. You're in more of a position to know than I am.
It seems to me that Blakesley has some idea that we're considering
him for that vice-presidency vacancy. Do you know anything about
this, Charles? (NANCY *looks at* CHARLES.)

NANCY—What did Blakesley think you were considering him for?

BURTON—That vice-presidency vacancy. I hadn't given it much
thought until the other day when we were talking about your going
up to Clyde. But Roger said a few things—and I got to thinking
back and—well, when anyone gets ideas like that it's a problem to
know what to do with him later. (*He looks at* CHARLES, *suddenly.*)
You never thought any of us were considering Blakesley, did you,
Charles?

CHARLES—Why, yes, Tony, I did.

BURTON (*astonished*)—Good Lord! (*He looks at* NANCY.) You
did?

NANCY—Now that you mention it, I think it did cross our minds.

BURTON—You amaze me! Roger is quite useful, but he's not the
right material at all. Your name comes up before the directors on
Monday. I've spoken to them, of course. There won't be any
trouble.

CHARLES—Thanks, Tony—that's—that's fine . . .

BURTON—That's what I meant when I said before—now that we'll
be working together more closely, I hope we'll all be friends.

But Charles is not as overjoyed as Tony expected him to be. He
confesses that a few moments ago he and Nancy thought they weren't
going to get the job—and now, suddenly, he feels "like that time at
Dartmouth when I won the half mile at Freshman track. A little
dull—a little tired and a little curious why I ran so hard."

Now Burton is doing the apple polishing. He admonishes Charley
that he is really obligated to take the job; the bank has invested a
lot of time in him. He can't turn back now. It's too late.

"That's true, isn't it," Charles agrees. "Tony, don't think I don't
want the job. It means a lot to us. And I'm glad you want me.

It's just that—from here on in—I want to be myself. The rest of my life I want to walk straight up and down—this way—vertical. I don't want to creep any more—I don't want to ever polish another apple. . . ."

The maid comes into the living room and nods at Nancy. Dinner is ready. They go toward the dining room, the Grays following the Burtons. Nancy gives her husband a quick kiss.

He inquires, "What's that for?"

"That's for free."

THE CURTAIN FALLS

BAREFOOT IN ATHENS *

A Play in Two Acts

BY MAXWELL ANDERSON

THIS is Maxwell Anderson's seventeenth Best Play—the seventeenth of his works to be represented in these Best Plays volumes. This puts him ahead of George S. Kaufman, who has had fifteen, and Eugene O'Neill, who has had eight. There have been very few seasons since 1924-1925, when "What Price Glory?" appeared, in which Anderson has not had a piece for the New York theatre either alone or in collaboration. His works have included comedy, musical comedy, historical drama and contemporary drama, and his method has ranged from prose to verse. In "Barefoot in Athens," Anderson seeks to combine history with the present. In the preface to the published version of his play, Anderson observes, "Our age is not the first which has seen democracy and communism in open conflict. The latter half of the life of Socrates was lived during a long quarrel between a communist state and a democratic state. Sparta was a complete, thorough and conscious communist society. Athens was the first conscious attempt at a democracy.

"Sparta was a closed, hard, grim slave state, in which the men and women lived in separate barracks and the children were appropriated and indoctrinated by the authorities as soon as the mother's milk was out of them. Sparta had neither commerce nor art, and nothing has come down to us from that stolid city except a fable about a boy who allowed his entrails to be eaten by a fox rather than cry out. No vase, no sculpture, no architecture, no literature was produced by Sparta in the great period of the Greeks.

"Athens, a commercial city, trading by land and sea, during the same period invented democracy, named it, defined it, and turned loose a flood of creative work in every field that has set the pace for western civilization ever since. . . . Not till the Renaissance was comparable work done in the arts, and even then the creators and

---

craftsmen looked back to the Mediterranean society founded by Athens for their models.

"These startling achievements of the Athens which Socrates knew have blinded many scholars to the imperfections of her political structure. To us it would seem a mockery to call a city a democracy when the vast majority of its inhabitants were slaves, yet this was the case in Athens. . . . The courts of Athens, growing raggedly and without plan out of the old aristocratic councils, consisted of huge paid juries (quite often of 500) with only a cloudy concept of what the law might be and a liking for flowery and misleading oratory. Trials frequently had the appearance of amusements staged for the entertainment of the jury. . . .

"The trial of Socrates had some of this character. He had begun as a sort of Will Rogers of the market place, homely, witty, unbeatable in argument, afraid of nobody, too shrewd to make enemies, too honest to make powerful friends. . . . He invented a question-and-answer game which he played with such skill that it seems to have ended almost invariably with his antagonist impaled on a verbal spit. The young-men-about-town began to keep him company for the fun of these sessions, and some of them became his followers and disciples."

The play begins at breakfast time in the home of Socrates, near the end of the Fifth Century B.C. Xantippe, Socrates' wife, is serving meager food to her three sons—Lamprocles, about 18; Lysis, 11 or 12, and Phoenix, a youngster. Xantippe tells the children they may as well eat; their father will come to breakfast when he has thought it all over. Lamprocles volunteers, "He's thinking of shaving. Somebody made him a present of a bronze razor." Xantippe calls off, "Are you shaving?"

Her husband calls back, "I'm thinking of it." Lysis earnestly wishes his father would shave, for in the field the boys make fun of Socrates' bare feet and funny whiskers. Lysis' father appears—bearded; he tells the disappointed boy he has decided against it. "Fear of the unknown, I suppose. Who knows what's underneath? It might be worse." His wife comments that at least he might *trim* his beard, and wear sandals and proper clothes. Amusedly, Socrates regards his Grecian garb—"the chiton or himation or whatever it is" —which seems inefficient to him: it doesn't keep one warm in Winter or cool in Summer, it doesn't shed rain or turn wind, and it trips one up when one runs. Of course, a new one would be better than what he's got. . . . "Is there money for a new one?" he asks.

"Not unless you brought money home with you last night," says his wife.

"That's what I forgot! Simmias owes me ten drachmas, but we stood so long talking about the war that I forgot to ask for it."

This would be a fortune in the Socrates family, which now is down to two obols; one obol will buy one fish for dinner. And Lamprocles informs his father that with three drachmas he could buy a second-hand sword and shield and join a contingent of foot soldiers who are leaving for the south tomorrow.

"Well," says Xantippe, "for once I thank Zeus for our poverty! Why would you want to go with the army?"

"To fight for Athens," her eldest son says simply. Xantippe recalls when her husband once fought for Athens—barefoot. Others were freezing in the ice and snow, but Socrates, in his one ragged garment, filled his comrades with courage and the enemy with despair. That was twenty-six years ago, and the war is still going on—and they are twenty-six times worse off than when they started.

Socrates goes on with his breakfast and his middle son, Lysis, summons courage to ask his father if he will wear sandals—the sandals Alcibiades gave him for a joke one time. "Once a day, just for me," the boy pleads. "When you walk down to the city in the morning you pass the athletic field where I am with the other boys. And they laugh at you because you don't wear shoes or sandals. Couldn't you put them on—and wear them when you pass the field—and then take them off?"

The boy's father debates this problem at length, aloud, with himself, and reaches a solution: He will simply take another path when he walks to the market. He will start this very morning. Lysis is made most happy. Lamprocles, armed with a coin from his mother, has gone to the market. Xantippe, worn and worried, says, "We're at rock bottom, Socrates." He suggests that he might go back to work as a stonecutter, which was his trade thirty years ago.

XANTIPPE—No, you couldn't. You could no more do that than you could wear sandals; but there's one thing you could do, you could take money for the lessons you give.

SOCRATES—I give no lessons.

XANTIPPE—You have a large following, and you are held in greater esteem than any other teacher in Athens. You are offered money by handfuls and you won't take it! (*He lifts his hand.*) Be quiet! Let me finish: I know of at least five other teachers in Athens —Hippias, Prodicus, Gorgias, Polus, and Callicles—and every one of them is well paid, well dressed, well fed and solvent. And you could be!

SOCRATES—If I took money for what I say I'd be cheating my

listeners, for I truly know nothing. All I have is a kind of skill in argument—

XANTIPPE—And that's what they go to you for! That's what they use you for! Alcibiades did it, and Critias, and dozens of others! These young men spend a few years with you, and suddenly they're great orators and powers in the state, while here you sit just as before, in the same old shirt and probably the same old dirt, because you've never been quite sure that bathing was good for people!

SOCRATES—When you are searching for truth, my dear, money can only corrupt you. Once get into the habit of taking it and you'll steer toward where the money is, not toward the truth.

XANTIPPE—I know your intentions are good—Hades, as we know, is paved with good intentions—

SOCRATES—I'm happy to hear that it's paved at all. I'll probably spend a good deal of time there.

XANTIPPE—You will not charge money for lessons?

SOCRATES—No, I will not.

XANTIPPE—How are we to live?

SOCRATES—I'll sell those sandals Alcibiades gave me. The workmanship is fabulous.

XANTIPPE—And after that?

SOCRATES—Who knows?

XANTIPPE—It's not only the money, Socrates. It's that you're not liked. You're hated by many people. Hated because you refuse to fit in.

SOCRATES—Perhaps because they have no hold over me.

XANTIPPE—You see—I'm afraid for you. If you'd set up as a teacher and were paid you'd be one of them—they'd accept you. But as it is you're completely uncontrollable. You're known as the horsefly of Athens, and you sting the most respectable people on their least respectable parts. You can't expect to be popular.

Now the complaining wife, she accuses her husband of never having loved her. "Xantippe," he assures her, "you come right after Athens—next to the city of Athens I love you best." Yes, she sniffs —after the whole city, and after a particular perfumed woman whose scent she has more than once detected on her husband. That, says the old man, was years ago; now he is in love with a city—a city of slaves and free men, of artists and traitors, of poets and generals— "such a city as the gods must have been thinking of when they first made men—a city drowned in sunlight and dancing and music and wisdom and deviltry, and crowned with the mystic marbles of the Parthenon!"

Lamprocles comes home, breathless from running, and crying, "Father! There's an indictment of you hung up in the government building!" The young man is followed by Crito and Phaedo, well-to-do gentlemen of Socrates' age, and Crito's son, Critobulus. As soon as he saw the indictment, Crito tore it down, it is related. Crito tells his friend what the charge was: "We three citizens of Athens, Meletos, Anytas and Lycon, bring this charge against Socrates—that he is guilty of crime, first because he does not worship the gods of our city, but introduces new divinities of his own; second, because he corrupts the thinking of our young men. We make this charge and demand an immediate trial. The penalty due is death."

Xantippe, ever the pessimist, is appalled and frightened, but her husband seems quite pleased, saying, "It's a heaven-sent opportunity to defend my way of life in open court." He is confident that, in a city like Athens, he will win.

A pretty woman of 35 or 40 comes into Socrates' house, slowly and gravely. She is Theodote, and she says she has come to bring terrible news. No, it isn't news of the indictment. "We have lost the war," she says. "Our city, which has ruled so long, is at the mercy of Sparta. I come to tell this to the one great man left out of the great age of Athens. Pericles is dead, Herodotus is dead. Sophocles, too, and Euripides—and Alcibiades. I bring the message to Socrates." King Pausanias of Sparta, she adds in detail, offers no terms and demands abject surrender.

The men hurry off to the government building, where there must be a meeting. Xantippe has a brief clash with Theodote, who seems obviously a strumpet. The wife seizes the hem of the woman's garment and smells it. "Yes," she declares, "it was your perfume he brought home." Theodote denies the accusation, but Xantippe is sure she is right. The curtain falls as the little boy, Phoenix, runs in to say there are strange soldiers in the street. The Spartans!

Scene II

Several months have passed; Socrates, Phaedo, Crito, Anytas, Lycon, Crassos, Meletos and Critobulus, now slaves of the Spartans, are working with crowbars to overturn a section of the city wall, according to the terms of surrender. A gigantic thug, Satyros, carries a whip and keeps them at their work. He threatens a whipping for any loiterer—for Critias and King Pausanias are on an inspection tour and may be here any moment.

These two gentlemen appear, deep in conversation, and Satyros drives the workers off to a distance. Critias is an elegant and intelligent Athenian; King Pausanias is unpolished, slow-moving, hesitant in speech—and astonishingly self-deprecating. "Lord love you," he says, "don't call me King Pausanias. The name's long enough without the handle. Call me Stupid. In Sparta all the kings are called Stupid, and they *are* stupid. . . . My family has an almost perfect record—nobody closer than a second cousin has learned to read during the last three centuries. . . . Stupid I was born, stupid I live, stupid I shall die, and the better king for it!" On his part, Pausanias will call Critias Brilliant—and perhaps Critias is.

Now the Athenian representative of the Spartans, Critias reports to the king that destroying democracy has been easy enough, but his substitution of thirty oligarchs to rule, with himself as the head oligarch, is not popular. However, Critias expects to win by the simple method of giving a little authority—and a little money from the treasury—to those who oppose him; after this, their hands aren't too clean, and this shuts them up. There is one man, however, named Socrates, who remains the most outspoken and venomous opponent.

Pausanias would like to hear a sample of Socrates' talk, and the old man is brought forth by Satyros, along with the rest of the labor gang. Critias orders Socrates to do some talking.

SOCRATES—With whom shall I speak, my dear Critias?

CRITIAS—With anybody.

SOCRATES—Very well. King Pausanias—

PAUSANIAS—No, no, I don't want to be tied up in knots! Choose a social equal.

SOCRATES—Surely. Anytas, we began a conversation a moment ago—

CRITIAS—Good. Complete it—for the king.

SOCRATES—I believe the last thing you said was that you were my enemy?

ANYTAS—It was! You've spent your whole life pulling Athens down, stone by stone, and this is a fitting climax to your work! The defeat of Athens, the thousands dead of famine and pestilence, the pestilential government that rules us now under Sparta's orders, these are all the result of Socrates' teachings!

SOCRATES—Please answer my question, Anytas, and do not make orations. Are you my enemy?

ANYTAS—I am!

SOCRATES—Anytas, is a man's enemy one who does evil to him?

ANYTAS—He is.

SOCRATES—And is a man's friend one who does good to him?
ANYTAS—He is.
SOCRATES—Now, Anytas, my friends tell me that I am a wise teacher and a philosopher of parts. Is that true?
ANYTAS—It is not. It's a lie.
SOCRATES—Then my friends flatter me and lie to me?
ANYTAS—They do.
SOCRATES—Is that good for me? (ANYTAS *hesitates*.) Is that good for me?
ANYTAS—No.
SOCRATES—My enemies, on the other hand, tell me bluntly to my face that I am a fool and a windbag. Is that good for me?
ANYTAS—It's the truth!
SOCRATES—But is it good for me?
ANYTAS—How do I know?
SOCRATES—Are you afraid to answer?
PAUSANIAS—By the gods, if he answers he'll contradict himself!
CRITIAS—That's true. That's what always happens.
SOCRATES—Is it good for me to be told that I am a fool and a windbag?
ANYTAS—Yes, damn you, yes! Because you are!
SOCRATES—But you began by saying that a friend was one who did good to a man and an enemy was one who did evil—and you end by saying that the friend does evil to him and the enemy does good.
PAUSANIAS—Wonderful! Now *that* I understand! Philosophy without one two-syllable word!

Critias warns the king not to be misled by this clever old man, who is a mortal enemy, but Pausanias is fascinated. He engages Socrates in a debate over which city did good when Sparta conquered Athens, and the old man bests the monarch in a few short moves of logic, ending with the argument, "When you took our freedom from us, then for the first time we realized what a precious thing freedom is!"

"But democracy," Pausanias objects, "is as stupid as I am."

"As stupid as all of us put together, O King. But free!"

Critias orders Satyros to take away all the laborers but Socrates, whom he now seeks to win by flattery and unction. "You were my first teacher, Socrates," he says. "You are still my master, even though I am by accident master of Athens for this moment. . . . We both want the same thing: the best government that can be had for our great and beloved city."

The old man asks, "What do you want of me?"

"Nothing. Only your good will."

"If you wanted nothing you would not spray me with this expert nonsense."

Xantippe comes on the scene, bringing her husband a noonday meal—a stone jug and some food wrapped in a cabbage leaf. Critias orders her away and continues his campaign with Socrates . . . while Pausanias, bored, yawns and looks about. "On the island of Salamis," Critias tells the philosopher, "there is a rich and unscrupulous man named Leon who openly defies Athens and has sworn that he will contribute nothing to the treasury while the Thirty are in power. The Thirty wish you to sit in judgment at his trial."

Xantippe creeps up, unseen, to listen. Socrates says he will be willing to act as a judge—if Leon has been indicted under the laws. "His crimes," says Critias, "are so open and flagrant that there seems no need for formal indictment." Socrates, he continues, will be one of a panel of five judges. The old man reasons, "I should be one among five. My voice would hardly count. . . . No, Critias, I shall not sit on such a court. . . . I am listening. . . . There is a little fellow, invisible and nameless, who sits on my ear at such moments and whispers to me. He is saying something now."

Theodote appears, carrying an elegant flask, a basket of food and a bunch of grapes. King Pausanias, who has been paying no attention to the duel between Socrates and Critias, halts her—because she is attractive and because the provender she carries reminds him he is hungry. "Sit down, dearest," he commands. "Let's see what we have here." Theodote indignantly orders him to let it alone; she has brought this food for Anytas, who paid for it.

PAUSANIAS (*taking her by the arm*)—Be more courteous to outlanders.

THEODOTE (*striking him with her free hand*)—It's not for Spartans.

PAUSANIAS (*forcing her to sit*)—A little service, please. (*He takes the food.*)

THEODOTE—You're horrible.

PAUSANIAS—I know. (*He sits.*) Stupid, too, don't you think?

THEODOTE—Yes, stupid.

PAUSANIAS—That's what they all say. But I am the king of Sparta.

THEODOTE—The king of Sparta! And I said you were stupid! Oh, forgive me! (XANTIPPE *crouches, listening.*)

SOCRATES—The three most gifted young men I have ever known sat talking with me through the whole of a Summer night, about twenty-five years ago. Their names were Alcibiades, Charmides, and Critias, for you were one of the three. We talked of Athens and of the arts and of government . . . and of the chances of this world. And we concluded—I think it was you, Critias, who summed up for us, and we were happy in what you said—we concluded that the most valuable thing a man or a state could have was freedom. We concluded that if a man or a state was to retain freedom three things were needed: power and incorruptibility and frugality—the art of wanting little for yourself. And the more frugal and honest you are the less power you need.

CRITIAS—Must we go back so far?

SOCRATES—I had great hope for you three, and for Athens because of you. A democracy must have leaders and perhaps another Pericles might come from among you. You were very gay, and witty and elated, and somebody proposed that we swear an oath to support democracy whatever might come. We made up such an oath, and swore it, all four of us. The oath was to this effect: "I will kill with my own hand, if I am able, any man who subverts the democracy of Athens, or who shall hold any office in the city after the democracy has been destroyed, or shall rise in arms to make himself a despot, or shall help a despot to establish himself. And if anyone else slay such an enemy of our democracy I will account the slayer holy before the gods and give him friendship and love." Do you remember this?

CRITIAS—I remember. Men do silly things when a little drunk.

SOCRATES—And when drunk with power—or the thirst for power. That was twenty-five years ago. Charmides is dead. He was among the first to plot the destruction of democracy, and he is dead. Alcibiades—you know his history. He set out to gain power at any price. He poured out money. He offered the most extravagant displays of games and horse racing and costly celebration in our city's history. He took money, in vast quantity, from the king of Persia, promising Athens to him. He was banished, and set out to destroy the city that banished him. He was a brilliant statesman and general, and he betrayed every talent and every trust till he was universally hated—and at last his enemies caught up with him and he was killed. The history of Athens reeks with such men, brilliant and unscrupulous, committed to success at any price, serving on three sides of every cause—and they have not ended well. Themistocles, our greatest general, saved Athens from Persia, and then sold out to Persia—and died dishonored. In all our history there has never been a time when brilliant men have been lacking to betray our city and change coats for money—and die young. You are still young,

Critias, and you, like the others, have sold out—and you follow after
Alcibiades.

CRITIAS—You lie. I have not sold out.

SOCRATES—Leon is guilty of no crime. You wish to kill him to
consolidate your power and to confiscate his fortune. You have
killed many because they were rich and fat and tempting prizes.
You will die young.

Critias takes a step toward Socrates to deliver some sort of ultimatum about serving on his "court," but is interrupted by the return
of the rest of the labor gang. Several have food in their hands,
brought by their women; Anytas goes to Theodote, expecting to receive his collation from her, but the woman explains that the king of
Sparta has appropriated it. "I'm sorry, friend," Pausanias mumbles
while eating.

"Here's a drachma," says Anytas to Theodote; "bring me something."

"I'm sorry, friend," repeats Pausanias. "She stays with me." So
Anytas has to go find himself something, and Satyros, the guard,
warns him to return before the sun crosses the wall. Critias gives
Socrates a warning: "Before the sun touches the west pillars of the
Acropolis you will be at the Senate chamber, ready to join the other
four judges." The oligarch orders Satyros to stay with Socrates.
"If he goes to the Senate, do not touch him. If he goes home, or
elsewhere, follow him and do the needful." Critias leaves and the
old man says good-humoredly to his guard, "You are to be my constant companion."

"To the death, Socrates," Satyros replies.

Xantippe approaches her husband to urge him to start for the
Senate chamber. He takes the food she has brought and begins eating, and answers her, "I am going home." King Pausanias puts in,
"Better do as you're told, friend. Critias will have Leon killed anyway." "All my life," says Socrates, "I've been saying it is better
for a man to die than to do what his soul believes to be wrong. Shall
I now do wrong to save my life?" He calmly goes on eating.

The curtain falls.

SCENE III

About a half hour later, Socrates is at home with his wife and two
of his sons, Lysis and Phoenix. Satyros and some assistant thugs
have followed, and Socrates offers his ugly guard a drink of wine.
Unbelieving, Satyros says, "You wouldn't drink with me. I'm a

slave. And an executioner." "Nonsense," the philosopher retorts, and he asks Xantippe to pour for both of them. The old man notes the absence of his eldest son, Lamprocles, and young Lysis informs his father that the youth has gone to Piraeus, where a rebellion against Critias is starting.

Pausanias and Critias arrive—Pausanias to witness the end of Socrates and Critias coming along at the king's bidding. Theodote follows. The king suggests that the women and children retire to the women's quarters of the house, but Theodote is allowed to remain when she brashly declares, "I'm only supposed to mix with men!" She has a way with men—even with a king. Critias is impatient to get the execution over, but Pausanias appears to be in no hurry; he is interested in the little divinity that clings to Socrates' ear and occasionally helps even so intelligent a man by warning, "Wait a minute. Not so fast."

SOCRATES—He says something like that, yes.

PAUSANIAS—Now I'm just the opposite. I'm dull. You go in and out of that rathole in front of my eyes and I can't even see where you went. I can't figure anything out. So what happens? I'm a king and I have to make decisions because people come screaming at me. And what do I do? I wait.

SOCRATES—And somebody whispers in your ear?

PAUSANIAS—No. Nobody whispers in my ear. No such luck. I just wait and let them scream. And if I wait long enough, and sleep on it, and maybe sleep on it two or three times, why I wake up some morning and there it is, plain as morning, what to do.

SOCRATES—Why, that's wonderful!

PAUSANIAS—And I'm stupid! Dumb!

SOCRATES—Just beyond words wonderful!

PAUSANIAS—Isn't it?

CRITIAS—Could we abbreviate these felicitations?

PAUSANIAS—Isn't it wonderful?

SOCRATES—Beyond description! Enchanting!

PAUSANIAS—Now take a case like this: Critias says Socrates is the worst enemy of the state and we must be rid of him at once. At once, mind you. Now that's what I don't like. Maybe we should get rid of you, but why all this hurry? Why not sleep on it?

SOCRATES—Surely. Why not?

PAUSANIAS—If need be, why not sleep—well . . . two or three nights on it?

SOCRATES—Of course I'm not a young man. If you wait too long I might die.

PAUSANIAS—Now you're going round corners. Now you're too fast for me.

SOCRATES—I wonder.

PAUSANIAS—Tell me, what is your little angel-demon whispering to you this afternoon?

SOCRATES—Let me see. Something very strange. For the first time since I have known him he's whispering a warning about somebody else—not about me at all.

PAUSANIAS—A warning?

SOCRATES—Just a warning that somebody is in danger.

PAUSANIAS—Not you?

SOCRATES—Not me.

PAUSANIAS—Me?

SOCRATES—Not you.

PAUSANIAS (looking round)—Theodote?

SOCRATES—No.

PAUSANIAS—Your wife? Your children?

SOCRATES—No.

PAUSANIAS—Leon of Salamis?

SOCRATES—No.

PAUSANIAS—I can tell you something about Leon of Salamis. He's dead. Critias had him killed before he asked you to act as judge over him.

SOCRATES—Is this true, Critias?

CRITIAS—I am not here to be questioned.

PAUSANIAS—It's true.

SOCRATES—This is most strange and disturbing. Critias, the warning I receive concerns you, and it's so definite and immediate that I feel like urging you to run—run until you can surround yourself with heavy-armed troops and ward off what seems to be coming. . . .

Critias, sneering, is unimpressed—and he would like the execution to be got on with because his time is limited. He stands at the door, inviting everybody out. When they have gone, Theodote goes to the door of the inner room and calls Xantippe, telling her that Critias, Pausanias and Socrates have gone out, with Satyros and the executioners following. Theodote, sobbing, asks if she can come into Xantippe's room. At the door Xantippe puts her arm around the woman and leads her inside. The stage is empty for a moment, and then from outside a man's cry is heard. The women run in, apprehensive. "He's probably lying in the street," Xantippe wails, and she begs Theodote, "Will you help me carry him in?"

The women make for the outer door, but at this moment Pausanias walks in slowly—followed by Socrates. Xantippe, with incredulous relief, asks what happened and her husband, bewildered, answers, "I don't know, my dear. The usual governmental inefficiency. They killed the wrong man. . . . They killed Critias." Xantippe moves violently away from Theodote, crying, "We were about to go out and carry you in, I and this scented doxy of yours!"

Pausanias puts in, "I had no intention of having him killed today but he forced my hand."

Socrates asks in amazement, "His death was not a mistake?" No, quite regular but a little early, the king declares. In the next few days Critias would have gathered in several large and luscious plutocrats. "The kings of Sparta have sunk pretty low," Pausanias explains. "My family needs a fortune, preferably in gold. I was counting on Critias. He'll still bring me quite a chunk. Leon of Salamis alone was worth near half a million."

Socrates cannot understand this taking of money by murder; surely such money should go to the families of the deceased, he argues. Pausanias has simpler reasoning: Critias stole the money first, and now the king steals it. Why should he try to return it? "How," he argues, "do I know who they stole it from? Or who *they* stole it from? It's an endless chain. Much simpler to keep it."

Now, Pausanias continues, he must return home; the occupation is over. All that remains is to put somebody in his place here. He asks Socrates for a suggestion, and the old man answers, "Give us back our democracy." The king refuses; he wants to find a man who can be trusted and set him up in power before he leaves. The old philosopher observes that nobody can be trusted with power— only the citizens, the voters. Pausanias scoffs that democracy is an ugly and disorderly form of government, and the one in Sparta is much better. Socrates is curious about it, so the king describes its beauties: All property is common, so no man can attempt to get ahead of the others and there is no unseemly scramble for wealth and honors.

"You've invented paradise," says Socrates drily. Then he adds, "Who governs this paradise?"

"A small group of men take the whole burden of the government on themselves, so that the average citizen never has to worry about it at all." There is, for instance, the case of Socrates himself. Pausanias worried about him, so he had Critias killed—and lost money by murdering him too soon.

Socrates argues, "You're not consistent, O King! Why should you lose money to save my worthless neck?"

"That's my weakness. I like a man, I like to keep him alive."

Xantippe, admiring, says to the king, "You're only pretending you're a fool," and he chuckles, "Woman, do you want to ruin me?"

Satyros arrives to report that Critias has been laid in his house, and his money, a hundred and four bags each labeled "one talent," is now aboard Pausanias' trireme, ready for the return to Sparta. Also, the king's occupation forces are now marching toward their boats. Satyros is dismissed, and Pausanias turns again to Socrates. "If Athens goes back to a democracy," he warns, "you won't be safe here. You'll be tried on the same old charge they nailed up against you once before. And if it comes to a vote you could be found guilty. So choose some honest, stupid man, with no more brain than I have, and in he shall go as despot here. And choose a friend of yours. You may need protection."

"I rather like you, Stupid," Socrates laughs. "You have the endearing qualities of the frankly criminal class—but the courts are my protection."

The king will not give up. He argues that a despot such as he recommends could do a little quiet looting for the philosopher. "I've never needed money," says Socrates—but Xantippe argues differently; she'd like money, no matter how they got it.

Pausanias tries another tack, quoting history very well for so stupid a man. The greatest statesman Athens ever had, Pericles, had a teacher—Annex something or other. "Anaxagoras," Socrates supplies. Well, even with Pericles protecting him, he was banished because he said the sun was not a god but a ball of fire. Banished by popular vote. And Protagoras was exiled by popular vote for writing that he didn't know whether the gods existed or not. "Athens has been pretty rough on philosophers," Pausanias warns. "I understand you too have said a few things about the gods."

Socrates admits this is so. When he makes his daily sacrifices at the temple he does so "believing devoutly that no man knows where he came from or what he should do while here or where he is going, and that he should search without rest for the answers to these questions—in books and at the altars of gods and in his own mind."

"They'll have you up for it," Pausanias is certain.

"Not Athens, not my city of Athens!"

Pausanias, ready to go, promises to have a bag of silver sent to Socrates' house. Theodote takes his arm to go with him, but they are stopped when Critobulus rushes unrecognizing past them with news of the rebellion. With Critias dead, the rebels are returning to Athens and the Spartans are retreating to their ships. He exults, "There's nobody between us and freedom except King Pausanias! He's hiding somewhere and we're going to find him and kill him!"

Backing up Critobulus are Crito, Lamprocles, Anytas, Crassos, Lycon and Meletos. Lycon suddenly descries Pausanias, pulls his dagger and leaps—but Socrates stops him.

Lycon turns his knife toward the old man, but the thrust is stopped by Crassos, who cries, "Father—would you kill Socrates?"

"Yes, I would kill Socrates!"

The old man takes the dagger from Lycon's hand, coolly saying this may not be necessary. In fact, the revolution can be concluded without killing anybody. They can probably persuade the Spartan king to re-establish Athenian democracy and go home.

Pausanias again warns, "The old charge will be brought up against you. You will go to trial for your life."

Socrates suggests that they form a guard of honor and conduct the king to the Senate, where he can formally surrender possession of the city to its citizens. "A guard of honor? He's our prisoner," Anytas objects hotly. But the wise Socrates observes, "It's hard to tell the difference between a police guard and a guard of honor. But let's escort him. Otherwise some hothead might murder him before he goes through the ceremony." The escort forms up and leaves, with only Xantippe and Theodote remaining.

Shyly, Xantippe questions Theodote on her perfumes—do men like them?

"They're mad about perfumes."

"What was between you and Socrates?" Xantippe demands.

"Not much. Long ago. But it was Alcibiades I loved. And he's dead. . . . Sometimes I like to see Socrates because he was Alcibiades' friend. Do you mind?"

Xantippe, mollified, says no, then sighs, "Am I a fool to be in love when I'm old?"

Theodote answers, "What better is there to do, old or young?"

The curtain falls.

ACT II

A few days, perhaps weeks, later, Socrates, Xantippe, Lamprocles and Phoenix are at the breakfast table and Lysis, who has been out playing, runs in late. The lad runs his fingers through his hair and something drops on the table—something he must have got running through the bushes.

"It looks like a tick," says Lamprocles. "Shall I kill it?"

"Not on the table," his mother warns.

Lysis allows that the bug could be a plain harmless little beetle. His father, amused, suggests that the bug be given a fair trial; if it's a tick, kill it, and if it's a beetle, let it off—that's the Athenian way.

"A man isn't guilty until he's found guilty. And neither is a bug."

Xantippe bursts out, "But why must they try you now? There's plenty to do just to re-establish the democracy and clean up after the way things were under the Thirty! Why don't they just do that?"

"I don't know," her husband answers, "but I do know that history doesn't come at us the way it should. It comes at us any old way, higgledy-piggledy, and every day when you look at it it looks like a mess. The next day a new mess is poured on top of the old mess, and nothing is ever cleaned up. The whole thing stratifies and petrifies down below, so underneath it's a petrified mess and on top it's a fresh mess and it goes on that way forever."

Lamprocles, Phoenix and Lysis continue their mock trial of the bug, and Lamprocles brings up a new accusation—being a female Athenian under 30 and guilty of violating the law governing the rules of dress. It is not wearing its chiton in such fashion as to expose one leg as far as the thigh. Xantippe has never heard of such a law, and her husband explains that it is a new one. Since the war ended there have been too many unmarried girls and too many bachelors, so now every girl on the street must slip along with one leg twinkling.

Now the insect has escaped, and Phoenix proclaims that it wasn't guilty anyway—it was showing all six legs up to its bottom.

Theodote comes for a visit and tells of the excitement on the streets. "Every vendable maid in Athens is being walked up and down by her mother, her best leg foremost."

Xantippe inquires, "And the men?"

"Oh, the men walk up and down and gape as if such wonders had never been seen! Girls are going like hotcakes."

"This," says Xantippe sarcastically, "has destroyed your business, no doubt?"

"Oh, no—licit and illicit business have improved together!" Theodote herself is wearing the new garb and excuses herself for doing so by saying, "Every single woman is a maiden, naturally. And what woman is over thirty?" But more exciting than fashion is the news that Theodote has received a message from the king of Sparta: The king is coming here, and Theodote should prepare herself for a journey. This means only one thing to Xantippe—Theodote will become the king's mistress and live in a palace and have many servants. "I hate you," she cries. Turning on her husband, she rails, "Everybody goes around praising temperance and moderation and poverty and all that nonsense! You go around praising them— you most of all! And nobody wants them—nobody! What people want is luxuries, and loads of money, and loads of everything, and people waiting on them—and that's what I want! You're always looking for the honest truth and there it is! People don't want to be poor. They want to have everything, and so do I!"

SOCRATES—Of course, not everybody can have everything.

XANTIPPE—Of course not! Let them do without. I've done without long enough! Let other people try it. How many do you know that aren't trying to get rich or stay rich or climb out of the hole they're in? I only know one, and that's you! One man in all the world! And, God help me, it just happens to be my priceless luck to be married to that one man.

SOCRATES—You say it well, Xantippe. I have never heard such a clear and passionate statement of the position. The only trouble is that you don't mean it. . . .

XANTIPPE—Don't mean it?

SOCRATES—If you had Theodote's chance you wouldn't take it.

XANTIPPE—When offered servants and a palace?

SOCRATES—You would think the matter over for a few days and in the end you would decide to remain here and eke out an existence on the same three obols a day—

XANTIPPE—That's what you would do!

SOCRATES—Think how we'd waste those three obols if you weren't here.

XANTIPPE (*a bit shaken*)—The spending of the money I'd turn over to Lysis. He has some sense—

THEODOTE—And so far you haven't received any offers.

XANTIPPE—True. And I won't.

This discussion of how far Xantippe would go in her quest for luxury is halted by the arrival of Socrates' friends, Crito and Phaedo. They have come to discuss preparations for the trial tomorrow morning. For instance, says Crito, in trials involving the death penalty it is usual to have the defendant's wife and children appear with him and ask for clemency. It is usual, even, to borrow tattered cloaks for the whole family and rehearse a scene of weeping.

"This," says Socrates, "we can't do."

Phaedo brings up another matter—choice of a spokesman for the defense. He recommends a rhetorician, Zephyros, who has conducted thirty-four cases and lost not one. Again Socrates objects, arguing that, no matter how successful, there is always some sly perversion of the truth in a professional defense. And public grieving by the family is no better than an attempt to corrupt the court. "I am accused of being the kind of man who corrupts and falsifies and distorts and destroys. . . . How can the jury tell what kind of man I am if I go before them speaking words that are not mine and hiding behind a crying wife and children? Do you think they are likely to think me guilty if they see me as I am?"

Crito answers, "Not likely to think you guilty, but likely to *find* you guilty."

"It's my day," Socrates insists. "And I go toward it with a very light heart." He tells his friends he will speak in his own defense, *extempore* as always, and they leave. When they have gone his wife tells him, "I think you're wrong—I think one might just as well give up and have things like the rest of the world. But that doesn't mean I don't love you. I do." Suddenly tender, she murmurs, "Do you know that it's—it's a long time since you've put your arms round me? . . . When I go to the trial I want to watch you and remember that you love me a little."

Xantippe asks her man if he would do what he did long ago—lie with his head in her lap. She sits, and with his head in her lap she strokes his hair and looks into the distance. Socrates likes it—it makes him feel almost young. Sniffing, he asks, "When did you take to wearing perfumes?"

"Only lately. Do you like it?"

"Yes, I rather like it. I have in mind to say a prayer."

"You used to say a prayer to the god Pan when you lay thus long ago."

Socrates begins it:

"Beloved Pan, and all you other gods who haunt this city, give me beauty in the inward soul, for outward beauty I'm not likely to have. May I reckon the wise to be the wealthy and those who need least to be most like the gods. Make me content with what I have but not self-satisfied. Let me give more than I get, love more than I hate, and think more of living than of having lived. . . . Anything more? This prayer, I think, is enough for me."

Xantippe continues stroking his hair as the curtain falls.

SCENE II

The trial has run half its course. The audience in the theatre now becomes the jury, listening. On the stage a magistrate sits, and near him sits Socrates. Xantippe and the children are nearby, and so are Theodote, King Pausanias, Crito and Phaedo. On the opposite side is Meletos, and standing, speaking, is Anytas.

Anytas summarizes the accusations: First, Socrates teaches a new religion, with gods of his own devising which are not gods at all, for he has no belief and is not sure that the earth is here and men are walking on it. Second, he corrupts the young men by cynically questioning all precepts and patterns of conduct. Third, all the great enemies of Athens have been his pupils and friends. He warns the jury, "Beware of him. Don't let him trick you or make the worse appear the better cause, for that is his vocation and he has done it all too well."

MAGISTRATE—Socrates will now speak in his own defense.

SOCRATES (*rising, taking his place*)—Men of Athens, if Anytas wished to be believed he should never have said that I'm an orator, for you'll soon discover that I'm not. I'm afraid you'll hear from me only the first plain words that come to hand. I'm not used to speaking from a platform and I've never before been in a lawsuit. I'm a stranger to the language of this place. I shall have to speak as I have always spoken in the streets. . . . Now I am accused of ruining Athens, and those who accuse me ask that I be put to death. They may be right, but let me tell you how I became the kind of fellow I am. My father was a sculptor—no, he was a stonecutter, and I took the same trade and I was a stonecutter. There are some marbles in the sanctuary of the Parthenon that I remember working on. But I had what was known as a shrewd wit—a workman's wit— and it was my habit to talk while I chiseled the stone. I talked and cracked about politics and public affairs and statesmen and kept the whole workroom in good humor. After a while people began to drift into the factory to listen to me, and the crowds around my bench were large enough to become a nuisance. The day arrived when I had to stop talking or quit work, and so I moved my conversations into the street. By this time I was nearly forty years of age, and married, and my wife brought me a bit of money—not a fortune, three obols a day—and talking to the men in the streets became my work. And what did I talk about? Well, I'm afraid I was just a joker at first, because it amused people, but I sometimes joked about important men and questions, as we all do—and it happened after a while that I met some of these important men. Now I was only an irresponsible ignoramus, but I began to find that I knew as much about many things as the important people did. And I began to question them and stick needles in them—and sometimes I showed them up as ignoramuses—and they were angry. And I invented a sort of question-and-answer game for getting people into corners, and my following grew larger, because there's nothing people like better than seeing public men confused and unable to answer. I was just as unable to answer as they were, but I was asking the questions, not answering them, and so I acquired a reputation for wisdom which I didn't deserve and don't deserve now. . . . The next thing that happened, though, seemed to me very serious. A friend of mine, now dead, a man well known to many of you, named Chairephon, went to Delphi and had the audacity to ask the oracle if there were any wiser man than Socrates. And the priestess answered no. This was heard by many citizens and when the news came to me I was stunned, for I had never pretended to wisdom and still don't. Yet I couldn't help taking the matter seriously and I asked myself, "What can the god mean?" For a long while I was at a loss, but then I decided to continue my question-and-answer game, testing every man I met till I found somebody wiser than myself. And that search has gone on from that day to this, making me many enemies, no doubt, among those who were stumped by my questions, and getting me just about nowhere. I have not found one man who knows what holiness is, or wisdom, or courage or loyalty or faith. And I still don't know. I have put in a lifetime of Herculean labor to prove the god wrong, and I have not proved him either wrong or right.

MELETOS—Do you deny that you questioned the existence of the gods?

MAGISTRATE—Let us be orderly, Meletos!

SOCRATES (*to the judge*)—This I can answer now, sir. Meletos, I am nearly seventy years old. In the course of the last thirty or forty years I have asked questions on nearly every subject. By the dog, I have not spared anything or anybody, myself included, and if matters of religion ever came up for discussion I pursued my usual course. It has been my fixed principle that the uncovering of truth could do no harm. I have believed that questioning could injure only what is false among workmen, businessmen, Sophists, statesmen or gods. The air of a democracy is only healthy when inquiry bites constantly at the heels of every proposal and every project, even at the foundations of our way of life.

MELETOS—You have bitten into them and you have destroyed them!

Socrates now drags the unwilling Meletos into a philosophical argument and quickly has him bested. He forces Meletos to declare he is in favor of free discussion and opposed to censorship—yet Meletos angrily insists he would enforce censorship on people like Socrates—people who don't believe in the gods. This gives Socrates another opening; again he forces an admission that Meletos has heard the philosopher praying to demigods or to Pan. "Demigods," says Soc-

rates, "are the offspring of gods and mortals. Could a man believe
in demigods without believing that the gods exist?" He has Meletos
there. Anytas jumps into the argument, and the philosopher soon
has them both out of their depth over a definition of piety as opposed
to impiety.

Socrates addresses the jury, "Men of Athens, I am a man of doubt,
as my accusers have said. All my wisdom is in knowing how little
I know. None of my questions has been answered, none of the defi-
nitions I sought has been found. We live our lives, it seems to me,
in such mystery and darkness that I was quick to take the one hint
I thought might have come my way from a god, the answer made by
the Delphic Apollo to a question about myself. Since that answer I
have continued to seek, sometimes gaily, sometimes ironically, but
always seriously, for somebody wiser than I am. Perhaps I was
wrong, but this is the closest I have ever come to hearing a mandate
from any god, and I wished to do as the god directed. You see before
you then, a man who is not sure of his faith but has tried hard to
serve Apollo, and in his accusers you see men of complete faith who
have not heard even a hint as to whether they are serving the gods
or only themselves. By Meletos' own admission these men are more
guilty than I."

Anytas and Meletos voice angry denials. Anytas proclaims that
he himself learned about the gods on Olympos from Homer. Socrates, asking where Homer learned about the gods, says, "Homer was a
poet, and he wrote gloriously. . . . But were not the gods he wrote
about the gods as he imagined them?" Anytas counters by asking,
"Do you believe the gods of Olympos to be sure and solid and real?"

The old man replies simply, "As sure and solid and real as anything in this world!"

Meletos jumps in with, "Only how sure and real is this world?"

"Of different degrees of reality, Meletos. Sometimes it seems to
me that the gods in the pages of Homer are vividly alive, and that
by comparison they are shadowy and indistinct on Mount Olympos.
Sometimes it seems to me that your figure and mine, speaking here,
are shadowy and indistinct, and will be quickly forgotten, while the
scene of this trial, remembered and written down, say by young Plato
there, who is always writing things down, may come vividly alive and
remain so for a long time. Which then would be the more real,
Meletos, the vivid scene written down or the shadowy one that actually takes place and then drifts away from men's minds and is lost?"

Lycon, the third accuser, now shifts the prosecution from philosophy to reality. He charges that since the Peloponnesian War Athens
has been led by the pupils of Socrates. Alcibiades was an evil spirit.

Charmides led the rebellion that overthrew democracy. Critias completed the wreck of Athens. And, he adds, Socrates' followers also number a whole rabble, the worst men of three generations. Socrates objects that Lycon has shown no connection between his words and the disasters Lycon has mentioned. Lycon insists that there is a connection—that, by teaching his listeners to question everything, Socrates sowed in them seeds of doubt and corruption . . . and he did it out of pure love of evil, destruction, tearing down; out of hatred for Athens.

Angry for the first time, the old philosopher shouts, "You lie! I love Athens. . . . And the thing I have loved most about my city is its freedom, its willingness to look at all the evidence there is and live in the same world with it. . . . The evidence will not destroy a free city, Lycon. Far from destroying it, the truth will make and keep it free. A despotism dies of the truth, a democracy lives by it!"

Seeking to trap the old man, Lycon asks, "If you had to choose between Athens and the search for truth, to which of these would you give your allegiance?"

"They are one and the same, fortunately. Yet if you wish me to say which I would choose if they were not the same—and I see that you do wish it, Lycon—I must say that the search for truth is more sacred than any god, more desirable than any woman, more hopeful than any child, more lovely than any city, even our own. (*To the jury.*) If you have not seen this you will vote against me, and you should. But you are men of Athens, and you have seen it or Athens would not be here, would not from the beginning have been possible! The unexamined life is not worth living! The unexamined life is built on lies, and a free world cannot live by lies. Only a world of slaves can live by lies!"

Lycon moves that the case may be put to the vote. Phaedo and Crito embrace their teacher and Pausanias approaches him with outstretched hand, saying, "I shall never understand democracy. If they want to kill you why do they talk till they let you talk yourself clear out of it?" Socrates has a feeling he has won. The lights dim while the jurors' ballots are taken up and counted. When they come up again, the magistrate is holding a piece of paper from which he reads, "The outcome of the trial—the vote stands at—let me make sure of this—279 for conviction and 221 for acquittal."

Xantippe gasps a choked, "No!"

"Then I'm found guilty," says Socrates, sadly. "I thought it would go the other way." The magistrate says he thought so, too. The old man looks slowly round at the crowd, saying, "I have not known my city, then. More than half of these faces that look up at me are the faces of men who have said, 'No more of Socrates.' "

The magistrate informs the philosopher that it is his right to propose a punishment alternate to death. The convicted man once again addresses the crowd, beginning, "My accusers think, no doubt, that my death would be a great victory for them and a calamity for Socrates. This is not the case. My death would be of enormous benefit to me, but a disaster to my accusers . . . and to Athens. . . . I shall be famous, and my accusers shall be infamous for all time! . . . If you were to let me die quietly in bed I should be quietly forgotten. But a martyr's death sends a man off in a blaze of excitement and a blare of argument! . . . I love Athens more than myself. Though this sentence means only good fortune to me it means evil fortune to my city, and I plead with you: Do not do this: Reverse your judgment: Let me die the unknown death I deserve! The alternate punishment I propose is that you fine me one mina—or thirty minae, or some such nominal sum—and maintain me henceforth at the public charge as a man serviceable to the state. That way I shall pass unnoticed into oblivion, and Athens will keep her good name."

Gently the magistrate declares that if Socrates gives the jury no other choice than this, the vote will go against him again.

Looking at Satyros, who has stepped up to take the prisoner in charge, the philosopher says to the magistrate, "In that case, sir, who at seventy—who at seventy ever looked on a more beautiful visage than the face of this sad and ugly slave who brings men death?"

The curtain falls.

SCENE III

Socrates, legs chained, sleeps on a pallet on the floor of his cell. It is before dawn some weeks later. Xantippe kneels beside him, and the three children are there. Socrates awakens, asks why they are there so early—then realizes why: It is his last day. The sacred ship, *Phoenix,* has returned from its annual voyage to the shrine of Apollo at Delos. While it goes and returns no criminal can be executed in Athens, which is why the old man has had a long stay of execution.

"What does one talk about on a last day?" muses Socrates. "It's not a time for banter, I suppose, and yet I don't want to get off the usual stupid apothegms about loving your mother and being good citizens." He talks lightly with Lamprocles, the eldest, about his not being enough of a rascal to succeed as a soldier. He asks Lysis, the middle boy, if he is still studying ticks—but Lysis has graduated to geometry. He has heard that there's even a way to measure the earth now, by marking how the sun's rays fall in one city or another. The boy's father comments that by the time he grows up perhaps it won't be atheistic to say such things. Little Phoenix he advises, "When you grow up and get married don't keep your wife penned up in the women's quarters. Let her out for a run once in a while."

"Anyway," chirps Phoenix, "you're not going to die today." Xantippe reveals that Pausanias has come back to get him out of prison. Satyros, two thugs, Pausanias and Theodote enter the cell. "We do a cash business here," Satyros reminds the king. Pausanias produces a sack, saying, "Take it. Three hundred silver owls." Satyros takes it and starts out, and the king asks where he is going. "To count it," says the executioner flatly. Pausanias pleads, "Take the leg irons off first," and Satyros orders the thugs to remove the irons from the prisoner's aching limbs.

The king explains his presence: He got bored hunting, making war and dispensing justice in Sparta, and finally he realized that he missed his Socrates and his Theodote—so he has come back to get them.

"And Xantippe and the boys?"

"It's all arranged, and there's room for as many as you want to take with you. Xantippe wants a palace. Well, she shall have it."

SOCRATES—Xantippe, when a woman buys a fish in the market does she look at it before she pays?

XANTIPPE—Now he's going to say we must examine into this offer.

SOCRATES—Shouldn't we?

XANTIPPE—You're being offered life in place of death!

SOCRATES—Well, a life is more important than a fish, Xantippe. And it's not only I who should examine what I am to receive. The king should examine me before he buys me from Satyros, for it may be that he won't like what he's getting.

PAUSANIAS—I know what I'm getting. I'm getting Socrates.

SOCRATES—But now remember what Socrates is. He is an obnoxious old fellow without sandals, badly dressed, walking up and down the streets putting annoying questions to the inhabitants.

PAUSANIAS—You won't have to go outside to talk, Socrates. You will sit in my palace with me and talk to me and my friends. None of this wandering about the streets.

SOCRATES—But suppose I grew tired of talking with important people and wanted to have a chat with shoemakers or weavers or the athletes in the palaestra?

PAUSANIAS—Hm.

SOCRATES—What do you say?

PAUSANIAS—Well, you know, this hadn't occurred to me, but it is a difficulty. Nobody goes about asking questions in Sparta. And if you asked them nobody would answer you.

SOCRATES—Why not, O King?

PAUSANIAS—They—they wouldn't be interested.

SOCRATES—I might . . . at length, after a while . . . rouse some interest.

PAUSANIAS—It wouldn't be encouraged. You'd do better just staying in the palace and talking there. You see, Sparta is not a democracy. We don't do things that way.

SOCRATES—In other words I wouldn't be allowed to talk?

PAUSANIAS—Not in the streets, no. But mind you, you might have a great deal of influence on me.

SOCRATES—Do you mind if I call you Stupid?

PAUSANIAS—From now on call me Stupid, nothing else.

SOCRATES—This is how it stands, Stupid. If the judge and the jury had told me they'd let me off if I'd stay at home and quit my question-and-answer game, I'd have said "Proceed, gentlemen; I'll live as I've always lived, and if that's incompatible with the laws why put me out of the way." In Sparta, as in Athens, I must wrangle and make inquiries in my accustomed fashion. Otherwise I prefer the hemlock. I'm old and set in my ways.

Xantippe, seeing a streak of gray in the sky, makes an anguished appeal to her husband—he's all they have, and the king would never hurt him. "Think of us!" she begs. He asks the king, "If I die here, will you take care of Xantippe?"

"Whether you come or stay she shall have her palace."

Socrates' mind is made up as he asks, "Shall I dwindle now into a king's buffoon, hanging to the ragged end of life by saying the right things and keeping Stupid amused?"

Satyros comes back with the money sack, reporting that forty-seven drachmas of the bribe are in Corinthian coin or worse. He wants Athenian ones, or Socrates dies. Hastily, Theodote produces fifty drachmas of her own and gives them to the executioner, who starts out, saying, "Now go. All of you. But be quick about it."

Socrates stops Satyros in his tracks by saying quietly, "You'd better give that money back. I'm not leaving."

The slave reminds him, "The hemlock is prepared and ready. You're to drink it this morning." The old man chuckles, "So we are to be together at the end, after all!"

Satyros has a strange change of heart. He gives back the money to Pausanias and Theodote and then orders, "And now go. You're free. It's a gift from Satyros to Socrates! Now go!" But the old man does not move. "I don't . . . understand it," falters the slave. "I don't want to give you the hemlock."

"Just bring it and I'll drink it." Crito and Phaedo arrive, and Socrates says he will converse with them over the cup. The others had better go. His wife asks, "Do you have . . . no last word for me?"

SOCRATES—Do you think we can better now what we have given each other over all these years?

PAUSANIAS (*to* XANTIPPE)—Come.

XANTIPPE—Then I have a last word for you. I shall not go to Sparta. I shall live in our old house on the three obols a day.

SOCRATES—You do this for the children?

XANTIPPE—No, for you. I can remember you there. It's the only way I can keep you. Any of you. Will you be with me there sometimes?

SOCRATES—Perhaps I shall not be there or anywhere, Xantippe. Nowhere at all.

XANTIPPE—But in spirit—if I could have your spirit with me—

SOCRATES—My spirit you can certainly have, and anyone can have it who remembers it and wants it.

XANTIPPE—Yes. You escape me now as before.

SOCRATES—We all escape when we die, Xantippe. From everybody. But you will live in the old house on the three obols?

XANTIPPE—Yes.

SOCRATES—Then— (*He goes close to her.*) Will you sometimes say my prayer for me?

XANTIPPE—If I remember it.

SOCRATES (*putting his arm round her*)—Say it now, and I'll prompt you if you forget, and then you'll have it all.

XANTIPPE—Now?

SOCRATES—Yes, now.

XANTIPPE—"Beloved Pan, and all you other gods who haunt this city"—oh, no, no, no! I can't lose you! I can't live!

SOCRATES—Go on, Xantippe. "Give me beauty in the inward soul"—

XANTIPPE—"Give me beauty in the inward soul"—

SOCRATES—"For outward beauty I'm not likely to have"—

XANTIPPE—"For outward beauty I'm not likely to have"— (*The lights begin to dim down and during the next speeches go out entirely.*)

SOCRATES—"May I reckon the wise to be the wealthy"—

XANTIPPE—I know the rest. "May I reckon the wise to be the wealthy and those who need least to be most like the gods." (*The lights are out.*)

SOCRATES—"And those who need least to be most like the gods."

THE CURTAIN FALLS

VENUS OBSERVED *

A Comedy in Three Acts

By Christopher Fry

CHRISTOPHER FRY, the British dramatist who writes in verse, had considerable impact on the New York theatre during the season 1951-1952. His "Venus Observed" won the Critics Circle award as the best foreign play of the season. This was his second Critics' prize, the first having been for "The Lady's Not for Burning" two years previously. Also, in 1951-1952, New York and many road cities saw his drama, "A Sleep of Prisoners," which had been commissioned as a religious work to be played in churches during the Festival of Britain. "Venus Observed" was commissioned by Sir Laurence Olivier. The jacket of the published version of the comedy states the case for the play and its author succinctly: "Christopher Fry, who now holds a unique place in the contemporary theatre and dramatic literature, has demonstrated that poetry preserves its force as a universal language—significant, important and immensely enjoyable—whether it is heard in the theatre or read for recreation or for study. Though Mr. Fry is a writer of plays with a serious metaphysical content, his invaluable achievement consists in the long-needed reinstatement of the comic spirit in English poetic drama." In the New York production of "Venus Observed," the comic spirit was nicely maintained by its stars, Rex Harrison and Lilli Palmer.

The Duke of Altair is handsome, suave, well-clad, getting on toward middle age, and wealthy. He is wealthy enough to inhabit and maintain a mansion and to follow an interesting and unusual hobby. When we first meet him he is in a room at the top of his mansion; this chamber once was a bedroom, but it has been reconstructed into a celestial observatory, and an imposing telescope pokes its long, thick barrel skyward through a slit in the observatory's revolving dome. Here, the Duke is found arguing with his son, Edgar, a good specimen of young English sporting blood. Also present is

* Copyright, 1941, by Christopher Fry. Published by Oxford University Press, New York and London. Author's agent, Leah Salisbury, 234 West 44th Street, New York City.

Herbert Reedbeck, a not-too-elderly fellow who is the Duke's agent—
the overseer and manager of the ducal properties.

DUKE

Anyone would think I had made some extraordinary
Suggestion. But in fact how natural it is.
Aren't you my son?

EDGAR

Yes, father, of course I am.

DUKE

Then it's up to you to choose who shall be your mother.
Does that seem to you improper, Reedbeck?

REEDBECK

No,
Your Grace; it's not, perhaps, always done,
But few parents consider their children as you do.
I don't dislike the plan at all.

EDGAR

I sweat

With embarrassment.

DUKE

You have been
Too much with the horses. This, that I ask you to do,
Is an act of poetry, and a compliment
To the freshness of your mind. Why should you sweat?
Here they will be, three handsome women,
All of them at some time implicated
In the joyous routine of my life. (I could scarcely
Put it more delicately.) I wish to marry.
Who am I, in heaven's name, to decide
Which were my vintage years of love?
Good God, to differentiate between
The first bright blow on my sleeping flesh,
The big breasts of mid-morning,
And the high old dance of afternoon—
Value one against the other? Never, not I,
Till the eschatological rain shall lay my dust.
But you, dear boy, with your twenty-five impartial years,
Can perform the judgment of Paris,
Can savor, consider, and award the apple

With a cool hand. You will find an apple
Over there by the spectroscope.

EDGAR
          But why must you marry?
Or, if that's an impertinence, why do I have to have
A mother? I've been able to grow to a sizable boy
Without one.

DUKE
      Why? Because I see no end
To the parceling out of heaven in small beauties,
Year after year, flocks of girls, who look
So lately kissed by God
They come out on the world with lips shining,
Flocks and generations, until time
Seems like nothing so much
As a blinding snowstorm of virginity,
And a man, lost in the perpetual scurry of white,
Can only close his eyes
In a resignation of monogamy.

EDGAR
Anyway, it would be an impossibly hasty
Judgment. Honor you as I may, I don't
See how I can do it.

DUKE
      If Paris had no trouble
Choosing between the tide-turning beauty,
Imponderable and sexed with eternity,
Of Aphrodite, Hera, and Athene,
Aren't you ashamed to make heavy weather of a choice
Between Hilda, and Rosabel, and Jessie?
And if you can't make up your mind about a woman
At first meeting, all hope of definition has gone;
Prejudice, delirium, or rage
Will cock their snooks, and the apple will go bad.
No, boy, no; go and water your horses
And come back and choose your mother.

EDGAR
          At what time?

DUKE

What is it now?

REEDBECK
Five past eleven.

DUKE
They should
Be here. At eleven twenty-nine we're to have
The total eclipse of the sun, to which I've invited them.
The mouth of the moon has already begun to munch.
We shall all feel ourselves making a north-west passage
Through the sea of heaven, and darkness will cover
The face of the earth. In that moment
All women will be as one.

EDGAR
That's what I was going
To ask you. I don't want to play the heavy son,
But would you say you loved these women equally?

DUKE
Equality is a mortuary word. Just choose.
Shall I be happy on Tuesdays, Thursdays, and Saturdays,
Or on Mondays, Wednesdays, and Fridays? Some such difference
Is all that your choice involves.

Another of the servants in Stellmere Park, which is the name of
the Duke's abode, has climbed four flights up to the observatory to
deliver a telegram to Reedbeck. This fellow, Captain Fox Reddleman, looks like a lion tamer—and it so happens he once was just
that, before he lost his nerve. The telegram incites great pleasure
in the Reedbeck breast; it reads, "Am in England hope to kiss you
before lunch Perpetua." It means, the agent explains to the Duke,
that his daughter is arriving—a daughter whom he has not seen
since ten years ago, when Mrs. Reedbeck left him for America. The
Duke cordially suggests that the girl join them in seeing the eclipse—
a change for her after America, he fancies. The Duke goes to dress
for the celestial phenomenon and the ensuing luncheon; his son has
left to change from riding clothes, and Reedbeck, alone in the observatory, uses the house telephone to ask the housekeeper to prepare
a room for his daughter.

Reedbeck's fatherly joy is dampened by the appearance of his son,
Dominic, a serious and studious young fellow who would have serious
but not studious words with his father. Dominic accepts the news of
his sister's impending arrival in silence. "Oh, dear," his father sighs,

"it's one of your knock-the-bottom-out-of-everything mornings." And indeed it is. "Why," the young man asks, "are we so rich? You, a Duke's bailiff, an agent: where did our money come from?" Reedbeck vaguely mentions an Uncle Hector who passed on in Tasmania, and a former employer, Lady Bright, who passed on herself to heaven and the rest to Reedbeck; but Dominic wants solider facts and some figures. When his father squirms and equivocates he accuses, "You've stolen the money, haven't you?" He mentions raising rents and pocketing the difference, and selling produce and timber at prices higher than his books have recorded. Dominic seems sure of his facts, for Bates, the footman, has been throwing out hints.

"Come now," argues Reedbeck; "Bates is a common burglar and sees, of course, his reflection in all about him. He was caught redhanded with the silver and his Grace, being short of staff at the time, asked him to stay and clean it." Dominic stands up for Bates as quite a decent fellow who used to suffer from a pathological lust for climbing ladders and had to rationalize it when he got to the top. The young man assures his father that Bates is now determined to be honest—and he, Dominic, now feels that he can no longer stay at Cambridge when any morning he might wake up and find himself the son of a convict.

Bates, showing signs of a recent punch in the nose from Captain Reedbeck, appears and announces the presence of one of the guests, Rosabel Fleming, an actress. Reedbeck introduces himself and his son, but Dominic says he can't look anyone happily in the eye and excuses himself. His father explains to Miss Fleming, "The paradoxes of virtue have confused him." Soon there appears another of the guests, Mrs. Jessie Dill, who has come up by herself. Both she and Miss Fleming give the impression that they have been in the room before, but not since it became an observatory. Reedbeck explains, "This was one of his Grace's bedrooms, as perhaps . . . But now, as you see, he prefers to regard the skies here, scavenging through the night for knowledge. He also uses the room for experiments."

"He always did," adds Jessie Dill.

The Duke, handsomely turned out, comes in to greet his guests; Jessie says he doesn't look a day older, but he turns aside this flattery, saying, "I have to consider my years and decline with the sun." Edgar appears and is introduced to the two women. "I've known your father," says Jessie pleasantly, "ever since I was ever so slim. Though, of course, properly speaking, it was my husband who was really his friend." Reedbeck, by the window, sings to himself, for his daughter is coming home; and when Bates appears to announce another guest the overseer starts happily, thinking it may be Perpetua. But the newcomer is a Mrs. Taylor-Snell, first name, Hilda. "A party, Hereward?" she inquires doubtfully of the Duke. It is obvious that each of the three women has been thinking that she alone had been invited.

Reedbeck, who has been hanging far out the window hoping for a sight of his daughter, pulls back in and hands Mrs. Dill a piece of darkened glass, suggesting that she have a look at the sun; by now, the moon has half obscured it. He passes the glass also to Miss Fleming, who appears to be emotionally overwrought and not much interested in celestial phenomena. At this moment Edgar announces, "Father, I'm going to make the decision now and pin the future down for you." To Miss Fleming the young man declares, "Before you go to the window, I wonder if you'd mind accepting this apple?"

Unaware of the significance of this offer, Rosabel declines it politely; she must go and see what's to be seen at the window before it is too late. The Duke's son presses the fruit upon her and calls his father's attention to the deed—but the Duke seems to have missed it and is making a disquisition on the eclipse. Edgar takes another piece of fruit from a bowl and exclaims, pointedly, "Father, for God's sake, look! I am giving Miss Fleming an apple." The father acknowledges, disinterestedly, that he has seen his son plying the lady with fruit—but now they should turn their attention again to the sun.

EDGAR

So a revolutionary change begins
Without raising a hand's turn of the dust.
Ah, well; give me some dark glass.

HILDA
What a shame

If that cloud spoils the climax for us.

REEDBECK
No,

It avoids, you see; it glides mercifully
And dexterously past. I hope and pray
The same will be true of the cloud that hangs over my own
Sunshine: but young men can be so ruthless,
So ruthless; it's terrible to think about.

DUKE

What now, Reedbeck?

REEDBECK
                    Ah, yes; to the cosmos it doesn't
Matter; I suppose I agree.

JESSIE
                    To think
We're in the shadow of old Lunabella.

DUKE
                                        To think
JESSIE
When she moves over will she see us
Coming out of her shadow? Are we really
As bright as a moon, from the moon's side of the question?

DUKE
We have a borrowed brilliance. At night
Among the knots and clusters and corner boys
Of the sky, among asteroids and cepheids,
With Sirius, Mercury, and Canis Major,
Among nebulae and magellanic cloud,
You shine, Jessie.

JESSIE
                    You're making me self-conscious.

DUKE
Here we're as dull as unwashed plates; out there
We shine. That's a consideration. Come
Close to paradise, and where's the luster?
But still, at some remove, we shine, and truth
We hope is content to keep a distant prospect.
So you, Jessie, and the swamps of the equator,
Shine; the boring overplus of ocean,
The Walworth Road, the Parthenon, and Reedbeck
Shine; the dark tree with the nightingale
At heart, dockyards, the desert, the newly dead,
Minarets, gasometers, and even I
Fall into space in one not unattractive
Beam. To take us separately is to stare
At mud; only together, at long range,
We coalesce in light.

JESSIE

I like to think I'm being
A ray of light to some nice young couple out there.
"There's the Great Bear," they'd say, and "Look,
There's old Jessie, tilted on her side
Just over the Charing Cross Hotel."

HILDA

You both
Chatter so. It's a moment for quiet. Who knows
If ever I'll see this again.

EDGAR

The end of our lord
The sun.

ROSABEL

It's no good. I must get out into the air!
It's impossible to breathe up here!

DUKE

What is it,
Rosabel? Claustrophobia on the brink
Of the free heavens? Come now, think of it
As the usual dipping of day's flag. You used
To love this room at night.

ROSABEL

How do you know?
How can you tell who loves, or when or why they love,
You without a single beat of heart
Worth measuring? You sit up here all night
Looking at the stars, traveling farther and farther
Away from living people. I hate your telescope!
How can you know, and what, if you knew, can it mean,
What can the darkest bruise on the human mind
Mean, when nothing beats against you heavier
Than a fall of rain? And out you whip
Your impervious umbrella of satisfaction!
How you prink across every puddle, and laugh
To think that other men can drown.
You would never believe there are some affections
Which would rather have decent burial

Than this mocking perpetuation you offer them.
You're a devil, a devil, a devil, a devil!

DUKE
Only
On one side of the family, Rosabel,
Please believe that.

EDGAR
(*Taking the apple from her hand*)
I beg your pardon; I think
I've made a mistake.

ROSABEL
Now I must go.   I've spoilt
The eclipse.   For that I'm sorry.

DUKE
It's frankly impossible
To spoil the eclipse.

Miss Fleming is weeping.   Hilda chides the Duke, "I must say, Hereward, you certainly seem to have been coruscating on thin ice." Jessie Dill, plump, imperturbable and good-natured, remains undisturbed.   To Hilda's scolding the Duke answers:

"I've behaved according to my lights of love
Which were excellent and bright and much to be
Remembered.   You have all of you been my moments
Of revelation.   I wish I understood why
You want to behave like skeletons in my cupboard."

Mrs. Dill interjects, "Not Jessie, alas; her weight is all against it."
Edgar makes another decision—a second choice: "I'd like it, Father, if Mrs. Dill would have this apple."
Somehow, the Duke is not as interested as he had planned to be; he feels that all he has got himself into is an embarrassment.   He declares, "I shall plow up the orchard, Edgar; it was never a great success."
The eclipse has become total, and now, just as the moon traverses the sun's face and the murky room becomes lighter, there stands in the doorway Reedbeck's daughter, Perpetua, a girl of vivid beauty and quick intelligence.   Father and daughter run toward each other and embrace just as the emotional Rosabel stumbles out of the room and is followed by Hilda Taylor-Snell, who is worried about her and

wants to help if she can. Proudly Reedbeck introduces Perpetua to
his Grace, the Duke of Altair. Perpetua, pleasant and graceful, comments, "I've spent four days on a wicked October sea. . . . I'd
scarcely expected quite so much impenetrable murk in the middle of
morning. Surely there must be something out of sorts about your
daylight?"

"Nothing time won't mend," replies the gallant Duke. He turns
to introduce Hilda and Rosabel and sees that they have gone, so he
introduces Jessie Dill and then his son, Edgar. Perpetua is happy;
"I'm really out of prison," she declares. With a start, her father
asks, "Of prison, my darling?"

The girl catches herself nicely and answers, "I mean, of course, the
boat was a prison and the frowning sea was Dartmoor." The Duke
offers the newcomer refreshments—wine, perhaps, or cider, or bis-
cuits . . . and a view of "our English sun, convalescent after passing through the valley of the shadow of the moon." Perpetua thus
at last realizes there has been an eclipse. Edgar, unusually attentive,
offers the girl something to drink, but she will have none at the moment. Her father, enormously happy, thinks there may be a catch
to his happiness; is Perpetua ill, perhaps, and come home for her
health? "I've come home to be home," she answers simply.

"And so you emerged," the breathless Edgar adds, "like Venus
from the sea." His father interrupts the young man's ecstasy by
commanding, pointedly, "I should like you to offer Miss Reedbeck
an apple, Edgar."

Edgar declines, saying he will offer anything but an apple—a
peach, a pineapple, a pear, an orange, an apricot . . .

"Then," says the Duke, "as Paris abdicates, I must offer the sweet
round robin fruit myself." He holds an apple up between his fingers
and begins a fine poetic address to it—but his apostrophe is most
surprisingly punctuated by a pistol shot and the apple vanishes from
his hands. Perpetua has whipped a very small firearm from a pigskin
holster at her belt and with one dead shot has shattered the piece of
fruit. Then she says, "That was thoughtless of me. Perhaps you
wanted to eat it."

The Duke's nerves are good; he says there are more apples, and
he is glad she let him keep his fingers. Her father exclaims, "You
might have been the death of him!" "No," Perpetua assures Reedbeck, "it was quite safe. To please, I always aim." Having heard
the shot, Rosabel and Hilda hurry back into the room and are reas-
sured when the Duke tells them that only an apple has come to grief.
Perpetua feels it is time she should make a confession, and her distracted father demands what it might be.

PERPETUA

I've lately been in prison. But not
For what we should call a crime.

REEDBECK

They put you in prison
Without rhyme or reason?

PERPETUA

There may have been
A little rhyme. I was thought to be unsafe
For democracy, because I broke, or shot,
Or burnt, a good many things, or rather—and this
Is the reason—a bad many things: the unsightly,
The gimcrack, the tedious, the hideous, the spurious,
The harmful. Not I alone, of course;
We were all students, and called ourselves
The Society for the Desecration
Of Ancient and Modern Monumental Errors.
We destroyed, or tried to destroy, whatever we loathed
As bad.

ROSABEL

Whatever you loathed, you destroyed?
Why, that was admirable, superb, the most
Heavenly daring!

PERPETUA

No, I think it was only
Exasperation. And then we went to prison.
And there I knew it was all no use.
The more we destroyed, the worse the bad sprang up.
And I thought and thought, What can I do for the world?
I was wearing the prison drab. My name was a number.
Inside or outside the prison, Perpetua
(I thought), you're no one, you're everybody's color.
You must make good, before you break the bad,
Perpetua. And so I came home to England
Simply to trace myself, in my own way.
(*She offers the pistol to the* DUKE.)
I'd better surrender this. I only kept it
For a kind of memento. And I apologize
Again for destroying the apple. Still half at sea
As I am, it appeared to be, in a misty way,
Like a threat to my new-come freedom.

DUKE

I hope you will think so again, some other time.

ROSABEL
(*Taking the pistol*)
May I have it, to remind me of your story,
To know there has been someone in the world
Who dared to do such things! If only I
Could be such a brave one, there might be
Some justification for me.

DUKE
(*Taking it from her*)
Caps for you,
Dear Rosabel, not bullets. I'll have it
Filled for your next big scene.
(*A gong booms from below.*)

EDGAR

Luncheon! Can we be supposed to eat
On a day when the sun is drowned by the moon,
And apples meet such a strange end?

DUKE

I see nothing strange. If we can move and talk
Under the sun at all, we must have accepted
The incredible as commonplace, long ago;
And even the incredible must eat.
Shall we go down?

The curtain falls.

ACT II

The vast grounds of Stellmere Park include a large, ancient, stone-columned outdoor edifice beside the ducal lake, called the Temple of the Ancient Virtues, and here, in the afternoon, the studious Dominic and the attractive Perpetua are conversing. Brother has told sister of their father's peculations, but it has been no shock to the girl. What seems to concern her is whether her father would be happy in prison. Dominic explodes, "He wouldn't, but what difference does that make? Would you be able to look anyone in the face, with a father jailed?"

"Oh, yes, if he were comfortable. But I think he might feel shut in. . . . If someone has to go to prison, I must." Then Perpetua explains to her puzzled brother that he, himself, has just now suggested that she make herself agreeable to the Duke, who seems to be inclined toward matrimony. No gentleman, surely, would try to incriminate his own father-in-law—so Perpetua has made up her mind. She tells her brother, "I see my carefree hours already numbered. . . . I'm no longer a woman after my own heart." She doesn't like it, but for their father's sake she will try. Dominic breathes a relieved, "God bless you, then." He adds, "A coronet's no martyrdom, particularly when it sits on a man whom women find easy to like." Looking about her, Perpetua wonders how many women have stood perplexed in this temple during the last two centuries.

Their father, out of wind from running after a hat blown off by the wind and now floating in the lake, approaches. Worried, he asks Perpetua if Dominic has been talking to her and the daughter says she has been hearing unimaginable things about Reedbeck. "Tell me why you've been cheating the Duke," she commands blandly. The old man protests that he has not been exactly cheating, and his daughter suggests, "Suppose I put it this way: What made you supercherify with chousery the Duke?"

Reedbeck is an interesting man, and not an unintelligent one. He tells his daughter that the banquet of civilization is over; dignity has dropped upon all fours, and someone must be found to keep alive the quality of living which separates us from the brutes. Reedbeck has simply proposed to himself that it should be himself who must keep alive this quality of living. He, for instance, cares so much for the patrician charm and nobility of civilization, whereas the Duke cares so little. His daughter suggests, "Perhaps if you had gone to the Duke and explained all this, he would have eased the path. . . ."

Dominic warns that the Duke is approaching. "Be cheerful if you can," he begs his sister, and she answers that her smile will be like the glint of handcuffs. The Duke is jovial and he is carrying a bow and quiver of arrows; ceremoniously he asks Reedbeck if his little girl may come out and play.

PERPETUA

I've never handled a bow.
How shall I manage?

DUKE

Beautifully.
The light will hang fire to see you; you might
Even hear the flash of the foliage

Where Artemis parts the leaves to patronize
And praise you; but take no notice, and watch what you're doing,
And do what I tell you.

PERPETUA
Implicitly.

DUKE
Take notice
Of the excellent marksmanship of the year, whose arrow
Singing from the April bow crossed over the width
Of Summer straight for the gold, where now, if you look,
You will see it quivering.

PERPETUA
The year has a world of experience.
But still, show me; and I'll try not to shame the shades
Of all the arching duchesses and ladies
Who played on these lawns before.

DUKE
They'll arch the more,
Adoring what you do, feathering their shafts
And shooting until doomsday's Parthian shot.
Be confident; and, if you miss,
The fashion of the game will be to miss,
Until you change your mind and hit.
(*He begins to instruct her in the use of the bow, holding it with her,
and speaking low into her ear, so that* REEDBECK *and* DOMINIC *cannot hear.*)
And then, Perpetua, tonight
If a clear sky inclines you to it, and the heavens
Remain suspended, how would it be
If we trained the telescope on the infinite
And made what we could of what we could see of it?
Are you still as interested as you were
This morning?

PERPETUA
Yes. I come from a city. The stars
Are new to me.

DUKE
They shall answer you
By numbers. But we'll not tell the world

What we mean to do. There's a little tension today
Already, nerves perhaps not ready to accept
The quiet session of scientific study
You and I propose. So let's be as mute
As we're mutable, and avoid misapprehension.

PERPETUA

I—if so—if so—yes, very well.

DUKE

You can tell the world you need a long night of sleep.

PERPETUA

Yes, yes, I can. But here's the good afternoon light
Fading to waste unless we make use of it.

DUKE

I know that thought so well. Come on, then,
Let the trial begin.

PERPETUA

Watch me, Poppadillo.
Come and judge what a huntress I should make,
What a rival for Artemis, and what chance Actaeon
Would have if I pursued him.

The assignation has been agreed upon, and Perpetua and the Duke
stroll off for their game of archery, leaving father and son alone.
"What did you say to her?" demands the father. "I simply told her
you were crooked," says the son. But, Dominic adds, he has suggested that Perpetua can save her father by marrying the Duke.
Instead of being relieved, Reedbeck is angry that Dominic thus considers selling his sister. He shakes his son in a burst of rage, calling
him "a vain, vexing, incomprehensible, crimping, constipated duffer—
a spigoted, bigoted, operculated pig."

Upon this scene the placid Jessie Dill wanders, carrying writing
materials and intending to write a letter in the repose of the Temple
of the Ancient Virtues. Ignoring the scuffle prettily, she asks, "Am
I in the way?" Dominic, who has been thrown to the ground by his
father's shaking, scuttles off, and Jessie observes, "It was lovely exercise for both of you." Jessie settles down to write a letter to her
eighty-seven-year-old father, to whom she drops a few lines every
day even though he cannot read her handwriting, and Reedbeck departs.

Hilda Taylor-Snell saunters beneath the shade of the temple roof. She has seen the Duke and Perpetua at their game of archery and now she interrupts the letter-writing by commenting, "I see Hereward has made another backward flight into his heyday." Hilda is seeking Jessie's confidence and understanding. "Why did I come here today," she asks, "and what did I expect? And why did he ever invite us here together?" Matter-of-factly, Jessie answers that, for herself, she likes being here so much that she never even wondered.

HILDA

When I first met him, I remember, he seemed
At once to give my spirits a holiday,
Though (like a first holiday abroad) almost too unlike
The daily round of the roundabout life I led—
And lead still, O my heavens—which had, and has,
All the appearance of movement without covering
Any ground whatsoever. I know I have
No particular heights or depths myself;
No one who thought me ordinary or dull
Would be far wrong. But even I despair
For Roderic, my husband, who really is
The height of depth, if it doesn't sound unkind
To say so: not deep depth, but a level depth
Of dullness. Once he had worn away the sheen
Of his quite becoming boyhood, which made me fancy him,
There was nothing to be seen in Roderic
For mile after mile after mile, except
A few sheeplike thoughts nibbling through the pages
Of a shiny weekly, any number of dead pheasants,
Partridges, pigeons, jays, and hares,
An occasional signpost of extreme prejudice
Marked "No thoroughfare," and the flat horizon
Which is not so much an horizon
As a straight ruled line beyond which one doesn't look.

JESSIE

Keep him warm and fed. They bloom
Once in seven years.

HILDA

Not Roderic.
(*Enter* EDGAR, *carrying a bow and quiver.*)

EDGAR

Are either of you ladies any good
At taking out a thorn? I took a look
In a mirror for some reason or other, and there it was.
A bramble slashed me when I was out riding yesterday.
I've brought my own needle.

HILDA
Am I hurting you?

EDGAR

Yes, but how nice of you. Isn't it strange?
For the first time in my young life
I'm jealous of my father. I thought I'd better
Mention it before I begin to brood.

HILDA

Jealous of him, why?

EDGAR
To me he's a man
Once and for all; once, once only,
And certainly for all. And any man
Who has to follow him (me, for instance)
Feels like the lag-last in a cloud of locusts:
By the time I come to a tree it's as bare
As a hat stand. Talent, conversation, wit,
Ease, and friendliness are all swallowed up
In advance. And just at present
I feel depressed about it.

HILDA
Now, take heart.
You have those virtues, too. There's room for both of you.

EDGAR

Not, I think, at the moment.

JESSIE
Do you mean
Only two can play at bows and arrows?

The ex-burglar servant, Bates, comes looking for Hilda Taylor-
Snell; he has an important telephone message to give her. There

has been a bit of an accident, the message goes, and they'd be glad
if she could make it convenient to find her way back home. Alarmed,
Hilda cries, "Roderic!" Bates soothes her with further information:
her old man has got hisself throwed off his horse, but it may be only
a front toof a bit loose. Edgar offers to take Hilda to her car, but
she prefers slipping off alone. "If you want to do something for me,"
she tells Edgar, "put your shoulders to your father and make yourself your own success."

Bates, talkative, observes to Jessie that he likes Mrs. Taylor-Snell
very much, but the other one, Miss Fleming, is another matter.
"What's she doing snooping about the east wing all the afternoon?
I tell you, Miss, I knows an undesirable character when I see one;
I've been one myself for years." Finally Bates wanders away and
Edgar stands looking in the distance. "I wonder if I should," he
says, as if to himself.

"If you should what?" asks Jessie.

"From here I think I could send an arrow right past him into the
target." Edgar takes an arrow from his quiver, fits it in his bow,
and shoots. There is a distant cry of remonstrance from the Duke,
and a cry of exultation from Edgar. He jolly near hit his father, but
he did manage to hit the target which the Duke and Perpetua have
been aiming at. The Duke steams in, indignant, demanding, "Did
I beget you to be shot from behind? . . . I had quite supposed the
contest was between Miss Reedbeck and me." Edgar puts in, pointedly, "When all the time it was really between you and your loving
son. . . . You've had a long innings, and a Summer of splendid
outings, and now I must ask you, father, not to monopolize every
heart in the world any longer." Jessie goes placidly on with her
letter, as father and son continue their verbal bout. Edgar pleads
with his father to desist from his attentions to Perpetua, but the
Duke smilingly declines. "The field is still open," he says.

Perpetua, now a little bored with outdoor sport, strolls to the
Temple. Edgar boldly seizes the opportunity and asks her if she
will go with him tonight to a dance at Mordernbury. It's All Hal-
lowe'en, he reminds her, temptingly. Perpetua would like to go, but
she dissembles; after four days at sea and such a homecoming she
is ready to rest and has promised herself she will sleep early. She
suggests, instead, that Edgar take her now to see the stables, and the
young man glumly does so.

For a moment the Duke and Jessie are left alone, but Jessie is
absorbed by the writing of a long letter to her father. After a while
Rosabel Fleming wanders back to the Temple, and the Duke suggests that she join him and perhaps Jessie and follow Edgar and the

girl to the stables. Rosabel says vaguely that she may follow and makes a sharp inquiry: "When do you mean to show her how to observe the stars through your telescope? Is it tonight? . . . I hate your telescope!" The Duke says he is going to bed early and steps off in pursuit of his son; Rosabel, forgetting that the quiet Jessie is still there, remarks aloud to herself, "So no one at all will be there. Now I know why all day long life has been tilting and driving me towards tonight. . . . He hurts whomever he touches. He has to be touched by fire to make a human of him, and only a woman who loves him can dare to do it."

JESSIE
Listen, love,
You'll be sending yourself silly. I always think
When someone knocks you down, it doesn't improve things
To knock yourself up. The way a thing is, is often
The way you happen to look at it. He's as kind
As anybody living, if you take a running jump.
And if you only had a stamp we could go together
And put this in the box.

ROSABEL
I'm over-run
By the most curious thoughts. I believe I was kept
From quite succeeding in anything I set
My heart on, so that now I should give all
My heart to this, tonight. The girl Perpetua
Has the courage that makes a person come true.
Did you hear her say how she went to war on things
She hated? I think she came to show me
What it is I have to do; indeed, I can't do less!
And nothing less will do to open his eyes
On to the distances that separate him
From other people.

JESSIE
Look at me: I've put Cumberland
When I mean Northants.

ROSABEL
Tonight, no one is there.
You'll see, I shall send his Observatory
Where Nero's Rome has gone; I'll blaze a trail
That he can follow towards humanity!

JESSIE

Now I wonder who's the most likely person to have a stamp?

The curtain falls.

SCENE II

It is night in the Observatory Room; in the dark the Duke lies on a day-bed, and Perpetua enters, standing uncertain. He speaks from the dark, "Does anyone know you're here?"
"No one."

He lights an oil lamp, and Perpetua, looking about the room, asks, "What happiness do you get up here with your telescope?"
"You came to see my stars. I have them here." He leads her to the eyepiece of the machine and tells her they are now trained on Senator Saturn, "white-hot with gravity. His moon, out of love for his gray steel brow, streamed away her life into a circle of tormented arms. You see them there, you see how they circle and never touch. Saturn is alone, for all their circling round him." But Perpetua would rather hear about him, and not the loves of Saturn. The Duke tells fleetingly of a wife. "Death," he relates, "chose to interrupt us while we were still careening together high above the spires of common sense."

"With your mind so full of inquiry, I'm surprised you've had any time for love."

DUKE

It takes no time.
It's on us while we walk, or in mid-sentence,
A sudden hoarseness, enough to choke the sense.
Now isn't that so?

PERPETUA

Not so with me.

DUKE

You must try
To use longer sentences. Then you would certainly feel
The fumbling in the quiver behind every syllable
And so to the arrow string, like a sudden
Swerving parenthesis.

PERPETUA

Do you think I should?

DUKE

No doubt of it.

PERPETUA

There isn't any reason
Why a sentence, I suppose, once it begins,
Once it has risen to the lips at all
And finds itself happily wandering
Through shady vowels and over consonants
Where ink's been spilt like rivers or like blood
Flowing for the cause of some half-truth
Or a dogma now outmoded, shouldn't go
Endlessly moving in grave periphrasis
And phrase in linking phrase, with commas falling
As airily as lime flowers, intermittently,
Uninterrupting, scarcely troubling
The mild and fragile progress of the sense
Which trills trebling like a pebbled stream
Or lowers towards an oath-intoning ocean
Or with a careless and forgetful music
Looping and threading, tuning and entwining,
Flings a babel of bells, a caroling
Of such various vowels the ear can almost feel
The soul of sound when it lay in chaos yearning
For the tongue to be created: such a hymn
If not as lovely, then as interminable,
As restless, and as heartless, as the hymn
Which in the tower of heaven the muted spheres
With every rippling harp and windy horn
Played for incidental harmony
Over the moldering rafters of the world,
Rafters which seldom care to ring, preferring
The functional death-watch beetle, stark, staccato,
Economical as a knuckle bone,
Strict, correct, but undelighting
Like a cleric jigging in the saturnalia,
The saturnalia we all must keep,
Green-growing and rash with life,
Our milchy, mortal, auroral, jovial,
Harsh, unedifying world,
Where every circle of grass can show a dragon
And every pool's as populous as Penge,
Where birds, with taffeta flying, scarf the air
On autumn evenings, and a sentence once
Begun goes on and on, there being no reason
To draw to any conclusion so long as breath

Shall last, except that breath
Can't last much longer.

DUKE

Now point me out the comma

Where you loved me.

PERPETUA

Not at any.

When she has caught her breath, the girl asks, "Why are you so
sure that I must love you?"

"Do you know what night this is? . . . All-Hallows Eve. . . .
Tonight the gravity of mirrors is so potent it can draw the future
into the glass, and show shadows of husbands to girls who sit and
comb their hair." He suggests, "Suppose you try it." Perpetua goes
to an antique mirror on an antique table and sits before it, looking.
The Duke quietly follows her across the room and stands behind her,
until his reflection is caught and she sees it. She stares into the
mirror, then turns to the Duke and says, "It seemed to be your son."

The Duke begs, "Am I, before God, too old? Consider the rocks
of Arizona, and then consider me. . . . Don't deliver me up to my
gray hairs."

The girl laughs, "It's rather that I wonder whether you're not
almost too young to be lived with." Then, with meaning, she asks,
"Do you know anything against my father?"

"In my heart, nothing. . . . No doubt he'll have to stand in a
corner of heaven with his face to a jasper wall, but here let him
thrive."

"So," says the knowing Perpetua, "this is how you know I shall
marry you."

"This is how."

The girl tells the Duke he has been mistaken; she is not going to
marry him, and she was glad when Edgar's reflection appeared in
the mirror. He sighs, "I seem to have come to the end of myself
sooner than I expected."

"Show me one more star and I must go."

"I think they're falling."

"When they fall," the girl inquires, "do they scorch the air in
passing? Is that what I can smell? . . . Something *is* on fire. I can
hear the flames crunching on wood." She runs to the window and
sees flickering light on the garden. "Look!" she exclaims. "It's the
house, this wing of the house is on fire!" The Duke hastens to the
door, flings it open and is flung back by the heat of a blaze which
has engulfed the stairway. Perpetua looks out the window, and sees

how far it is to the ground. The Duke tries to pick her up and make a dash for the burning stair, but she thrusts him away, saying, "I'd rather jump to the garden, and die fair and broken. I'll make my own death as it suits me."

The Duke remains unruffled; on the telephone he makes a call: "A fire at Stellmere Park. Two people trapped; neither anxious to die. I suggest you should make remarkable speed." After such a display of aplomb, the least the terrified Perpetua can do is kiss him when he asks her to. She has just about reconciled herself to a blazing death when Captain Reddleman bursts in from the doorway, quite unaccountably. "I thumbed a lift on the rising heat," he explains. "Didn't God make sinners of you and trap you here for the decent purpose of putting me back in the way of salvation?"

The rescue the old lion-tamer proposes is a little too daring for his clients: He will jump down to a stair landing and they will jump into his arms, and thus, by dropping from time to time, they will reach bottom. There seems to be no alternative, however—until the surly face of Bates appears at the window. Bates is on a ladder. He urges Perpetua to come on out and take a look at the panorama. Reddleman, roaring jealous of such competition, howls, "He spoils me night of glory. Send him about his business, if you love me, your Grace." Bates and Reddleman engage in a debate over the various merits of jumping and leaving by ladder. Bates wins; Perpetua puts herself in his arms and is taken below, and the Duke crosses the window threshold and follows. Reddleman races to the window and bellows out, "H'wot do you think the dear God gave me back me nerve for? To come crawling after heathen like spittle down a window? B'Jason, I've a better opinion of meself." In a great burst of courage he dashes across the room, throws open the door, meets the glare of fire—and jumps.

In an instant the Duke climbs back in the window, races across the room to the door and yells, "Reddleman, you hell-raking maniac! Who would have the heart to disappoint you?" The Duke jumps after Reddleman.

The curtain falls.

ACT III

An hour or so later the light from the burning house is pleasantly reflected in the ducal lake, and in the Temple of the Ancient Virtues Rosabel crouches, sobbing in the dark. Dominic appears, carrying two chairs and a table lantern, and stops when he hears the sobbing. "May I," he asks politely, "interrupt your unhappiness just to bring in one or two things? It's begun to rain. Everyone is safe, you know; they're all accounted for, except Miss Fleming. Do you know where she is?"

"No," sobs Miss Fleming. "No one must ever see her again. . . . I'm here. I wish I were dead. . . . It was I who started the fire. I did it deliberately. . . . Oh, what shall I do?"

Dominic makes a sound suggestion: "There's Sergeant Harry Bullen, the policeman. He's a very reasonable chap; I'm sure he'd arrest you willingly if you went and asked him." Rosabel, in enjoyable despair, determines, "I'll find him, and give myself up. Yes, out of this ditch of despair. No one need think of me again. . . . But, please God, help me avoid the Duke."

Rosabel's last plea is too late, for at this moment the Duke arrives, heavily laden with things salvaged from the fire and with a string of Chinese lanterns over his shoulder. He has heard some of what Rosabel has said, but affects not to have; casually he asks her to hold some of the lanterns while he hangs the rest. Dominic leaves, but before leaving urges the woman, "You must tell him now." Bravely, Rosabel declares to the Duke, "I started the fire," and he makes a joking rejoinder about a careless flash from her incendiary eyes. "You must believe me," she insists. "I fired the wing, to destroy the observatory, to make you human. . . . But I didn't know you were there; believe me, I didn't know any living soul was there!"

DUKE

O,

O, O, O, Rosabel:
If you had only asked me first.
I could have told you no fire would be enough
To burn down heaven, and while it's there
I shall find some wide-eyed place where I can sit
And scrutinize the inscrutable, amazed
That we can live in such a condition of mystery
And not be exasperated out of our flesh,
As we might be, were it not that flesh
Is interesting, too.
Your fire was too small, Rosabel, though enough
To singe my butler into ecstasy,
And smoke tears into eyes unaccustomed to them,
Mine, I mean. So much I delighted in
Is now all of ash, like a dove's breast feathers
Drifting dismally about the garden.

ROSABEL

Time and I both know how to bring
Good things to a bad end, all
In the course of love. No wonder
"God be with you" has become "Good-by,"
And every day that wishes our welfare says
Farewell. Tonight will go past, as a swan
Will pass like a recurring dream
On the light sleep of the lake,
And I shall be smoothed away in the wake of the swan;
But I can never return what I've lost you, or lose
What I gave, though the long steadiness of time
May long to make us well.

DUKE

So much I delighted in is all of ash.
(ROSABEL, *giving a moan almost too low to hear, goes out. Her
place is taken by* PERPETUA, *but the* DUKE, *now hanging the lanterns,
hasn't seen the change.*)
But the lost world of walls and stairs,
Where I could cosset ghosts for their melancholy
Charm, has let the daylight into me
With a straight left of love. So no remorse,
Rosabel. I love my love, and my love loves me.
Everything goes but everything comes.
We fall away into a future, and all
The seven seas, and the milky way
And morning, and evening, and hi-cockalorum are in it.
Nothing is with the past except the past.
So you can make merry with the world, Rosabel.
My grateful thanks.

PERPETUA

I have to make you understand.

DUKE

                    I forgive you:
You can mine the lake so that it bursts
In a hundred and one torrential rainbows
Over the roof of the Carpenters' Arms; you can shatter
Conservatories into a deluge of crystal,
And shoot the cowman's nine insufferable
Children: I forgive you in advance.
I've achieved the rare, benevolent place

Where the irk of the lonely human state
Is quite unknown, and the fumbling fury
We call our life— It wasn't Rosabel
Who spoke then. It was surely Perpetua?

PERPETUA
I have to make you understand. You must
Be patient with me.

DUKE
God so, it's the little firebird.
Are you rested? Lanterns, you see, to light our love.
I thought we could sit by the cinders
And toast our hearts, if Bates, as he was told to,
Brings the champagne.

The girl still is pleading for the Duke's attention, with no success,
when Bates arrives with champagne and glasses in a basket. Bates
also is carrying another lantern and a grudge—a grudge against
Captain Reddleman, who has taken the edge off his rescue work in
the fire with his going "in and out, in and out, in and out of the
burning building." The Duke, busy hanging Chinese lanterns about
the Temple of the Ancient Virtues, and lighting them, pays no heed
to Bates and none either to Perpetua, who still is pleading, "Let me
talk to you."

It appears that *everybody* wants to talk to the Duke. Captain
Reddleman, having lugged a table on the top of his head to the
Temple, fumes about the smallness of soul of the footman Bates—
a demi-semi soul, he says. The Duke advises the two to straighten
their laurel wreaths and remember one another in their prayers; at
the moment he has something else to listen to. But before he can
do any listening, Reedbeck and his son Dominic arrive, and Reedbeck is in an almost religious mood for confession. "I must tell
you plainly," he advises the slightly interested Duke, "I'm not all
what you thought me." Reedbeck hints that he would like to be
alone with his employer, and Reddleman and Bates remove themselves—but Perpetua and Dominic still remain. The girl has a prior
claim on the Duke's attention and begs her father, "Darling, not now.
. . . Just this night, and for just these five minutes of this night,
leave me to talk to him alone."

Perpetua's father will not be put off; being driven more by his son
Dominic than by his conscience, he is impelled to deliver a confession to the Duke. Perpetua tries to quiet her father, saying "He
knows, he knows," but Reedbeck won't stop, even when the Duke

offers champagne. "It wouldn't be correct," the agent says in accents of heavy guilt, "to drink with you before I give myself up to Sergeant Bullen."

The Duke urges, "Drink up"—and then, to Dominic, he declares, "If what appear to be discrepancies in your father's books afflict you, let me tell you though they seem unusual they're as much in order as Sergeant Bullen's collar and tie. There exists a document assigning to your father all those percentages from rents and sales which you seem to have thought are misbegotten." Dominic cannot quite believe this, nor can his father, who asks incredulously, "Made it legal?"

DUKE

There now. Shall we drink
To the babe born in the fire, the crowning of souls
In extremity? As long as we live, Perpetua,
We shall be able to tell how, at midnight,
We skated over death's high-lit ebony
And heard the dark ring a change of light,
While everywhere else the clocks
Were sounding the depths of a dark, unhappy end.
And then we shall be able to say
How an autumn duke—

PERPETUA

—found that fear could seem
Like love to a silly girl, who now knows
It was fear and not love, wishes you to forgive her,
Wishes she could sink away with the night
Where she won't any more trouble you.

DUKE

(*After a long pause, raising his glass*)
Then the toast is: Fear.

PERPETUA

I had to tell you.

In silence they all drink, and then the Duke says to Perpetua, "Do you think I can't forgive you? I forgive both of us for being born of the flesh. . . . I forgive everything, my most dear Perpetua, except that I wasn't born something less ambitious, such as a Muscovy duck."

Reedbeck, with guilt and confession still heavy upon him, protests irrelevantly that he could not think of accepting his Grace's generosity in legalizing the thefts from the estate; but nobody is listening, and weighing still more heavily on the old man is fatigue. Drooping, he mumbles to his daughter and the Duke, "You're both talking in my sleep, evidently."

Edgar, Jessie and Hilda appear in belated excitement. "We saw the fire on the clouds," says Edgar, "and guessed it could only be here." "I saw it from home," adds Hilda. "I tried to telephone but I couldn't get through." To Hilda's query if everybody is safe, the Duke gives an affirmative answer; he tells about the fire in the observatory and how Perpetua and he were rescued by Bates and Reddleman. "God bless them," the sleepy Reedbeck cheers; "I've never liked either of them, but God bless them."

Not so thankful or full of blessing is the Duke's son, Edgar, who accuses, "And so you meant to meet there, even this afternoon." The Duke adroitly changes the subject by asking Hilda how her injured husband is. Cheerfully she reports, "Two ribs broken, and a slight concussion, nothing worse." And then, revealing herself, she confesses that it has been bad enough to see her husband hurt, but it would be intolerable to see him maimed, or dying day by day. "I must get back home," the newly appreciative wife declares. "I only wanted to be quite certain no one was hurt."

The Duke puts in unexpectedly, "Rosabel is hurt."

EDGAR

But we saw her with Harry Bullen;
She seemed most vigorous, talking his helmet off;
He was mopping his head with a handkerchief.

DUKE

                                        Rosabel,
Why? With Harry Bullen? Why should she be?

DOMINIC

Because she thought it was necessary
To her peace of mind. She has given herself up.

DUKE

And I give you up! How, by hell's grand canyon,
Do you know she has?

DOMINIC

                        She was really very unhappy;
I think I helped her to decide.

JESSIE

But why?
Given herself up for lost, or what?

DUKE

You strapping,
Ice-cold, donkey-witted douche of tasteless water!
I could willingly—Dominic, dear boy,
God would tell me He loves you, but then God
Is wonderfully accomplished, and to me
You seem less lovely, and for this good reason:
You think more of the sin than of the sinner.
Poor Rosabel. Where shall we find her?

HILDA

When
We saw them they were standing by the sundial.
What has she done?

DUKE

Loved me beyond her strength.
We go and get her out of the arms of the law,
However attractive Bullen's arms may be.
Dear Rosabel! And after that we must find
Beds for ourselves away from the smell of smoldering
Memory. Bring along some of the lanterns.
Excellent, blessed Rosabel. Ros-a-bel!

The Duke hurries out of the Temple into the rain, still calling,
and Hilda follows him. "Beds," mumbles Reedbeck to Jessie. "Yes,
yes, beds, quite important. There's at least one at my house if you'd
care to oblige it. No more sleep for me tonight." He holds a lantern
and follows Jessie out of the Temple.
    Dominic asks his sister, "Aren't you coming, Perpetua?"
    "I'll stay in the dry and rest."
    Dominic tarries, trying to tell the girl how responsible he feels for
all the fear and danger she had tonight; then he, too, goes into the
rain, leaving Perpetua and Edgar alone. Edgar wants to forget this
afternoon, and this night which found Perpetua in the observatory
with his father. Passionately he declares, "Over and over again I see
you for the first time. I round some corner of my senses, and there,
as though the air had formed you out of a sudden thought, I discover
you. . . . My whole body stammers with surprise. I imagine I love
you."

Perpetua is not ready to accept this declaration—nor does she want to reject it. "Tell me," urges Edgar, "do I seem to you to be only a sort of postscript to my father?"

"No, Edgar, across and across my heart never at all."

This sentimental tête-à-tête abruptly ends with the return of the Duke and Reedbeck. Reedbeck hints that it is time his daughter went to bed; the Duke protests, "She will stay for a moment's peaceful conversation." Edgar, showing some spirit, suggests to the girl that they go and see the dying flames of the fire.

"Our peaceful conversation, Perpetua," the Duke insists.

"Perpetua?" Edgar's one-word question is more a command than a query. The girl tries an easy way of escape by saying she will find her way to bed, and Edgar firmly declares, "I shall take the liberty to light you there. . . . Tomorrow, then, Father." The Duke has been bested. "Tomorrow to you," he rejoins. His son and the girl depart, and the Duke is left with Reedbeck, who is almost asleep in a chair. The Duke, also relaxed in a chair, asks himself, "Shall I be sorry for myself?"—and answers his own question in the affirmative. He admits he is in the Autumn of his own life. The dozing Reedbeck mutters disjointedly in a half-dream.

DUKE

Shall I be happy for myself?
In the name of existence I'll be happy for myself.
Why, Reedbeck, how marvelous it is to molder.
Think how you would have felt when you were lying
Grubbing in your mother's womb,
With only a wall to look at,
If you could have seen in your embryonic eye
The realm of bryony, sloes, rose-hips,
And a hedge's ruin, a golden desuetude,
A countryside like a drowned angel
Lying in shallow water, every thorn
Tendering a tear. Think, Reedbeck,
Think of the wonder of such glimmering woe;
How in a field of milk-white haze the lost
Apollo glows and wanders towards noon;
The wind-blown webs are brighter,
The rolling apples warmer than the sun.
Heavens! you would have cried, the womb
Echoing round you: These are the heavens, and I,
Reedbeck, am stillborn. Would you not?

REEDBECK
(*Waking slightly*)
And la Duchesse de Condé, I think.

DUKE
So with ourselves; imagine: to have the sensation
Of nearness of sight, shortness of breath,
Palpitation, creaking in the joints,
Shootings, stabbings, lynching of the limbs,
A sudden illumination of lumbago.
What a rich world of sensation to achieve,
What infinite variety of being.
Is it not?

REEDBECK
Dominic not fond . . .
Perpetua. . . .

DUKE
Reedbeck, I have to tell you
I mean to marry. I can still remember,
In my ebbing way, how pleasant it is to love;
An ancient love can blow again, like Summer
Visiting St. Martin. A breath will do it,
If the breath comes deep, and deep it has come.
You must give me your felicitations. I marry
Rosabel, when Rosabel
(After six months, I understand)
Is disengaged from custody.
          (*Only deep breathing comes from* REEDBECK.)
Thank you, dear fellow. Rosabel
Would thank you, too, if she were here.
She and I, sharing two solitudes,
Will bear our spirits up to where not even
The nightingale can know,
Where the song is quiet, and quiet
Is the song. Tell me, Reedbeck, before
We leave each other in sleep, where would you say
The lonely moment is coaxing us to go?
          (REEDBECK *gives a gentle near-whistling snore.*)
Well, yes, yes, quite so, my little one,
It comes to that in the end.

THE CURTAIN FALLS

JANE *

A Comedy in Three Acts

By S. N. Behrman

BY output alone and without considering his undisputed gift, S. N. Behrman is the American theatre's leading practitioner in the realm of high, parlor, drawing room or smart comedy. There are and have been other dramatists in this field—Philip Barry, Rachel Crothers, R. E. Sherwood and George Kelly, to name important ones —but none has had quite the output Behrman has managed in a quarter-century. His works include "The Second Man," "Serena Blandish," "No Time for Comedy," "Biography" and "Amphitryon 38." His last play previous to "Jane" was a tailor-made affair for the Lunts' twenty-fifth anniversary as an acting team, "I Know My Love." "Jane" is, so far as Broadway records are concerned, his seventeenth and most recent work; actually, it is quite an old play, having first been written in 1947. Behrman adapted the comedy from a short story by his friend, W. Somerset Maugham, and in it the character of William Tower bears more than a superficial resemblance to Maugham. The play was first produced in England and in Sweden; in Sweden it had a long run, and the New York stage setting was a duplicate of the one used in Sweden. In London, "Jane" was, in intent and successful achievement, quite farcical; but, since Londoners seem to like farce better than New Yorkers do, Behrman made a new adaptation for the Broadway trade which was much closer to high comedy.

Mrs. Tower—Millicent Tower—is an Englishwoman who lets off steam by constantly redecorating her house at Hyde Park Gate, London. At the moment, her large living room features a wall made of antique glass in panels, and Mrs. Tower likes to touch up her hair in the wavy reflections of this wall. These reflections seem kinder. For the rest, the room is furnished with gaiety and charm; there are flowers everywhere, and in one corner is an elaborate cage of canaries, which Mrs. Tower feeds when she has nothing else to do. The time is September, 1937. Into the room come Ann Tower, a lovely young girl, and Peter Crewe, a keen and negligently dressed young man of 23.

Ann rings for the butler, Wilson, and when Wilson appears she asks if her father has been here. She is very much relieved when Wilson says Mr. Tower has not yet appeared. Ann explains to Peter that she has always been a little scared of her father, and now she hasn't seen him in two years. Her mother, too, is out. Ann declines Wilson's offer to serve tea and pours Peter a drink. "Well," she challenges, "you haven't said anything about Father's play yet. Didn't you like it?"

Peter is no man to beat about the bush. The play, he says, is beautifully written, but has the flavor of a period piece—a perfectly articulated fossil. Nor is Ann a woman to beat about the bush. Unruffled, she asks, "If you weren't already married—would you marry me?" With humorous tenderness Peter answers that he doesn't think so; it wouldn't be sensible for Ann.

"I don't want a sensible marriage. I want a love marriage."

"We have love now."

Ann exclaims that she feels so frustrated—she can't even hate Peter's wife. "Where is she now, do you suppose," she asks.

"Hard to say. When I last heard from her she was in Vienna. Maybe she's in a concentration camp somewhere."

"I think it was wonderful of you," says Ann adoringly, "to marry her—just to give her a passport." Peter reminds her that unfortunately the passport didn't work. He also reminds Ann that, although he loves her, Ann's mother can't bear him. Peter thinks Ann's mother is a very silly woman, but he must admit that her antagonism is understandable; he's a semi-employed journalist with a passion for writing poetry. He also has a strong belief that England is sitting on a cauldron which will blow up any moment—and when it happens he will enlist.

Peter is in need of a steady job, and Ann has an inspiration—Lord Frobisher, chain-paper publisher. He's a great friend of Mother's; in fact, it is popularly supposed that he broke up her marriage. Ann won't listen to Peter's objection that Frobisher is on the wrong side of everything; she is going to try for the job.

The butler announces the arrival of William Tower. "The actor who plays William Tower," it is counseled in the stage directions, "would do well to study the portraits and read the works of W. Somerset Maugham. . . . Tower wears a monocle on a broad black ribbon with which he habitually fixes people." Father and daughter embrace, and Tower is introduced to Peter. "How's Africa?" asks Ann.

"Enormous!"

There is an awkward pause, which Tower does nothing to ease. Peter soon leaves, and the girl chides her father for not being cordial to her young man.

"Oh, is he your young man?" Tower points out that journalism is the most insecure of professions, and poetry is simply a luxury. Can Peter afford it? Ann's father looks about the room and inquires if it hasn't been altered. The girl explains, "Everything that Mother could pickle, she pickled; and what she couldn't pickle, she painted." Still trying to make conversation with her parent, Ann learns from brief replies to her questions that he will be in London about a month and will then go to India. She is shy with him—and he seems to be shy with her. "I often wonder why you don't marry again," she ventures. "Is there anyone on the horizon?"

"Even if there were I shouldn't marry it. One reason is I can't afford to marry again because your mother gets most of my income." Rather grimly he adds, "Your mother drove a hard bargain, but, had she known it, she might have driven an even harder one."

Ann, with a little scheme in the back of her head, tells her father that Allan Frobisher is coming today. He seems pleased, and asks amiably, "How is the old pirate?"

"I have a feeling," says the girl hesitantly, "that Allan and Mother —will get married one of these days." Tower ejaculates prayerfully, "Speed the day. If Allan married your mother I could afford a few luxuries in my declining years."

Mrs. Tower comes in with a springy walk. She is chic, gay, assured and well-preserved—but at the moment she seems upset. She greets her husband with a "Hello, Willie," observes that he looks well, then cries, "I'm really upset." She waves a telegram. "She's coming! She's coming again!"

ANN—Who, Mother?

MRS. TOWER—Who? Who would put me in such a state? Jane, of course. Jane Fowler. It really is naughty of her. I have so many engagements, I really don't know where to turn.

TOWER—Jane Fowler? I seem to remember the name.

ANN (smiles)—Jane is Mother's cross.

MRS. TOWER (tragically)—She's coming tomorrow!

TOWER—Jane Fowler? Isn't that your sister-in-law and doesn't she live in Liverpool?

MRS. TOWER—Not enough! I never saw her after Harry and I

had that row. But when he died Jane fastened herself on to me. I'm
her only living relative and she makes a fetish of it.

Ann—But, Mother, she *is* kind. She does bring you tea-cozies
and doilies. She knits them with her own hands.

Mrs. Tower—She's worthy, she's dowdy, she's provincial. She
looks twenty years older than I do and she's perfectly capable of telling anyone she meets that we were at school together. When she
comes to London it never occurs to her to stay anywhere but here—
she thinks it would hurt my feelings—and she says for three or four
weeks. Entertains all her Liverpool friends here—just as dowdy as
she is. Thank God it's tomorrow and not today.

Tower—I should think, Millicent, that a woman with your social
experience would find a way to deal with a situation like this.

Mrs. Tower—But don't you see, Willie, I haven't a chance.
Jane's so unbearably kind. She bores me to death, but I wouldn't
for a moment let her suspect it. It's the kind of thing you could do,
but I couldn't.

Tower—I have never believed in encouraging bores.

Mrs. Tower—I know. You retire behind that mask.

Tower (*to* Ann)—Shall I lend your mother my mask?

Mrs. Tower—Tomorrow! Of all days! Just when I've asked
dozens of people to dinner.

Tower—Everything goes on quite as usual, doesn't it?

Mrs. Tower (*with some asperity*)—I hope, dear, you don't think
life stops in London just because you choose to go to Africa. This
is all I needed! And she'll expect to see her tea-cozies! She'll expect
to see her doilies!

Tower—Can't you just put them on to grace her visit?

Mrs. Tower—I've burnt them!

Ann—I don't care how funny she looks. I adore her. She has a
heart of gold.

Mrs. Tower—I can't bear people with hearts of gold. If this
continues I shall have to leave London. (*To* Tower.) Jane will
force me into going back to Africa with you.

Tower (*to ward off such a possibility*)—I'm going to India.

Mrs. Tower tells her ex-husband about Jane; she is not, as he
has surmised, elderly; she is Mrs. Tower's age. Jane and her husband, Mrs. Tower's brother, built up the largest department store
in Liverpool, and when he died Jane sold it for millions—an aca-
demic fact so far as Mrs. Tower is concerned, for this lady is certain
that Jane, who takes such care of herself, will live forever.

Ann goes upstairs, and Mrs. Tower tells Willie he has come home in the nick of time—to do something about Ann and that awful man she is involved with, Peter Crewe, who is so arrogant. "That," says Tower, "will pass when he has something to be arrogant about." Ann's mother complains that the penniless Peter is keeping the girl from marrying somebody else; she suggests that Tower, with his flair for deflating people, make Ann see that Peter is shallow. He objects that in order to do this he should have to see Peter, and that would be a trivial use of his time.

Mrs. Tower confides what Ann has already hinted—that Allan Frobisher is trembling on the brink. Calmly Tower rejoins, "I think I may trust you to push him over."

"Nothing will induce me to marry Allan. He's always rushing off to Birmingham or Manchester or some place to buy a newspaper. . . . You know, Willie, it's not easy to forget you. Your books keep reminding me. I know you so well—I see you in all of them." He suggests, "Why don't you simply not read them?"

Wilson appears at the door to announce Mrs. Fowler and the horrified Mrs. Tower almost screams, "Jane!" The woman has come a day early. At first sight, Jane Fowler is indeed an odd bundle—a vital little middle-aged lady in a mass of old-fashioned and excessive clothing. Over everything else she wears a cloak that oddly combines severity with fussiness. Her shoes are stout; her hat is the last century's. Yet, on closer inspection, Jane shows an extraordinary freshness of complexion and clear, candid eyes. She has a winning smile, and now she turns it on her sister-in-law. They embrace, and Millie Tower exclaims, "But I wasn't expecting you until tomorrow!"

"If you looked at the date on my telegram," says Jane forthrightly, "you would have seen that I sent it yesterday. It said, 'Arrive tomorrow.' That's today." Tower is introduced, and Mrs. Tower suggests tea. Jane makes quite a business of taking off her cloak and a scarf and folding them neatly. She is wearing a black cardigan sweater, and around her neck is a large silver locket on a black ribbon. She inquires how Ann is, and is told that the girl has found a young man who is a left-wing maniac who wants us to go to war over Czechoslovakia. The butler and a maid serve tea, and Jane invites Tower to sit beside her on a sofa. The butler adds that Lord Frobisher telephoned that he can't come to dinner but will drop in for tea.

Jane's habit of asking direct questions and making direct statements is highly amusing to William Tower; he enjoys the discomfort Jane arouses in Millicent. The tea-cozy, for instance—what happened to it? Burnt? Very well, she will make another one. Jane shows Tower the picture of her late husband in the locket. "Millie was at the wedding," she recalls. "It will be thirty-one years ago next Wednesday. I remember because the next day was Millie's birthday and I saved her a piece of the wedding cake. Do you remember that birthday party, Millie? It was your twenty-first. . . ."

Jane and Tower get along famously. She decides she will call him William; Willie is too informal for so famous an author. Jane does not always talk; she devotes herself thoroughly to the tea, and there are stretches of silence in the room. She remarks comfortably that it's nice not to have to talk; it gives one time to collect one's thoughts. Indeed, she is collecting hers now, so that she may tell some news. "I am about to be married," she announces. "What?" exclaims Mrs. Tower, jumping up. "Jane, you're not serious."

But indeed Jane is. The wedding will be at the registrar's tomorrow morning, and she wants them both to come. Moreover, she has invited her young man to come here this afternoon. Millicent chuckles, "It's too sweet to hear you talk about your young man!" Jane giggles. "And tell me," her sister-in-law pursues, "are you going to live in Liverpool?" A chasm yawns before her as Jane says her young man's profession requires that they live in London—so they will be able to see a lot of each other. Having devoured her tea, Jane goes up to her room to change out of her traveling clothes. On the stair landing she pauses, smiles winningly and declares, "I'm so pleased to have met you at last, William. I always thought you'd be rather formidable. You're not a bit. You're, if I may say so, you're quite—cozy!"

The next visitor is not the "young man," but Lord Frobisher. He is in his early fifties, medium-sized—and looks and acts larger than life. He is crusty, sadistic and humorous, and knows it; he enjoys being a salty character. He is pleased to see Willie, and when Willie inquires how he manages to keep so young he answers, "Women! Try them." Frobisher declines tea for whiskey and explains he has canceled his dinner date because he must stay close to his office on account of the European situation. "I say, Willie," he ventures, "while you're doing nothing, why don't you go to work for me? Biggest circulation in London, you know."

Tower counters suavely, "I know your circulation is big, Allan, but can it read?"

Jane comes down, wearing a black dress in the style of the early 1900s; her hair, parted in the middle, covers her ears. Discommoded, Mrs. Tower introduces Lord Frobisher, and Jane decides immediately that she disapproves of him because he has stared at her so. She reproves him for being rude, and Frobisher, his back up a

bit, says, "Of course I stared. When she came down I thought it
was Queen Victoria. Now by God I see I was right." Jane further
disapproves of the man because he has just bought a wretched newspaper in Liverpool and has filled it with sensational photographs.
   Mrs. Tower, floundering for conversation, informs Frobisher of
Jane's impending marriage. He asks, "Is it Prince Albert?" With
benign mildness, Jane addresses herself to her sister-in-law: "It
amazes me, Millie, that you could have left a mature man like my
dear William for an elderly adolescent like Lord Frobisher." Mrs.
Tower totters, but William is in ecstasy. Sinking to his knees before
Jane, he asks Millicent to remarry him so that he may once again be
Jane's brother-in-law—and at this moment Gilbert Dabney, Jane's
affianced, appears. He is not what anybody expected; he is about
30, slight, tallish, attractive and rather engaging. He looks with
mock consternation at Jane and Willie. Jane performs the introduc-
tions, and Mrs. Tower is speechless. Jane doesn't make her any
happier by explaining, "You know, Gilbert, Millie and I were at
school together."
   Gilbert is charming and frank as he answers interested questions.
He and Jane will have two months in Italy. He could never before
afford so long a vacation.

FROBISHER (*he has had enough*)—Well, thank you, Millicent, for
a most diverting afternoon.
   MRS. TOWER—I've hardly seen you at all.
   FROBISHER—I'll ring you tomorrow. You must get your sister-in-
law over her prejudice against me. By the way, Willie, I'm seeing
your play tonight and taking Muriel Kerr to supper afterwards.
Won't you join us? It'll be a big thrill for Muriel to meet the author.
   TOWER—Thank you very much but unfortunately I'm busy.
   MRS. TOWER—It's Muriel now, is it?
   FROBISHER—I hope it will be.
   TOWER (*eager to whip things up*)—You know, Jane, Lord Fro-
bisher is the most expert philanderer in London.
   JANE (*objectively*)—At his age? Is it becoming?
   TOWER (*keeping the fire going*)—He has a sort of vintage boyish-
ness, don't you think?
   FROBISHER (*nettled to open attack*)—Your sense of decorum is
extremely acute, Mrs. Fowler. You are very critical of other people's
indulgences. Doesn't it—in the circumstances—(*He looks from her
to* GILBERT.)—show a lack of humor?
   JANE (*with dignity, takes* GILBERT's *hand*)—Gilbert and I are
about to be *married*, Lord Frobisher.

FROBISHER (*helpless*)—I give up!

TOWER (*simmering with delight*)—This is the second time I've seen Allan so frustrated.

JANE (*not above wanting instances*)—Really? What was the first time?

TOWER—The first time was when he was staying with me in my villa in the South of France. A highly respectable American lady novelist was staying with me also. Allan came down to the swimming pool stark naked. She didn't bat an eyelash!

JANE (*gravely*)—I hope she managed to conceal her disappointment.

The publisher flees—a one-man rout. Mrs. Tower, in a savage mood, wants to talk with Jane alone and suggests that Willie take Dabney into the library. Willie protests, but does so. Millicent asks Jane if she is crazy, wanting to marry this young man? Where did she meet him?

"I advertised for him."

"In Cupid's Column, I suppose."

"No, in the *Times*. I advertised for a young architect, without an expensive reputation, to re-do my house in Liverpool. And Gilbert came."

Millicent argues that Dabney is simply marrying Jane for her money, but Jane doesn't think so; she thinks he is very fond of her—and she is not in love with him. Calmly she explains, "I've been a widow a very long time. I thought I'd like a change." Millicent weeps in pity for Jane, but Jane's confidence is unshaken.

Millicent would now like to talk to Willie, so Dabney comes out of the library and she goes in. Gilbert takes Jane's hands and remarks that they seem to have caused a sensation. "They make me feel as if—as if instead of marrying you—I should adopt you," says Jane. "It's obvious they think you're marrying me for my money." Gilbert is sure of this, too—but he is confident that they will enjoy their marriage. Arms locked, they go for a stroll in the garden just as Millicent and Willie emerge from the library.

Millicent still is on the subject of the impending marriage—Jane, so old and dowdy and dull. Tower disagrees, observing that what Jane says is very much to the point. "Fancy finding a young man like that in Liverpool," she fumes. "And she advertised for him!"

Tower, who has poured himself a sherry, inquires blandly, "Well, why don't you do the same, Millicent? In one of Allan's papers. I'm sure he'd give you a reduced rate."

She slaps him with her floppy straw hat. She is out of sorts with everything. Tower happily sips his sherry.

The curtain falls.

ACT II

It is March, 1938—six months later, late in the afternoon. The butler shows Tower in, and when Millicent comes into the room she is surprised to see him. They kiss lightly and she asks if he had a good time in India.

"Fascinating."

There is envy in her voice as she says, "You always have a wonderful time, don't you, Willie?" As for herself, she confesses she is in a state. Partly over that awful Peter Crewe; she takes it as a personal affront that the young man has had a book of poems published, and the critics raved about it. And what is even worse, she reveals bitterly, Jane is now the reigning social success of London! Also, something very mysterious must be going on between Allan Frobisher and Jane, for they quarrel all the time. Furthermore, Gilbert and Jane are living here while Gilbert is redecorating the house Jane has bought on Belgrave Square. She adds, "Not only has Gilbert redecorated Jane's house. He's reupholstered Jane!"

Mrs. Tower frankly admits that she is galled, because people who never came here before now do so on account of Jane—cabinet ministers, royalty—film stars, even! They all think Jane is so amusing, but Millicent can't see where Jane is so funny. Reverting to the topic of their daughter, she expresses the hope that Willie will do something about the situation, "but instead of that, I suppose you'll be popping off to Afghanistan at any moment."

TOWER (*in the interest of accuracy*)—I am not going to Afghanistan. I am going to Tibet.

MRS. TOWER—While you're playing around with all those lamas . . . (TOWER *laughs*.) What are you laughing at?

TOWER—My dear Millicent, the lamas are rather exclusive. You can't play around with them.

MRS. TOWER—Well, while you are playing around with whatever they have in Tibet, I suppose I shall be left here wrestling with Ann's problems. Oh, dear, life *is* difficult!

TOWER—It's practically impossible. The moment you're born you're done for.

MRS. TOWER (*one of her abrupt transitions*)—Jane prophesies that you and I will remarry.

TOWER (*interested*)—Does she?

MRS. TOWER (*tantalizing*)—Yes. Do you believe in prophecy?

TOWER (*laconic*)—I believe in free will.

MRS. TOWER—In your stories people are always swallowed up by a destiny they can't escape.

TOWER—I never read my stories.

MRS. TOWER (*still in pursuit*)—Jane says if you're not careful you'll let yourself in for a lonely old age. Aren't you afraid of that?

TOWER—My dear Millicent, I do not have to wait for old age to know loneliness. I have known it since I was a child.

MRS. TOWER (*frustrated*)—I can't cope with you.

TOWER (*with a charming smile*)—Isn't it nice you don't have to?

MRS. TOWER—The truth is you're vindictive. Sometimes I think you took advantage of the incident with Allan to leave me high and dry.

TOWER (*with a glance around the charming room*)—Many people wouldn't mind being left high and dry in these surroundings.

MRS. TOWER—You're such a materialist! You worship success.

TOWER (*quiet but accurate in aim*)—If my worship were unrequited, you might be even more bitter.

Gilbert comes down the stairs, dressed in tails. Jane is still up, changing. With a touch of petulance, Gilbert declares that he could be annoyed with his wife at this moment. He has been round to see Lady St. Earth, and Lady St. Earth has called off his commission to do her new house—all on account of one of Jane's pointed cracks at a party which made the woman furious. Millicent Tower is all sympathy toward Gilbert. "And when you do start disciplining Jane," she says, "you might ask her to stop encouraging that awful Peter Crewe." Then she suggests that Tower take them to dinner, since it is cook's night off, and he gallantly agrees. She goes up to look for Ann.

When the two men are alone, Tower quizzes Gilbert about Jane and himself, and the young man seems to enjoy it, although he protests there is no rift in the lute. Tower, seeking to analyze Jane's particular gift, puts it this way: "She just tells the truth. And in our world this is so unusual that people think it's outrageously funny!" Gilbert agrees, with a hint of bitterness, that his wife certainly doesn't mind telling the truth. He explains being upset about the loss of his commission: "In my profession, connections are everything. I have become ambitious. In a world of opportunities, I am an opportunist."

Jane—a new Jane—descends the stair. Her iron-gray hair is cut short and clustered thickly round her well-shaped head in tight curls. She wears very little makeup, and her face looks remarkably fresh. On her is an audacious, but somehow perfectly right, evening dress. Tower does not conceal his amazement. "Millicent tells me," he says, "that London regards you as a humorist. Were you a humorist in Liverpool?"

"Ah, but, William, Liverpool is much more difficult to impress than London."

Gilbert, interrupting, fishes a handful of invitations from his pocket, all for the weekend, and asks his wife to help decide which to accept. Lord Duffield? "That's horses," Jane checks off. Tower inquires how she gets on with the horsey set. "I talk to them about easy books and I pass for an intellectual."

Anson Dykes? The effervescent historian. Jane continues, "I simply let him bubble. He is dazzled with his own identity." Lord Shillinghurst? "He *is* a problem," Jane confesses to Tower. "He's a Labor peer, and he is very self-conscious because he has never been a workingman." Gilbert excuses himself for a moment—he wants to go up and bring some new plans he has made for Jane's house, so she may see them.

The admiring Tower declares to her, "You are unique, and you are radiantly happy. Aren't you?"

"I must tell you, William—since our last meeting I have read you. . . . I shouldn't try to pretend to you because I can see from your books that you understand women too well."

"Does that mean you are going to confess to me?"

"Only partially. One thing I have discovered—the young have no conversation."

"I have just been talking to Gilbert and he is extremely glib," Tower objects.

"He has no silences."

Jane puts no blame on Gilbert; it's the difference in ages. Tower points out that he has heard that Jane gets on well with young Peter. "Peter is more adventurous than Gilbert. . . . Gilbert is a dear, but he's a bit . . . a bit . . . old-fashioned."

And now Jane wants to talk to him about his daughter, Ann, who is in love with Peter. Tower asks why they don't marry, then. "Because," Jane reveals, "he is already married." She tells of Crewe's marrying a girl in Austria who was being persecuted because of her father's political opinions—just to give her a passport. But it was too late, and now she is in a prison camp. "I saw her," says Jane, astonishingly. She managed it through Lord Frobisher, which was nice of him because personally he can't bear Jane. Jane warns

Tower that Millicent must not know any of this, because she'd get hysterical.

Tower can't see that there is any future for Ann, with Peter married, but Jane hints that she has plans which she will not talk about. Ann runs down and greets her father; bluntly Jane declares, "Ann, I've told him." She suggests that the girl take her father into the garden and have a nice cozy talk with him. When she is alone, Jane moves swiftly to the telephone, dials it, and asks Lord Frobisher's secretary if Lord Frobisher received her message. "Oh, he did . . . Oh, he is. Thank you very much." Gilbert, on his way down with a set of blueprints, has heard the call and asks if she is badgering Allan again about giving Peter a job. Then he takes her to a chair, spreads blueprints on the floor, kneels by them and begins telling her about her new house, which is going to be a wonderful setting for her.

"You see this exquisite circular staircase?"

"It's charming. But who will walk up those stairs?"

"Crowds."

She laughs, "And I'll have to receive them! . . . What will I do if, instead of receiving them, I feel a tremendous impulse to say, 'Please go home!'?"

"You'll say it and they'll only laugh and walk right in."

Jane tells her husband it has been fun being "the rage of London," but all it amounts to is amusing mildly a lot of people one doesn't know very well and doesn't want to know any better. It's the sort of fun that can't last forever. She asks Gilbert, "Don't you know what is threatening England today—the world today? Don't you read the papers?"

"Oh, I read the theatre and society columns once in a while."

Jane drops her bombshell: "I don't want to go on with the plans for our house, Gilbert." He protests that she can't be serious, but she is; when she looks at those plans and thinks of the parties he is so eagerly anticipating, she longs for those evenings in Liverpool when she sat before her fire and read Jane Austen.

Gilbert, hard now, accuses, "This is the second commission you have cost me today!" His voice rises as he continues, "I am perfectly aware and so are you what people think of me—that I married for money. Well, this commission from Lady St. Earth, which incidentally would have led to others, would have made me independent of you financially."

Lord Frobisher is announced and Jane exclaims to him, "How nice of you to come so quickly." Tower wanders in from the garden and inquires with pleasant malice, "How's the elderly adolescent?"

Then, more genuinely solicitous, "How's your asthma?"

Jane remembers she has a wonderful asthma remedy upstairs; her late husband used to suffer from it and this prescription worked wonders. She asks Gilbert to go up and try to find it in her morocco case. Frobisher asks, "What did your husband die of, Jane?"

"Asthma."

Tower remarks that Frobisher hasn't changed in thirty years and asks how he does it. Allan explains, "I have two devotions—my body and women. I pay infinite attention to the requirements of both."

Peter Crewe is announced, and Jane introduces him to Lord Frobisher. Bluntly Allan says, "I've read some of your things, my boy, in those bloody Socialist papers. You wouldn't do for me at all." Peter bows and thanks him, as if this were a compliment. "I do appreciate your efforts in my behalf, Jane," the young man says, "but actually the last thing I want to do is work for Lord Frobisher." Allan, piqued, gruffly states, "He thinks he will provoke me into hiring him. He is mistaken." Peter inquires for Ann, is told she is in the garden, and goes to find her.

Now, Jane wants Frobisher to herself, so she pointedly invites William also to go into the garden. Frobisher goes to the sideboard and pours himself a drink. "Now tell me what it is you want and let me know. I've got a date," he urges. For once, Jane does not come to the point; instead she asks how it is that Allan has avoided matrimony, and he answers, "Somehow all the women I've ever been attracted to were already married—or else they were actresses." Jane analyzes his pride in his conquests: "It must be easier to conquer many than to constantly reconquer one. There, one cannot rely on novelty." Frobisher pours himself another drink, and a third, and a fourth, as Jane continues her analysis of him and voices the final conclusion that Allan goes after so many women because he is lazy.

At last Jane comes to her point—the reason she asked Lord Frobisher to come here: She wants him to get Peter Crewe's wife out of the prison camp, so that they may get a divorce and enable Peter to marry Ann. Mulling it over, Frobisher allows that there have been instances where it's been done—but it would be expensive. "I am ready to supply all it will cost," Jane assures him.

He sizes her up: "You're pretty cool!"

With a bewitching smile she rejoins, "At our age we *should* be cool, don't you think?"

Frobisher is getting somewhere between rage and despair, what with the drinks—which he keeps on taking because Jane warns him that he is far too kind and important to kill himself with drink. He sinks to a settee, complaining that she has made him feel something like rigor mortis.

JANE—You're the most determined rake I ever met. It must be very exhausting. And I'm not at all sure it's good for your asthma.

FROBISHER—I wish you to know, Mrs. Dabney . . . I wish you to know that I'll go on living as I have been living. Do you mind? I'm far too old to change.

JANE—Are you as old as all that?

FROBISHER (*at bay*)—Yes, I am!

JANE—I'd hate to be too old to change. Look at me. Look how I've changed.

FROBISHER—I won't do it. I will *not* do it!

JANE—What?

FROBISHER—What you asked me. I could do it, probably, if I put myself out. But I won't. And do you know why I won't? Because you asked me. I won't do a damn thing about it.

JANE—Oh, yes, you will. Your kind heart will make you—when you are sober.

FROBISHER (*thrashing about*)—And don't you write me any more letters. The next letter you write me I'm going to throw right in the waste-paper basket.

JANE—This one good deed which you are going to do may be the most comforting thing in your life to look back on—your immortality.

FROBISHER—I don't give a good God damn for immortality!

JANE—Don't be blasphemous.

FROBISHER—Not a damn. I live for the moment, do you hear? I don't give a hoot what comes after me. I shan't be here to see it. You can decide in your calm way whether you'll have azaleas or calla lilies at your funeral. But I don't give a damn! At *my* funeral they can have ragweed for all I care. Let them bloody well sneeze their heads off!

Tower, coming in from the garden, comments, "Why, Allan, you're as noisy as one of your newspapers!" Mrs. Tower descends in evening dress from upstairs and is surprised to see Frobisher there—and miffed when she learns that he came to see Jane, not her. Frobisher shouts, "Jane, this is my last word to you. If you think you're going to make a do-gooder out of me you are very much mistaken. I'm getting no girls out of prison camps—and especially not for you!"

Jane is aghast. Mrs. Tower asks, "Allan, what are you saying?"

"That young bounder's wife," he begins, pointing toward the garden—and then, in his high pitch of anger, he spills the beans about Peter's wife. He huffs out, passing Gilbert, who has come down with the asthma prescription, saying to Gilbert, "I no longer need it. Your dear wife has already buried me without it."

The import of what Frobisher has said begins to dawn on Mrs. Tower. Peter—a bigamist! And Jane—a meddler. Millicent makes a scene. She has had about as much of Jane as she can stand. "Gilbert," she demands, "why don't you exert your marital authority—what's left of it!" The unhappy Gilbert tells Jane he is on Millicent's side, and, moreover, he is now in no mood to go with his wife to the opera tonight. He goes upstairs in a pet.

JANE—Millie, dear, I know that you're very angry with me.

MRS. TOWER—That's putting it mildly.

JANE—But I'm going to ask you to do something for me. I know Gilbert has set his heart on going to the opera. It's an opening night and he does so love to be seen. Why don't you make him go with you? You're looking so lovely and you'll see all your friends in the intermission. And when Gilbert comes home he will have forgotten how upset he is with me.

MRS. TOWER—You don't deserve it! (*Abruptly.*) Where are the tickets?

JANE—Here. (*She gives them to her.*)

MRS. TOWER—I don't know why I'm sacrificing myself for you.

JANE—Because you're an angel.

MRS. TOWER—I suppose that must be it. I must confess, Mr. Richard Wagner gives me the fidgets—but the intermissions *are* rather fun. (*With a twinge of martyrdom.*) Still—think what you have to go through to get to them! (*She goes upstairs.*)

TOWER—Millicent seems to have completely forgotten that she was to dine with me. May I take you to dinner, Jane?

JANE—That would be lovely. I'm very hungry.

TOWER—To borrow your favorite word—it will be *cozy*.

FROBISHER (*his voice is heard booming off stage*)—All right, Wilson, you needn't announce me. (*He is back again.*)

JANE—Why, Allan—what have you come back for? I thought you had a date.

FROBISHER—I did. Thanks to you I've missed it. You not only ruined my afternoon—you've ruined my evening! Willie, I'd even go to dinner with you!

TOWER—I've asked Jane to go to dinner with me. Won't you join us? (*Can't resist the final barb.*) With you around, Jane will appreciate me all the more.

FROBISHER (*defiantly*)—I'll take my chances!

JANE (*as she looks from one to the other*)—Oh, it will be such a relief for once . . .

TOWER—What?

JANE (*as the two men flank her she links her arms through theirs*) —To spend an evening with two men of my own age!

They start off gaily as the curtain falls.

ACT III

Ten days have passed, and it is another late afternoon. Jane, with shoes off and wearing glasses, has been propped up on pillows on the settee, reading Peter's poems, when William Tower disturbs her and apologizes for doing so. He confesses that, as a father, he is rather conventional and he has been worrying about Ann. He wants her to make a reasonably good marriage, and he cannot see much financial future for Peter Crewe. "I appeal to you," he addresses Jane, "to help get her out of this impossible situation."

"I'm taking steps to get her out," Jane informs him. "I am going to adopt Peter's wife." He stares at her. "How will Gilbert enjoy all this?" he asks.

"I don't know. I haven't told him yet."

William warns her that Gilbert won't care for it, and she might lose him. Tranquilly she replies, "Gilbert is bound to leave me sooner or later." She hopes he will marry again—a girl of his own age. The butler comes in to tell her she has a phone call from Peter Crewe, and Jane goes to her room to take it. In a moment Mrs. Tower appears from the library; evidently she has been waiting there, for now she asks, "Well, Willie—did you get anywhere with her?" He says he is afraid not, and Millicent fairly bursts with righteous indignation at Jane. "I haven't spoken to her for weeks," she adds.

Tantalizingly, Tower says he *does* have a bit of news about Jane and Gilbert. When he has teased Millicent with enough mystery he announces crisply, "Gilbert is leaving Jane." Millicent fairly gasps with joy, chortling, "It's happened at last!" Now she switches to pity for Jane, whom she considers already abandoned at an advanced age. Willie must be very nice to her, she counsels. She wonders whom Gilbert is leaving for, or going to. She is determined she will find out—she'll find out from Gilbert.

Gilbert comes down the stairs in headlong flight. Brimming with consolation, Mrs. Tower coos, "Dear Gilbert!" He seems mystified.

Tower, seeing a new situation to exploit, says mischievously to Jane's husband, "My congratulations . . . on the forthcoming addition to your family!"

Gilbert is now at sea—but Millicent isn't; she is transfixed with horror. "It's a trick! It's a contemptible trick—to hold you, Gilbert," she shrieks. "Isn't that just like Jane! At her age! Gilbert, how could you! . . . At her age! She'll never survive!"

Gilbert finally gathers that Millicent thinks Jane is approaching motherhood, and he asks, "Willie, have you been pulling Millicent's leg?"

Tower has had his fun; now he explains that, in the interests of accuracy, Jane did tell him there was to be an addition to the family, but that she was going to adopt it. Gilbert and Millicent babble "Who" and "Why." Tower answers the "who": "Peter's wife." He goes upstairs to see Ann. Millicent, wasting no time, demands, "Are you going to stand for this, Gilbert?"

"This time," he announces, "Jane has gone too far."

Millicent is all sympathy, saying Jane never belonged to *their* world; he is young, attractive, clever—and an artist. Gilbert at least is clever enough to see a new haven looming, and he plays up to Millicent; she plays back. "You will be the most welcome guest in this house," she declares with unction. "And I'll see that you get all the commissions you want. I see no reason why you shouldn't design my dresses for me—for as long as Willie can pay for them."

Jane returns from her phone call. "Oh, Jane, my heart goes out to you," says Millicent—who has a very going-out heart. "Thank God," Millicent adds as she goes upstairs, "my conscience is clear!"

Gilbert furiously accuses Jane of a determination to make him ridiculous with this adoption of Peter's wife. He scoffs at any altruistic motive she may claim as very satisfying to the ego. As if studying her husband anew, Jane observes, "You're very hard, aren't you?"

"I'm realistic and not sentimental."

"You're selfish, aren't you?"

Gilbert admits it, declaring that anybody who says he isn't is either a liar or a hypocrite. Jane seems to be looking past him in a trance, and he asks, "What's the matter?"

"I was just wondering," she confesses, "if you're not too old for me!"

Just as Tower comes down from seeing Ann, Gilbert tells his wife, "As you find me too old for you, you are now perfectly at liberty to marry someone younger!" He slams out of the room and out of the house. It's a busy living room, however, and soon Lord Frobisher is there, looking liverish. He has seen Gilbert bounding out the door and asks what is amiss. Dramatically, Tower announces, "Jane is bereft, abandoned. Gilbert is deserting her."

"Serves her right," says the ungallant Frobisher.

Tower sees another situation which he may develop into something amusing. "You know, Jane," he remarks, "Allan is so rude I think he must be very taken with you."

"I'm very taken with Allan," Jane replies.

Tower—And now that you're going to be free again, Jane, the field is open, isn't it? I was just thinking—it might be very amusing to be married to you, Jane. It would certainly keep one on one's mettle. (JANE *and* TOWER *exchange looks. Now that he has thrown out the hint,* TOWER *cannot resist exploring its possibilities.* JANE *plays along with him.*)

JANE—Thank you, William. I can return the compliment. It would be fascinating to be married to you.

FROBISHER (*to* JANE)—Marry Willie! Last man on earth for anyone to marry.

JANE—Why, Allan?

TOWER—Why, indeed? I feel a reckless impulse to propose to you, Jane.

JANE—Why suppress it?

TOWER—But I can't propose to you in front of Allan.

JANE—Why not? It might give him some idea of how it's done. It's the one form of approach in which he's had very little experience.

TOWER (*in complete cahoots with her*)—You wouldn't seriously consider marrying Allan, would you?

JANE (*a glance at* TOWER, *then a look at* FROBISHER. *She nudges* FROBISHER *farther along on the sofa to make room for* TOWER)— Let's talk about it! (TOWER *edges himself in beside her. The three sit in a row very close together.*) Now, William—why not?

TOWER—For one thing, Allan's scarcely housebroken.

JANE (*demurely*)—That would give me something to do.

TOWER—I could offer you a more advanced form of occupation.

JANE—Could you, William? What would it be?

FROBISHER (*very jealous actually*)—I hope it happens! You deserve each other. The coldest man in England . . .

JANE—Oh, I think you're wrong there, Allan. I think William is very emotional, really.

FROBISHER (*scornfully*)—That's a joke!

JANE—You, Allan, are passionate. William is emotional.

FROBISHER—You deserve each other. I'll go to your wedding and laugh my head off!

TOWER—Pagliacci! (*To* JANE.) Obviously he is so annoyed at the prospect, he must really be interested in you. His is not an original mind and the fact that I'm involved makes him feel that perhaps there are possibilities in you he hadn't suspected. (*He takes* JANE's *hand.*)

JANE—You are naughty, William. Don't mind him, Allan. He is a dramatist and he cannot resist what he considers a "situation."

TOWER (*he gets up*)—I certainly can't resist this one! I'll give you exactly five minutes, Allan. Get rid of your business with Jane, during which time I shall collect my thoughts in the garden. Then I shall return and propose to Jane with consummate grace and ultimate efficiency! (*He blows her a kiss and goes into the garden.*)

At once Jane drops her playful air and asks of Allan, "Any news?" "Yes. I've done it. The girl is out. In fact, she arrives in London at seven o'clock this evening. Once I get started I work pretty fast. Somebody'd better go to Croydon to meet her."

Jane puts a hand on his arm and ejaculates a fervent "Bless you!" He removes her arm, saying, "I did not do this for you! . . . It was that bloody German ambassador. He got my back up." Awkwardly he asks her permission to pour himself a drink, and she grants that he has earned the right to all his indulgences.

"I may have earned the right," he says bitterly out of his glass, "but thanks to you—I've lost the knack!" Ever since she made that first remark about his being an elderly adolescent . . . "You've undermined me!" he bursts out. In profound misery he tells Jane he has lost his confidence with girls. Today a girl stood him up, saying she had another date—something that never happened before. Jane comforts, "Dear Allan. Perhaps you're growing up."

Frobisher finds some cruel satisfaction in the fact that Jane is being deserted. "What are you going to do now, All-Wise, All-Seeing Jane?" he taunts.

"Marry someone of my own age—if I can find him."

The publisher makes a step in retreat. Then, with a quick look toward the garden, he recovers himself and bellows, "Oh, my God! Of course—Tower!" He begins laughing uncontrollably.

"He's the most fascinating man I ever met," Jane admits, but then terrifies Frobisher by adding, "Perhaps it would be safer to marry a simple man—like you!" He runs to the liquor table and pours a quick one.

Tower, returning from the garden, orders, "Clear out, Allan. Your five minutes are up." In a kind of panic Frobisher goes to him and asks, "Willie, you're always going some place. Where are you going this time?"

"Tibet."

"Will you take me with you?"

"Really, William," Jane interjects, "for a professional Don Juan, your friend Allan is the most easily frightened man I ever met."

Frobisher is more than frightened; he is panicked. He yells that he is going to his club for a drink. And at the door he shouts, "Also, Mrs. Dabney—I am going to call up a girl!" She calls back, "Good luck!"

As a result of Jane's telephone conversation a few minutes ago, Peter Crewe appears. "Wonderful news," Jane informs him. "Your wife's in England!" Ann has run downstairs and hears the news; the young people can scarcely believe it's possible. Jane explains that Lord Frobisher did it—and now, she advises, Peter and Ann should go to the airport and meet this miraculously liberated wife. As they start out, Tower calls his daughter back.

"Ann," he says, with unaccustomed softness, "will you accept my blessing? And you, Peter, will you accept it, too? Can you find it in your hearts to be generous to the defeated?"

Peter accepts Tower's handshake and says, simply, "Thank you very much, Mr. Tower. Please don't think me superior; because, although I couldn't afford to admit it to my own advanced circle, I do admire you very much." Ann and Peter leave, hand in hand.

And now Tower is left with the problem of Lord Frobisher, who seems to be in love with Jane, but remains afraid. "Shall we knock him out of his panic?" he suggests. Jane impulsively puts her arms around him, kisses him, and exclaims, "I adore you, William"—just as Frobisher bolts back into the room and views the tableau. "I won't have it, Jane," he roars. "You can't undermine me and then abandon me!" He has telephoned another girl and has discovered that his knack is still lost; hence his return.

Tower moves to the attack. "I was just about to propose to Jane. Will you please go into the garden and wait?"

Indeed Frobisher will not. Gardens give him hay fever. "Never mind him," says Jane, and she tosses a pillow in front of Tower for him to propose from. His knee creaks as he begins to kneel, and Jane has to help him down.

Tower suggests, "Shall we merge forces?"

Jane considers, "Together we might have too much character. Don't you think we ought to distribute some of it?"

Frobisher cuts in morosely, "I pity those that get it."

Tower continues his proposal. Mrs. Tower, coming downstairs, takes in the sight and asks what's going on. Frobisher explains, "He's proposing to Jane."

Millicent, who specializes in hysteria, cries, "Marvelous! Perfect! Isn't it just like Jane—coming between husband and wife like this?"

"Millicent's time-sense," Tower comments, "is defective." Frobisher wishes to God Willie would go to Tibet. Tower goes on with his proposal, promising a villa in the South of France. "It's beautiful, William," Jane admits, "but I'm going back to Liverpool."

Tower, rising and picking up the pillow, tells her, "I withdraw my offer." This is a relief to Millicent, who now inquires, "But, Jane, what will you do with your house in Belgrave Square?"

Jane supposes she may give it to some charity. "What do you think, Allan? A home for wayward girls?"

Tower exclaims, "Admirable! Allan will fill it!"

Lord Frobisher is galvanized into action. "Jane and I will fill it," he roars. "We're going to live in it!" Millicent starts to babble again, but Frobisher ignores her and addresses himself to Jane: "You owe it to me. You've robbed me of my confidence. You've got to give it back to me."

Tower has had a pretty good afternoon. He lies down on the settee and covers his face with a pillow. To the uncomprehending Mrs. Tower, Jane explains, "I love Allan." Millicent, laughing hysterically, snaps the pillow from Tower's face and asks, "Did you hear that, Willie—love!"

Willie has heard of the word.

Millicent continues, "I've never heard anything so grotesque, so fantastic, so unbelievable!"

Frobisher asks, "Why is it unbelievable?"

Jane goes to him and says, "Perhaps, dear Allan, it is unbelievable because it is the truth!" Frobisher kisses her hand.

THE CURTAIN FALLS

GIGI *

A Comedy in Two Acts

By Anita Loos

IN the 1920s the playwriting and screenwriting team of John Emerson and Anita Loos was a busy one, and successful; the Broadway end of their work resulted in comedies for A. H. Woods and Edgar Selwyn, including "Gentlemen Prefer Blondes." Then, for a number of years, Miss Loos left Broadway to its own devices and did not reappear until the season of 1946-1947, when she wrote "Happy Birthday" for Helen Hayes. Next, being familiar with the subject, she did the book for the very successful musical version of "Gentlemen Prefer Blondes." Her next effort was the adaptation of a novel, "Gigi," by the French author, Colette. Gilbert Miller gave it an extraordinarily handsome production, and the appearance in the title role of Audrey Hepburn, a young English actress known here for her screen work, was such a personal triumph that soon after the opening Miller ceremoniously anointed her with stardom.

The time is about 1900 and the setting is the modest living room of Mme. Alvarez' apartment in Paris. There is a fireplace with a small coal stove fitted into it. A high arch, draped with heavy red plush curtains, opens into a dining alcove and the main entrance; from the alcove a large window looks down on the street. On one side of the room, two doors lead into the kitchen and into the remainder of the apartment. In the alcove there is a large round dining table with a red cover; the furnishings of the main part of the room include a low pouf, a Victorian sofa and an upright piano. The apartment is heavy with pictures, mostly photographs of Gigi's mother, Andrée, at various stages of her singing career, and a large portrait of Gigi as a younger child hangs over the piano. While the room is clean, it is cluttered and disordered. Gigi now is in the awkward stage of adolescence; she is at the piano practicing her scales, and from off in the bedroom her mother is doing vocal exercises which later turn into off-key strains of the Bell Song from "Lakmé." The front door opens and in comes Mme. Alvarez, the lady-of-the-house and Gigi's grandmother. In her shopping bag she has a modest quantity of provisions. Although born and bred in Paris, Mme. Alvarez had long ago assumed the foreign name of a departed lover and acquired a butter-like Spanish paleness. As she comes in she calls, "Gilberte!" There is no answer. "Gilberte!" And finally, in a tone of command, "Gigi!"

Gigi gives a start and turns from the piano, saying she didn't hear her grandmother call because Mama is making such a noise. Soon Mama will be on her way to a rehearsal. Mme. Alvarez tells Gigi to take the groceries into the kitchen, but to bring in the carrots. While the girl does so, the grandmother hangs coat and hat on a rack, assembles a curling iron and papers on a table in front of the sofa and lights an alcohol stove. "And don't forget you've got to go to your Aunt Alicia's," Grandma calls. Gigi returns with the carrots and is eating one; she asks if she couldn't wait until tomorrow to see Aunt Alicia—and if she must go today, couldn't she go without having her hair curled?

Mme. Alvarez voices a firm no, so Gigi sits on the stool by the table. She has to bend her long legs so that her skirt discloses her cotton stockings clear to her knees. "Sometimes," says Grandma, "when I look at those nice, long legs of yours, I regret that you never learned to dance."

"But I wanted to learn, Grandma. Why didn't you let me take lessons?"

Mme. Alvarez, busy now with curling hair, answers, "Your mother took lessons in singing—and look where she's ended up. Slaving away at the Opéra Comique, and not even in principal roles. . . . You see, my Gigi, lessons can give a girl ideas of a career. And a career is the ruination of any woman."

Andrée comes from her bedroom, humming and feeling her delicate tonsils. She is 31, faded and discouraged; she is wearing a worn negligée and carries a shirtwaist; the other parts of her street clothes are draped on a dining-alcove chair, and her hat is on the mantel. At sight of her mother, Gigi remembers she forgot to get a magazine at the kiosk for her mother—a theatre magazine which, Andrée has heard, has a picture of her in it. Taking a coin from her mother, the girl runs, curl papers and all, to do the errand. Gigi almost always runs anywhere, and is usually eating something. Mme. Alvarez calls after her, "And pick up a copy of *Gil Blas* for me!"

ANDRÉE (*to her mother, amused*)—You and your scandal magazine! (MME. ALVAREZ *blows out flame in alcohol stove, and exits to kitchen for apron, while* ANDRÉE *removes her negligee, revealing her bloomers and corsets. She begins to adjust stockings and garters.*) Poor little monkey! She's so backward.. Now, at her age, I was . . .

MME. ALVAREZ (*returning from kitchen, and tying her apron*)— Don't throw roses at yourself for what you were at her age! If memory serves me right, at her age you threw over a rich flour magnate, to run away with a singing teacher!

ANDRÉE—Oh, let's not go into that now, Maman! (*Gets into position for* MME. ALVAREZ *to lace her corset.*) . . . Please, Maman!

MME. ALVAREZ (*proceeding to tighten corset*)—A singing teacher —and when I think how that delightful old gentleman with flour mills all over the place, actually hired the scoundrel . . . (*Presses her knee against* ANDRÉE, *in order to draw corset tighter.*) Stop breathing . . . and paid for the singing lessons!

ANDRÉE—Poor Georges—he wasn't really so bad at heart, Maman.

MME. ALVAREZ—Not bad—huh!

ANDRÉE—But as soon as he found out he'd gotten me into trouble, Georges wanted to . . . (*Goes to chair to get remaining clothes.*)

MME. ALVAREZ—Wanted to marry you! (*Sits on sofa and starts cleaning carrots.*) Well, at least I saved you from that dishonor. Are there any signs at the theatre that you're going to get the lead in this new operetta?

ANDRÉE (*starts putting on clothes*)—Oh, I'm sure they'll give it to Tiphane. Everything goes to her. What a life!

MME. ALVAREZ—Well, you chose it! Even so, you'd be able to stand things better if you had an admirer with a little dignity.

ANDRÉE—It's going to be hot today! (*Puts on hat.*)

MME. ALVAREZ—You know what I'm talking about!

ANDRÉE—Yes, Maman! But, you see, I don't feel that M. Durand is undignified. To be a clerk in a Post and Telegraph Office isn't such a bad career. At least, we can look ahead to a pension.

MME. ALVAREZ—Oh, we can, eh? So you expect to have him hanging around till then, do you?

ANDRÉE (*getting gloves and purse from mantel*)—Is it my fault, if I can't care for anyone else, Maman?

MME. ALVAREZ—It certainly is! It shows a complete lack of self-control!

ANDREÉ—Oh, well! You know, Maman, if we only had a telephone, I could have called up Leclerc and found out what was decided about the new operetta. Don't you think we should have one put in, Maman? A telephone?

MME. ALVAREZ—I know why you want a telephone. ! . .

ANDRÉE—If you think it's because . . .

MME. ALVAREZ—It's because you want to keep in touch with that no-account lover of yours!

ANDRÉE—But, Maman . . .

MME. ALVAREZ—A telephone is only useful to men who have big business affairs, and women who have something to lie about. Now, if you'd get a lover with even a little money, I'd be the first to say, "Let's have a telephone." But as matters stand, we'll wait until Gigi is old enough to have an admirer.

The girl returns from her errand, delivers the magazines, helps herself to a piece of licorice from the buffet and submits to having her curl papers removed. Andrée has found her picture in the magazine and now she slams it on the table; the picture is a group photo of a musical finale and Andrée is barely visible behind a large grenadier. "That's the way it always is," she sighs, and goes out to her rehearsal.

Gigi is ready for the visit to her aunt. At Grandma's command she puts on her navy blue coat and her sailor hat and assures Grandma that she has gloves in her pocket. Grandma speaks disapprovingly of her awkward appearance: "You haven't the single shadow of a stomach, and yet you find some means of sticking it out!"

There are three sharp rings of the doorbell and the girl, running to the door, cries, "It's Tonton!" She flings herself ecstatically at Tonton, who is a very chic young man of 30—real name, Gaston Lachaille. He is deeply dejected—and Gigi knows why without his telling her, for she has read it in *Gil Blas* at school. "You've broken it off with Liane," she says. "But nobody at school blames you, Tonton," she comforts him. "They all say Liane's behavior hasn't been what it should be—ever since you first started to keep her."

Grandma reaches for her copy of *Gil Blas* and confirms the news; there's a spicy story about "a certain bitterness seeping into the beet-sugar fortune of Gaston Lachaille . . ."

Gigi must be off for her lesson at Aunt Alicia's, and Gaston tosses her into seventh heaven by suggesting that she take his new De Dion-Bouton landaulet to her aunt's and then send it back. Mme. Alvarez makes camomile tea in the kitchen for herself and the dejected Gaston. "Anything new with Alicia?" he asks.

"You know how it is with my sister," says Mme. Alvarez. "She's always the same. Says she prefers to live in her beautiful past rather than in an ugly present. . . . Alicia and her King of Spain, her Duke of Milan, her Khedive, her Rajahs, in packages of six if you want to believe her."

Gaston informs, "According to the stories my father told me, she really knew them." He reminds Mme. Alvarez, whom he calls Mamita, that she has made romantic history herself. "Dear Mamita," he declares with affection as he sips his tea, "you've been better than a mother to me, always. That's why I came here today—the one place in all Paris where I can relax and forget that, with all my money, I had to catch Liane in bed with someone else."

The curtain falls.

Scene II

Aunt Alicia lives in a small but exquisite house and her second-floor boudoir looks like a jewel case; it lacks warmth and exudes discreet luxury. The woodwork is gilt. One door leads downstairs, the other to the bedrooms. A large window looks onto the streets of Paris. Alicia's impeccable butler, Victor, ushers in Gigi and brings with him a box of headache *cachets* on a silver tray. Says Gigi, "I'll bet you were surprised, when I pointed out my car down there, weren't you, Victor?" Indeed he was. She runs to the window to have another look at the car—for she has bidden the chauffeur to wait a bit because she wants her aunt to see it.

Aunt Alicia appears from a bedroom—an exquisite old lady of 70, dainty as porcelain, and robustly healthy even though she affects frailty. Her pink chiffon dressing gown is exquisite, and on her head is a lace *fichu*. Aunt Alicia kisses Gigi's forehead and the girl observes that her aunt must have another headache because she's wearing that lace thing on her hair. "That lace thing, Gilberte, is called a *fichu*," Alicia instructs. "This one happened to belong to a Queen of France."

Gigi points out Gaston's car below, and Alicia is surprised that he is in town, for this is the week of the flower *fête* in Nice. "He didn't go this time because he's broken with Liane," Gigi explains.

A properly instructed young girl is not supposed to repeat gossip, but this time Alicia permits Gigi to tell all she knows—which seems to be everything. Liane waited for her birthday present—thirty-seven monstrous pearls—and then skipped out with a skating professor named Sandomar. Poor Tonton found them in a small inn in Normandy. And now Gigi is sad, for this means that Tonton will have to spend all his time picking out someone new, and he won't come to the house any more to play piquet or drink camomile or bring her licorice. This will be pretty gloomy for Gigi.

Since Aunt Alicia has a headache, Gigi thinks the lesson should be postponed and Alicia agrees, counseling her, "You'll go straight home, dear, won't you?"

"Of course I will. Why, now I can have a game of piquet with Tonton."

"Tonton!" exclaims Alicia. "Will Tonton still be there?"

"Of course! He can't leave without his car, Aunty."

An idea is born to Alicia. Perhaps it is wrong of her to neglect Gilberte's lessons. She orders the reluctant girl to take off her coat and turn around. She views Gigi's dress with distaste; it's an old one of her mother's that Grandma made over. Alicia instructs Gigi to summon Victor with the bell-pull and have him dismiss the car. The old woman goes to her room for a moment, returning with a rather large jewel box. Victor is still there and his mistress tells him, "You may serve luncheon today for two, but give us a half hour for Mlle. Gilberte to have her lesson first."

The lesson begins with an examination, in which Aunty learns that Gilberte, at 16, has no men hanging about because Grandma has forbidden her to accept invitations. Why does Grandma do that?

"Because," says Alicia, "you'd only be asked out by very ordinary people, who wouldn't be of any use to you."

"But what makes us different from those ordinary people, Aunty?"

"In the main, Gilberte, it's because they marry."

The lesson has begun—and now it continues with the jewel case. Alicia holds up a ring for inspection and asks what it is. "A diamond," says Gigi.

"What kind?"

"An oblong one."

"Yes"—she puts the ring on the girl's finger—"and the weight of it is five carats."

Another sample is a pin with diamonds set around a ruby. "Their weight," says the instructress, "is half a carat each. Anything less than that I call a chip."

Gigi does make some mistakes; she calls a jonquil diamond a topaz, for instance. The girl admires an emerald ring and asks who gave it to Aunty. "A king," is the answer. Putting jewels back in the box, Alicia counsels, "Hold firmly to your ideals. Better to wear a ring that costs 100 sous than a bad diamond costing 3,000 francs. At least you can say it's a memento from some female relative."

Gigi wants to know who *does* give away the most valuable jewels, and is told, "Men who are timid—men who are conceited. Climbers, because they think giving away monstrous jewels is proof of culture.

And, speaking of culture, never, under any circumstances, wear artistic jewels. And *always* protect yourself against family heirlooms."

Now Alicia gives Gigi a thorough physical examination. Teeth, excellent. Nose, impossible. Mouth, undistinguished. But even so, her eyes, eyelashes, teeth and hair are all the equipment necessary—and her figure has very nice possibilities. Alicia takes a pad and pencil from the table and says, "I'm going to give you a note to the head saleswoman at Paquin. Paquin is an old colleague of mine—she failed and had to go to work." Gigi's delight at the prospect of having a dress from Paquin is vast; she throws her arms about Alicia.

Victor announces lunch and Alicia goes to put away her jewels. "What do I have to learn how to eat today?" asks Gigi, worried.

"For the first course there will be eggs brouillés mousseline à l'Impératrice," the butler replies.

"Are they going to be very complicated?"

"Merely scrambled. The entrée will be ortolans."

"Oh, those nasty little birds!"

Victor says they aren't complicated, either. One cuts each bird in two, and then pops a half in the mouth, bones and all.

When Alicia returns, she and her protégée move ceremoniously down to luncheon, with the old lady counseling the girl to hold her head up and walk gracefully.

The curtain falls.

SCENE III

An hour has passed in Mme. Alvarez' living room, and Gaston is pacing agonizedly as he gives the details of his rupture with his mistress. "What is it they require, these women, in order to be faithful?" he cries. He has always tried to be generous, but sometimes he thinks he has a thief for a roommate. Sometimes he hides his diamond cuff links and his cigarette case. From his pocket he takes a case that makes Mamita's eyes pop—a gold affair studded with jewels.

Making money, Gaston continues, is easy; it's keeping it that is difficult, with everybody wanting some. And now, since he has a date at the Jockey Club, he starts to leave—but collides at the door with the galloping Gigi, who begs him to stay for just one rubber of piquet. He gives in. As Gigi prepares the cards she tells her grandmother of the Paquin dress Aunty is giving her—"one to play cards in with Tonton—Aunty said so!"

Gaston suggests that they play for ten pounds of sugar, but Gigi objects that he always wants to bet with sugar because he gets it for nothing. She wants something expensive, like a Nile-green corset with garters embroidered in moss roses, or a music roll. She settles for the music roll. The play begins.

GASTON—Look out, my friend, I don't need a single card.

GIGI—Don't let that fool you, my partner—I couldn't have picked mine better if I'd stole them! (ANDRÉE *enters, carrying the evening paper,* Figaro.)

ANDRÉE—Well, heavens above, if it isn't Gaston! (GASTON *rises, shakes hands with her, during which time* GIGI *steals a quick glance at the cards in his other hand.*)

GASTON—Oh, good afternoon, Andrée.

ANDRÉE—Please sit down!

GIGI—What's so unusual about Tonton being here, Maman?

ANDRÉE—Nothing. But it is a coincidence because everybody was talking about Gaston backstage today. You and your break with Liane. (MME. ALVAREZ *fakes a distracting cough.*) Have you a cold, Maman? (MME. ALVAREZ *glares at her.*)

GASTON—I wish they'd leave the whole subject alone.

MME. ALVAREZ—But what a compliment, Gaston! The Opéra Comique isn't generally up on the gossip of the *past* century!

GIGI—Your play, idiot!

GASTON—Oh, beg pardon, half-wit!

ANDRÉE—If I could only have telephoned you, Maman, I wouldn't have come home today to dinner.

MME. ALVAREZ—And why not?

ANDRÉE—I had an invitation to dine out.

MME. ALVAREZ—With someone new? Who is he?

ANDRÉE—Madame Leclerc.

MME. ALVAREZ—Oh.

ANDRÉE—It was a wonderful chance to go to work on her, and get her to work on her husband, about that part in the new production. . . . Don't you think we ought to have a telephone?

GASTON—Sure! Why don't you, Mamita?

MME. ALVAREZ—Because Andrée would forever be talking to some no-account.

ANDRÉE—Mama says we've got to wait until Gigi's grown up to have admirers. (GIGI *has just trumped a play of* GASTON'S.)

GASTON—Does she? Just a moment, my friend, you're cheating!

GIGI—Liar!

ANDRÉE—Mama says that telephones are useful to women when they want to lie to men. (*Standing behind* GASTON, *she signals to* GIGI *which card to play.* GIGI *takes her cue and plays another card.*)

MME. ALVAREZ—Did you sing well at the matinee, dear?

ANDRÉE (*approves of* GIGI's *strategy*)—Yes, very well, Maman—as usual.

GASTON—You little robber—you've got that fourth king up your sleeve!

Gigi, kicking Gaston playfully under the table, cries, "I have not—you big, stupid parrot-nose!" They both are acting like children.

Andrée, heedless of her mother's glares, chatters about Gaston's misfortune and what his prospects might be for another mistress, until Mme. Alvarez warns her that her voice is getting husky, and Andrée goes to gargle. Gigi trumps Gaston's best play and he humorously accuses her of cheating again. The girl takes an end of the table cover, throws it over his head, pulls him off his chair and tussles with him on the floor. At last he struggles up and straightens his disheveled clothes. He must go now. Gigi reminds him she has won a music roll and some licorice, then asks where he is going to eat dinner tonight. He supposes Maxim's, as usual. And what will he eat? Oh, filet of sole and breast of pheasant.

"Mmmmm!" the girl exclaims. Then, "We're going to have warmed-over cassoulet tonight." Gaston says it sounds delicious and Mme. Alvarez is quick to invite him to stay and have some, but he declines and starts out. Gigi runs to him, saying, "Just a moment, Tonton! Your hair got rumpled." She wets both palms with her tongue and plasters his hair in place. Then she lifts his chin and straightens his necktie. For a moment their eyes meet, and there is silence. The clock strikes five. Grandma covertly watches them.

Self-conscious, Gaston steps back and bumps into a chair. "You're blushing!" cries Gigi. Gaston seizes hat, coat and stick and stands in the doorway, saying, "Dash it all! I don't know why I ever made that dinner date. I never hated leaving anything so much"—he looks quickly at Gigi—"as that cassoulet of yours, Mamita." He promises to see them again as soon as he comes back from Switzerland.

Andrée comes into the room when Gaston has left, still gargling camomile. Gigi picks up the cards, puts them away, and asks, "Do you think Tonton will remember my music roll, Grandma? He's so forgetful."

"Well," Mme. Alvarez replies, "if he forgets any more, you can telephone him." Andrée and Gigi are very happy at this news.

The curtain falls.

ACT II

A telephone has been installed on the wall near the fireplace at Mme. Alvarez' apartment, and it is ringing. Sidonie, a part-time maid, laundress and garment-presser, comes from the kitchen to answer it. It is Monsieur Lachaille, back from Switzerland. Sidonie says she is dying to meet him because he is the talk of the whole neighborhood. No, Mme. Alvarez is out—gone to bring Gigi from school. Yes, Sidonie will tell Mme. Alvarez that he is coming.

The doorbell rings, and here is Victor with a wicker basket containing four bottles and two splits of champagne. He is tired of lugging stuff here; last week it was a couple of baskets of china, some silver and some cases of *pâté de foie gras* and anchovies. "Little One," Victor observes drily, "is being launched with all the trimmings!"

Gigi comes home in a mood of dreamy dignity, carrying an elaborate leather music roll with large silver clasps. Victor, departing, asks Gigi if there is any message for her aunt, and the girl says, "No, thanks." Sidonie asks, "Do you want Victor to tell her that Monsieur Lachaille is back?" This is news, good news, to Gigi. Sidonie suggests that she put on her new dress, but Gigi says there is no hurry—and adds, "To think that he came back from his holiday ahead of time!" Sidonie says she felt he would all along, ever since he began delaying his trip so he could bring Gigi the music roll personally, instead of merely having it sent. "The music roll plus two dozen boxes of licorice," Gigi counts up. "Twenty-four boxes of rat-tails!" Gigi shows Sidonie something else: a cigarette case—the jewel-studded gold one. "I won this from him at piquet. So I've been taking it to school every day, filled with rat-tails. I pass them around, just carelessly."

Sidonie predicts, "You'll end up covered in jewels, like Mademoiselle Liane."

"Oh! Do you think I will, Sidonie?"

"Yes, indeed. You're going to be a real credit to your family."

Andrée comes in from her bedroom, in dressing gown and slippers, carrying her part for a new operetta and complaining that she just can't seem to learn it, she feels so dull today. Sidonie suggests champagne, which Victor has just brought, and Andrée brightens. While the maid goes for the wine, Gigi's mother attacks her role, and Gigi reads the cues for her—a role which consists entirely of singing, in answer to questions, "No" on a long, high note. There are several "No's" and Andrée has trouble with remembering them all. Mme.

Alvarez, having stopped off to shop after bringing Gigi from school, comes home with the daily provisions. She has already heard from the concierge, who had it from Victor, that Gaston is coming, and she hurries Gigi to her bedroom to dress.

Sidonie comes from the kitchen with a tumbler of champagne, silently sidles around Mme. Alvarez and hands it to Andrée. "What is that?" demands Mme. Alvarez, and the maid answers, "Pommery, 1882, sent over by Madame Alicia." Mme. Alvarez, angry, says the wine was sent here for the sole purpose of entertaining Monsieur Lachaille—but as long as a bottle has been opened Andrée may as well have some. Andrée, anxious to change the subject, jolts her mother by saying that she heard at the theatre last night that Liane followed Gaston to Switzerland. Then she resumes practicing her role until her mother yells, "Will you please stop studying that two-letter word you've got to learn and listen to me? Did anyone say whether or not Liane made up with Gaston in Switzerland?" Andrée replies that last night the opinions were divided, yes and no.

This is a crisis in which Mme. Alvarez needs help. She orders her daughter to go in and put on a dress, then telephones her sister Alicia. While she is thus occupied on the phone, Andrée sneaks into the kitchen, steals a large bottle of champagne and tiptoes to her bedroom. Mme. Alvarez, getting Alicia on the wire, tells the old lady of Gaston's impending arrival and of the report about Liane pursuing him to Switzerland. This is going to need the sort of delicate treatment that only Alicia can supply, so will Alicia hurry right over?

Barely has this conversation ended when Gaston's familiar triple ring on the doorbell is heard. Sidonie drops some dishes in the kitchen and hastens to the door. Mme. Alvarez welcomes him, and he hands her some flowers. "And flowers for Gilberte!" she exclaims. "How chic!"

Gaston says no, the flowers are for her. "I brought *this* for Gigi," he says—and from his pocket takes a rubber ball with a rubber string attached. Mme. Alvarez asks Sidonie to bring the champagne and she and Gaston sit for a chat. He reveals that he hasn't just got back; he's been back for several days, and a few nights ago he gave a really bang-up party at the Pré-Catelan. He hired a number of acts, and a strange little dwarf, Count Lautrec, got tight and was very amusing, and his grand finale was having Rita del Erido, from the Hippodrome, ride among the tables on horseback in a silver riding habit trimmed with ostrich plumes.

Mme. Alvarez cannot understand how a party like this could have escaped publicity; she hadn't read anything about it. Gaston explains he has been learning about publicity; he let *Gil Blas* know that he would withdraw the subsidy he granted them if they ever mentioned a word about it. Gaston adds, "I bought Del Erido a lavallière, Mamita—bigger than the one I gave Liane last Christmas." Gaston begins bouncing Gigi's rubber ball, abstractedly. Mme. Alvarez knows what is wrong: "You're not thinking of Del Erido, Gaston. You're thinking of Liane." He admits it, dejectedly, but adds with spirit that he has his pride and nothing would ever make him take her back.

Sidonie brings champagne and glasses and Gaston, glad of something to do, volunteers to open the bottle. Andrée, still in her dressing gown and tight from champagne, teeters in from her bedroom to greet the guest. She begins babbling about Gigi—about her being moody, and eating too much—particularly garlic sausages, which gave her a pimple on her nose last week. . . . Mme. Alvarez cannot shut her daughter up, either by glares or protests. Gaston has opened the champagne and poured it, and Sidonie passes it. Gigi comes in, wearing her Paquin dress and carrying an ivory fan her aunt has given her. In her best ladylike manner she makes a complete turn, and Gaston gazes at her speechless.

GIGI—Well, Tonton? Why, what's the matter?

GASTON—Matter?

MME. ALVAREZ—Gaston has neglected us so long, dear, he doesn't recognize you any more.

GIGI (*her childlike enthusiasm breaking through all her efforts to be a lady*)—Look, Tonton! My skirt is four meters and twenty-five around. And that isn't all! I've got a box coat, just like Mademoiselle de Merode's. And two new hats, and another pair of high-heeled shoes. (*Strikes a pose and curtsies.*) Well, what do you think of me?

GASTON—You look exactly like an organ-grinder's monkey!

MME. ALVAREZ—Gaston!

ANDRÉE (*attempting to hit table with her hand, misses it, and lunges forward*)—I side with you, Gaston! You're absolutely right! (*GASTON goes to GIGI.*)

GASTON—You see? Your mother knows! Come over here! (*Takes GIGI by the arm, holds her in front of him, and makes her look in the mirror.*) That collar makes you look just like a hen that's eaten too many chick-peas!

GIGI—Tonton!

GASTON—I liked you a lot better in your old blue dress!

GIGI—You pretend to know a lot of things, Tonton, but I never heard of your having any taste in dress!

GASTON—Now, really! (ANDRÉE *breaks into the "Bell Song," moves to* GASTON, *and dances with a sinuous motion of the hips.* MME. ALVAREZ, *seeing that* ANDRÉE *is completely out of control, grabs her by the left arm, and struggles to get her off into the bedroom. Hearing the noise,* SIDONIE *enters, takes in the situation.*)

SIDONIE—Well, here we go!

MME. ALVAREZ (*pulling* ANDRÉE, *who is still singing the "Bell Song" and wriggling her hips*)—That's enough! We've seen everything we want! (*The doorbell rings.* SIDONIE *starts for door, but* MME. ALVAREZ, *who has now succeeded in pushing the still-singing* ANDRÉE *into the bedroom, starts to answer the door.*) Never mind, Sidonie; I'll answer it! (SIDONIE *exits into kitchen.* MME. ALVAREZ *pauses for a second, to get her breath, then opens the door. During this,* GIGI, *at the point of tears, sits in the armchair by the fireplace, her back to* GASTON *who is dazed by the whole performance.* ALICIA *enters.* MME. ALVAREZ *kisses* ALICIA *on the cheek.*) Alicia!

ALICIA—Inez, my dear! Gaston! How well you look, my boy.

GASTON (*kissing her hand*)—Madame!

ALICIA—A little bit thin, perhaps, but it only brings out those fatal eyes of yours, Gilberte! Is that a new dress I see?

The crushed Gigi, bursting into tears, tells her aunt that Tonton says it makes her look like a monkey. Gaston hastens to make amends. Going to Gigi, he offers her the rubber ball. With bitter sarcasm, she says it's too awfully, dreadfully nice of him—and she throws the ball at him. Then she pushes him in the chest, shouting that as far as what *he* looks like goes, he's gotten so scrawny his nose looks perfectly enormous. To punctuate her opinion, she pushes his nose upward—and then flees to her room. Gaston, with almost all the poise knocked out of him, leaves with what dignity he can, flinging at Mme. Alvarez, "Well, Mamita! You have my compliments! A fine bringing-up you've given that child!"

Alicia has been astounded by the scene. Now she takes from her muff a clipping which she has just torn from the afternoon paper. She tells her sister, "Mademoiselle Liane has committed suicide." The experienced Mme. Alvarez inquires, "Is she dead this time?" Alicia snaps, "Certainly not!" It was laudanum, as usual, and Mme. Alvarez predicts that Liane will be getting gunnysacks under her eyes from all those doses of laudanum. Alicia, however, is worried: Liane's is Gaston's first experience with suicide and it may make him feel all puffed up—particularly after Gigi's recent insulting performance.

Alicia determines that Gigi must come stay with her, beginning tomorrow, where she can be brought up properly.

There are three rings at the door—Gaston has come back because he has forgotten his hat. Also, he thought he'd take Gigi to the Pré-Catelan and buy her an ice. Mme. Alvarez is all for it, but Alicia uickly steps in; Gilberte is not the little girl Gaston knew, but a oung lady, and it would never do for her to be seen with him at the ré-Cat.

Gaston suggests that Alicia come along as chaperone and she laughs, "Me? With *my* reputation as a *grande cocotte?* Why, people might think I was putting the child on the market! . . . No, Gaston, before Gilberte ever sets foot in the great world she must enter into a formal liaison with some nice man, who will ensure her future."

Gigi has taken off her new dress and put on her old one and now she comes back. She wanly acknowledges Gaston's presence. Aunt Alicia tells her to cheer up, and reveals that Gigi is coming to stay with her for a nice long visit. When Alicia has left, Gigi cries violently to her grandmother that she doesn't want to leave here. Gaston picks up his hat, ready to go; then he looks at Gigi and puts his hat on the dining table, where it covers the clipping Alicia has left there, and goes to the girl and apologizes for what he said. Gigi says it's all right—she can't be mad at him forever. In new high spirits, Gaston asks Mme. Alvarez if Gigi can't go out with him—to the Bois, for an ice. Gigi pleads, "Grandma, may I?"

MME. ALVAREZ—Not this time, dear. Run into the kitchen, and see if Sidonie has put the kettle on, will you?

GIGI—Oh, all right, Grandma. (*Exits into kitchen.*)

MME. ALVAREZ—I hate to seem difficult, Gaston, but you understand my position, don't you?

GASTON—Can't say that I do. It seems to me you're making an elephant out of a flea.

MME. ALVAREZ—But, my dear boy, I'm only acting as a mother would. I have a sacred trust, to guard Gigi like a tender flower.

GASTON—Well, I won't argue about it. Just go on protecting your brat. (*From the kitchen comes the sound of the tea-kettle crashing to the floor.*)

MME. ALVAREZ—Oh, that wretched Sidonie! What is it this time? (*She exits.*)

GIGI's voice—Me, Grandma! I dropped the tea-kettle, that's all. (GASTON *picks up his hat, revealing the newspaper clipping, which he takes and reads. From the kitchen we hear:*)

MME. ALVAREZ—You didn't hurt yourself?

GIGI—No, Grandma, I guess I was a little bit nervous.

MME. ALVAREZ—Well, be careful now!

GIGI—I will! (MME. ALVAREZ *enters, sees* GASTON *reading the clipping about Liane.*)

MME. ALVAREZ (*trying to appear casual*)—Imagine the faker! Trying to commit suicide! (GASTON *looks at her, replacing paper on table.*) Lucky escape you had from that one!

GASTON—Think so? Well, I've got to get along.

MME. ALVAREZ (*following him*)—I'll just fetch Gigi, to say good-by.

GASTON (*quickly*)—Don't bother; I'll see her some other time.

MME. ALVAREZ—Tomorrow, perhaps?

GASTON—Perhaps. I'm afraid I'll be pretty busy the next few weeks. Good-by! (*Exits and closes door.* SIDONIE *enters from kitchen, just in time to see* GASTON *leave.*)

SIDONIE—This may not be my business, Madame—but I think you've gone one step too far with that young man.

MME. ALVAREZ (*shortly*)—It's not your business—and nobody pays you to think! (*Takes clipping from table, starts to read.*)

SIDONIE—Very well, Madame, but what in the world could he be doing that would take him several weeks? (*Picks up half-empty champagne bottle.*)

MME. ALVAREZ—Shut up! And get along with your work!

SIDONIE—Better look out, Madame— If Monsieur Lachaille can leave you, *I* can! (*Exits, looking into bottle, hopefully. As lights dim,* MME. ALVAREZ *crumples clipping, sits at table, worried and apprehensive.*)

The curtain falls.

SCENE II

In her boudoir, Alicia is on the telephone with her sister, Mme. Alvarez, and she doesn't know that Gigi is in the doorway listening as she says:

"I do wish you'd leave this affair to *me!* I'm telling you, you almost lost the man for good; so from now on, you'll just keep out of things, if you don't mind. . . . What if he didn't go back to Liane? He didn't go back to you, either—he came to *me.* And what's more important, he's coming this afternoon—and I think he's going to make a proposition—for Gilberte, not *you,* dear! Yes, and I've spent the last three hours working out a counter-proposition that will be absolutely water-tight. . . . But of course, Lachaille will protect his own interests, down to the last penny. Don't forget he has one of the best business brains in France. . . . No, please, Inez, don't come over here again! I hate to sound inhospitable, but you've been running in here, two and three times a day, and upsetting Gigi. She appears to hanker for that run-down flat of yours, and the perfume of stale cooking. If you have anything important to say, you have a telephone—*use* it. (*Conscious of* GIGI's *presence, turns and sees her.*) Ah, Gilberte, my dear—how sweet you look! (*Into phone.*) Gilberte—she's wearing my rose chiffon negligee. . . . Yes, ravishing! Very well, dear, you may call up later. Good-by!"

Gigi does not feel well and has come to ask her aunt for a headache powder. Victor knocks, enters, and announces that Monsieur Lachaille is downstairs. Alicia asks that he be shown up, tells Victor also to bring Gilberte a headache powder in her room, and leads the girl off.

Victor brings Gaston up, then, speaking in a low tone, says, "She's got the strategy of twenty rattlesnakes—so be on your guard, Monsieur." Gaston assures Victor he needn't worry; "I'll remember what you told me—one can clip a sheep every year, but you can only skin him once."

Alicia reappears and Victor departs. After a few preliminary *politesses*, the old lady and the young millionaire get down to business, with Alicia setting the terms. Gaston has discovered that little Gilberte has grown up, and he would like the privilege of—well— that she'll be taken care of. . . . Alicia prescribes, first, a roof over the girl's head—a suitable house on the Avenue du Bois, which she will find for them. Then, of course, there must be a competent staff, and a motor car. And in case Gaston should be killed in one of his motor cars, some provision for Gilberte . . .

Alicia suggests that they meet tomorrow in her lawyer's office. Gaston blandly submits that they meet in *his* lawyer's office, with *her* lawyer along. Alicia agrees.

Victor knocks, enters and says, "Forgive me, Madame—but Mademoiselle Gilberte asked me to bring you this." He hands her a diamond ring with a piece of note-paper rolled up in it. "She's gone, Madame," Victor adds. "She said she was returning to her own home." Alicia reads the note, then takes refuge in acting feeble again. She begs Gaston to excuse her. She will not be able to see the lawyers tomorrow—in fact, she's afraid things will have to be dropped for the moment. Gaston tries to find out what is in this note of Gigi's, but Alicia, sinking to her chaise-longue, fends him off and bids him good-by. The instant he has left she is on the telephone trying to reach Mme. Alvarez, but the line is busy. Frantically she summons Victor and tells him she wants the carriage at once. Victor has already provided the carriage. "I smelled trouble in the air," he explains. "Trouble, you idiot," Alicia shouts as she goes toward the stairs. "It's disaster!"

The curtain falls.

Scene III

It is later the same day and Gigi is back home. As the curtain rises, the girl is discovered at the telephone with her coat draped about her head to keep her grandmother, who is in the kitchen, from hearing her. Gigi has put in a call for Gaston at the Jockey Club. He isn't there. She leaves a message saying that she would like to see him at her own home. The doorbell rings viciously, and Gigi runs to her room.

Mme. Alvarez opens the door, and it is Alicia, in a fury of excitement. Where is Gigi? Mme. Alvarez hasn't seen her. Alicia details the recent events—how she had Gaston all ready to talk to her lawyer, and then Gigi runs out, leaving an ultimatum. In her note, Gigi has told Alicia that the only way she might possibly consider Gaston would be to talk things over with him—alone. A silly child couldn't possibly handle so delicate and complicated an affair!

Gigi comes in and calmly asks, "What do you want with me, Aunt Alicia?"

ALICIA—Come here! I want an explanation!

MME. ALVAREZ—Please don't scold the child, Alicia! Can't you see she's nervous! (*To* GIGI.) Don't you worry about anything, my darling. Nobody's going to torment you about Tonton! (GIGI *looks over her shoulder at* MME. ALVAREZ.)

ALICIA (*trying more gentle tactics*)—No, of course not! But at the same time, I do wish you'd use a little common sense. Some women don't fall in love before thirty—or even later. And it really might have been a pity for you to have started out your career with a grand passion. Fascinating as it would be to go to the end of the world with a man who knows everything there is to know about life. To lose one's self in the arms of a divine creature like Gaston Lachaille . . . To listen to love songs under a sky of eternal springtime! (GIGI *slowly looks at* ALICIA.) Of course, if that doesn't appeal to you, there's nothing more to be said!

GIGI—There's something more that I can say, Aunty. I can say that when the eternal springtime is over, Monsieur Lachaille may go off with another woman—perhaps the woman, even I, may run away from Monsieur Lachaille, and Monsieur Lachaille will tell the story to everyone at the Jockey Club. And the woman, who could still be I, might have nothing to do but go straight into the bed of some other man!

ALICIA—Inez! She's speaking the language of the gutter!

GIGI—I'm sorry, Aunty. But I just don't care for that way of living. I'm not that changeable.

ALICIA—Very well, then, if you want to end up working at a dress-making shop, or in the chorus of the Opéra Comique, go ahead and do it!

GIGI—You think you know so much, Aunt Alicia! You think you've done so brilliantly in life! Well, do you know what *I* think? I think that you're a failure!

ALICIA—What?

GIGI—What have you got out of that elegant career of yours, except a house full of silly knick-knacks? Why, you're so bored you have to trump up headaches, just to keep yourself company!

ALICIA—That will do, Gilberte!

MME. ALVAREZ—Don't scold her, Alicia! I've never believed much in those headaches myself!

GIGI (*quickly interrupting*)—And *you*, Grandma! You've sided with her about Tonton—you *know* you have!

MME. ALVAREZ—I only wanted to save you from poverty, my child.

GIGI—But *why?* We've always been poor, you and Mama and I—and has it been so bad? Why, Tonton himself has to come here for a decent cup of camomile! Both of you! With your plans and schemes and your advice—maybe I can work some way out myself that will be better.

There are three rings on the doorbell. Gigi, a suddenly aroused Gigi, is in command; she orders the two women to go into the bed-room so she may see Gaston alone. As the bell rings again, she hastily fixes her hair in a mirror, then admits Gaston. He hasn't been to the Jockey Club and hasn't got her message; he has come on his own, to see if she got home safely from her aunt's. Hesitantly he asks if Gigi knows what he had gone to see Aunt Alicia about. Gigi knows. He pleads, "Just tell me what it is you don't want. And then tell me what it is you *do* want. I'll give it to you if I can."

Gigi indignantly details the future he has in store for her: She will sleep in his bed, and have her picture in the newspapers, and go to the flower festival at Nice and the races at Trouville, and every time they have a quarrel *Gil Blas* will chronicle it, and then one day he will leave her for good, as he has left others. . . .

Gaston protests that this kind of thing is finished for him, but Gigi says she doesn't believe him. She has another proposition: He can come here as usual, only more often. He can bring licorice and champagne for her birthday, and they can play monstrous games of piquet.

This is not what Gaston wants at all. He points out that Gigi has missed one little thing—the fact that he loves her. The girl seems dazed at this declaration—and then she reacts oddly: She denounces him for wanting to drag her into a life of suffering, a life where everybody talks viciously about everybody else, a life which will end with a separation and quarrels and revolvers and laudanum —and another woman for him and another man for her. She begins to sob. "Go away!" she shrieks. "Get out—get out!"

Mme. Alvarez and Alicia run in in a panic. "Your niece," Gaston informs Alicia, "has just ordered me to leave the house! She doesn't want me! It's the first time it has ever been said to my face." He departs, slamming the door angrily, and the women turn to Gigi, who is sobbing on the mantel, for an explanation. "He said he was in love with me," she manages to say.

For Alicia this is the end—and for the indignant Grandma, too. But suddenly there are three rings at the doorbell. Gigi commands, "If it is Tonton, I can't see him again." She leaves the room. "Let the child go," Alicia advises her sister. "Can't you see she's got a method in her madness?"

Grandma admits Gaston, who is carrying a box of licorice. It was in his car, and he thought Gigi might as well have it. Suddenly he throws the box to the floor, drops to one knee and pleads, "Mamita! Will you grant me the honor, the favor, the infinite joy of Gigi's hand?"

Mme. Alvarez collapses, stunned, on the sofa, and Alicia remarks, "Well, it's rather unconventional, dear boy. Let's see what Gilberte has to say about it." She opens the bedroom door and calls her grand-niece. Gigi, thinking Gaston has left, appears. Gaston urges, "I want you to be my wife, Gigi"—and the girl begins to cry again— but this time, she confesses, because she loves Gaston too. She throws her arms about him, still weeping and exclaiming, "I love you! You don't have to marry me!" Mme. Alvarez and Alicia show a new alarm, but Gaston assures them it is all right—this is the only way he could ever have taken Gigi. He kisses her.

In comes Andrée, wanting to know what's up, and when she is told that Gaston wants to marry her daughter *she* begins weeping. Gaston protests, "Listen, Andrée, we're happy! We want you to help us celebrate!" Andrée's sobs increase until Mme. Alvarez comes up with a fine suggestion. "How," she says to her daughter, "would you like to sing something?"

Andrée's sobs subside as she invites, "Anything special?"

Grandma makes the supreme sacrifice. "The Bell Song," she suggests. Andrée goes to the piano and begins, as usual, off-key.

THE CURTAIN FALLS

REMAINS TO BE SEEN *

A Comedy in Three Acts

By Howard Lindsay and Russel Crouse

THE writing team of Lindsay and Crouse seems happily willing to try anything. They have turned out the librettos of many musicals, the most recent of which was a political satire, "Call Me Madam." They have collaborated on joyful comedies like "Life with Father" and have won a Pulitzer prize for a serious play on politics, "State of the Union." They seem to have written "Remains to Be Seen" just for fun, with no other aim than to provide the theatre with a comedy-melodrama. It was welcomed in the season of 1951-1952 because the theatre can always use a comedy-melodrama and it hasn't been getting many in recent seasons.

The setting is the living room in the Park Avenue apartment of Travis Revercombe; it's a man's room, but rather luxuriously furnished. In one wall is a door to the bedroom, and the bath can be entered either from the bedroom or through a door out of sight in the foyer. In the foyer is a house telephone. In another wall is a door leading to the other rooms of the apartment. Tall bookcases occupy part of the back wall. There is a couch, and above it hangs a collection of African masks. There is a television set which can be closed with double doors. Other decorations and furnishings include a painting of Revercombe, an African tom-tom, a desk with telephone, chairs and side tables. It is shortly after ten o'clock at night; the room is almost dark. On the television screen a prize fight is in progress, and somebody has a chair drawn up before it, back to the audience. When a round ends, a figure is seen getting up from the chair and moving to a light switch on a wall. The lights go up and reveal Edward Miller, a uniformed policeman. The front door buzzer sounds, and Miller hurries to the chair, picks up and puts on his cap, turns off the television set, puts the chair back in its proper place and opens the door. In comes Benjamin Goodman, distinguished-looking and middle-aged, looking puzzled at Miller's presence.

Says the officer, "I was ordered to wait until you got here." Goodman is more puzzled. Miller asks, "Aren't you the medical examiner?"

"No. Why? What's happened? I came here to see Mr. Revercombe."

"If you're a friend of his I've got some bad news for you. He's dead," the officer declares. "They found him in the bedroom about an hour ago." Goodman starts for the bedroom but the policeman says he can't get in that way because the body is lying against the door. Anyhow, he shouldn't even go in by way of the bathroom—not until the medical examiner comes.

Goodman inquires how Revercombe died and the policeman informs him, "Heart attack. That's what his doctor said." Goodman goes to the telephone on the desk, calls his secretary at her home, and asks her to telephone an undertaker. In a moment there is an incoming call on the phone—the New York *Times*. Goodman takes the call, says he is Revercombe's attorney, and gives what facts he can. The door buzzer sounds and the policeman admits Dr. Charles Gresham, physician to the deceased, who has offices in the building. He is carrying a folder containing Revercombe's medical record. He and Goodman discuss notifying the family, but the only family Goodman knows of is a niece about whom he didn't know until just recently. The doctor tells the lawyer that Revercombe had had a serious heart attack about a year ago, and was also diabetic—a bad combination. The lawyer tells the doctor that Revercombe fancied himself as a guardian of public morals and had recently taken up watching the morals of television programs. The bookshelves, Goodman indicates, contain the finest collection of pornography and erotica in the country. Gresham and Goodman pull out a few samples to glance at, and the policeman helps himself to one. "Oh, boy—pictures!" he ejaculates. He sits down, absorbed in the book.

Goodman tells the doctor that Revercombe was an odd man—he enjoyed these books, but didn't want anybody else to. "I loathed him," he adds. Miller, rising with his book, asks if either of the gentlemen could tell him where he could buy a copy. Goodman takes it from him, looks at it and says it's a pretty rare item; might cost three or four thousand dollars. Miller reaches for the volume, but the lawyer withholds it and advises the officer to go back to his television prize fight and cool off.

Waldo Walton enters, having let himself in with a key from a bunch he is carrying. He is the apartment house manager—but surprisingly young for such a post. Waldo brings in Dr. Chester De-lapp, the medical examiner, who says he was at the fight at the

Garden when he got the call to come here. Now he seems more interested in the rest of the fight on television than he is in Waldo's recital of his discovery of the body. Waldo explains that the apartment building is co-operative, and Revercombe had called a meeting of the board for nine o'clock and failed to show up. So Waldo let himself in here with his passkey, found the body in the bedroom, telephoned on the house phone for help, fainted, and was ultimately brought to by Dr. Gresham. "I must confess," says Waldo, "I never liked Mr. Revercombe, but when I saw him lying there I just could feel sorry for him."

After watching a bit more of the fight, the medical examiner and Dr. Gresham go to the bedroom, with Gresham explaining that his patient had diabetes. "The hypodermic is right there beside him. He might have given himself an overdose of insulin." Delapp asks the policeman to keep an eye on the fight while he's gone.

Goodman introduces himself to Waldo, explaining that he wants to wait here until a Miss Revere arrives and asks for him. "You see that she gets here," he instructs, "and ask the hallman not to mention Mr. Revercombe's death. Or even that this is his apartment." Goodman joins the others in the bedroom. Waldo watches the fight with the policeman for a moment, and then the cop says he'd rather do a little reading. He has his eye on the picture book Goodman has put back in the shelves. "If you don't want to watch the fight there's a dance band I'd like to get," says Waldo, reaching for the television dial, but the policeman says, "Leave the fight on. I promised Doc I'd keep an eye on it for him."

The examination hasn't taken long and Delapp and Gresham soon return. Gresham is saying he had just warned Revercombe yesterday not to take more than twenty-five units of insulin a day. The case is clear enough to the medical examiner, who says he will sign the death certificate. Waldo goes back downstairs. Goodman asks and gets the medical examiner's permission to move the body to a bed and Dr. Gresham offers to help. As soon as the pair have gone to the bedroom the policeman edges toward the book case, but before he can reach his picture volume there is a roar from the television crowd. "One of them's down. I think it's Wilson." The policeman comes back for a look and opines that it is Kramer. The officer suggests that if they turned out the lights they might get a clearer picture. He switches off all the lights, just as Goodman enters from the bedroom door. He wants the policeman and the medical examiner to help him and Gresham move the body, and they reluctantly join him.

The bedroom door closes and the room is dark except for the television screen—which now shows a referee counting a knockout. The silhouette of a hand feels its way across the screen. Then a human figure passes in front of the screen and disappears through the foyer in the direction of the bathroom and the front door.

Miller opens the bedroom door, admitting some light, and hurries toward the book case; but Goodman follows him closely and catches him with the red book in his hand. Again the lawyer takes the volume and puts it back in place, observing, "I'm getting a bad impression of you, Officer." He turns up the lights as Gresham and Delapp emerge from the bedroom. Gresham asks the examiner to sign the certificate, but Delapp is more interested in the fight. He is enormously disappointed to find that it is over and nobody knows who won; now he will have to go to Toots Shor's to find out. Gresham reminds him of the death certificate and Delapp finally signs it and hurries out. Gresham tears a tab off the certificate and puts the rest of it in a large envelope on a table. Goodman says, pointedly, "Good night, Officer"—for this is not a police case. Miller, reluctant to leave his book, gets an idea. The district attorney's office ought to be very interested in all this obscene literature and he is going to take along some evidence. He takes the book again, but Goodman sharply orders him to put it back. Miller grudgingly does so and reluctantly leaves the apartment.

GRESHAM—I believe you are going to wait here for someone, Mr. Goodman?

GOODMAN—(*glancing at watch*)—Yes, I'm afraid I may be here an hour or more. I have to wait for Mr. Revercombe's niece.

GRESHAM—She's coming from out of town?

GOODMAN—Yes. I had a difficult time tracking her down. She sings with a band. Have you any idea how many bands there are in this country and how fast they move?

GRESHAM—No, that's a little out of my line.

GOODMAN—This particular aggregation, led by a Mr. Pee Wee Baker, plays in a different town every night.

GRESHAM—I can see how she'd be hard to find.

GOODMAN—And it didn't exactly help that she changed her name from Josephine Revercombe to Jody Revere.

GRESHAM—Well, I should be down in my office. Would you mind giving this to the undertaker when he comes? (*He starts, hesitates, returns.*) There's something I'd like to talk to you about.

GOODMAN—Yes?

GRESHAM—It seems a little indelicate at this moment, but I've been waiting for a long time to buy an apartment in this building.

I'd like to be considered if this one goes on the market.

GOODMAN (*with a twinkle in his voice*)—You didn't plan this, did you, Doctor? (*They both laugh.*) What do you think it's worth?

GRESHAM—I don't know how large it is. I've only been in this room and the bedroom.

GOODMAN—Well, let's look around.

But before they can look around Waldo lets himself in and brings an undertaker. In a moment the buzzer rings, and another undertaker appears; for Dr. Gresham also has called one. Since Goodman is the executor of the deceased's estate, the first undertaker, named Clark, wins the body and the other one leaves, amiable but disappointed. Waldo starts to go, but Dr. Gresham stops him, saying, "I'm hoping to buy this apartment. While you're here can you show us the rest of it?" Waldo would be glad to; there's only a dining room, kitchen and linen closet left to see. He starts the tour. Undertaker Clark calls, "Oh, Doctor, have you the certificate?"

"It's there on the desk. You'll find Mr. Revercombe in the bedroom," says Gresham, and he follows Waldo and Goodman. Clark uses the house phone and asks that his men come up in the freight elevator, then goes to the bedroom. He is there only for a few seconds when he comes running out. Waldo, Gresham and Goodman have finished their tour and stand astonished as the undertaker dials the phone on the desk and says, excitedly, "Hello . . . Medical Examiner's office? I was called in on the death of Mr. Travis Revercombe, 412 Park Avenue. That's where I'm phoning from now. The certificate was signed by Delapp. It says natural causes. . . . What's the matter? There's a carving knife sticking in his chest!"

The curtain falls.

SCENE II

It is later that night, and officer Miller has returned—with reinforcements in the persons of Detectives Rosenberg and Minetti. Goodman is nervously pacing. Waldo is listening to a band record on the phonograph part of the television set, and pretty soon he takes from a coat pocket a pair of drumsticks and begins drumming with the band in pantomime. Rosenberg is leafing through Patrolman Miller's favorite book. Testily Goodman suggests that the detectives do a little detecting—after all, somebody was hidden in the apartment or got into it, with a knife. Rosenberg says they'll have to wait until the medical examiner returns.

Delapp appears, demanding, "What the hell do you want me here for?" Rosenberg identifies himself, then asks Delapp sarcastically if he happened to notice a carving knife sticking in the stiff's chest. Delapp is mystified, and Goodman puts in, "We've told you, Officer, the knife wasn't there at the time."

The phone rings; it's the morgue, where Mr. Revercombe has been taken, calling the medical examiner. Delapp takes the phone and spends some moments listening and asking questions. Then he hangs up and turns triumphantly to Rosenberg, saying, "This man was dead long before the knife was stuck into him and there is every evidence that he died just as I said he did—heart shock."

"That settles that," says Rosenberg, and he and his partner start to go, but Delapp detains them, saying the case isn't closed yet: it's against the law to stab a dead body, and he has ordered an autopsy. Reluctantly the detectives decide they'd better look around, and the medical examiner leaves after announcing that he is going to report the case to the D.A. Dr. Gresham asks nobody in particular, "But who would want to do such a thing?"

Waldo leaves, and Rosenberg and Minetti go into the bedroom. A call on the house phone announces that a young lady is downstairs to see Mr. Goodman, and he asks that she be sent up. Gresham wants to leave, but Goodman asks him to stay until the girl comes, because it might be awkward at first. He explains, "There was a coolness between the two branches of the family. We hoped to effect a reconciliation."

GRESHAM—Men with bad hearts are apt to have bad consciences.

GOODMAN—But he was afraid she might refuse to see him. So I wired her asking her to come to New York and meet me here. I made it sound important to her future. As a matter of fact, it is. He wrote her into his will last week.

GRESHAM—Oh? Well, you've got a lot to tell her.

GOODMAN—Yes, fortunately. Oh, there's one little detail I'd like to avoid— Any mention of the knife.

GRESHAM—Of course. Why should anyone want to stab a dead body? (*We hear voices off stage by the front door.*)

WALDO (*off stage*)—Here we are! Is that really so?

JODY (*off stage*)—Yes, this is the first time I've ever been in New York.

WALDO (*off stage*)—You'll like it. Right through here.

JODY (*off stage*)—Oh—a mirror! Tell Mr. Goodman I'll be right in. I've been on that plane since noon. (WALDO *enters, carrying a suitcase. He speaks back to her.*)

WALDO—You look fine! I noticed! (*He goes into the room and speaks to* GOODMAN.) She's here. She'll be right in. (JODY REVERE *enters with her best smile.* JODY *is a pretty, attractive girl in her middle twenties. She comes briskly into the room. As she enters* WALDO *speaks and indicates.*) This is Mr. Goodman!

GOODMAN—How do you do? (*She starts toward* GOODMAN, *then stops. The expectancy drains out of her face.*)

JODY—You ain't Benny Goodman!

GOODMAN—Yes, I'm Benjamin Goodman.

JODY—But you're not Benny Goodman, the band leader.

GOODMAN—Oh, no! (*The bedroom door opens abruptly, and* MILLER, ROSENBERG *and* MINETTI *walk in. They stare at* JODY.)

JODY (*backing up*)—What's going on here? What's the idea?

ROSENBERG—Who's this dame? Who are you? What's your name?

GOODMAN—This is Mr. Revercombe's niece.

JODY—Oh, so my uncle is mixed up in this! What is this—a frame-up?

GOODMAN—No. Please let me explain. Miss Revercombe, I'm your uncle's attorney. I have some news for you—some of it's good news, some of it's bad news.

JODY—Give me the bad news first.

GOODMAN—Your uncle dropped dead this afternoon.

JODY—That's good news.

GOODMAN—But you figure rather importantly in his will.

JODY—That's bad news. I wouldn't take anything off of him.

GOODMAN—We'll talk about that later. I regret you've arrived under these circumstances, but it's rather fortunate you are here at this time.

JODY—Oh, it is, eh? I come here all steamed up to meet Benny Goodman and you ain't even Benny Goodman!

GOODMAN—I'm sorry you're disappointed, but my name is Benjamin Goodman.

The disappointed Jody, fearing she may have lost her job by making this trip, asks permission to use the phone and puts in a call for Pee Wee Baker at the Iceland Skating Rink at Lawrence, Kansas. Gresham departs and Goodman goes to the foyer to see him off. Waldo is bug-eyed at meeting Jody Revere in person; he heard her on the radio once from Omaha and he has one of her records, "Somebody Stole My Gal." Waldo says he will dig it out of his collection, and goes to do so as Goodman returns to the room.

The lawyer tells Jody that her uncle changed his will last week, leaving her a life income from more than a million dollars; after her death the principal will go to an institution Revercombe was interested in. Jody wants no part of the million; all she wants is to get back with Pee Wee Baker. She tells bitterly of her father's hard life and ultimate death, and Revercombe's proposal to take care of her father during his long illness—if her mother would spend her nights with the uncle.

Goodman ejaculates, "Why, the son of—"

"Shake," says Jody. She is beginning to warm to the lawyer, and he to her. Her freshness, her enthusiasm for the gypsy life of a band singer, are fascinating. He is a little annoyed when Waldo bursts back in, bringing the phonograph record. The young man puts it on the machine and soon, "sent" by the music, begins jitterbugging. Jody takes fire, too, and begins singing, while Waldo whips out his sticks and begins drumming on a table-top. Goodman is fascinated.

After the record ends the phone rings; it is long distance, reporting that Pee Wee Baker doesn't answer. She says, "Keep ringing" and asks the lawyer if she can wait here, even if it takes all night. She can sleep on the couch if she has to. It's all right with Goodman, and Waldo hurries to the linen closet to get sheets and blankets for the girl.

"I'll telephone you in the morning," says Goodman. "I'd like to show you around town. . . . And I want to arrange for some trombone lessons."

"You're all right," Jody approves. Goodman leaves. Waldo returns with bed things and he and the girl begin making up the couch. She admires his drumming and he boasts that he has a full set of drums down in the furnace room. He practices down there. "I'm quite a student of the drums," he adds. "Savage tribes used to use them to send messages." He points to the tom-tom hanging on the wall. "I even know some of the drum language."

Waldo starts to leave, but Jody asks him to play the record again. This time they start dancing, and coming into close contact with the girl makes Waldo self-conscious. When the number is over he says he'd better say good night.

JODY—I hope none of my uncle's girl friends come barging in on me. (*She lifts her suitcase to a chair, where she opens it.*)
WALDO—Oh, Miss Revere, your uncle didn't have any girl friends!
JODY—That's what you think.
WALDO—I'm positive—no woman ever came up to this apartment.
JODY—Then he went to hers.
WALDO—Oh, I don't believe that!
JODY—He had a biscuit hidden somewhere.

WALDO—A girl? Oh, no, he was the most respectable man I ever met. (JODY *has taken out a dressing gown and mules and a nightgown which she holds up and shakes out.* WALDO *is embarrassed.* JODY *starts turning out the lights, leaving on one at the head of the bed. The room becomes quite dark.*) Oh, now I do have to go. I hope you get a good night's sleep.

JODY—Thanks, but I don't expect to do much sleeping.

WALDO—Would you like me to bring you a sleeping pill?

JODY—I never took one.

WALDO—I never did either but Mother used to.

JODY—Do they work?

WALDO—Oh, yes, and you ought to get some sleep.

JODY—O.K. I'll try anything once. (*The phone rings.* JODY *goes to the phone.* WALDO *waits. Into phone:*) Hello . . . You're sure? O.K. (*She hangs up.*) They can't get Pee Wee. They don't answer. (*She opens her bag and gets out a piece of paper.*) Where are we tomorrow? (*She consults the paper.*) Coffeyville, Kansas. They ought to get there by noon. I'll wire Pee Wee tomorrow morning to call me here as soon as he gets in.

WALDO—I'll get the pills. I'll be right back. (*He exits.* JODY *returns paper to her purse. She moves to a chair, slips off her shoes; sits down as if to relax, stretching a bit, then leans down and slips off her stockings. She stands up, puts her stockings on the back of the chair. She is standing with her back to the section of the bookcase in the back wall. The chair is to her left. She reaches for the zipper on her dress and has a little trouble with it. A section of the bookcase on the back wall noiselessly and slowly swings open into the room, disclosing a passageway. A woman in a chiffon negligee enters the passageway. She is rather handsome, in her thirties. The presence of* JODY *evidently comes as a surprise and shock to this woman. She freezes, as if wondering what to do.* JODY *has now unzipped her dress and begins to pull it over her head. The woman behind her tenses, as if to spring on* JODY. JODY *gets the dress off, shakes it out and is about to turn to put it on the chair. Had she turned, she would have seen the woman. But at this second the doorbell rings; so that although she completes the gesture of throwing the dress on the chair, her face is turned, right, toward the door. Being now in only panties and bra, she quickly slips into her negligee and hurries to the door, disappearing through the arch. The woman draws back through the passageway, and the bookcase swings back into place. We hear* JODY *off stage.*)

JODY (*off stage*)—I thought it was you, but I wasn't taking any chances. (*She enters, followed by* WALDO.)

WALDO—Here's the nembutal—I brought you two of them.
JODY—Thanks. I'll take them both.

While Waldo is out, the girl takes her nightgown from her bag, slips it over her head, removes panties and bra and climbs under the covers on the couch. Waldo, returning, tells her she will have to use the foyer entrance to the bathroom because the police have locked off the bedroom until they find the carving knife.

"What carving knife?" the startled Jody cries.

"The one they found sticking in your uncle." Waldo explains about the posthumous stabbing and the girl is frightened. She demands that Waldo stay and keep her company; ever a one for propriety, the young man suggests that he take a chair and sit out in the hall. His eyes catch the tom-tom and he takes it off the wall. "If you get frightened," he says, "just do this." He beats one rap, pauses, then two more. "That's the danger signal."

Jody would rather have him right here, but she agrees to the scheme—if he will stay here until she falls asleep. He might read her to sleep, she suggests, and Waldo, taking a book from the shelves, opens it and begins:

"My maiden name was Fanny Hill. I was born in a small village, near Liverpool, in Lancashire, of parents extremely poor. . . ." Soon Jody is asleep. Waldo reads to himself for a moment, skipping through the book, until he comes to something which seems to startle him. He closes the volume abruptly, goes to the bookcase, takes out several books and hides the copy of "Fanny Hill" behind them. He turns out the reading lamp, tiptoes past the couch, comes back and tenderly kisses Jody's brow, turns out the foyer lights and eases out of the apartment. The room is in total darkness. The audience sits tensely for a few seconds—and is taken completely by surprise when the house lights go up.

The curtain has fallen.

ACT II

It is the next afternoon. Hideo Hayakawa, a middle-aged Japanese houseman, is indignantly folding up the sheets and blankets that were on the couch. He is indignant that a girl should have stayed there, and made use of his kitchen to make herself breakfast, too. He also is indignant at the presence of the police, who have returned —Patrolman Miller, Rosenberg and Minetti. Hayakawa's indignation further increases when he is told that a carving knife has been stuck in his employer and he discovers that his carving knife is missing from the kitchen drawer. Jody is packing her bag. When Waldo lets himself in, thus arousing police suspicions, Jody asks him if he moved her suitcase last night. He says he didn't touch it. "This morning," says Jody, "it looked as though somebody had been going through it."

Fingerprints have been found on the knife, so now the detectives, who really aren't interested in the case, must fingerprint everybody. They set up apparatus in the kitchen and the houseman is the first client, even though he protests that he wasn't here yesterday, it having been his day off. Jody is next, even though Waldo protests that the girl didn't get to New York until after it happened. While Jody is in the kitchen, Waldo goes to the house phone and makes a deal with somebody named Dan, downstairs, to take over the job for the rest of the day; in return, Waldo will work for Dan tomorrow. When Jody returns he is dancing joyfully. "I just made a big deal," he starts to explain—but the detectives come from the kitchen and lead him away to be fingerprinted. The patrolman, alone with Jody, casually asks if he can borrow one of the books and she says it's all right so far as she's concerned. He has just removed his favorite volume when Lawyer Goodman is admitted by one of the detectives. Back the book goes on its shelf.

Goodman tells Jody that her renouncing her uncle's will has made a great deal of difference to another woman. The girl asks, "Some dame of my uncle's?"

"No," the lawyer replies, "just the executive secretary of the organization that will inherit the estate. A Miss Chauvel. She's a very excited and happy woman. She wants to see you, to thank you. She'll be here shortly."

The telephone rings—Western Union with a telegram for Miss Jody Revere. The girl listens, then explains to Goodman that Pee Wee Baker's schedule has been mixed up and he's had to high-tail it for Wichita. He will call her from there tonight—at 2 A.M. New York time. "That's perfect," says the lawyer. "That gives me a chance to carry out a certain plan of mine."

The plan is a dazzling one to a girl like Jody—a progressive dinner, with a different band for every course . . . Irving Conn, Frankie Carle, Dick La Salle, Wingy Manone, Xavier Cugat. . . . And after dinner they will go to Eddie Condon's. Also, there may be another surprise Goodman won't tell about.

Minetti comes to get Goodman for fingerprinting, and Waldo comes back in. The detectives have given him quite a grilling just because he has a passkey. Which reminds Jody: Could he get her one? She wants to come back late tonight and take a call from Pee Wee Baker.

Waldo asks, "Then you're not leaving right away? That's great." He outlines a plan he has made: They will have dinner at a little joint called the Stovepipe, which has a pretty good little combo and where the leader sometimes lets Waldo sit in. This way, Jody can hear him play the drums.

Jody breaks the news that she is dated up for dinner with Mr. Goodman. But she has an idea. It will be an hour before they start—so why couldn't Waldo bring his drums up here right now and play them? He considers it, and decides he can do it because Mrs. Bright, a tenant who always complains about noise, is out of town for the weekend. On the house phone he calls a man named Al and asks Al to bring up his drums and things.

Jody turns back to her suitcase and remembers her suspicion that somebody went through it last night. She also vaguely remembers somebody standing over her and looking at her. "I guess I owe you an apology," Waldo falters—and he tells about kissing her while she was asleep. Sternly she beckons him to come to her and orders him never to do that again—while she is asleep. She takes his face in her hands and murmurs, "You're sweet, for a drummer." She is about to kiss him, but thinks better of it, saying, "Nope, I've got to get back to the band." The doorbell rings, and Waldo opens it to Al and a great assortment of drums and things. He and Al begin setting it up.

Behind them appears Valeska Chauvel. She is the woman who was in the hidden passageway behind the bookcase. She speaks with a slight foreign accent and with the intensity of the dedicated as she introduces herself to Jody and begins a torrent of thanks. Jody, while listening, begins selecting a dress from another piece of luggage—a valpack. "The hope of mankind," Valeska continues, "is Unalingua." One language—a universal language which will bring universal peace, she explains to the disinterested Jody, who asks, "What's the matter with English? It's easy to talk—it's easy to understand—I never have any trouble with it."

VALESKA (*sharply*)—There are some things we must take on faith —even if you can't understand them.

JODY—Now wait a minute—don't get hincty. I understand it all right, I just think it sounds like a lot of hooey.

VALESKA—Let's not quarrel—just take my word for it—the money will be spent in a great cause.

JODY—I know a good cause when I see one. I've played plenty

of benefits.   Take the Red Cross . . . take the March of Dimes—
and the best one of them all—the welfare fund of AGVA . . .

VALESKA—What is this AGVA?

JODY—The American Guild of Variety Artists.

VALESKA—Variety Artists!   I am trying to save the world!   Are
you comparing the needs of night-club entertainers with that?

JODY (*with angry pride*)—Let me tell you something.   Last year
when I had my operation they advanced me the dough for my hospital bill.   And once they got me back to Chicago all the way from
Missoula, Montana, where I was flat on my canetta.   You talk about
good causes!   Say, I've got an idea . . . AGVA could make very
good use of this dough.

VALESKA—Oh, no—!   (AL *wheels on a xylophone.* VALESKA
stops and waits for him to place it and exit, then speaks.)   This
money belongs to Unalingua!

JODY—Not yet it don't.

VALESKA (*aghast*)—But it's in your uncle's will.

JODY—He left it to me first.   I guess I can do what I please with it.

VALESKA—No, no—you mustn't!   I won't allow it!

JODY—For somebody who's asking for a freebie you're getting
pretty biggity.   (WALDO *comes on with snare drum.   He is followed
by* DR. GRESHAM.)

VALESKA—You don't want this money for yourself.   (*She turns
to* DR. GRESHAM.)   You must help me.   This stupid, ignorant little
girl . . .

GRESHAM—I beg your pardon!

VALESKA—Oh, yes, forgive me.   (WALDO *exits.* GOODMAN *enters,
followed by* MINETTI.)

GOODMAN (*seeing the drums*)—What's all this?

VALESKA—Mr. Goodman.

GOODMAN—Oh, Miss Chauvel . . .

VALESKA (*emotionally*)—Mr. Goodman, you must—   (*She stops
as she sees* MINETTI.)

MINETTI—Doctor, do you mind stepping out in the kitchen?   It'll
only take a minute.   (MINETTI *and* DR. GRESHAM *exit, left.   As
soon as* MINETTI *is off stage* VALESKA *speaks.*)

VALESKA—Mr. Goodman, you can't let this happen.

GOODMAN—What has happened?   (JODY *is carrying an evening
dress from the valpack over her arm.*)

JODY (*calmly*)—Just I changed my mind.   This new language
she's dreaming up.   I got a better idea where the money should go.

Jody informs the lawyer she is going to accept the income and
donate it to the AGVA Welfare Fund.   Hysterically angry, Valeska

warns that she will break the will; she's not going to let that stupid little idiot stand between her and what's rightfully hers. Jody goes to the bathroom with her dress, to change. Rosenberg, coming from the kitchen, sees a possible fingerprint client in the newcomer, Miss Chauvel, but Goodman assures him that she is remote from the case. Valeska storms out, with Goodman following her and offering to get her a cab.

Al has finished setting up the drums and leaves. Jody returns in an attention-calling semi-evening dress and Waldo is spellbound. He also is puzzled about Valeska Chauvel. He has never seen her before, he tells Jody, but a minute ago the woman tried to get Goodman to talk privately with her in the bedroom—and she knew right where the bedroom was! Perhaps it was she who put the knife into Revercombe—to kill him to get the money.

The joke, says Jody lightly, is on Valeska—for she doesn't get the money until Jody is dead.

Waldo stares queerly at the girl, repeating, "Until you're dead. For her to get that money—you've got to be dead." Now Jody begins to feel creepy.

When he comes back from fingerprinting, Goodman looks uneasily at Jody's dress, but finally shrugs it off. A telephone call comes for him—and it is the surprise for Jody he has been hoping for. He talks pleasantly with somebody, makes a note on a memo pad of an address and says, "I should say in about ten or fifteen minutes. I'm very grateful." He hangs up and says smilingly to the girl, "You're not going back to Pee Wee Baker without being able to say you met Benny Goodman." It was Benny Goodman who called, and he's waiting for them.

Waldo, who is all ready to give his concert, generously gives it up. Jody, getting her bag and a wrap, says, "You're a sweet kid. . . . Look, I got to be back late tonight to get that call—"

Waldo asks eagerly, "Could I be here waiting for you?"

"Swell!" exclaims Jody. "Plant you now and dig you later!" She leaves with the lawyer. Waldo disconsolately starts the record player. It is Jody, singing "Somebody Stole My Gal."

The curtain falls.

Scene II

It is long past midnight. Waldo is waiting, with his traps, and the two detectives and the patrolman are still there. Rosenberg telephones the morgue and learns there is no new development yet. He picks up an address book, finds the address of the Japanese houseman and makes a note of it. The front buzzer sounds and

Waldo leaps to answer it. Goodman has brought Jody home. The lawyer, pleading that he has a case to try in the morning, does not come in. Jody is a bit tight, and annoyed to find Rosenberg at the phone. "I'm expecting a telephone call, and when it comes, I go." Waldo taps the danger signal on one of his drums as Rosenberg quickly asks, "Where do you go?" Waldo again signals, and Jody, who is smart, answers the detective, "If I get a telephone call I go to the telephone."

Rosenberg and his partner depart, to try to find the Jap at his home, and when Waldo and the girl are alone he explains that the detectives have warned against anybody leaving town. This means that if Jody gets her call from Pee Wee she'll have to move fast.

With enthusiasm she tells of her wonderful evening, starting with meeting Benny Goodman and singing for him—he told her to work hard and get in touch with him in two or three years—and detailing the dinner round with Lawyer Goodman. She starts to take off her dress and get into a negligee and Waldo flees to the hall until she is properly clad—a shyness which amuses her. And now she is ready for his concert.

Waldo puts on her record and, because it is so late, begins drumming softly. He doesn't sound so hot to Jody. She goes behind him and strokes his hair, and Waldo's drumming picks up sharply. She keeps on rubbing, and he throws caution to the winds and goes to town. Jody, feeling hot, too, begins singing the number. The house phone stops them abruptly. Mike, down below, warns Waldo that Mrs. Bright has returned and is raising hell about noise—so the concert is over.

Jody thinks back to Valeska, and reasons aloud that her uncle must have put Jody in the will just to get even with Valeska. He must have found her cheating. . . .

Long Distance rings. It's Pee Wee at last, calling from a pay station. Jody tells of her adventure with Benny Goodman, and says she is now free to come back. With a sudden new idea she tells the band leader that she has found a hot new drummer—he's right here with his drums. He can audition for Pee Wee right now. Waldo is fearful, but the girl urges him to take a chance and once again he goes to town, while Jody holds the telephone instrument toward him. She kisses his ear, just to make sure he drums well. When the number is finished, Jody shouts to Pee Wee, "How about it? A gasser, eh?" But Pee Wee isn't there—he has run out of coins for his phone.

The tenant, Mrs. Bright, is heard in the foyer. She has succeeded the late Revercombe as head of the building, and has a passkey. "Waldo," she is heard commanding, "you come with me to my apartment." The young man meekly obeys, saying he will be back as soon as he can. Jody, tired, stretches on a couch, riffles a magazine, gets up and turns off the light and falls asleep. The room is dark—until a flashlight beam emerges from the bedroom door. In a moment it snaps off. There is the tingle of a triangle, then a sound of two chimes bumping together. Jody awakens and whispers in fright, "Is that you, Waldo?" There is a tremendous crash of drums falling over. Jody, screaming madly, turns on the light, which reveals Patrolman Miller on the floor, clutching his red book. His head has somehow got stuck through the slats of the xylophone. Jody, in true hysterics, keeps screaming for the police until Waldo rushes in. He takes the book from Miller, orders him out, and tries to calm the sobbing Jody, but her hysteria is still uncontrolled. On the house phone he asks Mike, downstairs, to find Dr. Gresham right away.

Dr. Gresham appears quickly, with his bag, which he opens to prepare a sedative for Jody. Waldo goes back up to continue his interview with Mrs. Bright, and Jody runs to the hall after him, begging him not to leave her. The phone rings and Gresham answers it: "Who wants him? . . . The morgue? . . . Just a moment." When Jody returns, the doctor, thinking fast, asks her to go to the bathroom and bring a glass of hot water—very hot. When she has gone and he hears the water running, he returns to the phone and, imitating Rosenberg's voice, says, "Rosenberg at this end . . ." He listens, then hangs up. He is thinking fast and desperately. He dives into his bag and takes out his narcotics case.

When Jody returns with the water he seats her on a heavy chair, takes a stethoscope and asks her to slip her gown over her shoulders so he can listen to her heart . . . and to put her hands behind her. The girl obeys—and Gresham swiftly ties her arms to the chair with the sleeves of her gown. "I just want you to sit quietly while I tell you about your uncle," he says. "I killed him. . . . And now I have to kill myself." While he prepares a narcotic in a bottle, he explains that Revercombe didn't have diabetes, and the insulin Gresham prescribed was intended as a fatal shock to a weak heart. And now he is trapped, for the morgue has discovered that Revercombe didn't have diabetes.

Jody pleads with him not to kill himself. Nobody's sorry about her uncle. He should take it on the lam. But why, she asks, did he kill Revercombe? He replies, "I happen to be in love with Valeska." He begins writing a confession at the same time he is making his confession to Jody. With Revercombe dead, he continues, he could have Valeska and Valeska could have her money. Jody assures him that Valeska will have her money—when Jody dies. Again she begs the doctor not to kill himself . . . and now he has a new idea. He strips off his coat and gags the girl with his handkerchief and bow tie, saying, "I can make sure she gets the money now. That means, my dear, you have to die, too."

By now the water in the glass has cooled, so he goes to the bathroom to get more. With great effort Jody hitches the chair toward the drums and with her foot beats out the danger signal. Gresham swiftly appears, moves the drum out of reach, pours hot water into a bottle of pills and shakes it, then fills a hypodermic syringe. He seizes the squirming Jody, trying to hold her still enough to insert the needle, when Waldo whirls in and knocks Gresham off balance. The hypodermic falls to the floor. Gresham hurls Waldo across the room, grabs the needle again—and sees that it is broken. He dashes out toward the kitchen, with Waldo pursuing.

In a moment Waldo returns; the doctor has got away. He ungags and unties Jody, who cries, "He was trying to kill me! He killed my uncle! Get the police!" Waldo goes to the phone. Jody runs to him and the negligee falls to the floor, leaving her clad in panties and bra. She throws herself into Waldo's arms. He reaches the police and tells them there has been an attempted murder at Apartment 3C, 412 Park Avenue. Jody has slumped in a faint, and on an impulse Waldo kisses her passionately on the lips. Then, sensing his own danger, he says to the police, "You'd better hurry!"

The curtain falls.

ACT III

It is half an hour later. Jody is in a kimono in an armchair, Waldo beside her. Goodman is looking through the telephone book. Miller and three plainclothesmen are in the room watching their officer, Lieutenant Casey, who is talking on the telephone. Casey is ordering a general alarm for a man in a white shirt and black pants, without a coat. He orders a watch put on Gresham's car at its garage. He hangs up—and Jody tells him not to use the phone any more because she is expecting an important call.

Goodman has been looking in the book for a home address for Valeska Chauvel. He has found the address of the office of Unalingua, but no home listing for her. Casey orders a man to get into the office and look for a home address. Goodman remembers that she must live near here, because when he offered to call a cab for her when she angrily left the apartment, she said she'd walk. Casey orders two men to search every house for four blocks around. Miller remains, and Jody suggests that the lieutenant send him—he's good at breaking into apartments. Instead, Casey puts Miller to search-ing the floor for the broken tip of the hypo needle, and Miller uses the maneuver to snitch his book again. He orders Waldo to let him-self into Gresham's office and try to find an address for Valeska. He orders Jody to get some clothes on, because she will have to make a statement down town. Jody, protesting that she is waiting for a phone call, picks up her bag, goes to the bedroom and leaves the door partly open—so that she can hear the phone and also because she is still afraid.

Minetti and Rosenberg return, with Hayakawa in tow. Casey starts quizzing the Jap, but Hayakawa insists no woman ever came to this apartment. Rosenberg interrupts, "Will you let me work on this guy? I want to ask him about the knife that was sticking in the fellow's heart." "That's not this case," says Casey brusquely. "The doctor killed him with insulin." Rosenberg explains to the mystified lieutenant that the stabbing was done after death, and he goes to work on Hayakawa. Hayakawa says he knows nothing about the knife, even if it *does* have his fingerprints on it. "I no talk. I want lawyer," he says.

Goodman volunteers and is accepted. Goodman pleads with Hayakawa to help, adding that Revercombe must have been fond of the houseman because he left a bequest in his will—five thousand dollars.

There is a sudden change in Hayakawa as he cries that it should have been twenty-five or fifty thousand dollars.

HAYAKAWA—For fourteen years I work for him, I spy for him, I keep his secrets, I promise never to tell— (*He holds up his hand as if taking an oath.*) Five thousand dollars? Now I tell. (*Tele-phone rings.* JODY *enters.* CASEY *answers the telephone.*)

CASEY—Hello? (*To* JODY.) It's for you. (*He hands the re-ceiver to her.*)

JODY (*into telephone*)—Hello?

CASEY (*to* HAYAKAWA)—O.K., spill it! (JODY *concentrates on the telephone; the policemen on* HAYAKAWA.)

JODY—Yes, this is Jody Revere.

ROSENBERG—Let's have it.

JODY—I'll hold on.

MINETTI—Come on, shoot!

HAYAKAWA—I here yesterday. I see Mr. Revercombe dead. I think maybe Dr. Gresham—Miss Chauvel kill him.

CASEY—That Miss Chauvel! Where does she live?

HAYAKAWA—I tell everything.

JODY—Yes, I'm waiting.

HAYAKAWA—I swear to boss never to tell he had woman here. I can't tell police but I want police to find out if they kill boss so I stick knife in him.

ROSENBERG—I knew damn well you did.

CASEY—Come again. Why did you stick that knife in him?

HAYAKAWA—So somebody call police, so they find out if he die or get killed.

MINETTI—You're a damn smart Chinaman.

HAYAKAWA—Please! I am Japanese!

JODY—Hello, Pee Wee.

CASEY—Where does this dame live?

JODY—I knew you'd like him, Pee Wee.

CASEY—Will you tell us that?

JODY (to CASEY)—Pipe down, will you? I can't hear.

HAYAKAWA—I know where she live. I watch her house for boss. I see Dr. Gresham go in there. I tell boss last week.

JODY—Where do we join you?

CASEY—But where does she live?

HAYAKAWA—Doctor go to her house three times last week. I follow him.

CASEY—Where does she live, I'm asking you!

JODY—How do you spell it, Pee Wee?

HAYAKAWA—She live around the corner.

CASEY—Where?

JODY (to the others)—You guys will have to keep quiet a minute. I can't hear! (CASEY grabs phone out of JODY's hand and hangs it up.)

CASEY—For God's sake, shut up! (To HAYAKAWA.) Where?

JODY (dismayed and indignant)—Hey, you cut me off! (She picks up the phone again and taps the cradle, then dials.)

HAYAKAWA—Around the corner.

JODY—That was a hell of a thing to do.

GOODMAN—Number 72—is that it? Seventy-two East 55th?

HAYAKAWA—Yes, 72. How you know?

GOODMAN (to CASEY)—Mr. Revercombe owned that property and this too.

CASEY—Seventy-two—let's go. (He starts out.)

HAYAKAWA—She no come through front door—she come through wall—Mr. Revercombe fix—bookcase open up—she come through bookcase— (HAYAKAWA points to the bookcase. They all rush to the bookcase, including GOODMAN. They search for the mechanism to open it.)

JODY (*into telephone*)—Hello? I don't want Minneapolis; I was talking to Wichita.

ROSENBERG—Come here, Mac. Show us how this thing works.

MINETTI—Yes, open it up.

HAYAKAWA—Don't know how open up. Always open from other side. She open from other side.

They all rush out, just as Waldo bounces in. He, too, has discovered Valeska's address in the doctor's records. Jody cries, "Pee Wee's crazy about you! He wants us to join the band right away." She adds that she was disconnected before she found out where, but they've got to get the eight o'clock plane this morning to somewhere.

Waldo falters that he'll have to give Mrs. Bright two weeks' notice. "Waldo," says Jody, kissing him, "I just plain love you. We can't wait for two weeks' notice." Straightening his shoulders, the young man goes to face Mrs. Bright. "Make her fire you," she calls—and to help a little she begins banging furiously at the drums. Behind her the bookcase swings open. Valeska comes through, touches Jody on the shoulders, and Jody leaps up over the drums and behind the desk, brandishing drumsticks and screaming, "Stay away from me!"

"You're in danger," Valeska says desperately. The woman has seen Dr. Gresham, and now she pleads that she doesn't want any killing. Rosenberg comes through the bookcase, gun in hand, and is followed by the lieutenant and Patrolman Miller. They ask Valeska where Dr. Gresham is and she says she doesn't know where he has gone. Miller is left to guard Valeska and Rosenberg and Casey go back through the bookcase to Valeska's house to search it.

In a moment Gresham enters through the bookcase, with a gun. Valeska stands between him and Jody and he orders her to get out of the way, but the woman won't move. The telephone rings and Jody answers it. It's Pee Wee back on the wire. Waldo enters from the front door and Gresham is momentarily distracted. Seizing the advantage, Miller reaches for his gun, but before he can raise it the doctor shoots and Miller sinks to his knees, then falls on his face. Waldo rushes to Jody's side and helps Valeska protect her. The voice of Casey is heard in the passageway. Gresham flees through the foyer and out the front door, and in a moment a shot is heard. Valeska, screaming "Charles! Charles!" runs after him. Others pile through the passageway. Jody, on the telephone, says, "Pee Wee, where do we join you? Olathe, Kansas? I got it."

Detective Minetti takes the phone from Jody, cuts off her call, dials for an ambulance for the wounded Miller. Waldo informs Jody that Mrs. Bright won't let him go without two weeks' notice, and she yells, "The hell with Mrs. Bright!"

Rosenberg, who has followed Valeska in pursuit of Dr. Gresham, returns to report that the doctor has killed himself. The wounded Miller has regained consciousness and is protesting that he is all right. On the house phone, Mrs. Bright orders Waldo to come right up, and the young man says he will. Minetti and Goodman, ministering to Miller, notice a bullet hole in his coat and start unbuttoning the garment, with the patrolman protesting that he is all right. Under the coat they find the red-bound book, with a bullet imbedded in it.

Casey begins rounding up everybody, including the Japanese houseman, for a trip to headquarters to make statements, and orders Miller to remain and guard Gresham's body. Miller starts out, but Goodman stops him and takes his book from him. Then, ceremoniously, the lawyer gives it back, saying Miller has deserved a reward for his bravery—and perseverance. The patrolman, enormously grateful, starts out again, opens the book—and stops, almost in tears. "Aw, for God's sake," he mourns, "a bull's eye on every page!" He goes on out.

Valeska has gone to her apartment to dress for the trip down town, and Rosenberg informs Goodman that she has asked him to be her lawyer. Goodman says he thinks he can help her, and Jody adds, "I'd like to help her, too. Knowing my uncle, I feel she earned a piece of the dough. Could I take what's coming to me and divide it between her outfit and the AGVA?"

GOODMAN—We'd have to straighten out the tax problem. What is this AGVA?

JODY—American Guild of Variety Artists.

GOODMAN—Oh, yes, it was through them I got in touch with you.

JODY—They always know where I am.

GOODMAN—I'd like always to know where you are.

JODY—I'll keep in touch.

GOODMAN—That's not good enough. I'd like to have you right here with me.

JODY—I'll get to New York some day. I'm just not ready for it yet.

GOODMAN—I don't think you quite understand what I'm trying to say. I don't want you to go away. I don't want to lose you. (*She looks up at him.*) You may think I'm a little too old. But that's not true. I'm young. You've made me young.

JODY—Well, naturally, I'm glad if you got a kick out of going around with me.

GOODMAN—I never said this to anyone before. I never thought I would— But, Jody—(*He takes her hand.*)—will you marry me?

JODY—Gee, Mr. Goodman! That's something I never expected. (WALDO *bursts into the room.*)

WALDO—All right, Jody, let's go! There's a lot to do before we catch that plane.

JODY (*going to him*)—You quit your job?

WALDO—No. But she thought I did all that shooting. I got fired.

JODY (*with tender understanding*)—That makes you feel better, doesn't it?

WALDO—Yes. Come on. We've got to get down to the station-house.

JODY—You ring for the elevator and wait for me. (WALDO *exits.* JODY *turns to* GOODMAN.) Gee, Mr. Goodman, what you said—I can't get over it. It's a very high compliment. But there are lots of reasons—the band, my career—and the most important one of all. You see, Mr. Goodman, I think when you marry you should marry a virgin. (*We hear* WALDO *shout "Jody" off stage. She gives a quick look in his direction, then back to* GOODMAN.) And I'm going to. (*She raises herself on her toes and kisses* GOODMAN. *As they break,* WALDO *marches in and down to her. She takes his arm and they walk out together,* WALDO *looking wonderingly back at* GOOD-MAN.)

THE CURTAIN FALLS

THE PLAYS AND THEIR AUTHORS

MRS. MCTHING, by Mary Coyle Chase

Mary Coyle Chase was born in Denver forty-five years ago and lives there with her husband and three sons. Her husband, Robert Chase, is an editor of the *Rocky Mountain News*. She graduated from the University of Colorado with a Litt.D. and in 1924 took up newspaper reporting. Her first play, "Now You've Done It," was produced by the late Brock Pemberton and the late Antoinette Perry in 1937, and was a failure. The same producers presented her "Harvey" in the season of 1944-1945; it won the Pulitzer prize and had a run of 1,775 performances. In 1945 Max Gordon presented her "The Next Half Hour," written before "Harvey," and it was a failure. Mrs. Chase's newest play, "Bernardine," has been scheduled for production in 1952-1953.

THE SHRIKE, by Joseph Kramm

Joseph Kramm was born in South Philadelphia, the son of a druggist. He graduated from the University of Pennsylvania in 1928, and became a reporter and rewrite man on the *Philadelphia Inquirer* and the *Philadelphia Record*. While on the *Record* staff he went to New York to audition for Eva Le Gallienne and was appointed an apprentice at the Civic Repertory Theatre, and has been in the theatre since then. For six years he acted with the Civic Repertory. In World War II he served three years with the Army Signal Corps and earned five battle stars. After the war he turned to directing stock at Sayville, L. I., Toronto and Olney, Md. At Olney, in 1948, he directed José Ferrer in "Twentieth Century." He wrote eight plays which never found production. He wrote "The Shrike," his ninth, in eight weeks, starting Christmas Day, 1949. "The Shrike" won the Pulitzer prize. A new play by Kramm, "The Gypsies Wore High Hats," has been scheduled for production in 1952-1953.

I AM A CAMERA, by John van Druten

John van Druten was born in London in 1901, of a Dutch father and an English mother. He was a lawyer and a college professor before he took up playwriting in 1925 with "Young Woodley." His successes have included "Bell, Book and Candle," "The Voice of the Turtle," "I Remember Mama" and "There's Always Juliet." Van Druten, who has become an American citizen, took up a new field of the theatre when he directed the successful musical, "The King and I." "I Am a Camera" won the season's award from the New York Drama Critics Circle.

THE FOURPOSTER, by Jan de Hartog

Jan de Hartog was born in Holland in 1914, the son of a professor of theology. By the late 1930s he had made a name for himself in Holland as a novelist, playwright, screenwriter and actor. During World War II, de Hartog went underground against the Nazis, finally escaped to England, where he still lives. In 1945 he wrote "Skipper Next to God," which was produced in New York in the season of 1947-1948.

POINT OF NO RETURN, by Paul Osborn

Paul Osborn was born in Evansville, Ind., in 1901. He graduated from the University of Michigan with an A.B., later took an M.A. there. He studied playwriting under George Pierce Baker at Harvard, and taught English at the University of Michigan. His first play was "Hotbed," a failure of the 1928-1929 season. His first success was "The Vinegar Tree," in 1930, and was followed by "On Borrowed Time" in 1937. "Point of No Return" is Osborn's second successful adaptation of a book, the other having been the play made from John Hersey's "A Bell for Adano."

BAREFOOT IN ATHENS, by Maxwell Anderson

Maxwell Anderson was born in Atlantic, Pa., in 1888, the son of a Baptist minister. He attended Stanford University and after graduating became a member of the faculty there. Becoming a newspaperman, he worked on San Francisco journals until coming to New York in 1919. He became an editorial writer on the *World* and there met Laurence Stallings, with whom he wrote "What Price Glory?" He soon became the most prolific of American dramatists.

VENUS OBSERVED, by Christopher Fry

Christopher Fry was born in Bristol, England, forty-four years ago. His father was an architect named Charles Harris, who wanted to become a clergyman and a missionary in the Bristol slums. When his father died, Christopher took his mother's maiden name. He wrote his first play at the age of 11 and his first verse play at the age of 14. He alternated between acting and teaching after reaching young manhood. After World War II, Fry, wanting to write a play in verse, read a dozen volumes of short stories and finally found an old German short story about a man who wanted to be hanged. He transformed this into his great success, "The Lady's Not for Burning." He followed this with "Venus Observed." He lives in London.

JANE, by S. N. Behrman

Samuel Nathaniel Behrman was born in Worcester, Mass., in 1893. He studied at Clark College, Harvard and Columbia University. Out of Columbia with an M.A., he became an assistant in the book department of the New York Times. He began writing magazine fiction and articles. His first two plays, "The Second Man" and "Serena Blandish," were successes in 1927 and 1928. His most recent play—written after "Jane"—was "I Know My Love," in which Alfred Lunt and Lynn Fontanne starred. Behrman has also written many screenplays.

GIGI, by Anita Loos

Anita Loos was born in Sisson, Calif., in 1893. She attended school in San Diego, and in 1919 married John Emerson. With Emerson she became a screenwriter for David Wark Griffith, Douglas Fairbanks and Constance Talmadge. In 1925 she wrote a magazine series which became the novel, "Gentlemen Prefer Blondes," which since has been made into a play and a musical. She divides her time between novels, screenplays and plays. Prior to "Gigi," she had a success with Helen Hayes' vehicle, "Happy Birthday."

REMAINS TO BE SEEN, by Howard Lindsay and Russel Crouse

Lindsay and Crouse are habitual collaborators both as authors and as producers. Their productions have included "Arsenic and Old Lace," "The Hasty Heart" and "Detective Story." Their writing partnership has resulted in such hits as "Red, Hot and Blue," "Life with Father," "Life with Mother," the Pulitzer prize-winning "State of the Union" and the musical, "Call Me Madam." Lindsay can do one thing Crouse can't do—act. Lindsay frequently appears in their plays, as he did in "Remains to Be Seen." Howard Lindsay was born in Waterford, N. Y., in 1889. He became an actor in "Polly of the Circus" in 1909, and later became a director, staging such successes as "Dulcy," "To the Ladies" and "The Poor Nut." His first collaboration with Crouse was "Anything Goes," in 1934. He is married to Dorothy Stickney, the actress. Russel Crouse was born in Findlay, Ohio, in 1893. He became a reporter on the Cincinnati *Commercial-Tribune* in 1910, and followed a journalistic career in Kansas City and New York. He was a columnist on the *New York Evening Post* from 1925 until 1931, and for a short period was publicity man for the Theatre Guild. His first work for the theatre was the libretto of the musical, "The Gang's All Here," in 1931.

PLAYS PRODUCED IN NEW YORK

June 1, 1951—May 31, 1952

(Plays marked "continued" were still running on June 1, 1952)

COURTIN' TIME

(37 performances)

Musical comedy in two acts, based on Eden Phillpotts' play, "The Farmer's Wife"; book by William Roos; lyrics by Jack Lawrence; music by Don Walker; produced by James Russo and Michael Ellis, in association with Alexander H. Cohen, at the National Theatre, June 13, 1951.

Cast of characters—

Nell Rilling	Gloria Patrice
Cathy Rilling	Gloria Hamilton
Laura	Mary O'Fallon
George Mullins	Peter Conlow
Samuel Rilling	Joe E. Brown
Carl Stevens	Theodor Uppman
Fred Lawson	David E. Thomas
Araminta	Billie Worth
Harriet Hearn	Effie Afton
Mr. Hearn	Joseph Sweeney
Theresa Tapper	Carmen Mathews
Louisa Windeatt	Katherine Anderson
Polly	May Muth
Sadie	Rosemary Kuhlmann
Millie	Teddy Tavenner
Larry Walton	Earl William
The Brat	Patricia Poole

Singing Ensemble: Betty Jane Cocho, Peggy Gavan, Glynn Hill, Joan Keenan, Rosemary Kuhlmann, May Muth, Mary O'Fallon, Teddy Tavenner, Walter Brandin, Michael T. Carolan, John Michael King, Michael Kingsley, Charles Rule, Robert Strobel, John Taliaferro, Lawrence Weber.

Dancing Ensemble: Patricia Casey, Audrey Keane (Captain), Mary Martinet, Patricia Poole, Frances Sorenson, Elsa Van Horne, Edward Andrews, Hubert Bland, Peter Deign, William Maguire, Lou Yetter, Charles Zulkeski.

The action takes place in Maine in 1898. Scenes include Samuel Rilling's farm, Louisa Windeatt's apiary, the post office and general store, Theresa Tapper's garden and the railroad station.

Staged by Alfred Drake; dances by George Balanchine; sets by Ralph Alswang; costumes by Saul Bolsani; musical and vocal arrangements by Don Walker; musical director, Bill Jonson; stage manager, James Gelb.

Principal musical numbers—

ACT I

"Today at Your House, Tomorrow at Mine" ..Joe E. Brown, Theodor Uppman, David E. Thomas, Peter Conlow

"Fixin' for a Long, Cold Winter" ...Joe E. Brown and Billie Worth
"Araminta to Herself" ....Billie Worth
"An Old-fashioned Glimmer in Your Eye" ....Billie Worth, Gloria
                                             Hamilton and girls
"Goodbye, Dear Friend, Goodbye" ....Gloria Hamilton
                                             and Earl William
"The Wishbone Song" ....Billie Worth, Gloria Hamilton, Earl Wil-
         liam, Gloria Patrice, Peter Conlow, Theodor Uppman
"Smile Awhile" ....Billie Worth
"Too Much Trouble" ....Joe E. Brown
"Choose Your Partner" ....Gloria Patrice, Gloria Hamilton,
                                   Earl William, Theodor Uppman
"I Do, He Doesn't" ....Billie Worth
"Golden Moment" ....Carmen Mathews and Joe E. Brown

ACT II

"Johnny Ride the Sky" .....Theodor Uppman and Gloria Hamilton
"The Sensible Thing to Do" ....Billie Worth and Earl William
"Masculinity" ....Katherine Anderson, Carmen Mathews, Effie Afton
"Maine Will Remember the Maine" ....Earl William, Theodor
                                    Uppman, Joseph Sweeney
"Heart in Hand" ....Joe E. Brown and Billie Worth

(Closed July 14, 1951)

SEVENTEEN

(182 performances)

Musical comedy in two acts, based on the novel by Booth Tarkington; book by Sally Benson, music by Walter Kent and lyrics by Kim Gannon; produced by Milton Berle, Sammy Lambert and Bernie Foyer at the Broadhurst Theatre, June 21, 1951.

Cast of characters—

Genesis ....Maurice Ellis
Johnnie Watson ....John Sharpe
Willie Baxter ....Kenneth Nelson
Jane Baxter ....Betty Jane Seagle
Bert ....Greg O'Brien
Charlie ....Jim Moore
Dave ....Bill Reilly
Joe Bullitt ....Dick Kallman
Lester ....Richard France
Darrell ....Darrell Notara
Don ....Bob Bakanic
Lola Pratt ....Ann Crowley
Mrs. Baxter ....Doris Dalton
May Parcher ....Ellen McCown
Emmie ....Helen Wood
Ida ....Carol Cole
Madge ....Bonnie Brae
Sue ....Elizabeth Pacetti
Jenny ....Sherry McCutcheon
Nan ....Joan Bowman
Mr. Baxter ....Frank Albertson
Mr. Parcher ....King Calder
Mrs. Parcher ....Penny Bancroft
George Crooper ....Harrison Muller
Mr. Genesis ....Alonzo Bosan
Porter ....Joseph James
     The action takes place in Indianapolis in 1907. Scenes include the Baxters' house, Willie's room, the Parchers' house, the Parchers' lawn and the railroad station.

Staged by Hassard Short; book directed by Richard Whorf; dances by Dania Krupska; sets by Stewart Chaney; costumes by David Ffolkes; orchestrations by Ted Royal; choral arrangements by Crane Calder; Vincent Travers, musical director; stage manager, Robert Downing.

Principal musical numbers—

ACT I

"Weatherbee's Drug Store" ....Dick Kallman, Bob Bakanic, Richard France, Jim Moore, Darrell Notara, Bill Reilly and John Sharpe
"This Was Just Another Day" ....Ann Crowley and Kenneth Nelson
"Things Are Gonna Hum This Summer" ....Ann Crowley, Ellen McCown, Helen Wood, Dick Kallman, John Sharpe, Jim Moore, Joan Bowman, Richard France
"How Do You Do, Miss Pratt?" ....Kenneth Nelson
"Summertime Is Summertime" ......Helen Wood, Richard France, Ellen McCown, Dick Kallman
"Reciprocity" ....Ann Crowley, Bob Bakanic, Jim Moore, Richard France, Bill Reilly, Darrell Notara and John Sharpe
"Ode to Lola" ...Ellen McCown, Helen Wood, Joan Bowman, Bonnie Brae, Carol Cole, Sherry McCutcheon and Elizabeth Pacetti
"Headache and Heartache" ......Doris Dalton and Frank Albertson
"OO-OOO-OOO, What You Do to Me" ....Harrison Muller

ACT II

"The Hoosier Way" ......Harrison Muller, Helen Wood, Richard France, Jim Moore, Carol Cole
"I Could Get Married Today" ......Kenneth Nelson, Maurice Ellis and Alonzo Bosan
"After All, It's Spring" ....Ellen McCown, Dick Kallman
"If We Only Could Stop the Old Town Clock" ....Ann Crowley, Kenneth Nelson, Harrison Muller, Dick Kallman, Ellen McCown, Helen Wood

(Closed November 24, 1951)

TWO ON THE AISLE

(281 performances)

Revue in two acts, with music by Jule Styne and lyrics and sketches by Betty Comden, Adolph Green, Nat Hiken and William Friedberg, produced by Arthur Lesser at the Mark Hellinger Theatre, July 19, 1951.

The principals—

Bert Lahr	John Kelly
Dolores Gray	Bob Emmett
Elliott Reid	Jeannett Aquilina
Colette Marchand	Alan LeRoy
Stanley Prager	Richard Gray
Robert Gallagher	J. C. McCord
Larry Laurence	Vera Lee
Arthur Rubin	Gloria Danyl
Walter Kelvin	Margery Beddow
Frank Reynolds	Jane Mason

Kathryn Mylorie

Staged by Abe Burrows; musical numbers staged by Ted Cappy; sets by Howard Bay; costumes by Joan Personette; orchestrations by Philip Lang; dance orchestrations by Genevieve Pitot; musical director, Herbert Greene; general stage manager, John Sola.

Sketches and musical numbers—

ACT I

"HOLD ME TIGHT"

1st Suitor	Frank Reynolds
2nd Suitor	John Kelly
3rd Suitor	Bob Emmett
Maid	Jeannett Aquilina
The Girl	Dolores Gray

"HIGHLIGHTS FROM THE WORLD OF SPORTS"

Producer	Alan LeRoy
Announcer	Elliott Reid
Cameraman	Richard Gray and Robert Gallagher
Lefty Hogan	Bert Lahr

"EAST RIVER HOE-DOWN"

Danced by	J. C. McCord and Vera Lee

"THERE NEVER WAS A BABY LIKE MY BABY"

Wife	Dolores Gray
Husband	Elliott Reid
Danced by	J. C. McCord

"SPACE BRIGADE"

Hodgkins	Richard Gray
Hotchkiss	Larry Laurence
Hitchcock	Robert Gallagher
Captain Universe	Bert Lahr
Higgins	Stanley Prager
Radio Voice	Walter Kelvin
Queen Chlorophyl	Kathryn Mylorie

"IF YOU HADN'T, BUT YOU DID"

The Girl	Dolores Gray
The Other Woman	Gloria Danyl
The Man	Bob Emmett

"THE CLOWN"

Bert Lahr

"THE GUIDE BOOK"

Three Urchins	Frank Reynolds, Victor Reilley, John Kelly
The Girl	Colette Marchand
The Lovers	Paul Lyday, Betty Buday
Traveler	Bob Emmett
The American	J. C. McCord

"HERE'S WHAT YOU SAID"

Elliott Reid

"CATCH OUR ACT"

Two Vaudevillians	Bert Lahr and Dolores Gray

"AT THE MET"

Siegfried	Bert Lahr
Brünnhilde	Dolores Gray
The Dragon	Stanley Prager
Danced by	Colette Marchand

ACT II

"EVERLASTING"

Sung by	Kathryn Mylorie and Fred Bryan
Danced by	Dorothy Etheridge and Jerry Fries

"SCHNEIDER'S MIRACLE"

By Nat Hiken and William Friedberg

Schneider	Bert Lahr
Mrs. Higgleston	Patricia Tobin

Piper ....Stanley Prager
Miss Flaherty ....Kathryn Mylorie
Inspector ....Robert Gallagher
Man on Bench ....Alan LeRoy
Little Girl ....Jeannett Aquilina
Policeman ....Richard Gray
Passers-by: John Allen, Leila Martin, Frank Reynolds, Walter Kelvin

"GIVE A LITTLE, GET A LITTLE LOVE"

Dolores Gray

"DOG SHOW"
Choreographed by Ruthanna Boris

Judge ....Bob Emmett
Russian Wolfhounds .....Gregg Evans, Rosemary Kittelton, Dell
        Parker, Mira Stefan, Jeanne Tyler, Charlotte Van Lein
Their Trainer ....Jerry Fries
Pekinese ....Dorothy Etheridge
Her Trainer ....Paul Lyday
Cocker Spaniels ....Gloria Danyl, Jane Mason
Their Trainer ....Victor Reilley
Dalmatians ....Betty Buday, Doris Goodwin
Their Trainer ....John Kelly
French Poodle ....Colette Marchand
Her Manager ....Gordon Hamilton

"HOW WILL HE KNOW?"

Mr. Murdock ....Bert Lahr
Miss Travers ....Dolores Gray

(Closed March 15, 1952)

LACE ON HER PETTICOAT

(79 performances)

Play in three acts by Aimee Stuart, produced by Herman Shumlin at the Booth Theatre, September 4, 1951.

Cast of characters—

Mrs. Cahoon ....Jean Cameron
Mrs. Oliphant ....Muriel Aked
Elspeth McNairn ....Patsy Bruder
Alexandra Carmichael ....Perlita Neilson
Faith McNairn ....Neva Patterson
Hamish Cahoon ....Jeff Morrow
Mac ....Jock MacGregor

The action takes place in the kitchen-living room of a small cottage on the west coast of Scotland in Spring and Summer of 1890. Act I.—Scene 1—A Saturday afternoon. Scene 2—The next morning. Act II.—Scene 1—That evening. Scene 2—Six weeks later. Act III.—Later the same night.

Staged by Herman Shumlin; set by Samuel Leve; costumes by Hazel Roy; general stage manager, James Gelb.

Elspeth McNairn, about 12, a poor girl, becomes bosom friends with Alexandra Carmichael, a rich one. Class distinctions imposed by their elders break up the friendship.

(Closed November 10, 1951)

BAGELS AND YOX

(208 performances)

An "American-Yiddish revue" with songs by Sholom Secunda and Hy Jacobson, produced by Al Beckman and John Pransky in association with the Brandt Theatres at the Holiday Theatre, September 12, 1951.

Principals—

The Barton Brothers	Ricky Layne and Velvel
Lou Saxon	Mary Forrest
Marty Drake	Patrice Helene
Larry Alpert	Jan Howard

Orchestra conducted by Irv Carroll, with Curt Bell at the piano.

(Closed February 12, 1952)

DIAMOND LIL

(67 performances)

Play in three acts by Mae West, revived by George Brandt at the Broadway Theatre, September 14, 1951.

Cast of characters—

Jim	Richard King
Bill	Jack Howard
Ragtime	Arnold New
Spike	George Warren
Jerry	Harry Warren
Card Players	Jerry Ford, Les Colodny
Kitty	Linda King
Frances	Sally Lewis
Flo	Helen Waters
Flynn	Charles G. Martin
Kane	Patsy Perroni
Gus Jordan	Walter Petrie
Sally	Alice Martin
Rita	Zolya Talma
Juarez	James Courtney
Mike	James Fallon
Diamond Lil	Mae West
Charlie	Charles Brown
Bessie	Lois Harmon
Barbara	Marion Gates
Captain Cummings	Dan Matthews
Pete the Duke	Lester Laurence
Jacobson	Louis Nussbaum
Chic Clark	Val Gould
Sailor	Bert Remsen
Dan Darcy	Sid Lawson
Doheny	Harry Kadison
Lefty	Fred Ardath
Miss West's Accompanist	David Lapin
Bowery Musicians	Roy Johnson, Willie Creager, Adrian Tei, Bernie Friedland

This was the second revival of Miss West's comedy. The play was first produced April 9, 1928, at the Royale Theatre, and first revived February 5, 1949.

(Closed November 10, 1951)

BORSCHT CAPADES

(99 performances)

An "English-Yiddish musical revue," produced by Hal Ziegler at the Royale Theatre, September 17, 1951.

Principals—

Dave Barry
Barry Sisters
Raasche
Jack Hilliard
Patsy Abbott

Alan Shackner
The Ted Adair Dancers
Mickey Katz
Phil Foster

Staged by Mickey Katz; sets by Charles Elson.

(Closed December 2, 1951)

OUT WEST OF EIGHTH

(4 performances)

Comedy in two acts by Kenyon Nicholson, produced by Courtney Burr and Malcolm Pearson at the Ethel Barrymore Theatre, September 20, 1951.

Cast of characters—

Cecil Wulliver	Gene Darfler
Virgil Lavendar	Dennis Weaver
Delbert Moon	Charles Windell
Joe Varro	Jim Moreno
Eddie Todd	Richard Carlyle
Horace MacNamara	Cliff Dunstan
Everett Garner	Al Henderson
Clovis Garrett	Texas Jim Robertson
Lottie Vogel	Edna Preston
Skeeter Roach	Bill McCutcheon
Dad Offutt	Earl Jay Gilbert
Lash Castro	Robert Keith, Jr.
Virginia Beamer	Barbara Baxley
Booger Lowry	Charles Thompson
Gale Rambo	Margaret Hill
Blaine Rambo	Tommy Allen
Ginger Hornick	Mary Carver
Peaches Gomez	Patricia John Canty
Tony Demopolis	Martin Greene
Rita Crummitt	Irene Cowan
Harry Crummitt	Donald McClelland
Lyman Stack	Alan Jay Schnapier
Mrs. Otis Stack	Mary Perry
Mr. Ogilbie	Donald Bain

The action takes place in various parts of the Rialto Plaza Hotel, New York, beginning on an October morning.

No director credited in the program; sets by Ralph Alswang; costumes by Jocelyn; stage manager, Charles Durand.

The hotel is packed with cowboys during the Fall engagement of the Rodeo at Madison Square Garden. One of them steals a cute manicurist from a former bellhop, and the latter seeks revenge.

(Closed September 22, 1951)

TWILIGHT WALK

(8 performances)

Melodrama in three acts by A. B. Shiffrin, produced by Richard W. Krakeur at the Fulton Theatre, September 24, 1951.

Cast of characters—

Ronnie Brewster	Charles Proctor
Clark Wilson	Walter Brooke
Mrs. Kramer	Anna Berger
First Little Girl	Pauline Hahn
Second Little Girl	Rosemarie Sheer
Woman	Genevieve Frizzell
First Old Man	Joseph Leberman
Second Old Man	Nathaniel Sack
Shoeshine Boy	Philip Hepburn
Kate Scott	Nancy Kelly
Mrs. Brewster	Ann Shoemaker
Sam Dundee	Walter Matthau
Young Man	Joseph Roman
Rosie Callahan	Virginia Vincent
Policeman	Leo Lucker

Passers-by: Christopher Barbero, Edward Bucsko, William Camia, Ronald Cusack, Morris Kamhi, Lynne Lyons, John Pavelko, Gene Perlowin, Robert Sagalyn, Nina Seamans, Carol Steers.

Scene: Somewhere in Central Park, New York; time, the present. Act I.—Late afternoon. Act II.—Next' day; late afternoon. Act III.—Next day; twilight.

Staged by Paul Stewart; set by Paul Morrison; production stage manager, Herman Shapiro.

Police are after a sex-twisted killer in Central Park, and Kate Scott, a feature writer who believes that such killers should be treated as invalids and not criminals, is following the hunt. She finds the killer and her sympathy for him almost gets her strangled.

(Closed September 29, 1951)

REMAINS TO BE SEEN

(199 performances)

Comedy in three acts by Howard Lindsay and Russel Crouse, produced by Leland Hayward at the Morosco Theatre, October 3, 1951.

Cast of characters—

Edward Miller	Karl Lukas
Benjamin Goodman	Howard Lindsay
Dr. Charles Gresham	Warner Anderson
Waldo Walton	Jackie Cooper

Dr. Chester Delapp ....Ross Hertz
Robert Clark ....Hugh Rennie
Fred Fleming ....Joseph Latham
Tony Minetti ....Frank Campanella
Morris Rosenberg ....Paul Lipson
Jody Revere ....Janis Paige
Hideo Hayakawa ....Harry Shaw Lowe
Valeska Chauvel ....Madeleine Morka
Al, the Porter ....Ossie Davis
Lieutenant Casey ....Kirk Brown
Detective Davis ....Alexander Lockwood
Detective Watson ....Jonathan Brewster
Detective Weiner ....Lew Herbert
Patrolman Johnson ....John Bouie
Mrs. Bright ....Edith Bell

The action takes place in the living room of Travis Revercombe's Park Avenue apartment. Act I.—Scene 1—Evening, shortly after 9 o'clock. Scene 2—Later that night. Act II.—Scene 1—The following afternoon. Scene 2—Late that night. Act III.—Half an hour later.

Staged by Bretaigne Windust; set by Raymond Sovey.

See page 250.

(Closed March 22, 1952)

SAINT JOAN

(142 performances)

Play in six scenes and an epilogue by Bernard Shaw, revived by the Theatre Guild at the Cort Theatre, October 4, 1951.

Cast of characters—

Robert de Baudricourt (Squire of Vaucouleurs) ....James Daly
His Steward ....Burton Mallory
Joan ....Uta Hagen
Bertrand de Poulengey ....Preston Hanson
The Archbishop of Rheims ....Frederic Worlock
The Duke De la Tremouille ....Norman Roland
A Page ....Robert M. Casper
Gilles de Rais ("Bluebeard") ....Frederic Warriner
Captain La Hire ....Paul Ballantyne
The Dauphin (afterwards Charles VII of France) ...John Buckmaster
Duchess De la Tremouille ....Sylvia Farnham
Dunois ("The Bastard of Orleans") ....Robert Pastene
Page to Dunois ....Tom Hughes Sand
The Earl of Warwick ....Andrew Cruickshank
John de Stogumber ....Dion Allen
Peter Cauchon (Bishop of Beauvais) ....Alexander Scourby
Page to Warwick ....Tarry Green
The Inquisitor ....Frederick Rolf
Canon D'Estivet ....John Straub
Thomas de Courcelles (Canon of Paris) ....Frederic Warriner
Brother Martin Ladvenu ....Kendall Clark
The Executioner ....Preston Hanson
A Soldier in Warwick's Army ....James Daly
A Gentleman ....Paul Ballantyne

Ladies, Courtiers, Monks, Doctors, Assessors: Martine Bartlett, Joseph Dooley, Jill Melford, Martin Waldron, Nancy Wickwire, Van Williams, Sylvia Farnham, John Straub, Norman Roland, Jon Dawson, Burton Mallory.

Staged by Margaret Webster; settings by Richard Harrison Senie; costumes by Elinor Robbins; score by Lehman Engel; production under the supervision of Theresa Helburn and Lawrence Langner; stage manager, Thelma Chandler.

"Saint Joan" was given its first production by the Theatre Guild at the Garrick Theatre, December 28, 1923, with Winifred Lenihan in the title role. It was revived by Katharine Cornell at the Martin Beck Theatre March 9, 1936, where it had 89 performances.

(Closed February 2, 1952)

MUSIC IN THE AIR

(56 performances)

Musical comedy in two acts, by Jerome Kern and Oscar Hammerstein II, revived by Reginald Hammerstein at the Ziegfeld Theatre, October 8, 1951.

Cast of characters—

Mrs. Pflugfelder	Julie Kelety
Tila	Marybeth Fitzpatrick
Herman	Richard Case
Karl Reder	Mitchell Gregg
Burgomaster	Hal Frye
Sieglinde Lessing	Lillian Murphy
Dr. Walther Lessing	Charles Winninger
Schmidt	Carlo Corelli
Priest	Milton Watson
Pflugfelder	Walter Born
Ernst Weber	Conrad Nagel
Uppmann	Guy Spaull
Marthe	Terry Saunders
Frieda Harzfeld	Jane Pickens
Bruno Mahler	Dennis King
Waiter	John M. King
Zoo Attendant	Waldorf
Anna	Norah Howard
Porter	James Beni
Kirschner	Richard Bishop
Lilli	Muriel O'Malley
Sophie	Julie Kelety
Assistant Stage Manager	John M. King
Lawyer Baum	Gordon Alexander
Barmaid	Biruta Ramoska
Willi	James Beni
Frau Schreimann	Jean Ellsperman
Frau Moeller	Susan Steell

Staged by Oscar Hammerstein II; sets by Lemuel Ayers; orchestrations by Robert Russell Bennett; general stage manager, Paul Shiers.

"Music in the Air" was first produced at the Alvin Theatre, November 8, 1932, where it had 144 performances. In a return engagement ending the following year it brought its total to 342 performances. The run was interrupted by the depression and disputes with theatrical unions.

(Closed November 24, 1951)

GLAD TIDINGS

(100 performances)

Comedy in three acts by Edward Mabley, produced by Harald Bromley at the Lyceum Theatre, October 11, 1951.

Cast of characters—

Ethel Nash	Haila Stoddard
Mrs. McDonald	Fay Sappington
Henry	James Hagerman
Steve Whitney	Melvyn Douglas
Agnes Bell	Ann Sturgis
Maud Abbott	Signe Hasso
Claire Abbott	Patricia Benoit
Gus Kennedy	Rudy Bond
Terry Abbott	Henry Garrard

The action takes place on the terrace of Steve Whitney's house on the Connecticut shore. Act I.—A Summer morning. Act II.—That evening. Act III.—The next morning.

Staged by Melvyn Douglas; set by William and Jean Eckert; costumes supervised by John Derro; production stage manager, John Holden.

Steve Whitney, about to wed Ethel Nash, a wealthy magazine owner who has made Steve the editor, is confronted with a love of twenty years ago—temperamental film star Maud Abbott. Miss Abbott presents him with a 19-year-old daughter he didn't know he had, and he decides to make the lass legitimate.

(Closed January 5, 1952)

A SLEEP OF PRISONERS

(31 performances)

Religious drama in verse, in one act, by Christopher Fry, produced by Luther Greene at St. James' Church, Madison Avenue at 71st St., October 16, 1951.

Cast of characters—

Pvt. David King	Leonard White
Pvt. Peter Able	Donald Harron
Cpl. Joseph Adams	Stanley Baker
Pvt. Tim Meadows	Hugh Pryse

The church, which is presumed to be in a foreign country, is being used as a temporary prison. The action is continuous.

Staged by Michael MacOwan; lighted by Abe Feder; assistant director, Hugh Goldie.

Mr. Fry wrote this drama at the behest of an English church organization. In it, four war prisoners have successive dreams that they are various Biblical characters.

(Closed November 10, 1951)

BUY ME BLUE RIBBONS

(13 performances)

Comedy in three acts by Sumner Locke Elliott, produced by Jay Robinson at the Empire Theatre, October 17, 1951.

Cast of characters—

Maude	Kate Harrington
Norma Cusack	Cynthia Latham
Daisy Sable	Enid Markey
Liz Kendall	Audrey Christie
Jordan Sable	Jay Robinson
Professor Oscar Nimrod	Wells Richardson
Victor Hatfield	Gavin Gordon
Camilla Ransome	Vicki Cummings
Alvin Sable	Jack Hartley
Nurse Fiske	Philippa Bevans

Jordan Sable's duplex apartment on Park Avenue. Act I.—A morning in late Fall. Act II.—Late afternoon, two weeks later. Act III.—Scene 1—Early evening, three weeks later. Scene 2—The following morning.

Staged by Cyril Ritchard; set and costumes by Jack Landau; stage manager, Allen F. Collins.

Jordan Sable, rich, young and spoiled, thinks he is an actor and produces a play to prove it. He is so bad he is fired from his own show.

(Closed October 27, 1951)

FAITHFULLY YOURS

(68 performances)

Comedy in two acts by L. Bush-Fekete and Mary Helen Fay, produced by Richard W. Krakeur at the Coronet Theatre, October 18, 1951.

Cast of characters—

Vivian Harding	Ann Sothern
Thomas O. Harding	Robert Cummings
Stokes	Victor Wood
Susan	Marguerite Gould
Dr. Peter Wilson	Philip Bourneuf
Betty	Eileen Erskine
Miss Parker	Doreen Lang
Gracie	Florence Sundstrom
Joyce	Beverly Whitney
Vera	Barbara Barondess MacLean

Time: today. The action takes place in the living room of the Hardings' penthouse apartment in New York City.

Staged by Richard Whorf; set by Paul Morrison; production stage manager, Harry Howell.

Vivian Harding imagines that her husband, Tom, needs psychoanalysis, but she knows he'd never stand for it. So she volunteers to Dr. Peter Wilson to take the psychoanalysis for him.

(Closed December 15, 1951)

LOVE AND LET LOVE

(51 performances)

Comedy in two acts by Louis Verneuil, produced by Anthony B. Farrell at the Plymouth Theatre, October 19, 1951.

Cast of characters—

Dr. Fred Stevens	Tom Helmore
Shirley	Helen Marcy
Harlan	David Perkins
Charles Warren	Paul McGrath
Valerie King }	Ginger Rogers
Ruth Gage }	

The action takes place in Charles Warren's home in New York. Act I.—Scene 1—An evening in May. Scene 2—Later the same evening. Act II.—Scene 1—The following Sunday. Scene 2—That evening. Scene 3—Later the same night.
Staged by Louis Verneuil; set by Ralph Alswang; costumes by Jean Louis.

Two men, Dr. Stevens and Charles Warren, love Valerie King, an actress. One of them gets her.

(Closed December 1, 1951)

THE FOURPOSTER

(256 performances)
(Continued)

Comedy in three acts by Jan de Hartog, produced by the Playwrights' Company at the Ethel Barrymore Theatre, October 24, 1951.

Cast of characters—

Agnes	Jessica Tandy
Michael	Hume Cronyn

The action takes place in the bedroom of a home. Act I.—Scene 1—1890. Scene 2—A year later. Act II.—Scene 1—1901. Scene 2—Seven years later. Act III.—Scene 1—1913. Scene 2—Twelve years later.
Staged by José Ferrer; set by Syrjala; costumes by Lucinda Ballard; stage managers, William Weaver and Marjorie Winfield.

See page 107.

THE NUMBER

(87 performances)

Melodrama in three acts by Arthur Carter, produced at the Biltmore Theatre by Paul Vroom and Irving Cooper, October 30, 1951.

Cast of characters—

Dottie	Peggy Nelson
Sylvia	Martha Scott

Alice ....Louise Larabee
Maury ....Murvyn Vye
Lennie ....Luis Van Rooten
Bessie Berger ....Jennie Goldstein
Hyman Berger ....Anatole Winogradoff
Dominic Spizzilini ....Dane Clark
Waitress ....Diana Herbert
Dolly ....Bobby Vail
Guido ....Guy Thomajan

Act I.—Scene 1—Maury's office; a December afternoon. Scene 2—
The Berger kitchen; three weeks later, 7 P.M. Scene 3—Corner of a
restaurant on a highway miles out of town; a week later, 9 P.M.
Scene 4—Four telephone areas; three days later. Act II.—Scene 1—
A tourist cabin outside the city; several hours later. Scene 2—
Maury's office; thirty minutes later. Act III.—The Berger kitchen;
an hour later.

Staged by George Abbott; sets by Ralph Alswang; costumes by Jocelyn; stage manager, Robert Griffith.

Sylvia takes telephone bets in Maury's office. She falls in love
with smooth-talking Dominic Spizzilini and gets in trouble when
Dominic has the winning number in Maury's numbers game. Dominic is rubbed out. (*Editor's note:* "The Number" was a rare instance in which a play was revised after its New York opening.
After reading reviews, director George Abbott eliminated a scene
in Act II which showed Sylvia fighting to keep her small daughter
from her estranged husband. This simplified and tightened the
melodrama.)

(Closed January 12, 1952)

BAREFOOT IN ATHENS

(30 performances)

Play in two acts by Maxwell Anderson, produced by the Playwrights' Company at the Martin Beck Theatre, October 31, 1951.

Cast of characters—

Xantippe ....Lotte Lenya
Lamprocles ....Robert Brown
Lysis ....Judson Rees
Phoenix ....Robin Michael
Socrates ....Barry Jones
Crito ....Daniel Reed
Phaedo ....William Bush
Critobulus ....Stratton Walling
Theodote ....Helen Shields
Anytos ....David J. Stewart
Meletos ....Bruce Hall
Lykon ....William Hansen
Crassos ....Karl Light
Satyros ....Bart Burns
Guards ....Edward Groag, John McLiam
Critias ....Philip Coolidge
Pausanias ....George Mathews
Magistrate ....Joseph Warren

Act I.—Scene 1—In the house of Socrates; breakfast time. Scene
2—At the wall of Athens; around noon, several months later. Scene
3—In Socrates' house; a half hour later. Act II.—Scene 1—In Soc-

rates' house; a week or two later, morning. Scene 2—The trial of
Socrates; the next day.   Scene 3—Socrates' cell; before dawn, some
weeks later.   The action takes place in Athens near the end of the
Fifth Century B.C.
    Staged by Alan Anderson; sets by Boris Aronson; costumes by
Bernard Rudofsky; production stage manager, Scott Jackson.

See page 151.

(Closed November 24, 1951)

TOP BANANA

(246 performances)
(Continued)

Musical comedy in two acts; book by Hy Kraft; words and music
by Johnny Mercer; produced by Paula Stone and Mike Sloane at
the Winter Garden, November 1, 1951.

Cast of characters—

Danny	Eddie Hanley
Script Girl	Eve Hebert
Bubble Girls	Beverly Weston, Sara Dillon
Vic Davis	Jack Albertson
Tommy	Bob Scheerer
Walter	Walter Dare Wahl
Jerry Biffle	Phil Silvers
Cliff Lane	Lindy Doherty
Moe	Herbie Faye
Pinky	Joey Faye
Betty Dillon	Rose Marie
Sally Peters	Judy Lynn
A Man	Johnny Trama
Elevator Operator	Sara Dillon
Models	Marian Burke, Basha Regis
Sales Girls	Joy Skylar, Polly Ward, Florence Baum, Eve Hebert
Russ Wiswell	Zachary A. Charles
Mr. Parker	Brad Hatton
Announcer	Dean Campbell
Featured Dancers	Hal Loman, Joan Fields
TV Technician	Ken Harvey
Miss Pillsbury	Betsy Holland
Dr. Leroy	Doug Luther
Stagehand	Don Covert
Ted (Sport) Morgan	By Himself
Dance Team	Bob Scheerer, Polly Ward
Juggler	Claude Heater
A Passing Girl	Mary Harmon
The Widow	Judy Sinclair
The Magician's Assistant	Basha Regis
"Bubbles"	Gloria Smith

    Dancers: Florence Baum, Eve Hebert, Vivian Smith, Joy Skylar,
Gloria Smith, Thelma Tadlock, Polly Ward, Nikki Cellini, Bill Joyce,
John Laverty, George Marci, Walter Stane, Bill Sumner, Ken
Urmston.
    Singers: Marian Burke, Sara Dillon, Mary Harmon, Betsy Holland,
B. J. Keating, Laurel Shelby, Judy Sinclair, Beverly Weston, Dean
Campbell, Don Covert, Herb Fields, Ken Harvey, Claude Heater,
Bob Kole, Doug Luther, Don McKay.

Principal song numbers—

ACT I

"The Man of the Year This Week"	Ensemble
"You're So Beautiful That—"	Cliff

"Top Banana" ....Jerry, Vic, Cliff, Pinky, Moe
"Elevator Song" ....Ensemble
"Hail to MacCracken's" ....Ensemble
"Only if You're in Love" ....Cliff and Sally
"My Home Is in My Shoes" ....Tommy and Ensemble
"I Fought Every Step of the Way" ....Betty
"O.K. for TV" ....Jerry, Vic, Sally, Pinky, Moe, Danny, Russ
"Slogan Song" ....Jerry, Betty, Vic, Sally, Cliff, Tommy,
                              Pinky, Moe, Danny, Russ Parker

ACT II

"Sans Souci" ....Betty, Hal Loman, Joan Fields and Ensemble
"A Dog Is a Man's Best Friend" ..Jerry, "Sport" and the Grenadiers
"That's for Sure".......................Cliff, Sally and Ensemble
"A Word a Day" ....Jerry and Betty
    Staged by Jack Donohue; sets by Jo Mielziner; costumes by Alvin
Colt; dances by Ron Fletcher; musical director, Harold Hastings;
vocal arrangements and direction by Hugh Martin; orchestrations by
Don Walker; production associate, Harry Zevin; production stage
manager, Fred Hebert.

DINOSAUR WHARF

(4 performances)

Melodrama in five scenes by Joel Wyman, produced by Terese
Hayden at the National Theatre, November 8, 1951.

Cast of characters—

Timmy ....William Darrid
Thug ....Richard Castle
Charlie ....James Gregory
Pop ....Harrison Dowd
Sam ....John Marriott
Mike..Thomas Russino
John ....Stuart McIntosh
Paula ....Lois Wheeler
Clancy ....Barnard Hughes
Woman ....Sally Gracie
Boy ....Salvatore Mineo
Will ....Leo Penn
Chris ....Richard Venture
Mr. Brodie ....John Marley
Mr. Sherman ....Gregory Robbins
Capt. Swanson ....Stuart McIntosh
Second Thug ....John Marley
    The scene is a barge, moored at an abandoned wharf in the East
River, New York. Time, late September.
    Staged by Terese Hayden; set by Samuel Leve; production stage
manager, Burry Fredrik.

Paula lives with her father, Pop, on their barge, and works in a
library. She is interested in Will, a young longshoreman who leads
a revolt against gangster control of the dockmen's union, but she
abhors the violence of the waterfront. However, it is she who stabs
to death the gang leader, Charlie.

(Closed November 10, 1951)

PAINT YOUR WAGON

(233 performances)
(Continued)

Musical comedy in two acts; book and lyrics by Alan Jay Lerner; music by Frederick Loewe; produced by Cheryl Crawford at the Shubert Theatre, November 12, 1951.

Cast of characters—

Walt	Jack Sheehan
Jennifer Rumson	Ann Crowley
Salem Trumbull	Ralph Bunker
Jasper	Ted Thurston
Ben Rumson	Eddie Dowling
Steve Bullnack	Rufus Smith
Pete Billings	Scott Merrill
Cherry	Kay Medford
Jake Whippany	Robert Penn
Mike Mooney	John Randolph
Doctor Newcomb	David Thomas
Lee Zen	Chun-Tao Cheng
Edgar Crocker	Angus Cairns
Sandy Twist	Newton Sullivan
Reuben Sloane	Gordon Dilworth
Julio Valveras	Tony Bavaar
Jacob Woodling	Josh Wheeler
Elizabeth Woodling	Marijane Maricle
Sarah Woodling	Jan Sherwood
Dutchie	Jack Sheehan
Carmellita	Lorraine Havercroft
Yvonne Sorel	Gemze de Lappe
Suzanne Duval	Mary Burr
Raymond Janney	Gordon Dilworth
Rocky	James Tarbutton
Jack	Delbert Anderson
Ed	Edgar Thompson
Sam	Feodore Tedick
Johansen	John Anderson

Singers: Delbert Anderson, John Anderson, Gino Baldi, Edward Becker, Jack Dabdoub, John Faulkner, Robert Flavelle, John Schickling, John Schmidt, John Spach, Newton Sullivan, Feodore Tedick, David Thomas, Edgar Thompson, Ted Thurston, Norman Weise.

Dancers: Tamara Chapman, Gemze de Lappe, Joan Djorup, Katia Geleznova, Lorraine Havercroft, Dorothy Hill, Stuart Hodes, Jean Houloose, Carmelita Lanza, Ilona Murai, Paul Olson, Kenneth LeRoy, Martha Mathes, Evelyn Taylor, Duncan Noble, Naomi Boneck, James Tarbutton, Guy Stanbaugh.

The time is 1853; the locale, northern California. Act I scenes include a hilltop, the exterior of a store, a cabin, a saloon, mine diggings and the town square. Act II scenes include Jake's Palace, the diggings, Rumson's cabin and Rumson Square.

Production directed by Daniel Mann; dances staged by Agnes de Mille; sets by Oliver Smith; costumes by Motley; orchestrations by Ted Royal; dance music arrangements by Trude Rittman; Franz Allers, orchestra conductor; production associate, Bea Lawrence; production stage manager, Ward Bishop.

Principal numbers—

ACT I

"I'm on My Way" .... Sung by Steve, Jake, Mooney, Zen, Sandy, Crocker, Sloane and the miners
"I Talk to the Trees" ...... Sung and danced by Julio and Jennifer
"They Call the Wind Maria" .... Sung by Steve and the miners

"I Still See Elisa" ....Sung by Ben Rumson
"How Can I Wait?" ....Sung by Jennifer
"Whoop-Ti-Ay!" ....Sung and danced by Ben, Elizabeth
                                                  and the miners
"Carino Mio" ....Sung by Julio and Jennifer
"There's a Coach Comin' In" ....Sung by the miners

ACT II

"Hand Me Down That Can o' Beans" ..Sung by Jake and the miners
"Another Autumn" ....Sung by Julio
"Movin' " ....Sung by Ed, Sandy, Joe, Sam, Jack, Jasper,
                                                  Johansen, Zen
"All for Him" ....Sung by Jennifer
"Wand'rin' Star" ....Sung by Ben

"Paint Your Wagon" tells a story of the Gold Rush, from the beginning of a mining camp through its growth into a boom town and through its decline when the lode peters out, until it becomes a ghost town. But there still is a future for this town, for irrigation and agriculture have begun.

TO DOROTHY, A SON

(8 performances)

Comedy in three acts by Roger MacDougall, in collaboration with Otis Bigelow, produced by Herman Shumlin at the John Golden Theatre, November 19, 1951.

Cast of characters—

Evelyn Ridgeway ....Ronald Howard
Dorothy Ridgeway ....Stella Andrew
Hank Thompson ....Martin Rudy
Alice ....Hildy Parks
Taxi Driver ⎫
Postman   ⎪
2nd Taxi Driver ⎬ ....Neil Fitzgerald
Landlord   ⎪
Dr. Cameron ⎭
Nurse ....Rosalynd Avery

The action takes place in the Ridgeways' cottage in Chiswick, a London suburb. Act I.—A Spring morning. Act II.—Scene 1—The following morning. Scene 2—The next morning. Act III.—About five hours later.

Staged by Herman Shumlin; set by William and Jean Eckhart; clothes by Hazel Roy; general stage manager, Lucia Victor.

Evelyn Ridgeway, a young musician, is about to become a father, courtesy of his wife, Dorothy. His first wife, Alice, turns up from Texas to claim that her divorce was illegal in a scheme to inherit a million dollars from an uncle. But the uncle's will bestows the fortune on a male child Evelyn may have, if any, and Dorothy delivers just in time.

(Closed November 24, 1951)

NEVER SAY NEVER

(7 performances)

Comedy in three acts by Carl Leo, produced by Albert H. Rosen and Lester Meyer at the Booth Theatre, November 20, 1951.

Cast of characters—

Coralie Jones	Anne Jackson
Gloria Sampson	Nita Talbot
Alex Wesley	Hugh Reilly
Lester B. Sprawls	Don Briggs
Maxie Jordan	Haim Winant
Jasper Hornblower, III	Royal Beal

The action takes place in an apartment off lower Fifth Avenue, New York. Act I.—Scene 1—October; late afternoon. Scene 2— Later that night. Act II.—Scene 1—The next morning. Scene 2— Late afternoon, same day. Act III.—An hour later.

Staged by Robert B. Sinclair; set by Frederick Fox; costumes by Alice Gibson; production associate, Gilda Dahlberg; stage manager, Karl Nielsen.

Coralie Jones, a career girl, and Alex Wesley, a writer, are contentedly living in sin until Coralie's home-town friend, Lester B. Sprawls, comes to take her away from the wicked city. He fails, and Alex persuades Coralie to marry him.

(Closed November 24, 1951)

DON JUAN IN HELL

(105 performances)

Third act of "Man and Superman," by Bernard Shaw, produced at Carnegie Hall by Paul Gregory, October 22, 1951. After one performance at Carnegie Hall, the "First Drama Quartette" returned to the Century Theatre for a limited run beginning November 29, 1951, and after 38 performances there it went on tour and returned to the Plymouth Theatre, April 6, 1952.

Cast of characters—

Don Juan	Charles Boyer
The Devil	Charles Laughton
The Statue	Cedric Hardwicke
Donna Anna	Agnes Moorehead

Staged by Charles Laughton.

This long debate about Man's mind and destiny had played one- and two-night stands in meeting halls across the country, with the actors in evening dress and with no props except four stools and four microphones. New York interest in the novelty was so great that, after one performance in New York and one in Brooklyn, bookings in other cities were canceled or postponed and the Quartette was brought back for an engagement of four and a half weeks.

(Closed May 24, 1952)

GIGI

(219 performances)

Comedy in two acts by Anita Loos, based on a novel by Colette, produced by Gilbert Miller at the Fulton Theatre, November 24, 1951.

Cast of characters—

```
Gigi .................................................Audrey Hepburn
Mme. Alvarez .................................Josephine Brown
Andrée .............................................Doris Patston
Gaston Lachaille .............................Michael Evans
Victor .............................................Francis Compton
Alicia de St. Ephlam .......................Cathleen Nesbitt
Sidonie ...........................................Bertha Belmore
```
        Paris, 1900.   Act I.—Scene 1—Mme. Alvarez' apartment.   Scene 2—Alicia de St. Ephlam's boudoir.   Scene 3—Mme. Alvarez' apartment.   Act II.—Scene 1—Mme. Alvarez' apartment.   Scene 2—Alicia's boudoir.   Scene 3—Mme. Alvarez' apartment.
        Staged by Raymond Rouleau; settings credited to Raymond Sovey; stage manager, Richard Bender.

See page 230.

(Closed May 31, 1952)

I AM A CAMERA

(214 performances)

Play in three acts by John van Druten, based on stories by Christopher Isherwood, produced by Gertrude Macy in association with Walter Starcke at the Empire Theatre, November 28, 1951.

Cast of characters—

```
Christopher Isherwood ..........................William Prince
Fräulein Schneider ................................Olga Fabian
Fritz Wendel .....................................Martin Brooks
Sally Bowles .....................................Julie Harris
Natalia Landauer ..............................Marian Winters
Clive Mortimer ..............................Edward Andrews
Mrs. Watson-Courtneidge .....................Catherine Willard
```
        The action takes place in a room of Fräulein Schneider's flat in Berlin in 1930, before the rise of the Hitler regime.   Act I.—Scene 1—A Summer afternoon.   Scene 2—Three months later.   Act II.—Scene 1—A week later.   Scene 2—Five days later.   Act III.—Scene 1—Two days later.   Scene 2—Three days later.   Scene 3—Three days later.
        Staged by John van Druten; set by Boris Aronson; costumes by Ellen Goldsborough; production assistant, Paul Bigelow; stage manager, Jose Vega.

See page 83.

(Closed May 31, 1952)

NINA

(45 performances)

Comedy in three acts by André Roussin, adapted by Samuel Taylor, produced by John C. Wilson and H. M. Tennent, Ltd., at the Royale Theatre, December 5, 1951.

Cast of characters—

Gerard ....David Niven
Adolphe ....Alam Webb
Nina ....Gloria Swanson
M. Redon-LaMur ....William Le Massena
 The scene is Gerard's bachelor apartment in Paris; Spring. Act I.—Late afternoon. Act II.—The following morning. Act III.—That afternoon.
 Staged by Gregory Ratoff; set by Charles Elson; stage manager, Samuel Liff.

For some time Nina has been Gerard's mistress. One afternoon her husband, Adolphe, comes to shoot Gerard, but comes down with a cold and remains as a patient. Adolphe and Gerard become fast friends in the face of a common opponent—Nina.

(Closed January 12, 1952)

THE CONSTANT WIFE

(138 performances)

Comedy in three acts by Somerset Maugham, revived by Katharine Cornell at the National Theatre, December 8, 1951.

Cast of characters—

Mrs. Culver ....Grace George
Bentley ....Liam Sullivan
Martha Culver ....Gertrude Musgrove
Barbara Fawcett ....Eva Leonard-Boyne
Constance Middleton ....Katharine Cornell
Marie-Louise Durham ....Nan Martin
John Middleton, F.R.C.S. ....Brian Aherne
Bernard Kersal ....John Emery
Mortimer Durham ....Claude Horton
 The action takes place in Constance Middleton's drawing room, Harley Street, London. Act I.—June, present year. Act II.—The same, two weeks later. Act III.—The same, a year later.
 Staged by Guthrie McClintic; set by Donald Oenslager; stage manager, Seymour Milbert.

"The Constant Wife" was first produced by the Frohman office November 29, 1926, with Ethel Barrymore in the title role and C. Aubrey Smith, Frank Conroy and Veree Teasdale in supporting roles. It ran for 233 performances. Miss Cornell's revival was first staged for the drama and opera festival at Central City, Colorado, in the Summer of 1951.

(Closed April 5, 1952)

THE GRAND TOUR

(8 performances)

Play in two acts by Elmer Rice, produced by the Playwrights' Company at the Martin Beck Theatre, December 10, 1951.

Cast of characters—

Mr. Montgomery	John Rodney
A female traveler	Claire Justice
Nell Valentine	Beatrice Straight
A male traveler	Maury Tuckerman
Raymond Brinton	Richard Derr
A deck steward	Sam Bonnell
Professor Coogan	William A. Lee
Harvey Richman	Edwin Jerome
Adele Brinton	Louisa Horton

Act I.—Scene 1—New York. Scene 2—At sea. Scene 3—Still at sea. Scene 4—Paris. Act II.—Scene 1—Chartres. Scene 2—Montreux. Scene 3—Rome. Scene 4—Rome again. Scene 5—Back home.

Staged by Elmer Rice; sets by Howard Bay; costumes selected by Motley; production stage manager, Scott Jackson.

Nell Valentine, a schoolteacher who has inherited some money, goes on a European tour and falls in love with another tourist, Raymond Brinton, a bank embezzler. It is a tender romance, but it won't work out, and when Summer is over Nell is back in her classroom.

(Closed December 15, 1951)

LO AND BEHOLD

(38 performances)

Comedy in three acts by John Patrick, produced by the Theatre Guild at the Booth Theatre, December 12, 1951.

Cast of characters—

Milo Alcott	Leo G. Carroll
Mr. Wingate	George Englund
Daisy Durdle	Lee Grant
Dr. Robert Dorsey	Jeffrey Lynn
Minnetonka Smallflower	Doro Merande
Kenneth Moore	Roy Irving
Honey Wainwright	Cloris Leachman
Jack McDougal	Paul Crabtree

The action occurs in the library of Milo Alcott's home; time, the present. Act I.—Scene 1—Noon. Scene 2—Several days later; night. Act II.—Scene 1—A couple of days later; morning. Scene 2—Several weeks later; night. Act III.—A few hours later.

Staged by Burgess Meredith; set and costumes by Stewart Chaney; produced under the supervision of Theresa Helburn and Lawrence Langner; stage manager, Edmund Baylies.

Milo Alcott, rich, misanthropic author, tires of having been an invalid for forty years and commits suicide by eating a square meal. Before this act he arranges in a will that his home be kept as it is, but vacant, in case there is a life after death and he needs a place to stay. He does haunt his own home and is joined by other ghosts from other times and places. They watch a real-life romance develop between Daisy Durdle and Dr. Robert Dorsey without being able to influence it.

(Closed January 12, 1952)

POINT OF NO RETURN

(197 performances)
(Continued)

Play in three acts by Paul Osborn, based on the novel by John P. Marquand, produced by Leland Hayward at the Alvin Theatre, December 13, 1951.

Cast of characters—

Evelyn Gray	Susan Harris
Nancy Gray	Leora Dana
Bill Gray	Keith Russell
Charles Gray	Henry Fonda
Joe	James Jolley
First Teller	Davis Roberts
Miss Marble	Madeleine King
Miss Dingle	Katherine Hynes
First Clerk	Stanley Tackney
Second Clerk	Heywood Hale Broun
Roger Blakesley	Bartlett Robinson
Anthony Burton	Frank Conroy
Malcolm Bryant	Robert Ross
Conductor	James MacDonald
Jackie Mason	Phil Arthur
Jessica Lovell	Patricia Smith
Laurence Lovell	Colin Keith-Johnston
John Gray	John Cromwell
Esther Gray	Frances Bavier
Tailor	Pitt Herbert
Mrs. Burton	Madeleine Clive
Maid	Harriet Selby

Act I.—Time, the present. Scene 1—The living room of Charles and Nancy Gray in Sycamore Park, Connecticut. Scene 2—The Stuyvesant Bank, New York City. Scene 3—Same as Scene 1. Act II.—Scene 1—On the way to Clyde. Scene 2—Clyde, Massachusetts; 1929. Scene 3—On the way back from Clyde. Act III.—Same as Act I, Scene 1.

Staged by H. C. Potter; sets by Jo Mielziner; costumes designed by Main Bocher; production stage manager, David Gray, Jr.

See page 126.

CAESAR AND CLEOPATRA

(67 performances)

Comedy by Bernard Shaw, produced by Gilbert Miller by arrangement with Laurence Olivier Productions, Ltd., at the Ziegfeld Theatre, December 19, 1951.

Cast of characters—

Belzanor	David Greene
Persian	Edmund Purdom
Egyptian Guardsmen	
Nubian Sentinel	Cy Grant
Bel Affris	Robert Beaumont
Women of the Palace	
Ftatateeta	Pat Nye
Julius Caesar	Laurence Olivier
Cleopatra	Vivien Leigh
Charmian	Katharine Blake
Iras	Mairhi Russell
Roman Soldiers	
Pothinus	Harold Kasket
Theodotus	Timothy Bateson
Ptolemy	Dawson France
Achillas	Dan Cunningham
Court Ladies, Officials and Politicians	
Rufio	Niall MacGinnis
Britannus	Wilfred Hyde White
Lucius Septimius	Harry Andrews
Wounded Soldier	Jack Melford
Apollodorus	Robert Helpmann
Roman Sentinel	Colin Kemball
Four Porters	
Centurion	Anthony Pelly
1st Roman Auxiliary	Noel Coleman
2nd Roman Auxiliary	Max Gardiner
Boatman	Patrick Troughton
Musician	Ronald Adam
Harpist	Elizabeth Kentish
The Major-Domo	Donald Pleasence
Officials at Dinner	Clifford Williams, John Dearth
Priest	Terence Owen

Staged by Michael Benthall; sets by Roger Furse; costumes by Audrey Cruddas; music by Herbert Mengies; Jacques Singer, musical director; stage director, Rosemary Hill.

(Closed April 12, 1952)

ANTONY AND CLEOPATRA

(66 performances)

Play by William Shakespeare, produced by Gilbert Miller by arrangement with Laurence Olivier Productions, Ltd., at the Ziegfeld Theatre, December 20, 1951.

Cast of characters—

Philo Canidius	David Greene
Cleopatra	Vivien Leigh
Antony	Laurence Olivier
Mardian	Harold Kasket
The Messenger	Alec McCowen
Scarus Dercetas	Patrick Troughton
Charmian	Katharine Blake
Alexas Diomedes	Robert Beaumont
Lemprius Euphronius, a Soothsayer	Donald Pleasence
Enobarbus	Harry Andrews
Iras	Mairhi Russell
Octavius Caesar	Robert Helpmann
Lepidus	Wilfrid Hyde White
Maecenas	Jack Melford
Agrippa	Ronald Adam

Octavia ....Elizabeth Kentish
Pompey ....Niall MacGinnis
Menas ....Max Gardiner
Attendant on Octavia ....Pat Nye
Old Soldier ....Anthony Pelly
Eros ....Lyndon Brook
Dolabella ....Dan Cunningham
Thydeus ....Edmund Purdom
Nubian Messenger ....Cy Grant
A Soldier of Caesar ....Oliver Hunter
Sentries to Antony's Camp
Sentries to Caesar's Camp
Clown ....Timothy Bateson
Soldiers of Antony and Caesar, Attendants on Cleopatra, Pirates
    Staged by Michael Benthall; sets by Roger Furse; costumes by
Audrey Cruddas; music by Herbert Mengies; Jacques Singer, or-
chestra director; stage director, Rosemary Hill.

This limited engagement of Sir Laurence Olivier and Vivien Leigh
in a repertoire—with alternating performances—of Shaw's comedy,
"Caesar and Cleopatra," and Shakespeare's tragedy, "Antony and
Cleopatra," was an artistic highlight of the New York season. It
played at an unprecedented top price of $7.20, and the run was
almost entirely sold out before the opening nights.

(Closed April 12, 1952)

LEGEND OF LOVERS

(22 performances)

Play by Jean Anouilh, adapted by Kitty Black from the French
original, "Eurydice," and produced by the Theatre Guild, in association with H. M. Tennent, Ltd., at the Plymouth Theatre, December
26, 1951.

Cast of characters—

The Young Musician ....Richard Burton
His Father .. ..Hugh Griffith
The Young Actress ....Dorothy McGuire
Her Mother ....Edith King
The Cashier ....Ruth Volner
Station Waiter ....Byron Russell
Vincent ....Alexander Clark
Mathias ....Eric Sinclair
Another Actress ....Ludie Claire
Dulac ....Bruce Gordon
A Third Actress ....Jennifer Raine
Monsieur Henri ....Noel Willman
The Company Manager ....Roy Johnson
Hotel Waiter ....William Smithers
The Police Clerk ....Clem Fowler
    Act I.—The refreshment room of a French provincial station. Act
II.—A room in a Marseille hotel. Act III.—Same as Act I.
    Staged by Peter Ashmore; sets by Eldon Elder; costumes by
Mildred Trebor; music by John Hotchkis; production supervised by
Lawrence Langner and Theresa Helburn; stage manager, Arthur Mar-
lowe.

This was a version of the legend of Orpheus and Eurydice, with Orpheus a poor street musician and Eurydice an actress. After one day of ecstatic love, they face a choice between continuing this love on its rapturous plane in death, or risking the sordidness and unhappiness of life. Orpheus chooses death for them.

(Closed January 12, 1952)

THE WILD DUCK

(15 performances)

Drama in three acts by Henrik Ibsen, adapted by Max Faber, produced by the New York City Theatre Company at the New York City Center of Music and Drama, December 26, 1951.

Cast of characters—

Petterson	Wendell Whitten
Jensen	Raymond Johnson
Waiter	George Sullivan
Another Waiter	Wyman Kane
Old Ekdal	Philip Loeb
Mrs. Sorby	Nan McFarland
Flabby Gentleman	O. Tolbert-Hewitt
Bald Gentleman	Walter F. Appler
Short-sighted Gentleman	Bert Bartram
Haakon Werle	Robert Middleton
Gregers Werle	Kent Smith
Hjalmar Ekdal	Maurice Evans
Gina	Mildred Dunnock
Hedvig	Diana Lynn
Doctor Relling	David Lewis
Molvik	Leonardo Cimino

Guests at the Party: Charles Campbell, Frank Ford, Carl Harms, Jack Henderson, Philip Remer, Arthur Row

Staged by Morton DaCosta; George Schaefer, artistic director for the City Center; sets by Peter Larkin; costumes by Noel Taylor; production stage manager, Billy Matthews.

(Closed January 6, 1952)

PAL JOEY

(173 performances)
(Continued)

Musical comedy in two acts by Richard Rodgers, the late Lorenz Hart and John O'Hara, revived by Jule Styne and Leonard Key, in association with Anthony B. Farrell, at the Broadhurst Theatre, January 3, 1952.

Cast of characters—

Mike	Jack Waldron
Joey	Harold Lang

Kid ....Helen Wood
Gladys ....Helen Gallagher
Agnes ....Janyce Ann Wagner
Mickey ....Phyllis Dorne
Diane ....Frances Krell
Dottie ....Lynn Joelson
Sandra ....Eleanor Boleyn
Adele ....Rita Tanno
Francine ....Gloria O'Malley
Linda ....Pat Northrop
Vera..Vivienne Segal
Valerie ....Barbara Nichols
Janet ....Ina Learner
Fraser ....Ethel Martin
Amarilla ....Thelma Tadlock
Ernest ....Gordon Peters
Victor ....Robert Fortier
Louis (The Tenor) ....Lewis Bolyard
Melba ....Elaine Stritch
Ludlow Lowell ....Lionel Stander
O'Brien ....T. J. Halligan
    Dancers: Eleanor Boleyn, Bonnie Brae, Phyllis Dorne, Eleanor
Fairchild, Jean Goodall, Patty Ann Jackson, Lynn Joelson, Helene
Keller, Frances Krell, Ina Learner, Ethel Martin, June McCain,
Gloria O'Malley, Thelma Tadlock, Rita Tanno, Norma Thornton,
Janyce Ann Wagner, Harry Asmus, Hank Brunjes, Peter Holmes,
Ray Kyle, George Martin, Buzz Miller, David Neuman, Stanley Sim-
mons, George Vosburgh.
    Production supervised by Robert Alton; book directed by David
Alexander; dances by Robert Alton; sets by Oliver Smith; costumes
by Miles White; special orchestrations by Don Walker; Max Meth,
musical director; production stage manager, Neil Hartley.

Synopsis of scenes—

ACT I

Scene 1

Mike's South Side Night Club; a September afternoon

"You Mustn't Kick It Around" ....Joey, Gladys, Boys and Girls

Scene 2

The Pet Shop; that evening

"I Could Write a Book" ....Joey and Linda

Scene 3

Mike's Night Club; an evening a month later

"Chicago" ....Girls
"That Terrific Rainbow" ....Gladys, Robert Fortier, Boys and Girls

Scene 4

(a) A Phone Booth ⎫ the next afternoon
(b) Vera's Boudoir ⎭

"What Is a Man" ....Vera

Scene 5

Mike's Night Club; after closing time that evening

"Happy Hunting Horn" ....Joey, Helen Wood, Robert Fortier,
                    George Martin, Buzz Miller, Boys and Girls

Scene 6

The Tailor Shop; a few days later

"Bewitched, Bothered and Bewildered" .... Vera
"Pal Joey" .... Joey

ACT II

Scene 1

Chez Joey; a few weeks later

"The Flower Garden of My Heart" .... Tenor, Gladys, George
                                       Martin, Boys and Girls
"Zip" .... Melba
"Plant You Now, Dig You Later" .... Gladys, Robert Fortier, Boys
                                                    and Girls

Scene 2

Joey's Apartment; the next morning

"In Our Little Den" .... Vera and Joey

Scene 3

Chez Joey; that afternoon

A Dance Rehearsal .... Boys and Girls

Scene 4

Joey's Apartment; later that afternoon

"Do It the Hard Way" .... Joey
"Take Him" .... Linda and Vera

Scene 5

The Pet Shop; later that evening

"Pal Joey" was produced by George Abbott Christmas night, 1940, at the Ethel Barrymore Theatre. It was the first major role for Danny Kaye, and the company included Vivienne Segal, June Havoc and Van Johnson. The musical ran for 374 performances.

KISS ME, KATE

(8 performances)

Musical comedy in two acts, with book by Sam and Bella Spewack and songs by Cole Porter, revived by Saint Subber and Lemuel Ayers at the Broadway Theatre, January 8, 1952.

Cast of characters—

Fred Graham .... Robert Wright
Harry Trevor .... Nat Burns
Lois Lane .... Marilyn Day
Ralph (Stage Manager) .... Emory Bass
Lilli Vanessi .... Holly Harris
Hattie .... Lillyan Brown
Paul .... Bobby Johnson
Bill Calhoun .... Frank Derbas
Cab Driver .... Max Hart

Stage Doorman ....Bruce Laffey
First Man ....Hank Henry
Second Man ....Sparky Kaye
Harrison Howell ....Lionel Ince
Specialty Dancers...................Charles Cook, Ernest Brown

"TAMING OF THE SHREW" PLAYERS

Bianca (Lois Lane) ....Marilyn Day
Baptista (Harry Trevor) ....Nat Burns
Gremio (First Suitor) ....Jim Howard
Hortensio (Second Suitor) ....Alfred Homan
Lucentio (Bill Calhoun) ....Frank Derbas
Katharine (Lilli Vanessi) ....Holly Harris
Petruchio (Fred Graham) ....Robert Wright
Haberdasher ....Jan Kovac
    Singing Ensemble: Jean Cannon, Sylvia Chaney, Marilyn Hanson, Louise Hoffman, Janet Medlin, Pat Sayers, Bobra Suitor, Charles Adrian, Emory Bass, Frank Green, Joseph Gregory, Max Hart, Alfred Homan, Edward Whitman.
    Dancers: Esta Beck, Naomi Boneck, Doris Atkinson, Albertina Horstmann, Claire Mallardy, Julie Marlowe, Florence Miller, Charles Arnett, Harold Drake, Bill Harris, Jay Kleindorf, Jan Kovac, Roland Landry, Jess Ramirez.
    Staged by John C. Wilson; sets and costumes by Lemuel Ayers; dances by Hanya Holm; George Hirst, musical director; production stage manager, Milton Stern.

This was a touring company of "Kiss Me, Kate," brought to New York in expectation of a run at popular prices. The original production of the musical closed July 28, 1951, after 1,077 performances.

(Closed January 13, 1952)

ANNA CHRISTIE

(29 performances)

Drama in three acts by Eugene O'Neill, revived by the New York City Theatre Company at the City Center of Music and Drama, January 9, 1951.

Cast of characters—

Man-at-the-Bar ....Lou Gilbert
Johnny-the-Priest ....Frank Rowan
1st Longshoreman ....Ely Segall
2nd Longshoreman ....Matt Resnick
A Postman ....Arthur O'Connell
Larry, the Bartender ....Jerry Paris
Chris Christopherson ....Art Smith
Marthy Owen ....Grace Valentine
Anna Christopherson ....Celeste Holm
Mat Burke ....Kevin McCarthy
Johnson ....Robert Anderson
    Act I.—Johnny-the-Priest's saloon near the waterfront, New York; about 1910. Act II.—Scene 1—Ten days later. The stern of the barge, *Simeon Winthrop*, at anchor in the harbor of Provincetown. Scene 2—A week later; the cabin of the barge, at dock in Boston. Act III.—Two days later.
    Staged by Michael Gordon; sets and costumes by Emeline Roche; production manager, Billy Matthews.

"Anna Christie" was first produced November 2, 1921, at the Vanderbilt Theatre. This revival—the first by a professional company in New York—was scheduled for 16 performances in the City Center's play series, but a commercial manager, Harald Bromley, moved it to the Lyceum Theatre for an extension of the run.

(Closed February 2, 1952)

FANCY MEETING YOU AGAIN

(8 performances)

Comedy in three acts by George S. Kaufman and Leueen MacGrath, produced by Chandler Cowles and Ben Segal at the Royale Theatre, January 14, 1952.

Cast of characters—

```
Judge Patterson ................................Reynolds Evans
Martin Vellabrook ...............................Glenn Langan
Amanda Phipps .............................Leueen MacGrath
Lucy Bascomb ............................Margaret Hamilton
Millie .......................................Vera Fuller Mellish
A Visitor .......................................Richard Purdy
Sinclair Heybore ..............................Walter Matthau
Mrs. Cornelius .................................Ruth McDevitt
First Nubian .................................Ellsworth Wright
Second Nubian .......................................Earl Jones
```
The scene is the studio of Miss Amanda Phipps in New York City.
Staged by George S. Kaufman; setting by Albert Johnson; costumes by Kathleen Arkers; production associate, Ann Noyes.

Amanda Phipps, a sculptor, believes in reincarnation—and what's more, can remember all her previous incarnations. In her previous ones, Stone Age, Egyptian, Roman, she has been on the verge of accepting a stuffy suitor but is more interested in an aggressive admirer. In her modern incarnation she gets a warning from On High that this is her last chance, her last reincarnation, and she'd better make up her mind this time. So she chooses Sinclair Heybore, a plain-speaking art critic, over stuffy Martin Vellabrook.

(Closed January 19, 1952)

THE SHRIKE

(161 performances)

Play in two acts by Joseph Kramm, produced by José Ferrer with Milton Baron as associate producer at the Cort Theatre, January 15, 1952.

Cast of characters—

Miss Cardell	Phyllis Hill
Fleming	Tom Reynolds
Miss Hansen	Jeannette Dowling
Dr. Kramer	Stephen Elliott
Perkins	James Hawthorne Bey
Grossberg	William Bush
Dr. Barrow	Isabel Bonner
Patient	Vincent Donahue
Ann Downs	Judith Evelyn
Jim Downs	José Ferrer
Dr. Schlesinger	Somer Alberg
Sam Tager	Will Lee
George O'Brien	Martin Newman
Joe Major	Joe Comadore
Don Gregory	Philip Huston
John Ankoritis	Will Kuluva
Frank Carlisle	Leigh Whipper
William Schloss	Billy M. Greene
Dr. Bellman	Kendall Clark
Miss Wingate	Mary Bell
Harry Downs	Edward Platt
Tom Blair	Arthur Jarrett

The action takes place in City Hospital. Act I.—Scene 1—11:30 A.M. Scene 2—2 A.M.; next morning. Scene 3—Noon; three days later. Scene 4—Morning; three days later. Scene 5—Immediately following. Act II.—Scene 1—Just before lunch; the next day. Scene 2—2 P.M.; the next day. Scene 3—Close to 9 P.M.; the same day. Scene 4—2 P.M.; the next day. Scene 5—3 P.M.; five days later.

Staged by José Ferrer; set by Howard Bay; costumes by Edith Lutyens; stage manager, Thomas King.

See page 59.

(Closed May 31, 1952)

DESIRE UNDER THE ELMS

(46 performances)

Drama in three acts by Eugene O'Neill, revived by the American National Theatre and Academy at the ANTA Playhouse, January 16, 1952.

Cast of characters—

Eben Cabot	Douglas Watson
Simeon Cabot	Lou Polan
Peter Cabot	George Mitchell
Ephraim Cabot	Karl Malden
Abbie Putnam	Carol Stone
Young Girl	Jocelyn Brando
Man	Charles Aidman
Fiddler	Mark Gordon
Another Man	John McLiam
Old Farmer	Howard H. Fischer
Woman	Minette Barrett
Sheriff	Russell Gaige

Neighbors: Elwyn Dearborn, Colleen Dewhurst, Don Elson, Norma Hayes, George Hoxie, Barbara Schultz, Jutta Wolfe.

Staged by Harold Clurman; set by Mordecai Gorelik; costumes by Ben Edwards; stage manager, James Gelb.

"Desire Under the Elms" was first produced by the Theatre Guild November 11, 1924, for 208 performances.

(Closed February 23, 1952)

COME OF AGE

(30 performances)

Play in three acts by Clemence Dane, with music by Richard Addinsell, revived by the New York City Theatre Company at the City Center of Music and Drama, January 23, 1952.

Cast of characters—

A Boy	Robert Brown
A Shadow of Death	Robert Harrison
A Woman	Judith Anderson
A Man	Melville Ruick
A Close Friend	Marian Seldes
Friends of the Woman	Ethel Colt Richard Barbee June Jollie James Noble Lita Dal Porto Stephen Reese Muriel Rahn James Bronson Barbara Torrance Gerry Jedd Phoebe MacKaye Peter Brandon Bill Krach Jacqueline deWit
An Entertainer	Muriel Rahn

Staged by Guthrie McClintic; sets by Raymond Sovey, from the original designs by James Reynolds; Miss Anderson's costumes by Valentina; other costumes by Noel Taylor; musical director, Macklin Marrow; George Schaefer, artistic director for the City Center.

"Come of Age" was first produced January 12, 1934, for 35 performances.

(Closed February 17, 1952)

GERTIE

(5 performances)

Comedy in three acts by Enid Bagnold, produced by Herman Shumlin at the Plymouth Theatre, January 30, 1952.

Cast of characters—

Bianca	Anita Cooper
James	Robert Duke
Gertie	Glynis Johns
Sarah	Patricia Wheel
Mr. Ritchie	Alan Napier

Mrs. Candida Kaufman .... Polly Rowles
Rex .... Albert Dekker
　　The action takes place in the living room of the Ritchie family in
England, in the country. Time, the present. Act I.—Scene 1—A
Winter day before lunch time. Scene 2—Five-thirty that afternoon.
Act II.—After lunch the next day, Sunday. Act III.—Later that
same afternoon.
　　Staged by Herman Shumlin; setting by William and Jean Eckart;
costumes by Hazel Roy; stage manager, Lucia Victor.

Gertie is the youngest but clearest-headed of three children of an
absent-minded professor, Mr. Ritchie. When the household is visited by Mrs. Candida Kaufman, a script scout for the movies, and
Rex, a New York producer, Gertie maneuvers it so that she and
her sister Sarah, an ambitious writer, can get a chance in the New
World.

(Closed February 2, 1952)

JANE

(100 performances)

Comedy by S. N. Behrman, suggested by an original story by W.
Somerset Maugham, produced by the Theatre Guild at the Coronet
Theatre, February 1, 1952.

Cast of characters—

Ann Tower .... Adrienne Corri
Peter Crewe .... William Whitman
Wilson .... Al Collins
William Tower .... Basil Rathbone
Millicent Tower .... Irene Browne
Jane Fowler .... Edna Best
Maid .... Sarah Marshall
Lord Frobisher .... Howard St. John
Gilbert Dabney .... Philip Friend
　　The action takes place in Mrs. Tower's drawing room, Regents Park,
London. Act I.—Spring, 1938. Act II.—Late July, the same year.
Act III.—Ten days later.
　　Staged by Cyril Ritchard; setting and costumes by Elfi von
Kantzow; Miss Best's gowns by Valentina; production under the
supervision of Theresa Helburn and Lawrence Langner; stage man-
ager, George Greenberg.

See page 209.

(Closed April 26, 1952)

EMLYN WILLIAMS as CHARLES DICKENS

(48 performances)

Readings from the works of Charles Dickens, presented by S.
Hurok at the John Golden Theatre, February 4, 1952.

The program—

"Moving in Society"
  Scenes from "Our Mutual Friend" (1866)
"Paul"
  Scenes from "Dombey and Son" (1848)
"Mr. Bob Sawyer Gives a Bachelor Party"
  An Episode from "Pickwick Papers" (1837)
"The Signal Man"
  A Ghost Story from "Christmas Stories" (1866)
"Mr. Chops"
  A Story from "Christmas Stories" (1858)
"The Fancy Ball"
  An Episode from "A Tale of Two Cities" (1859)

Following a year's success in England, Emlyn Williams brought his "readings" across the Atlantic for an American tour, just as Charles Dickens himself had done in 1867. Mr. Williams made himself up to look like Dickens, with a fan-shaped beard and a costume of the period, and he used a replica of Dickens' own plush-covered reading desk, which had a built-up arm rest on its left side for the repose of the lecturer.

(Closed March 15, 1952)

COLLECTOR'S ITEM

(3 performances)

Comedy by Lillian Day and Alfred Golden, produced by Roger Clark in association with Lloyd Isler at the Booth Theatre, February 8, 1952.

Cast of characters—

Helen McCarthy ....Florida Friebus
Nick Galvani ....Don Grusso
Adrian Van Dyck ....Allyn Joslyn
Yousuff Birka ....Louis Sorin
Lydia Roberts ....Gaye Jordan
Mrs. Roger Blain ....Pamela Roberts
Doree Bennett ....Jane Middleton
Lucien Dulac ....Rene Paul
Sir Cecil Pond ....Erik Rhodes
Fatima Birka ....Adelaide Klein
U.S. Customs Examiner ....Mac McLeod
Glenway Trent ....James Gregory
Mr. Hochheimer ....Mitchell Kowal
Mr. Blanc ....Harold Grau
Photographer ....Ralph Hertz
Bobbysoxer ....Judy Hall
Mr. Bailey ....Fred Irving Lewis
    The action takes place in the Van Dyck Galleries in the East Sixties, New York. Act I.—A morning in June. Act II.—Scene 1—Later the same day. Scene 2—Saturday afternoon, three weeks later. Act III.—Morning, one week later.
    Staged by Alfred Golden and Roger Clark; scenery supervised by Charles Elson; costumes supervised by Michi Weglyn; general stage manager, Peter Xantho.

Glenway Trent, a modern, jeep-driving Leonardo da Vinci who has an instinct for art and doesn't want money, finds a job and a girl in an antique shop operated by a family of no less than intercontinental origins.

(Closed February 9, 1952)

VENUS OBSERVED

(86 performances)

Comedy in blank verse by Christopher Fry, produced by the Theatre Guild, by arrangement with Laurence Olivier Productions, Ltd., at the Century Theatre, February 13, 1952.

Cast of characters—

Hereward, The Duke of Altair	Rex Harrison
Edgar, The Marquis of Charlock	John Merivale
Herbert Reedbeck	John Williams
Captain Fox Reddleman	James Westerfield
Dominic	Hurd Hatfield
Bates	Stuart Burge
Rosabel Fleming	Joan Haythorne
Jessie Dill	Claudia Morgan
Hilda Taylor-Snell	Eileen Peel
Perpetua	Lilli Palmer

Act I.—The observatory room of Stellmere Park, the Duke's mansion. Act II.—Scene 1—The Temple of the Ancient Virtues, Stellmere Park. Scene 2—The observatory room. Act III.—The Temple.

Staged by Laurence Olivier; music by Herbert Menges; scenery supervised by Eldon Elder, after designs by Roger Furse; costumes by Valentina and Mildred Trebor; stage manager, Karl Nielsen.

See page 178.

(Closed April 26, 1952)

MRS. McTHING

(118 performances)
(Continued)

Comic fantasy in two acts by Mary Chase, produced by the American National Theatre and Academy at the ANTA Playhouse, February 20, 1952.

Cast of characters—

Mrs. Howard V. Larue II	Helen Hayes
Carrie	Mary Michael
Sybil	Paula Trueman
Evva Lewis	Enid Markey
Maude Lewis	Marga Ann Deighton
Grace Lewis	Mildred Chandler
Nelson	Ernest Borgnine
Boy	Brandon de Wilde

Chef (Ellsworth) ....Iggie Wolfington
Waiter (Virgil) ....William Lanteau
Dirty Joe ....Irwin Corey
Stinker ....Fred Gwynne
Poison Eddie Schellenbach ....Jules Munshin
Mrs. Schellenbach ....Minnette Barrett
Howay ....Brandon de Wilde
Mimi ....Lydia Reed
First Policeman ....Solen Burry
Second Policeman ....Robert Sagalyn
Crone ....Elsa Freed
Fairy ....Ann Buckles

Act I.—Scene 1—Morning room, Larue Towers; mid-afternoon of a Summer day. Scene 2—The Shantyland Pool Hall Lunchroom; a few minutes later. Scene 3—The same as Scene 2. Act II.—Scene 1—The Shantyland Pool Hall Lunchroom. Scene 2—The morning room at Larue Towers.

Staged by Joseph Buloff; sets by Lester Polakov; costumes by Lucinda Ballard; stage manager, Frederick de Wilde.

See page 39.

DEAR BARBARIANS

(4 performances)

Comedy in three acts by Lexford Richards, produced by Gant Gaither at the Royale Theatre, February 21, 1952.

Cast of characters—

Alexander Fiske ....Donald Murphy
Mr. Fiske ....Nicholas Joy
Alice ....Cloris Leachman
Mrs. Fiske ....Violet Heming
Lorraine ....Betsy von Furstenberg

The action takes place in two New York apartments near the East River. The time is the present. Act I.—Morning. Act II.—Late afternoon. Act III.—Five minutes later.

Staged by Gant Gaither; sets and costumes by Jack Landau; music by the Cy Coleman Trio; stage manager, Samuel Liff.

Although Alexander Fiske and Lorraine have separate apartments, they live more or less together but pursue their individual careers. Alexander thinks his father is ill-tempered and domineering, and is surprised when Alice finally manages to demonstrate to him that he is a chip off the old block.

(Closed February 24, 1952)

WOMEN OF TWILIGHT

(8 performances)

Play by Sylvia Rayman, produced by Joseph Kipness and Jack Hylton at the Plymouth Theatre, March 3, 1952.

Cast of characters—

Helen Allistair .... Mary Merrall
Christine .... Gwendoline Watford
Jess .... Lorraine Clewes
Rosie .... June Whitfield
Laura .... Gwynne Whitby
Viviane .... Betty Ann Davies
Veronica .... Mary Matthews
Olga .... Miriam Karlin
Sal .... Lynda Lee
Molly .... Joan Forrest
Nurse .... Marjory Hawtrey

The action takes place in Helen Allistair's living room, near London.
Act I.—Scene 1—Early evening. Scene 2—A few weeks later. Act
II.—Scene 1—About a month later. Scene 2—Two months later.
Act III.—Scene 1—Four days later. Scene 2—Three days later.

Staged by Anthony Hawtrey; setting by Mary Purvis; stage manager, Prudence Williams.

Helen Allistair runs a shabby boarding house for unwed mothers and their fatherless infants. None of the mothers or mothers-to-be is very jolly and the babies are undernourished. If an infant dies Mrs. Allistair would prefer conducting burial services in the back yard, so as not to bother the authorities.

(Closed March 8, 1952)

PARIS '90

(87 performances)

Monologues by Cornelia Otis Skinner, produced by Alden S. Blodget at the Booth Theatre, March 4, 1952.

Synopsis of scenes—

Act I.—Champs Elysées. 1—The "Nou-Nou." 2—A fashionable
Parisienne. 3—La Duchesse de Vertprés. 4—La Belle Conchita.
5—The New Woman. Act II.—Left Bank. 1—Niche in a portal of
Nôtre Dame. 2—The laundress. 3—A Boston school teacher. 4—
A woman of virtue. 5—A professor's wife. Act III.—Montmartre.
1—La Goulue. 2—A lion tamer of the Medrano Circus. 3—Berthe
la Sourde ("Deaf Bertha"). 4—Yvette Guilbert.

Staged by Alden S. Blodget; music and lyrics by Kay Swift; sets
by Donald Oenslager; costumes by Helene Pons; orchestrations by
Robert Russell Bennett; musical director, Nathaniel Shilkret.

(Closed May 17, 1952)

GOLDEN BOY

(55 performances)

Play in three acts by Clifford Odets, revived by the American National Theatre and Academy at the ANTA Playhouse, March 12, 1952.

Cast of characters—

Tom Moody	Art Smith
Lorna Moon	Bette Grayson
Joe Bonaparte	John Garfield
Tokio	William Hansen
Mr. Carp	Martin Greene
Siggie	Michael Lewin
Mr. Bonaparte	Lee J. Cobb
Anna	Peggy Meredith
Frank Bonaparte	Jack Klugman
Roxy Gottlieb	Rudy Bond
Eddie Fuseli	Joseph Wiseman
Pepper White	Arthur O'Connell
Mickey	Jack Warden
Call Boy	Sidney Kay
Sam	Gerald S. O'Loughlin
Lewis	Norman Brooks
Drake	Joe Bernard
Driscoll	Bert Conway
Barker	Tony Kraber

Act I.—Scene 1—The office of Tom Moody; late Spring. Scene 2—The Bonaparte home; that night. Scene 3—The office; two months later. Scene 4—A park bench; a few nights later. Scene 5—The Bonaparte home; midnight, six weeks later. Act II.—Scene 1—A gymnasium; five months later. Scene 2—The park bench; a few nights later. Scene 3—The office; the following day. Scene 4—A dressing-room in the Arena; six weeks later. Act III.—Scene 1—The office; six months later. Scene 2—The dressing-room; the following night. Scene 3—The Bonaparte home; several hours later.

Staged by Clifford Odets; sets and costumes by Paul Morrison; stage manager, James Gelb.

"Golden Boy" was first produced at the Belasco Theatre, November 4, 1937, by the Group Theatre, and ran for 250 performances.

(Closed April 6, 1952)

FLIGHT INTO EGYPT

(46 performances)

Play in two acts by George Tabori, produced by Irene Mayer Selznick at the Music Box Theatre, March 18, 1952.

Cast of characters—

Glubb	Zero Mostel
Hassan	Fred Williams
Tewfik Bey	David Opatoshu
Lili Engel	Gusti Huber
Franz Engel	Paul Lukas
Bubi Engel	Voytek Dolinski
Bartender	Chris Gampel
Mr. Kuglhof	Edgar Franken
Mrs. Kuglhof	Ellen Mahar
Miss Foster	Jo Van Fleet
Cpt. Fleure	John Rodney
Freund	Paul Mann
Bronson	Don Keefer
Ghoulos	Joseph Anthony
Policemen	Leon Bibb, Randolph Echols
Lipton	Fred Stewart

Time, 1949; place, Glubb's hotel in Cairo.

Staged by Elia Kazan; setting by Jo Mielziner; costumes by Anna
Hill Johnstone; stage manager, Jose Vega.

Lili and Franz Engel and their boy, Bubi, are Viennese refugees
awaiting a passport to America.   Franz was crippled during the war.
Lili strives bravely to keep her little family together and provide for
it, even at the cost of an assignation with an admirer, until the passport is allowed.   But Franz is turned down by a U.S. consul, and so
that his wife and child may be free to go he drinks poison.

(Closed April 19, 1952)

ONE BRIGHT DAY

(29 performances)

Play in three acts by Sigmund Miller, produced by Howard Lindsay and Russel Crouse at the Royale Theatre, March 19, 1952.

Cast of characters—

George Lawrence	Walter Matthau
Julian Prescott	Howard Lindsay
Frederick Newberry	Raymond Bramley
Stanley Archer	Kermit Kegley
Louise Gordon	Helen Harrelson
Tom McGowan	Bruce Evans
Ginny	Leora Thatcher
Margot Prescott	Marian Russell
Sheila Prescott	Bess Winburn
Arthur Mitchell	Glenn Anders
Paul LeBarca	Phillip Pine
John Hagerty	Bart Burns
Theodore Cahill	Addison Richards
Dr. Ferguson	Joseph Warren
Paul Rust	Raymond Van Sickle

Time, the present; place, a small town near Boston.   Act I.—The
living room in the Prescott home; late afternoon of a day in early
Autumn.   Act II.—Scene 1—Julian Prescott's office; two days later.
Scene 2—The same; the following day.   Act III.—Scene 1—The living room; 8:30 that night.   Scene 2—The same; later that night.

Staged by Michael Gordon; sets by Raymond Sovey; costumes by
Noel Taylor; stage manager, Del Hughes.

Julian Prescott is president of a drug manufacturing company
which is being sued by a poor father who claims his son was poisoned
by the company's pain-killing pills.   Julian learns that the pills have,
indeed, been toxic in certain instances, and that is why George Lawrence, a young company officer, has taken the liberty of changing
the formula without informing Julian.   George also is the lover of
Julian's daughter, Margot.   Prescott is faced with a moral decision:
shall he, as his stockholders urge, trust to luck that the old pills,
which are quietly being called back, will do no further harm, or shall
he warn the public of their toxicity and perhaps destroy his company?

(Closed April 12, 1952)

THE LONG WATCH

(12 performances)

Comedy in two acts by Harvey Haislip, produced by Anthony B. Farrell and Charles Coburn at the Lyceum Theatre, March 20, 1952.

Cast of characters—

Commander Harrison	Albert Bergh
Blanche Kelley	Gloria Evans
Susie Blake	Christine White
Ruth Spencer	Peggy Nelson
Selma Williams	Patricia Englund
Wolf Blankenship	Lloyd Knight
Ensign Jane Hilton	Anne Meacham
Lt. Lennox	Sonia Sorel
Lt. Dick Bennett	Carl Betz
Lt. Tex Connoly	James Wyler
Capt. Mike Dorgan	Walter Abel
Joe Davis	Harry Holsten
Coding Officer	Peg Menefee
Shore Patrol	Arthur Oshlag
Ann Sutton	Lois Harmon

The scenes are in the temporary headquarters of Air-Sea Rescue Forces and Naval Patrols in the Western Sea Frontier—two weeks in February, season of ocean storms, during the second half of World War II. Act I.—Scene 1—Communications room and Lieutenant Lennox's private office; morning. Scene 2—Several days later. Scene 3—The next afternoon. Scene 4—An enlisted WAVES' dormitory; that night. Act II.—Scene 1—Communications room; the following morning. Scene 2—Early evening. Scene 3—Early morning; following day. Scene 4—Two days later.

Staged by John Larson; sets and costumes by John Blankenchip; general stage manager, Alden Aldrich.

Lieutenant Lennox runs her communications room, which is manned by WAVES, sternly and impersonally, punishing infractions according to the rules. She will not permit Susie Blake to spend a night with the husband she has just married, so Susie goes AWOL, returns just in time to stand her watch, falls asleep and fails to hear a distress call. A transport is ditched in the ocean and the communications room sets up rescue operations. The survivors are located by a plane commanded by Susie's husband—but the rescue plane itself runs out of gas and crashes. Susie commits suicide, and Lieutenant Lennox realizes that even a naval officer should operate with human consideration.

(Closed March 29, 1952)

THREE WISHES FOR JAMIE

(83 performances)
(Continued)

Musical comedy in two acts, based on a novel by Charles O'Neal; book by Charles O'Neal and Abe Burrows; music and lyrics by

Ralph Blane; produced by Albert and Arthur Lewis at the Mark Hellinger Theatre, March 21, 1952.

The cast—

Tim Shanahan	Robert Halliday
Nora	Michele Burke
McCaffrey	Wilton Clary
Bridgie Quinn	Marie Gibson
Tirsa Shanahan	Charlotte Rae
Owen Roe Tavish	Bert Wheeler
Jamie McRuin	John Raitt
Power O'Malley	Walter Burke
Maeve Harrigan	Anne Jeffreys
Randal Devlin	Jeff Morrow
Aunt Bid	Grania O'Malley
Jess Proddy	Royal Dano
Big Patrick	Wilton Clary
Shiel Harrigan	Malcolm Keen
Dennis O'Ryan	Peter Conlow
Father Kerrigan	Ralph Morgan
Kevin	Billy Chapin
Sheriff Haines	Dick Foote

Dancers: Sandra Zell, Doris Atkinson, Estelle Aza, Ann Deasy, Mary Haywood, Elizabeth Logue, Mildred Ann Mauldin, Janet Sayers, Buddy Bryan, James Capp, Donn Driver, George Foster, Jerry Newby, Greg O'Brien, Joe Stember, Robert St. Clair.

Singers: Leigh Allen, Marion Baird, Michele Burke, Marie Gibson, Joan Kibrig, Nancy Price, June Reimer, Ann Richards, Tafi Towers, Robert Baird, Jerry Cardoni, Clifford Fearl, Robert Lamont, Richard Scott, Donald Thrall, Richard Vine.

Children: Pud Flanagan, Jackie Scholle, Alfred Catal, Martin Walker.

The scenes include a cottage in Ireland and a horse traders' camp in the State of Georgia; time, 1896.

A fairy princess has promised Jamie McRuin three wishes and Jamie wishes for travel, for the girl of his dreams, and for a son. He voyages to Georgia, here falls in love with and marries Maeve Harrigan, and finds that Maeve is barren. They adopt a boy who turns out to be a mute until, by a miracle, he gains the power of speech and can, as Jamie had wished, talk the ancient Gaelic tongue.

Staged by Abe Burrows; sets by George Jenkins; costumes by Miles White; orchestrations by Robert Russell Bennett; musical conductor, Joseph Littau; choreography by Ted Cappy, Herbert Ross and Eugene Loring; stage manager, Phil Friedman.

Principal musical numbers—

ACT I

"The Wake"	Old Tim, Tirsa, Tavish and Mourners
"The Girl That I Court in My Mind"	Jamie
"My Home's a Highway"	Maeve and Horse Traders
"We're for Love"	Tavish, Horse Traders and Women of the Camp
"My Heart's Darlin'"	Jamie
"Goin' on a Hayride"	Jamie, Maeve, Boys and Girls
"Love Has Nothing to Do with Looks"	Tirsa, Tim, Tavish
"I'll Sing You a Song"	Tirsa, Tim, Dennis, Tavish and Dennis' Brothers
"It Must Be Spring"	Maeve, Brides and Bridesmaids

ACT II

"The Army Mule Song"	Jamie, Men and Women of the Camp
"What Do I Know?"	Maeve
"It's a Wishing World"	Maeve and Jamie
"Trottin' to the Fair"	Jamie, Old Tim, Dennis, Men and Women of the Camp
"April Face"	Tavish, Maeve and Jamie

THE GRASS HARP

(36 performances)

Play in two acts by Truman Capote, based on Mr. Capote's novel, produced by Saint-Subber in association with Rita Allen at the Martin Beck Theatre, March 27, 1952.

Cast of characters—

Catherine Creek	Georgia Burke
Collin Talbo	Johnny Stewart
Dolly Talbo	Mildred Natwick
Verena Talbo	Ruth Nelson
Dr. Morris Ritz	Jonathan Harris
The Reverend's Wife	Susan Steell
The Reverend	Ralph Hertz
The Barber	Sterling Holloway
The Baker's Wife	Gertrude Flynn
The Postmaster	Jay Barney
The Sheriff	Val Dufour
Judge Charlie Cool	Russell Collins
The Choir Mistress	Jane Smith
Big Eddie Stover	Anthony McGrath
Brophy	Jules Racine
Sam	Larry Robinson
Maude Riordan	Lenka Peterson
Miss Baby Love Dallas	Alice Pearce

Act I.—Scene 1—The Talbo house; a Sunday afternoon in late September. Scene 2—The town; the following morning. Scene 3—An Autumn wood; the same day. Act II.—Scene 1—The wood; early the following morning and that night. Scene 2—The Talbo house; that evening.

Staged by Robert Lewis; music by Virgil Thomson; scenery and costumes by Cecil Beaton; production stage manager, B. D. Kranz.

Dolly Talbo, fearing that her sister, Verena, and Dr. Morris Ritz are planning to commercialize her home-made dropsy cure, flees her house and goes to live in a tree house. She is accompanied by her cousin, Collin Talbo; a Negro servant, Catherine Creek, and Judge Charlie Cool. Townspeople violently object to this attempt to flee from the world. In the end Dolly decides fleeing hasn't accomplished anything, and she and her companions return home.

(Closed April 26, 1952)

THE BRASS RING

(4 performances)

Play in two acts by Irving Elman, produced by Donald Wolin in association with Donald Flamm at the Lyceum Theatre, April 10, 1952.

Cast of characters—

George Westman	Sidney Blackmer
Margaret Westman	Carol Goodner

Herbert Westman (also young George) ....Douglas Watson
George's Father ....Paul Ford
George's Mother ....Margaretta Warwick
Joan Westman (also young Corliss) ....Bethel Leslie
Conductor ....Joseph Leberman
Rosemary Adams ....Patricia Benoit
Charlie Butler ....Conrad Janis
Spence ....Fred Irving Lewis
Cora Potter ....Helene Dumas

The action occurs during 24 hours in the life of George Westman.
The time is the present. Act I.—A.M. Act II.—P.M.
Staged by Stanley Gould; sets and costumes by Elfi von Kantzow;
incidental music by John Barrows.

George Westman, middle-aged business man, regrets the safe regularity of his life and dreams of what might have happened had he begun differently—married another girl and gone to Paris, for instance. He sees his son and daughter facing the same choices, and hopes they will grab life's brass ring.

(Closed April 12, 1952)

THE CHASE

(31 performances)

Play in three acts by Horton Foote, produced by José Ferrer at the Playhouse, April 15, 1952.

Cast of characters—

Sheriff Hawes ....John Hodiak
Rip ....Richard Poston
Tarl ....Lin McCarthy
Ruby Hawes ....Kim Hunter
Edwin Stewart ....Sam Byrd
Mr. Douglas ....G. Albert Smith
Anna Reeves ....Kim Stanley
Mrs. Reeves ....Nan McFarland
Knub McDermont ....Lonny Chapman
Bubber Reeves ....Murray Hamilton
Hawks Damon ....Ted Yaryan

Act I.—Scene 1—The office of the jail in Richmond, Texas; twilight. Scene 2—Knub's cabin; later that night. Scene 3—The jail; later the same night. Act II.—Scene 1—The jail; the next evening. Scene 2—Knub's cabin; later the same night. Scene 3—The jail; later the same night. Act III.—Scene 1—The jail; later the same night. Scene 2—Knub's cabin; later the same night. Scene 3—The jail; early the next morning.

Staged by José Ferrer; associate producer, Milton Baron; sets by Albert Johnson; costumes by George Bockman.

Bubber Reeves, a murderer, has escaped from prison, and Sheriff Hawes knows Bubber will sneak into town and try to kill him. The sheriff wants to take Bubber alive, but is forced to shoot him after he has tracked him to a cabin hideout.

(Closed May 10, 1952)

FOUR SAINTS IN THREE ACTS

(15 performances)

Opera in four acts with music by Virgil Thomson and libretto by Gertrude Stein, revived by the American National Theatre and Academy at the Broadway Theatre, April 16, 1952.

Cast of characters—

St. Stephen	Clyde Turner
St. Settlement	Martha Flowers
St. Plan	Calvin Dash
St. Sara	Doris Mayes
Commere	Altonell Hines
Compere	Elwood Smith
St. Theresa I	Inez Matthews
St. Theresa II	Betty Lou Allen
St. Ignatius	Edward Matthews
St. Cecelia	Leontyne Price
St. Electra	Ida Johnson
St. Jan	George Goodman
St. Chavez	Rawn Spearman
St. Eustace	Charles Colman
St. Vincent	Rayfield du Bard

Prelude.—A narrative of Prepare for Saints. Act I.—Avila: St. Theresa half indoors and half out of doors. Act II.—Might it be mountains if it were not Barcelona. Act III.—Barcelona: St. Ignatius and One of Two Liberally. Act IV.—The Saints and Sisters reassembled and re-enacting why they went away to stay.

Artistic and musical direction by Virgil Thomson; William Jonson, associate conductor and choral director; sets and costumes by Paul Morison, after original models by Florine Stettheimer; choreography by William Dollar; book directed by Maurice Grosser.

(Closed April 27, 1952)

CANDIDA

(31 performances)

Comedy in three acts by Bernard Shaw, revived by Thomas Hammond at the National Theatre, April 22, 1952.

Cast of characters—

Miss Prosperine Garnett	Pamela Simpson
Reverend James Morell	Ron Randell
Rev. Alexander Mill	Frank Leslie
Mr. Burgess	Bramwell Fletcher
Candida	Olivia de Havilland
Eugene Marchbanks	Terrance Kilburn

The action takes place in the parsonage of the Rev. James Mavor Morell; October, 1894. Act I.—Morning. Act II.—The same day; in the afternoon. Act III.—Past ten; that evening.

Staged by Herman Shumlin; set by Donald Oenslager; costumes by Motley; stage manager, Robert Woods.

(Closed May 17, 1952)

TO BE CONTINUED

(13 performances)

Comedy in three acts by William Marchant, produced by **Guthrie McClintic** at the Booth Theatre, April 23, 1952.

Cast of characters—

Claude Franklin	Neil Hamilton
Annie	Mary Gildea
Dolly	Dorothy Stickney
Silvie Martineau	Luella Gear
Ted Peacock	John Drew Devereaux
A Young Woman	Grace Kelly
An Older Woman	Jean Dixon

The studio living room of a house in East Tenth Street, New York. Act I.—Ten-thirty of a Friday morning in early May. Act II.—Scene 1—The following Monday afternoon, about 4:30. Scene 2—About 7:45 that evening. Act III.—Two-fifteen the following afternoon.

Staged by Guthrie McClintic; set by Donald Oenslager; costumes by Motley; stage manager, John W. Trell.

Claude Franklin and his mistress, Dolly, are happy in their 26 years of life together—but Dolly does not like Claude's going home to his wife for weekends, and tries to provoke the wife into a divorce action.

(Closed May 2, 1952)

HOOK 'N' LADDER

(1 performance)

Comedy in three acts by Charles Horner and Henry Miles, produced by Al Moritz at the Royale Theatre, April 29, 1952.

Cast of characters—

Sam Ross	Judson Pratt
Ulysses	Guy Raymond
Steve Barton	Charles Bang
Christine Rapp	Vicki Cummings
Caspar Armbruster	Harry Sothern
Doc Cornwall	Charles G. Martin
Mayor Tiddle	Leland Stanford Harris
Gail Carter	Loretta Price
Mr. Deaton	Humphrey Davis
Mr. Gilkens	Allan Hale
George Casey	Donald McClelland
J. B. Carpenter	Alan Lee

The action takes place in a corner room of the Majestic Hotel in the village of Cloverdale. Act I.—Summer; late morning. Act II.—The following morning. Act III.—Scene 1—Three days later; early afternoon. Scene 2—The same; half hour later.

Staged by Al Moritz; set by Eldon Elder; costumes by Jerry Boxhorn; production stage manager, Edward Strum.

The plot concerns rival traveling salesmen trying to sell a hook and ladder to a village fire department.

(Closed April 29, 1952)

THE MALE ANIMAL

(35 performances)

(Continued)

Comedy in three acts by James Thurber and Elliott Nugent, revived by the New York City Theatre Company at the City Center, April 30, 1952.

Cast of characters—

Cleota	Eulabelle Moore
Ellen Turner	Martha Scott
Tommy Turner	Elliott Nugent
Patricia Stanley	Nancy Nugent
Wally Myers	Charles Boaz
Dean Frederick Damon	Halliwell Hobbes
Michael Barnes	John Gerstad
Joe Ferguson	Robert Preston
Mrs. Blanche Damon	Leora Thatcher
Ed Keller	Matt Briggs
Myrtle Keller	Dorothy Blackburn
"Nutsy" Miller	Billy James
Newspaper Reporter	Peter Harris

Time, 1940; the living room in the house of Prof. Thomas Turner in a midwestern university town. Act I.—Late Fall; a Friday evening. Act II.—Scene 1—The following day; after lunch. Scene 2—Three hours later. Act III.—Two days later; noon.

Staged by Michael Gordon; set by Melville Bourne; costumes by Noel Taylor; production stage manager, Billy Matthews.

"The Male Animal" was first produced by Herman Shumlin, January 9, 1940. The revival, scheduled for two weeks at the City Center, was so successful that John Golden took over the management for a commercial run at the Music Box Theatre.

MUCH ADO ABOUT NOTHING

(4 performances)

Comedy by William Shakespeare, produced by Luther Greene in association with Jerry Tishman at the Music Box, May 1, 1952.

Cast of characters—

Hero	Deirdre Owens
Margaret	Peggy Nelson
A Boy	Herbert Coleman
Messenger	Preston Hanson
Ursula	Raimonda Orselli
Leonato	John W. Austin
Beatrice	Claire Luce

```
Don Pedro ....................................... Ernest Graves
Benedick ........................................ Antony Eustrel
Claudio ......................................... Eric Sinclair
Don John ....................................... Carl Harbord
Conrade ........................................ Bruce Barlow
Balthazar ................................... Edward Van Sickle
Borachio ........................................ Jay Robinson
Antonio ......................................... Evan Thomas
1st Watchman ................................... John Giroux
2nd Watchman ................................... Carl Harms
Verges ........................................ Barry Macollum
Dogberry ....................................... Melville Cooper
Friar .......................................... Joseph Macaulay
Sexton ......................................... Nat Burns
Ladies ........................................ { Diane Howard
                                                { Patricia McCarthy
Pages .............................. David Massey, Al Hedison
```
      The action of the play takes place in Messina.
      Staged by Antony Eustrel; sets and costumes by Stewart Chaney;
music by Raffaello de Banfield; production stage manager, Gerald
Phillips.

(Closed May 3, 1952)

OF THEE I SING

(32 performances)
(Continued)

   Musical comedy in two acts; book by George S. Kaufman and
Morrie Ryskind; music by the late George Gershwin; lyrics by Ira
Gershwin; revived by Chandler Cowles and Ben Segal at the Zieg-
feld Theatre, May 5, 1952.

Cast of characters—

```
Francis X. Gilhooley ........................... J. Pat O'Malley
Louis Lippman ................................. Robert F. Simon
Chambermaid ................................... Louise Carlyle
Matthew Arnold Fulton .......................... Loring Smith
Senator Carver Jones .......................... Howard Freeman
Senator Robert E. Lyons ......................... Donald Foster
Alexander Throttlebottom ......................... Paul Hartman
John P. Wintergreen ............................. Jack Carson
Beauty Contestant ................................ Jean Bartel
Mary Turner .................................... Betty Oakes
Sam Jenkins ................................... Jonathan Lucas
Diana Devereaux ............................. Lenore Lonergan
Emily Benson ..................................... Joan Mann
Announcer ...................................... Mort Marshall
Vladimir Vidovitch ................................ Abe Stein
Yussef Yussevitch ................................. Bob Oran
The Chief Justice ............................... Jack Whiting
Guide .......................................... Jack Whiting
A Sightseer .................................... Parker Wilson
The French Ambassador .......................... Florenz Ames
Chief Senate Clerk ............................. Mort Marshall
Senator from Massachusetts ...................... Jack Whiting
Attaché ........................................ Tom Wells
Chief Flunkey ................................. Al McGranary
Flunkeys .......... William Krach, Michael King, Ken Ayers
```
   Singers: Claudia Campbell, Louise Carlyle, Helen Rice, Jeanne
Schlegel, Joanne Spiller, Gloria Van Dorpe, Ken Ayers, Norman
Clayton, Warren Galjour, Jay Harwick, Keith Kaldenberg, Joe Ker-

rigan, Michael King, William Krach, James McCracken, Larry Weber.

Dancers: Vicki Barrett, Betty Buday, Georgine Darcy, Peggy Merber, Pat Stanley, Crandall Diehl, J. Corkey Geil, Skeet Guenther, Frank Seabolt, Bob Tucker, Parker Wilson.

Show Girls: Arlene Anderson, Jean Bartel, Gregg Evans, Charlotte Foley, Dorothy Richards, Siri, Jeanne Tyler, Charlotte Van Lein.

The scenes in Act I include Main Street, a smoke-filled room, Atlantic City, Madison Square Garden and Washington, D. C. Scenes in Act II include the White House, the Capitol and the Senate.

Staged by George S. Kaufman; musical numbers staged by Jack Donohue; sets by Albert Johnson; costumes by Irene Sharaff; musical director, Maurice Levine; orchestrations by Don Walker; musical supervision and vocal direction by David Craig; stage manager, Jerry Alder.

"Of Thee I sing" was first produced by the late Sam H. Harris at the Music Box, December 26, 1931. It was revived at the Imperial Theatre, May 15, 1933.

SHUFFLE ALONG

(4 performances)

Musical comedy in two acts; book by Flournoy Miller and Paul Gerard Smith; lyrics by Noble Sissle; music by Eubie Blake; produced by Irving Gaumont in association with Grace Rosenfield at the Broadway Theatre, May 8, 1952.

Cast of characters—

Bugler	William Dillard
M/Sgt.	James E. Wall
Cpl. Betty Lee	Thelma Carpenter
Lt. Jim Crocker	Avon Long
Col. Alexander Popham	Earl Sydnor
Major Joseph Gantt	William McDaniel
Capt. Frederick Graham	T. S. Krigarin
Sgt. Lucy Duke	Delores Martin
Cpl. Louie Bauche	Leslie Scott
Capt. Harry Gaillard	Napoleon Reed
Pvt. Cyphus Brown	Flournoy Miller
Pvt. Longitude Lane	Hamtree Harrington
Chaplain	Laurence Watson
Mable	Mable Lee
Fifeto	Henry Sherwood
Rosa Pasini	Louise Woods
SS Trooper	Harro Meller
Laura Popham	Urylee Leonardos
Sgt. Mabel Powers	Marie Young
Margie	Sara Lou Harris
Noble Sissle Eubie Blake	Themselves

Act I.—Northern Italy, Spring, 1945; a castle, an Alpine pass, a street in Genoa and a café. Act II.—New York, the following Spring; a fashion salon, a street, an office and a pier.

Staged by George Hale and Paul Gerard Smith; choreography by Henry Le Tang; additional music and lyrics by Joseph Meyer and Floyd Huddleston; sets by Albert Johnson; costumes by Waldo Angelo; orchestrations by Charles E. Cooke; vocal arrangements by Claude Garreau; stage manager, Lawrence Seymour.

Principal song numbers—

ACT I

"Jive Drill" ....Bugler, Rocky and Ensemble
"Bitten by Love" ....Betty, Jim and Ensemble
"Falling" ....Lucy and Harry
"I'm Just Wild About Harry" ....Lucy, Harry and Ensemble
"City Called Heaven—Juba-lee" ....Chaplain and Ensemble
"Bongo-Boola" ....Mable, Bugler, Drummer and Ensemble
"Swanee Moon" ....Betty and Singers
"Love Will Find a Way" .....Lucy, Jim, Louie, Rosa and Singers
"Rhythm of America" ....Lucy and Entire Company

ACT II

"It's the Gown That Makes the Gal That Makes the Guy" ..Ensemble
"You Can't Overdo a Good Thing" ....Lucy and Models
"My Day" ....Jim and GIs
"Give It Love" ....Betty and WACs
"Farewell with Love" ....Lucy
"Here 'Tis" ....Mable
"Reminiscing" ....Sissle and Blake

The first production of "Shuffle Along" opened November 14, 1921, at Daly's 63d St. Theatre; it was revived January 19, 1932, at the Mansfield Theatre.

(Closed May 10, 1952)

TOVARICH

(15 performances)

Comedy in two acts by Jacques Deval, adapted by Robert E. Sherwood; revived by the New York City Theatre Company at the City Center, May 14, 1952.

Cast of characters—

Billposter ....Arny Freeman
Prince Mikail Alexandrovitch Ouratieff ....Herbert Berghof
Grand Duchess Tatiana Petrovna ....Uta Hagen
Olga ....Sudie Bond
Count Feodor Brekenski ....John Heldabrand
Chauffourier-Dubieff ....Raymond Bramley
Martelleau ....Arny Freeman
Fernande Dupont ....Paula Laurence
Charles Dupont ....Romney Brent
Louise (the Cook) ....Edna Preston
Georges Dupont ....Peter Brandon
Helene Dupont ....Pat Crowley
Concierge ....William Hickey
Madame Van Hemert ....Elizabeth Dillon
Madame Chauffourier-Dubieff ....Julia Adler
Commissar Gorotchenko ....Luther Adler
  Act I.—Scene 1—A room in the Hotel de Quercy. Scene 2—
Fernande Dupont's boudoir; an hour later. Act II.—Scene 1—The
Duponts' drawing room; two months later. Scene 2—The Duponts'
kitchen; an hour later.
  Staged by Harry Horner; sets by Harry Horner; costumes by Noel
Taylor; stage manager, Bernard Gersten.

"Tovarich" was first produced October 15, 1936, at the Plymouth Theatre.

(Closed May 25, 1952)

CONSCIENCE

(4 performances)

Drama in two acts by Pedro Bloch, translated from the Portuguese by Claude Vincent and adapted by A. M. Klein; produced by the Messrs. Shubert, by arrangement with Joseph Kipness and Jack Small, at the Booth Theatre, May 15, 1952.

The cast—

Robert Burgos ....Maurice Schwartz
    Act I.—Garden and exterior of Robert Burgos' home; four o'clock on an Autumn afternoon. Act II.—Garden and interior of home; one hour later.
    Staged by Maurice Schwartz; set by Ralph Alswang; stage manager, Eddie Scanlon.

Robert Burgos returns home after a number of years spent with a mistress, expecting to find his wife and children there. But nobody is there, so he talks about the people and events of the last few years.

(Closed May 17, 1952)

NEW FACES OF 1952

(19 performances)

(Continued)

Revue in two acts, produced by Leonard Sillman at the Royale Theatre, May 16, 1952.

The company—

Virginia Bosler	Eartha Kitt
June Carroll	Joe Lautner
Robert Clary	Carol Lawrence
Allen Conroy	Paul Lynde
Virginia de Luce	Bill Mullikin
Michael Dominico	Carol Nelson
Alice Ghostley	Rosemary O'Reilly
Ronny Graham	Jimmy Russell
Patricia Hammerlee	

    Staged by John Murray Anderson; musical and dance numbers staged by Richard Barstow; sketches directed by John Beal; sets by Raoul Pène du Bois; costumes by Thomas Becher; orchestrations by Ted Royal; Anton Coppola, orchestra conductor; production stage manager, Arthur Barkow.

Principal numbers—

ACT I

"CRAZY, MAN!"

Counsellor Holly ....Paul Lynde
Senator Marble ....Joe Lautner
Senator Hutchinson ....Bill Mullikin
A Policeman ....Jimmy Russell
Dazz Rocco ....Ronny Graham

"Lucky Pierre"

Girls .....Virginia de Luce, Patricia Hammerlee, Rosemary O'Reilly
Pierre ....Robert Clary
Reporter ....Bill Mullikin

"Guess Who I Saw Today"

Sung by June Carroll

"Restoration Piece"

Lady Sylvia Malpractice ....Alice Ghostley
Simple ....Patricia Hammerlee
Sir Solemnity Sourpuss ....Paul Lynde
Sir Militant Malpractice ....Joe Lautner

"Love Is a Simple Thing"

Sung by Rosemary O'Reilly, Robert Clary, Eartha Kitt
and June Carroll

"Boston Beguine"

Sung by Alice Ghostley

"The Bard and the Beard"

Miss Leigh ....June Carroll
Sir Laurence ....Ronny Graham
Call Boy ....Bill Mullikin
Maid ....Rosemary O'Reilly

"Nanty Puts Her Hair Up"

Nanty ....Virginia Bosler
Father ....Joe Lautner
Mother ....Alice Ghostley
Brother ....Bill Mullikin
Highlander ....Allen Conroy

"Oedipus Goes South"

Ronny Graham

"Time for Tea"

Marcella ....Alice Ghostley
Lavinia ....June Carroll
Lavinia, the Girl ....Virginia Bosler
Marcella, the Girl ....Carol Nelson
Mother ..J....................................Rosemary O'Reilly
Father ....Joe Lautner
John ....Jimmy Russell
Guests ....Virginia de Luce, Allen Conroy, Michael Dominico

"Bal Petit Bal"

Sung by Eartha Kitt

"Of Fathers and Sons"

Mae ....Alice Ghostley
Harry ....Paul Lynde
Stanley ....Ronny Graham
Policemen ....Jimmy Russell, Allen Conroy

"Three for the Road"

Introduction ....Joe Lautner
"Raining Memories" ....Sung by Robert Clary
"Waltzing in Venice" ....Sung by Rosemary O'Reilly and

Joe Lautner, Virginia Bosler, June Carroll, Allen Conroy,
Michael Dominico, Patricia Hammerlee, Eartha Kitt,
Carol Lawrence, Paul Lynde, Bill Mullikin, Carol
Nelson, Jimmy Russell
"Take Off the Mask" .....Sung by Alice Ghostley, Ronny Graham

ACT II

"Don't Fall Asleep"

Wife ....Rosemary O'Reilly
Husband ....Jimmy Russell

"After Canasta—What?"

Dorothy ....June Carroll
Elsie ....Alice Ghostley

"Lizzie Borden"

Townspeople ..Rosemary O'Reilly, Carol Lawrence, Virginia de Luce,
Carol Nelson, Virginia Bosler, Allen Conroy,
Jimmy Russell, Michael Dominico
Man ....Bill Mullikin
Judge ....Paul Lynde
Lizzie ....Patricia Hammerlee
District Attorney ....Joe Lautner

"I'm in Love with Miss Logan"

Boy ....Robert Clary
Miss Logan ....Rosemary O'Reilly
Man ....Joe Lautner

"Trip of the Month"

The Explorer ....Paul Lynde

"Penny Candy"

Woman ....June Carroll
Gussie ....Carol Lawrence
Poor Kids ....Virginia Bosler, Jimmy Russell
Rich Kids ....Carol Nelson, Michael Dominico
Candy Vendor ....Bill Mullikin

"Convention Bound"

Ronny Graham   Joe Lautner
Paul Lynde   Patricia Hammerlee
Bill Mullikin   Allen Conroy

"Whither America? (Another Revival?)"
or "The Energy Contained in a Glass of Water Would Drive an Ocean Liner?"

Switchboard Operator ....Virginia de Luce
Stenographer ....June Carroll
Man ....Jimmy Russell

"Monotonous"
Sung by Eartha Kitt

"The Great American Opera"

Toby ....Ronny Graham
Madame Flora ....Alice Ghostley
Effie ....Rosemary O'Reilly

FIRST LADY

(5 performances)
(Continued)

Comedy in three acts by Katharine Dayton and George S. Kaufman, revived by the New York City Theatre Company at the City Center, May 28, 1952.

Cast of characters—

Sophy Prescott	Ona Munson
Charles	Frank Rowan
Emmy Paige	Peggy Ann Garner
Lucy Chase Wayne	Helen Gahagan
Stephen Wayne	Guy Spaull
Belle Hardwick	Margery Maude
Mrs. Ives	Regina Wallace
Ann Forrester	Althea Murphy
A Congressman's Wife	Genevieve Frizzell
Her Friend	Darthy Hinkley
The Baroness	Ulla Kazanova
Señor Ortega	Luis Martinez
A Chinese	Norman Chi
A General	Leonard Lord
Young Girl	Jean Jordan
Lal Rham	Richard D. Warner
Mrs. Creevey	Ruth McDevitt
Mrs. Davenport	Bette Ford
Senator Keane	Scott McKay
Tom Hardwick	Addison Richards
Irene Hibbard	Edna Best
Bleecker	Hal Cooper
Carter Hibbard	Frederic Tozere
George Mason	Will Hussung
Ellsworth T. Ganning	Howard Wierum
Jason Fleming	Richard Hamilton
Herbert Sedgwick	Richard Sterling

Act I.—Living room in the Secretary of State's home, Washington, D. C.; January. Act II.—Scene 1—Carter Hibbard's study; February. Scene 2—The Secretary of State's home; March. Act III.—Again the Secretary's home; April.

Staged by David Alexander; sets by Peter Larkin; costumes by Noel Taylor; stage manager, Leonard Auerbach.

"First Lady" was first produced November 26, 1935, at the Music Box.

SUNDAY BREAKFAST

(5 performances)
(Continued)

Play in two acts by Emery Rubio and Miriam Balf, produced by the American National Theatre and Academy at the Coronet Theatre, May 28, 1952.

Cast of characters—

Mary Jo Decker	Jada Rowland
Martha Decker	Margarey Feury

Anne Decker ....Cloris Leachman
George Decker ....Anthony Ross
Stanley Fredricks ....Duncan Baldwin
Mike Decker ....Douglas Watson
A State Trooper ....Jim Nolan
     Act I.—Scene 1—Eight o'clock on a fine Spring evening; the living room of the Decker flat in a small Connecticut town.   Scene 2—After midnight.   ACT II.—Scene 1—Early the next morning; Sunday.   Scene 2—One hour later.
     Staged by Stella Adler; sets and costumes by Ben Edwards; stage manager, James Gelb.

George Decker, who runs a small jewelry shop, is a mild and ineffectual head of a household which includes a nagging wife, an unsettled grown son, a hot-tempered grown daughter and a sensitive 8-year-old daughter. The family does have a few happy moments at Sunday breakfast before the usual differences arise.

THE DANCE

The principal news items in the ballet world during the season were the visits to Broadway of the Sadler's Wells Theatre Ballet and José Greco's Spanish Ballet. The Sadler's Wells company—not the great Sadler's Wells Ballet, but a young group—had a financial success, but New York ballet critics were not always enthusiastic about its artistic qualities.

In June, 1951, the New York City Ballet Company visited the City Center for three weeks. Among the novelties it presented were Jerome Robbins' "The Amazons," designed for Nora Kaye; George Balanchine's treatment for Mendelssohn's "Capriccio Brilliante," danced by Maria Tallchief and André Eglevsky; Ruthanna Boris' "Cakewalk" and Todd Bolender's dance version of Bartók's "The Miraculous Mandarin." In July the City Ballet Company offered another novelty, George Balanchine's "À la Français," set to the music of Jean Français.

In September the City Ballet returned to the City Center and Ballet Theatre took up a three-week stand at the Metropolitan Opera House. Ballet Theatre novelties included Jean Babilée's "Til Eulenspiegel" and Bronislava Nijinska's "Schumann Concerto."

José Greco's company arrived at the Shubert Theatre October 1. Greco, Brooklyn-born, had with him Nila Amparo, Carola Goya and La Quica as principal dancers. After a successful month at the Shubert, the company moved to the Century.

In November the New York City Ballet offered Balanchine's "Tyl Ulenspiegel"—not to be confused with the Babilée work—and an all-Stravinsky night with Stravinsky conducting.

December's ballet novelties included Jerome Robbins' "The Pied Piper," by the City Ballet, and a new treatment by Balanchine of "Swan Lake," by the same company.

In February, the busy New York City Ballet offered some more new numbers, including Jerome Robbins' "Ballade," George Balanchine's "Divertissement Classique" and "Bayou," Antony Tudor's "La Gloire" and Frederick Ashton's "Picnic at Tintagel."

In March, Angna Enters gave her first Broadway recital in eight years at the ANTA Playhouse, and Greco's Spanish Ballet had an engagement at the Palace Theatre. On March 25 the Sadler's Wells

Theatre Ballet opened at the Warner Theatre, a large movie house, for a two-week stand. Principal productions included "Pineapple Poll," based on Gilbert and Sullivan works; Frederick Ashton's "Les Rendezvous"; Ninette de Valois' "The Prospects Before Us"; John Cranko's "Beauty and the Beast," with Ravel's music; Cranko's "Harlequin in April" and Ashton's "Capriol Suite."

The outstanding dance event in April was a series of six performances at the Juilliard School of Music by Martha Graham, who had been inactive for two years. One of her principal offerings was "The Triumph of Saint Joan," with music by Norman Dello Joio.

OFF BROADWAY

Off Broadway theatre groups, numbering literally in the hundreds in Greater New York, were busy presenting revivals and new plays during the season. A few revivals were of more than neighborhood interest, but no new play seemed worthy of being promoted to a Broadway production. In fact, Broadway itself had some "Off Broadway" productions, all of which were failures, at the President Theatre. They were "Dark Legend," "The Victim" and "The Rehearsal." As usual, the Masque and Lyre Light Opera Company was continually busy, and successful, with its repertoire of Gilbert and Sullivan operettas at Jan Hus House.

The June offerings away from the commercial mart included Giraudoux' "The Enchanted," at the Circle in the Square, Greenwich Village; O'Casey's "Shadow of a Gunman" at the Provincetown Playhouse; Ibsen's "Ghosts," at the Provincetown Playhouse; and at the marine amphitheatre in Flushing Meadow Park Elliott Murphy's Aquashow was thriving.

In July an enterprising gentleman, Ivan Becker, took the ballroom of the Astor Hotel to present a play written by himself, "The King's Darling." An ambitious and deserving enterprise—the production of plays with Negro casts—began at the Apollo Theatre in Harlem when Charles Harrow presented "Detective Story," but patronage was insufficient to keep the project going long.

In August, an enterprise calling itself the Phoenix Theatre revived the 1906 melodrama, "Billy the Kid," at the Carnegie Recital Hall; the Circle-in-the-Square Theatre offered a new play by Susan Macpherson, "The Cruelest Month," and at the Bedford Theatre in Brooklyn there was an all-Negro production of "Rain." Actor Ken Parker wrote a play, "Yours Till Yesterday," which was produced simultaneously at the Provincetown Playhouse and in an arena theatre at Long Beach, and at the Carnegie Recital Hall the Phoenix Theatre offered "The Ladder."

In September Dorothy Raedler's Masque and Lyre company made plans for expanding into a touring Gilbert and Sullivan company to be known as American Savoyards, Inc. The perennial Davenport Free Theatre was offering "Difference in Gods," which the management described as "the psychology of a family." At the Provincetown, there was a production of "Ghosts," and the arena theatre, Circle in the Square, put on John Steinbeck's "Burning Bright." Both Equity and the Internal Revenue Department ruled that the Equity Library Theatre was a non-profit organization.

In October the New York Repertory Company began its season at the Cherry Lane Theatre with "Othello," and the Provincetown Repertory gave "Candida." The Sunday Theatre, playing Sundays only at the Hotel Sutton, offered a new play by Ben Morse and Louis Beachner, "The Daughters of the Late Colonel." The Rockefeller Foundation granted $47,000 to the New Dramatists Committee to aid in the development of new playwrights, and a workshop in the City Center building was dedicated in the name of the late Elinor Morgenthau, wife of Henry Morgenthau, Jr.

In November a new group, The Craftsmen, staged a production of "Desire Under the Elms" at the Barbizon-Plaza Theatre. At the Lenox Hill Playhouse, Equity Library Theatre attempted a *commedia dell' arte* titled "The Great Magician." A new play by Harry Wagstaff Gribble and James Proctor, "Ride the Right Bus," was tried out at the Bleecker Street Theatre and in Harlem.

In December the Living Theatre offered a Gertrude Stein play, "Doctor Faustus Lights the Lights," at the Cherry Lane; the Amateur Comedy Club gave a performance of "Laura," and the usual holiday entertainments for children abounded.

In January, 1952, the Provincetown Repertory essayed "Macbeth," the Lenox Hill Players put on Rose Franken's "Another Language," and a newcomer from England, Anna Russell, made a hit with a one-woman show at Town Hall. A play about Yucatan, Lynn Riggs' "The Year of Pilar," was presented by David Longstreet at the Amato Opera Theatre in Bleecker Street.

A February attraction was Charles Laughton, reading from Shaw, Shakespeare, Dickens and others at Town Hall. The Equity Community Theatre put on "Pygmalion" at the DeWitt Clinton Community Center, the Bronx, and scheduled "Blithe Spirit," "Lady in the Dark" and "The Pursuit of Happiness." This organization also reported a profit of 21 cents for the previous season, as against a loss of more than $2,000 the year before. The Lambs acted three O'Neill one-acters—"In the Zone," "Bound East for Cardiff" and "The Long Voyage Home"—at their clubhouse.

March was a busy time for the Living Theatre at the Cherry Lane Theatre, what with the presentation of three short plays grouped as "an evening of Bohemian theatre." They were Pablo Picasso's "Desire," Gertrude Stein's "Ladies' Voices" and T. S. Eliot's "Sweeney Agonistes." At the Greenwich Mews Playhouse the Community Theatre presented Edward Chodorov's "Decision," and a new comedy by Tad Mosel, "The Lion Hunters," was tried by the Journeymen at the Provincetown Playhouse.

Perhaps the greatest off Broadway success of the season was the production in March of Tennessee Williams' "Summer and Smoke," which had been a Broadway failure. This was presented by the Loft Players at the Circle-in-the-Square arena on Sheridan Square. The Blackfriars staged at their Playhouse a drama about St. Augustine, "The Restless Flame," by Louis de Wohl. The blind Lighthouse Players gave Noel Coward's "This Happy Breed," and in the Brooklyn High School for Homemaking the Kadimah Group of Hadassah presented "Die Yom Bonditten"—which was "The Pirates of Penzance" in Yiddish.

In April another amateur group of Savoyards, the Blue Hill Troupe, gave "The Sorcerer" as their twenty-eighth annual production at the Hunter College Playhouse. Equity Library Theatre put on "Chicago" at the Lenox Hill Playhouse—and was happily expected to show a season's profit of $1,000. The Amateur Comedy Club put on Lexford Richards' "Dear Barbarians," a recent Broadway failure.

In May, the School of Performing Arts, a part of the city's high school system, staged "The Madwoman of Chaillot." A group called the Mountebanks experimented with a midnight curtain at the Amato Opera House, offering "Dr. Jekyll and Mr. Hyde." The undaunted Living Theatre staged a new play by Paul Goodman, "Faustina," at the Cherry Lane Theatre.

STATISTICAL SUMMARY

Plays	Number Performances	
Affairs of State	610	(Closed February 26, 1952)
A Tree Grows in Brooklyn	270	(Closed December 8, 1951)
Bell, Book and Candle	233	(Closed June 2, 1951)
Call Me Madam	644	(Closed April 3, 1952)
Darkness at Noon	186	(Closed June 23, 1951)
Flahooley	40	(Closed June 17, 1951)
Gentlemen Prefer Blondes	740	(Closed September 15, 1951)
Gramercy Ghost	100	(Closed July 21, 1951)
Idiot's Delight	15	(Closed June 6, 1951)
Kiss Me, Kate	1,077	(Closed July 28, 1951)
Make a Wish	103	(Closed July 14, 1951)
Oklahoma!	100	(Closed July 28, 1951)
Season in the Sun	367	(Closed August 11, 1951)
The Autumn Garden	101	(Closed June 2, 1951)
The Country Girl	236	(Closed June 2, 1951)
The Happy Time	614	(Closed July 14, 1951)
The Rose Tattoo	306	(Closed October 27, 1951)
Twentieth Century	233	(Closed June 30, 1951)

LONG RUNS ON BROADWAY

To June 1, 1952

(Plays marked with asterisk were still playing June 1, 1952)

Plays	Number Performances	Plays	Number Performances
Life with Father	3,224	The Ladder	789
Tobacco Road	3,182	State of the Union	765
Abie's Irish Rose	2,327	The First Year	760
Oklahoma!	2,248	Death of a Salesman	742
Harvey	1,775	Sons o' Fun	742
Born Yesterday	1,642	The Man Who Came to Dinner	739
The Voice of the Turtle	1,557		
Arsenic and Old Lace	1,444	Call Me Mister	734
Hellzapoppin	1,404	High Button Shoes	727
Angel Street	1,295	Finian's Rainbow	725
Lightnin'	1,291	Claudia	722
* South Pacific	1,294	The Gold Diggers	720
Mister Roberts	1,157	I Remember Mama	714
Annie Get Your Gun	1,147	Junior Miss	710
Pins and Needles	1,108	Seventh Heaven	704
Kiss Me, Kate	1,070	Peg o' My Heart	692
Anna Lucasta	957	The Children's Hour	691
Kiss and Tell	957	Dead End	687
Carousel	890	The Lion and the Mouse	686
Hats Off to Ice	889	Dear Ruth	683
Follow the Girls	882	East Is West	680
The Bat	867	The Doughgirls	671
My Sister Eileen	865	Irene	670
White Cargo	864	Boy Meets Girl	669
Song of Norway	860	Blithe Spirit	657
A Streetcar Named Desire	855	The Women	657
You Can't Take It with You	837	A Trip to Chinatown	657
		Bloomer Girl	654
Three Men on a Horse	835	Rain	648
Stars on Ice	830	Call Me Madam	644
Where's Charley?	792	Janie	642

Plays	Number Performances	Plays	Number Performances
The Green Pastures	640	Floradora	553
* Guys and Dolls	639	Good News	551
Is Zat So?	618	Let's Face It	547
The Happy Time	614	Within the Law	541
Separate Rooms	613	The Music Master	540
Affairs of State	610	What a Life	538
Star and Garter	609	The Red Mill	531
The Student Prince	608	The Boomerang	522
Broadway	603	Rosalinda	521
Adonis	603	Chauve Souris	520
Street Scene	601	Blackbirds	518
Kiki	600	Sunny	517
A Society Circus	596	Victoria Regina	517
Blossom Time	592	* The Moon Is Blue	512
The Two Mrs. Carrolls	585	The Vagabond King	511
Detective Story	581	The New Moon	509
Brigadoon	581	Shuffle Along	504
Brother Rat	577	Up in Central Park	504
Show Boat	572	Carmen Jones	503
The Show-Off	571	The Member of the Wedding	501
Sally	570	Personal Appearance	501
One Touch of Venus	567	Panama Hattie	501
Happy Birthday	564	Bird in Hand	500
The Glass Menagerie	561	Sailor, Beware!	500
Rose Marie	557	Room Service	500
Strictly Dishonorable	557	Tomorrow the World	500
Ziegfeld Follies	553		

NEW YORK DRAMA CRITICS CIRCLE AWARDS

In their annual Spring assembly, the members of the New York Drama Critics Circle were in a generous mood (it was later when they proclaimed in a *Variety* poll that the season had been terrible). They had little trouble in voting John van Druten's "I Am a Camera" the best American play of the year, even though it had been based on an Englishman's stories. Mary Chase's "Mrs. McThing" was runner-up. An easy winner in the foreign play category was Christopher Fry's "Venus Observed." A *putsch* by some of the members swept "Pal Joey" into the best musical classification, and the critics did not seem to be chagrined when they later discovered that their constitution stipulates that awards be given only to new works. In another burst of gratitude they voted a special citation to Bernard Shaw's "Don Juan in Hell," claiming that so far as Broadway was concerned, it was a new play—or a new act, at least.

Circle awards have been—

1935-36—Winterset, by Maxwell Anderson
1936-37—High Tor, by Maxwell Anderson
1937-38—Of Mice and Men, by John Steinbeck
1938-39—No award.
1939-40—The Time of Your Life, by William Saroyan
1940-41—Watch on the Rhine, by Lillian Hellman
1941-42—No award.
1942-43—The Patriots, by Sidney Kingsley
1943-44—No award.
1944-45—The Glass Menagerie, by Tennessee Williams
1945-46—No award.
1946-47—All My Sons, by Arthur Miller
1947-48—A Streetcar Named Desire, by Tennessee Williams
1948-49—Death of a Salesman, by Arthur Miller
1949-50—The Member of the Wedding, by Carson McCullers
1950-51—Darkness at Noon, by Sidney Kingsley
1951-52—I Am a Camera, by John van Druten

PULITZER PRIZE WINNERS

The Pulitzer drama committee, which had turned in a "no award" report the previous season, gave its prize to Joseph Kramm for "The Shrike." The prize, incidentally, was back up to $1,000, after having been cut to $500 for a number of years.

Pulitzer awards have been—

1917-18—Why Marry?, by Jesse Lynch Williams
1918-19—No award.
1919-20—Beyond the Horizon, by Eugene O'Neill
1920-21—Miss Lulu Bett, by Zona Gale
1921-22—Anna Christie, by Eugene O'Neill
1922-23—Icebound, by Owen Davis
1923-24—Hell-bent fer Heaven, by Hatcher Hughes
1924-25—They Knew What They Wanted, by Sidney Howard
1925-26—Craig's Wife, by George Kelly
1926-27—In Abraham's Bosom, by Paul Green
1927-28—Strange Interlude, by Eugene O'Neill
1928-29—Street Scene, by Elmer Rice
1929-30—The Green Pastures, by Marc Connelly
1930-31—Alison's House, by Susan Glaspell
1931-32—Of Thee I Sing, by George S. Kaufman, Morrie Ryskind, Ira and George Gershwin
1932-33—Both Your Houses, by Maxwell Anderson
1933-34—Men in White, by Sidney Kingsley
1934-35—The Old Maid, by Zoë Akins
1935-36—Idiot's Delight, by Robert E. Sherwood
1936-37—You Can't Take It with You, by Moss Hart and George S. Kaufman
1937-38—Our Town, by Thornton Wilder
1938-39—Abe Lincoln in Illinois, by Robert E. Sherwood
1939-40—The Time of Your Life, by William Saroyan
1940-41—There Shall Be No Night, by Robert E. Sherwood
1941-42—No award.
1942-43—The Skin of Our Teeth, by Thornton Wilder
1943-44—No award.
1944-45—Harvey, by Mary Coyle Chase

1945-46—State of the Union, by Howard Lindsay and Russel
　　　　　Crouse
1946-47—No award.
1947-48—A Streetcar Named Desire, by Tennessee Williams
1948-49—Death of a Salesman, by Arthur Miller
1949-50—South Pacific, by Richard Rodgers, Oscar Hammerstein
　　　　　II and Joshua Logan
1950-51—No award.
1951-52—The Shrike, by Joseph Kramm

PREVIOUS VOLUMES OF BEST PLAYS

Plays chosen to represent the theatre seasons from 1899 to 1951 are as follows:

1899-1909

BARBARA FRIETCHIE, by Clyde Fitch. Life Publishing Co.
THE CLIMBERS, by Clyde Fitch. Macmillan.
IF I WERE KING, by Justin Huntly McCarthy. Samuel French.
THE DARLING OF THE GODS, by David Belasco. Little, Brown.
THE COUNTY CHAIRMAN, by George Ade. Samuel French.
LEAH KLESCHNA, by C. M. S. McLellan. Samuel French.
THE SQUAW MAN, by Edwin Milton Royle.
THE GREAT DIVIDE, by William Vaughn Moody. Samuel French.
THE WITCHING HOUR, by Augustus Thomas. Samuel French.
THE MAN FROM HOME, by Booth Tarkington and Harry Leon Wilson. Samuel French.

1909-1919

THE EASIEST WAY, by Eugene Walter. G. W. Dillingham and Houghton Mifflin.
MRS. BUMPSTEAD-LEIGH, by Harry James Smith. Samuel French.
DISRAELI, by Louis N. Parker. Dodd, Mead.
ROMANCE, by Edward Sheldon. Macmillan.
SEVEN KEYS TO BALDPATE, by George M. Cohan. Published by Bobbs-Merrill as a novel by Earl Derr Biggers; as a play by Samuel French.
ON TRIAL, by Elmer Reizenstein. Samuel French.
THE UNCHASTENED WOMAN, by Louis Kaufman Anspacher. Harcourt, Brace and Howe.
GOOD GRACIOUS ANNABELLE, by Clare Kummer. Samuel French.
WHY MARRY? by Jesse Lynch Williams. Scribner.
JOHN FERGUSON, by St. John Ervine. Macmillan.

1919-1920

ABRAHAM LINCOLN, by John Drinkwater. Houghton Mifflin.
CLARENCE, by Booth Tarkington. Samuel French.
BEYOND THE HORIZON, by Eugene G. O'Neill. Boni & Liveright.

DÉCLASSÉE, by Zoe Akins. Liveright, Inc.
THE FAMOUS MRS. FAIR, by James Forbes. Samuel French.
THE JEST, by Sem Benelli. (American adaptation by Edward Sheldon.)
JANE CLEGG, by St. John Ervine. Henry Holt.
MAMMA'S AFFAIR, by Rachel Barton Butler. Samuel French.
WEDDING BELLS, by Salisbury Field. Samuel French.
ADAM AND EVA, by George Middleton and Guy Bolton. Samuel French.

1920-1921

DEBURAU, adapted from the French of Sacha Guitry by H. Granville Barker. Putnam.
THE FIRST YEAR, by Frank Craven. Samuel French.
ENTER MADAME, by Gilda Varesi and Dolly Byrne. Putnam.
THE GREEN GODDESS, by William Archer. Knopf.
LILIOM, by Ferenc Molnar. Boni & Liveright.
MARY ROSE, by James M. Barrie. Scribner.
NICE PEOPLE, by Rachel Crothers. Scribner.
THE BAD MAN, by Porter Emerson Browne. Putnam.
THE EMPEROR JONES, by Eugene G. O'Neill. Boni & Liveright.
THE SKIN GAME, by John Galsworthy. Scribner.

1921-1922

ANNA CHRISTIE, by Eugene G. O'Neill. Boni & Liveright.
A BILL OF DIVORCEMENT, by Clemence Dane. Macmillan.
DULCY, by George S. Kaufman and Marc Connelly. Putnam.
HE WHO GETS SLAPPED, adapted from the Russian of Leonid Andreyev by Gregory Zilboorg. Brentano's.
SIX CYLINDER LOVE, by William Anthony McGuire.
THE HERO, by Gilbert Emery.
THE DOVER ROAD, by Alan Alexander Milne. Samuel French.
AMBUSH, by Arthur Richman.
THE CIRCLE, by William Somerset Maugham.
THE NEST, by Paul Geraldy and Grace George.

1922-1923

RAIN, by John Colton and Clemence Randolph. Liveright, Inc.
LOYALTIES, by John Galsworthy. Scribner.
ICEBOUND, by Owen Davis. Little, Brown.
YOU AND I, by Philip Barry. Brentano's.
THE FOOL, by Channing Pollock. Brentano's.

MERTON OF THE MOVIES, by George Kaufman and Marc Connelly, based on the novel of the same name by Harry Leon Wilson.
WHY NOT? by Jesse Lynch Williams. Walter H. Baker Co.
THE OLD SOAK, by Don Marquis. Doubleday, Page.
R.U.R., by Karel Capek. Translated by Paul Selver. Doubleday, Page.
MARY THE 3D, by Rachel Crothers. Brentano's.

1923-1924

THE SWAN, translated from the Hungarian of Ferenc Molnar by Melville Baker. Boni & Liveright.
OUTWARD BOUND, by Sutton Vane. Boni & Liveright.
THE SHOW-OFF, by George Kelly. Little, Brown.
THE CHANGELINGS, by Lee Wilson Dodd. Dutton.
CHICKEN FEED, by Guy Bolton. Samuel French.
SUN-UP, by Lula Vollmer. Brentano's.
BEGGAR ON HORSEBACK, by George Kaufman and Marc Connelly. Boni & Liveright.
TARNISH, by Gilbert Emery. Brentano's.
THE GOOSE HANGS HIGH, by Lewis Beach. Little, Brown.
HELL-BENT FER HEAVEN, by Hatcher Hughes. Harper.

1924-1925

WHAT PRICE GLORY? by Laurence Stallings and Maxwell Anderson. Harcourt, Brace.
THEY KNEW WHAT THEY WANTED, by Sidney Howard. Doubleday, Page.
DESIRE UNDER THE ELMS, by Eugene G. O'Neill. Boni & Liveright.
THE FIREBRAND, by Edwin Justus Mayer. Boni & Liveright.
DANCING MOTHERS, by Edgar Selwyn and Edmund Goulding.
MRS. PARTRIDGE PRESENTS, by Mary Kennedy and Ruth Warren. Samuel French.
THE FALL GUY, by James Gleason and George Abbott. Samuel French.
THE YOUNGEST, by Philip Barry. Samuel French.
MINICK, by Edna Ferber and George S. Kaufman. Doubleday, Page.
WILD BIRDS, by Dan Totheroh. Doubleday, Page.

1925-1926

CRAIG'S WIFE, by George Kelly. Little, Brown.
THE GREAT GOD BROWN, by Eugene G. O'Neill. Boni & Liveright.

THE GREEN HAT, by Michael Arlen.
THE DYBBUK, by S. Ansky, Henry G. Alsberg-Winifred Katzin translation. Boni & Liveright.
THE ENEMY, by Channing Pollock. Brentano's.
THE LAST OF MRS. CHEYNEY, by Frederick Lonsdale. Samuel French.
BRIDE OF THE LAMB, by William Hurlbut. Boni & Liveright.
THE WISDOM TOOTH, by Marc Connelly. George H. Doran.
THE BUTTER AND EGG MAN, by George Kaufman. Boni & Liveright.
YOUNG WOODLEY, by John Van Druten. Simon & Schuster.

1926-1927

BROADWAY, by Philip Dunning and George Abbott. George H. Doran.
SATURDAY'S CHILDREN, by Maxwell Anderson. Longmans, Green.
CHICAGO, by Maurine Watkins. Knopf.
THE CONSTANT WIFE, by William Somerset Maugham. George H. Doran.
THE PLAY'S THE THING, by Ferenc Molnar and P. G. Wodehouse. Brentano's.
THE ROAD TO ROME, by Robert Emmet Sherwood. Scribner.
THE SILVER CORD, by Sidney Howard. Scribner.
THE CRADLE SONG, translated from the Spanish of G. Martinez Sierra by John Garrett Underhill. Dutton.
DAISY MAYME, by George Kelly. Little, Brown.
IN ABRAHAM'S BOSOM, by Paul Green. McBride.

1927-1928

STRANGE INTERLUDE, by Eugene G. O'Neill. Boni & Liveright.
THE ROYAL FAMILY, by Edna Ferber and George Kaufman. Doubleday, Doran.
BURLESQUE, by George Manker Watters and Arthur Hopkins. Doubleday, Doran.
COQUETTE, by George Abbott and Ann Bridgers. Longmans, Green.
BEHOLD THE BRIDEGROOM, by George Kelly. Little, Brown.
PORGY, by DuBose Heyward. Doubleday, Doran.
PARIS BOUND, by Philip Barry. Samuel French.
ESCAPE, by John Galsworthy. Scribner.
THE RACKET, by Bartlett Cormack. Samuel French.
THE PLOUGH AND THE STARS, by Sean O'Casey. Macmillan.

1928-1929

STREET SCENE, by Elmer Rice. Samuel French.

JOURNEY'S END, by R. C. Sherriff. Brentano's.

WINGS OVER EUROPE, by Robert Nichols and Maurice Browne. Covici-Friede.

HOLIDAY, by Philip Barry. Samuel French.

THE FRONT PAGE, by Ben Hecht and Charles MacArthur. Covici-Friede.

LET US BE GAY, by Rachel Crothers. Samuel French.

MACHINAL, by Sophie Treadwell.

LITTLE ACCIDENT, by Floyd Dell and Thomas Mitchell.

GYPSY, by Maxwell Anderson.

THE KINGDOM OF GOD, by G. Martinez Sierra; English version by Helen and Harley Granville-Barker. Dutton.

1929-1930

THE GREEN PASTURES, by Marc Connelly (adapted from "Ol' Man Adam and His Chilllun," by Roark Bradford). Farrar & Rinehart.

THE CRIMINAL CODE, by Martin Flavin. Horace Liveright.

BERKELEY SQUARE, by John Balderston.

STRICTLY DISHONORABLE, by Preston Sturges. Horace Liveright.

THE FIRST MRS. FRASER, by St. John Ervine. Macmillan.

THE LAST MILE, by John Wexley. Samuel French.

JUNE MOON, by Ring W. Lardner and George S. Kaufman. Scribner.

MICHAEL AND MARY, by A. A. Milne. Chatto & Windus.

DEATH TAKES A HOLIDAY, by Walter Ferris (adapted from the Italian of Alberto Casella). Samuel French.

REBOUND, by Donald Ogden Stewart. Samuel French.

1930-1931

ELIZABETH THE QUEEN, by Maxwell Anderson. Longmans, Green.

TOMORROW AND TOMORROW, by Philip Barry. Samuel French.

ONCE IN A LIFETIME, by George S. Kaufman and Moss Hart. Farrar & Rinehart.

GREEN GROW THE LILACS, by Lynn Riggs. Samuel French.

AS HUSBANDS GO, by Rachel Crothers. Samuel French.

ALISON'S HOUSE, by Susan Glaspell. Samuel French.

FIVE-STAR FINAL, by Louis Weitzenkorn. Samuel French.

OVERTURE, by William Bolitho. Simon & Schuster.

THE BARRETTS OF WIMPOLE STREET, by Rudolf Besier.   Little, Brown.
GRAND HOTEL, adapted from the German of Vicki Baum by W. A. Drake.

1931-1932

OF THEE I SING, by George S. Kaufman and Morrie Ryskind; music and lyrics by George and Ira Gershwin.   Knopf.
MOURNING BECOMES ELECTRA, by Eugene G. O'Neill.   Horace Liveright.
REUNION IN VIENNA, by Robert Emmet Sherwood.   Scribner.
THE HOUSE OF CONNELLY, by Paul Green.   Samuel French.
THE ANIMAL KINGDOM, by Philip Barry.   Samuel French.
THE LEFT BANK, by Elmer Rice.   Samuel French.
ANOTHER LANGUAGE, by Rose Franken.   Samuel French.
BRIEF MOMENT, by S. N. Behrman.   Farrar & Rinehart.
THE DEVIL PASSES, by Benn W. Levy.   Martin Secker.
CYNARA, by H. M. Harwood and R. F. Gore-Browne.   Samuel French.

1932-1933

BOTH YOUR HOUSES, by Maxwell Anderson.   Samuel French.
DINNER AT EIGHT, by George S. Kaufman and Edna Ferber.   Doubleday, Doran.
WHEN LADIES MEET, by Rachel Crothers.   Samuel French.
DESIGN FOR LIVING, by Noel Coward.   Doubleday, Doran.
BIOGRAPHY, by S. N. Behrman.   Farrar & Rinehart.
ALIEN CORN, by Sidney Howard.   Scribner.
THE LATE CHRISTOPHER BEAN, adapted from the French of René Fauchois by Sidney Howard.   Samuel French.
WE, THE PEOPLE, by Elmer Rice.   Coward-McCann.
PIGEONS AND PEOPLE, by George M. Cohan.
ONE SUNDAY AFTERNOON, by James Hagan.   Samuel French.

1933-1934

MARY OF SCOTLAND, by Maxwell Anderson.   Doubleday, Doran.
MEN IN WHITE, by Sidney Kingsley.   Covici-Friede.
DODSWORTH, by Sinclair Lewis and Sidney Howard.   Harcourt, Brace.
AH, WILDERNESS, by Eugene O'Neill.   Random House.
THEY SHALL NOT DIE, by John Wexley.   Knopf.
HER MASTER'S VOICE, by Clare Kummer.   Samuel French.
NO MORE LADIES, by A. E. Thomas.

WEDNESDAY'S CHILD, by Leopold Atlas. Samuel French.
THE SHINING HOUR, by Keith Winter. Doubleday, Doran.
THE GREEN BAY TREE, by Mordaunt Shairp. Baker International
     Play Bureau.

1934-1935

THE CHILDREN'S HOUR, by Lillian Hellman. Knopf.
VALLEY FORGE, by Maxwell Anderson. Anderson House.
THE PETRIFIED FOREST, by Robert Sherwood. Scribner.
THE OLD MAID, by Zoe Akins. Appleton-Century.
ACCENT ON YOUTH, by Samson Raphaelson. Samuel French.
MERRILY WE ROLL ALONG, by George S. Kaufman and Moss Hart.
     Random House.
AWAKE AND SING, by Clifford Odets. Random House.
THE FARMER TAKES A WIFE, by Frank B. Elser and Marc Connelly.
LOST HORIZONS, by John Hayden.
THE DISTAFF SIDE, by John Van Druten. Knopf.

1935-1936

WINTERSET, by Maxwell Anderson. Anderson House.
IDIOT'S DELIGHT, by Robert Emmet Sherwood. Scribner.
END OF SUMMER, by S. N. Behrman. Random House.
FIRST LADY, by Katharine Dayton and George S. Kaufman. Random House.
VICTORIA REGINA, by Laurence Housman. Samuel French.
BOY MEETS GIRL, by Bella and Samuel Spewack. Random House.
DEAD END, by Sidney Kingsley. Random House.
CALL IT A DAY, by Dodie Smith. Samuel French.
ETHAN FROME, by Owen Davis and Donald Davis. Scribner.
PRIDE AND PREJUDICE, by Helen Jerome. Doubleday, Doran.

1936-1937

HIGH TOR, by Maxwell Anderson. Anderson House.
YOU CAN'T TAKE IT WITH YOU, by Moss Hart and George S. Kaufman. Farrar & Rinehart.
JOHNNY JOHNSON, by Paul Green. Samuel French.
DAUGHTERS OF ATREUS, by Robert Turney. Knopf.
STAGE DOOR, by Edna Ferber and George S. Kaufman. Doubleday, Doran.
THE WOMEN, by Clare Boothe. Random House.
ST. HELENA, by R. C. Sherriff and Jeanne de Casalis. Samuel French.

YES, MY DARLING DAUGHTER, by Mark Reed. Samuel French.
EXCURSION, by Victor Wolfson. Random House.
TOVARICH, by Jacques Deval and Robert E. Sherwood. Random House.

1937-1938

OF MICE AND MEN, by John Steinbeck. Covici-Friede.
OUR TOWN, by Thornton Wilder. Coward-McCann.
SHADOW AND SUBSTANCE, by Paul Vincent Carroll. Random House.
ON BORROWED TIME, by Paul Osborn. Knopf.
THE STAR-WAGON, by Maxwell Anderson. Anderson House.
SUSAN AND GOD, by Rachel Crothers. Random House.
PROLOGUE TO GLORY, by E. P. Conkle. Random House.
AMPHITRYON 38, by S. N. Behrman. Random House.
GOLDEN BOY, by Clifford Odets. Random House.
WHAT A LIFE, by Clifford Goldsmith. Dramatists' Play Service.

1938-1939

ABE LINCOLN IN ILLINOIS, by Robert E. Sherwood. Scribner.
THE LITTLE FOXES, by Lillian Hellman. Random House.
ROCKET TO THE MOON, by Clifford Odets. Random House.
THE AMERICAN WAY, by George S. Kaufman and Moss Hart.
    Random House.
NO TIME FOR COMEDY, by S. N. Behrman. Random House.
THE PHILADELPHIA STORY, by Philip Barry. Coward-McCann.
THE WHITE STEED, by Paul Vincent Carroll. Random House.
HERE COME THE CLOWNS, by Philip Barry. Coward-McCann.
FAMILY PORTRAIT, by Lenore Coffee and William Joyce Cowen.
    Random House.
KISS THE BOYS GOOD-BYE, by Clare Boothe. Random House.

1939-1940

THERE SHALL BE NO NIGHT, by Robert E. Sherwood. Scribner.
KEY LARGO, by Maxwell Anderson. Anderson House.
THE WORLD WE MAKE, by Sidney Kingsley.
LIFE WITH FATHER, by Howard Lindsay and Russel Crouse. Knopf.
THE MAN WHO CAME TO DINNER, by George S. Kaufman and Moss
    Hart. Random House.
THE MALE ANIMAL, by James Thurber and Elliott Nugent. Random House, New York, and MacMillan Co., Canada.
THE TIME OF YOUR LIFE, by William Saroyan. Harcourt, Brace.
SKYLARK, by Samson Raphaelson. Random House.

MARGIN FOR ERROR, by Clare Boothe. Random House.
MORNING'S AT SEVEN, by Paul Osborn. Samuel French.

1940-1941

NATIVE SON, by Paul Green and Richard Wright. Harper.
WATCH ON THE RHINE, by Lillian Hellman. Random House.
THE CORN IS GREEN, by Emlyn Williams. Random House.
LADY IN THE DARK, by Moss Hart. Random House.
ARSENIC AND OLD LACE, by Joseph Kesselring. Random House.
MY SISTER EILEEN, by Joseph Fields and Jerome Chodorov. Random House.
FLIGHT TO THE WEST, by Elmer Rice. Coward-McCann.
CLAUDIA, by Rose Franken Meloney. Farrar & Rinehart.
MR. AND MRS. NORTH, by Owen Davis. Samuel French.
GEORGE WASHINGTON SLEPT HERE, by George S. Kaufman and Moss Hart. Random House.

1941-1942

IN TIME TO COME, by Howard Koch. Dramatists' Play Service.
THE MOON IS DOWN, by John Steinbeck. Viking.
BLITHE SPIRIT, by Noel Coward. Doubleday, Doran.
JUNIOR MISS, by Jerome Chodorov and Joseph Fields. Random House.
CANDLE IN THE WIND, by Maxwell Anderson. Anderson House.
LETTERS TO LUCERNE, by Fritz Rotter and Allen Vincent. Samuel French.
JASON, by Samson Raphaelson. Random House.
ANGEL STREET, by Patrick Hamilton. Constable & Co., under the title "Gaslight."
UNCLE HARRY, by Thomas Job. Samuel French.
HOPE FOR A HARVEST, by Sophie Treadwell. Samuel French.

1942-1943

THE PATRIOTS, by Sidney Kingsley. Random House.
THE EVE OF ST. MARK, by Maxwell Anderson. Anderson House.
THE SKIN OF OUR TEETH, by Thornton Wilder. Harper.
WINTER SOLDIERS, by Dan James.
TOMORROW THE WORLD, by James Gow and Arnaud d'Usseau. Scribner.
HARRIET, by Florence Ryerson and Colin Clements. Scribner.
THE DOUGHGIRLS, by Joseph Fields. Random House.

THE DAMASK CHEEK, by John Van Druten and Lloyd Morris. Random House.

KISS AND TELL, by F. Hugh Herbert. Coward-McCann.

OKLAHOMA!, by Oscar Hammerstein 2nd and Richard Rodgers. Random House.

1943–1944

WINGED VICTORY, by Moss Hart. Random House.

THE SEARCHING WIND, by Lillian Hellman. Viking.

THE VOICE OF THE TURTLE, by John Van Druten. Random House.

DECISION, by Edward Chodorov.

OVER 21, by Ruth Gordon. Random House.

OUTRAGEOUS FORTUNE, by Rose Franken. Samuel French.

JACOBOWSKY AND THE COLONEL, by S. N. Behrman. Random House.

STORM OPERATION, by Maxwell Anderson. Anderson House.

PICK-UP GIRL, by Elsa Shelley.

THE INNOCENT VOYAGE, by Paul Osborn.

1944–1945

A BELL FOR ADANO, by Paul Osborn. Knopf.

I REMEMBER MAMA, by John Van Druten. Harcourt, Brace.

THE HASTY HEART, by John Patrick. Random House.

THE GLASS MENAGERIE, by Tennessee Williams. Random House.

HARVEY, by Mary Chase.

THE LATE GEORGE APLEY, by John P. Marquand and George S. Kaufman.

SOLDIER'S WIFE, by Rose Franken. Samuel French.

ANNA LUCASTA, by Philip Yordan. Random House.

FOOLISH NOTION, by Philip Barry.

DEAR RUTH, by Norman Krasna. Random House.

1945–1946

STATE OF THE UNION, by Howard Lindsay and Russel Crouse. Random House.

HOME OF THE BRAVE, by Arthur Laurents. Random House.

DEEP ARE THE ROOTS, by Arnaud d'Usseau and James Gow. Scribner.

THE MAGNIFICENT YANKEE, by Emmet Lavery. Samuel French.

ANTIGONE, by Lewis Galantiere (from the French of Jean Anouilh). Random House.

O MISTRESS MINE, by Terence Rattigan. Published and revised by the author.

BORN YESTERDAY, by Garson Kanin. Viking.
DREAM GIRL, by Elmer Rice. Coward-McCann.
THE RUGGED PATH, by Robert E. Sherwood. Scribner.
LUTE SONG, by Will Irwin and Sidney Howard. Published version by Will Irwin and Leopoldine Howard.

1946-1947

ALL MY SONS, by Arthur Miller. Reynal & Hitchcock.
THE ICEMAN COMETH, by Eugene G. O'Neill. Random House.
JOAN OF LORRAINE, by Maxwell Anderson. Published by Maxwell Anderson.
ANOTHER PART OF THE FOREST, by Lillian Hellman. Viking.
YEARS AGO, by Ruth Gordon. Viking.
JOHN LOVES MARY, by Norman Krasna. Copyright by Norman Krasna.
THE FATAL WEAKNESS, by George Kelly. Samuel French.
THE STORY OF MARY SURRATT, by John Patrick. Dramatists' Play Service.
CHRISTOPHER BLAKE, by Moss Hart. Random House.
BRIGADOON, by Alan Jay Lerner and Frederick Loewe. Coward-McCann.

1947-1948

A STREETCAR NAMED DESIRE, by Tennessee Williams. New Directions.
MISTER ROBERTS, by Thomas Heggen and Joshua Logan. Houghton Mifflin.
COMMAND DECISION, by William Wister Haines. Random House.
THE WINSLOW BOY, by Terence Rattigan.
THE HEIRESS, by Ruth and Augustus Goetz.
ALLEGRO, by Richard Rodgers and Oscar Hammerstein 2d. Knopf. Music published by Williamson Music, Inc.
EASTWARD IN EDEN, by Dorothy Gardner. Longmans, Green.
SKIPPER NEXT TO GOD, by Jan de Hartog.
AN INSPECTOR CALLS, by J. B. Priestley.
ME AND MOLLY, by Gertrude Berg.

1948-1949

DEATH OF A SALESMAN, by Arthur Miller. Viking.
ANNE OF THE THOUSAND DAYS, by Maxwell Anderson. Sloane.
THE MADWOMAN OF CHAILLOT, by Maurice Valency, adapted from the French of Jean Giraudoux. Random House.
DETECTIVE STORY, by Sidney Kingsley. Random House.

EDWARD, MY SON, by Robert Morley and Noel Langley. Random House, New York, and Samuel French, London.

LIFE WITH MOTHER, by Howard Lindsay and Russel Crouse. Knopf.

LIGHT UP THE SKY, by Moss Hart. Random House.

THE SILVER WHISTLE, by Robert Edward McEnroe. Dramatists' Play Service.

TWO BLIND MICE, by Samuel Spewack. Dramatists' Play Service.

GOODBYE, MY FANCY, by Fay Kanin. Samuel French.

1949-1950

THE COCKTAIL PARTY, by T. S. Eliot. Harcourt, Brace.

THE MEMBER OF THE WEDDING, by Carson McCullers. Houghton Mifflin.

THE INNOCENTS, by William Archibald. Coward-McCann.

LOST IN THE STARS, by Maxwell Anderson and Kurt Weill. Sloane.

COME BACK, LITTLE SHEBA, by William Inge. Random House.

THE HAPPY TIME, by Samuel Taylor. Random House.

THE WISTERIA TREES, by Joshua Logan. Random House.

I KNOW MY LOVE, by S. N. Behrman. Random House.

THE ENCHANTED, by Maurice Valency, adapted from a play by Jean Giraudoux. Random House.

CLUTTERBUCK, by Benn W. Levy. Dramatists' Play Service.

1950-1951

GUYS AND DOLLS, by Jo Swerling, Abe Burrows and Frank Loesser.

DARKNESS AT NOON, by Sidney Kingsley and Arthur Koestler. Random House.

BILLY BUDD, by Louis O. Coxe and Robert Chapman. Princeton University Press.

THE AUTUMN GARDEN, by Lillian Hellman. Little, Brown & Co.

BELL, BOOK AND CANDLE, by John van Druten. Random House.

THE COUNTRY GIRL, by Clifford Odets. Viking Press.

THE ROSE TATTOO, by Tennessee Williams. New Directions.

SEASON IN THE SUN, by Wolcott Gibbs. Random House.

AFFAIRS OF STATE, by Louis Verneuil.

SECOND THRESHOLD, by Philip Barry. Harper & Bros.

WHERE AND WHEN THEY WERE BORN

(Compiled from the most authentic records available)

Abbott, George	Forestville, N. Y.	1889
Abel, Walter	St. Paul, Minn.	1898
Adams, Maude	Salt Lake City, Utah	1872
Addy, Wesley	Omaha, Neb.	1912
Aherne, Brian	King's Norton, England	1902
Aldrich, Richard	Boston	1902
Anders, Glenn	Los Angeles, Cal.	1890
Anderson, Judith	Australia	1898
Anderson, Maxwell	Atlantic City, Pa.	1888
Arthur, Jean	New York City	1905
Ashcroft, Peggy	Croydon, England	1907
Bainter, Fay	Los Angeles, Cal.	1892
Bankhead, Tallulah	Huntsville, Ala.	1902
Barrymore, Ethel	Philadelphia, Pa.	1879
Barrymore, Lionel	Philadelphia, Pa.	1878
Barton, James	Gloucester, N. J.	1890
Behrman, S. N.	Worcester, Mass.	1893
Bellamy, Ralph	Chicago, Ill.	1904
Belmore, Bertha	Manchester, England	1882
Bergman, Ingrid	Stockholm	1917
Bergner, Elisabeth	Vienna	1900
Berlin, Irving	Russia	1888
Blackmer, Sidney	Salisbury, N. C.	1898
Bolger, Ray	Dorchester, Mass.	1904
Bondi, Beulah	Chicago, Ill.	1892
Bourneuf, Philip	Boston, Mass.	1912
Boyer, Charles	Figeac, France	1899
Braham, Horace	London, England	1896
Brent, Romney	Saltillo, Mex.	1902
Brown, Joe E.	Holgate, Ohio	1892
Burke, Billie	Washington, D. C.	1885
Byington, Spring	Colorado Springs, Colo.	1898

353

Cagney, James .... New York 1904
Cagney, Jeanne .... New York 1920
Calhern, Louis .... New York 1895
Cantor, Eddie .... New York 1892
Carnovsky, Morris .... St. Louis, Mo. 1898
Carradine, John .... New York City 1906
Carroll, Leo G. .... Weedon, England 1892
Carroll, Madeleine .... West Bromwich, England 1906
Caulfield, Joan .... New York City 1924
Chase, Ilka .... New York City 1905
Chatterton, Ruth .... New York 1893
Claire, Ina .... Washington, D. C. 1895
Clark, Bobby .... Springfield, Ohio 1888
Clift, Montgomery .... Omaha, Neb. 1921
Clive, Colin .... St. Malo, France 1900
Coburn, Charles .... Macon, Ga. 1877
Collinge, Patricia .... Dublin 1894
Collins, Russell .... New Orleans, La. 1897
Colt, Ethel Barrymore ..... Mamaroneck, N. Y. 1911
Colt, John Drew .... New York 1914
Conroy, Frank .... London, England 1885
Cook, Donald .... Portland, Ore. 1902
Cook, Joe .... Evansville, Ind. 1890
Cooper, Melville .... Birmingham, England 1896
Corbett, Leonora .... London, England 1908
Cornell, Katharine .... Berlin, Germany 1898
Coulouris, George .... Manchester, England 1906
Coward, Noel .... Teddington, England 1899
Cronyn, Hume .... London, Ontario 1912
Crothers, Rachel .... Bloomington, Ill. 1878
Crouse, Russel .... Findlay, Ohio 1893
Cummings, Constance ...... Seattle, Wash. 1911

Dale, Margaret .... Philadelphia, Pa. 1880
Dana, Leora .... New York City 1923
Daniell, Henry .... London 1894
Davis, Owen .... Portland, Me. 1874
Derwent, Clarence .... London 1884
Dixon, Jean .... Waterbury, Conn. 1905
Douglas, Melvyn .... Macon, Ga. 1901
Douglas, Susan .... Prague, Czechoslovakia 1925
Dowling, Eddie .... Woonsocket, R. I. 1894
Drake, Alfred .... New York City 1914

Dressler, Eric .... Brooklyn, N. Y. 1900
Duncan, Todd .... Danville, Ky. 1900
Dunning, Philip .... Meriden, Conn. 1890
Durante, Jimmy .... New York City 1893

Eldridge, Florence .... Brooklyn, N. Y. 1901
Evans, Edith .... London, England 1888
Evans, Maurice .... Dorchester, England 1901
Evans, Wilbur .... Philadelphia, Pa. 1908
Evelyn, Judith .... Seneca, S. Dak. 1913
Ewell, Tom .... Owensboro, Ky. 1912

Fabray, Nanette .... New Orleans, La. 1921
Fay, Frank .... San Francisco 1897
Ferber, Edna .... Kalamazoo, Mich. 1887
Ferrer, José .... Puerto Rico 1912
Field, Betty .... Boston 1918
Field, Virginia .... London 1917
Fields, Gracie .... Rochdale, England 1898
Fitzgerald, Barry .... Dublin, Ireland 1888
Fitzgerald, Geraldine ...... Dublin, Ireland 1914
Flemyng, Robert .... Liverpool 1912
Fletcher, Bramwell .... Bradford, Yorkshire, Eng. 1904
Fonda, Henry .... Grand Island, Neb. 1905
Fontanne, Lynn .... London, England 1887
Forbes, Brenda .... London, England 1909
Foy, Eddie, Jr. .... New Rochelle, N. Y. 1907
Francis, Arlene .... Boston, Mass. 1908

Gahagan, Helen .... Boonton, N. J. 1900
Gaxton, William .... San Francisco, Cal. 1893
Geddes, Barbara Bel .... New York 1922
Geddes, Norman Bel .... Adrian, Mich. 1893
George, Grace .... New York City 1879
Gershwin, Ira .... New York 1896
Gielgud, John .... London, England 1904
Gillmore, Margalo .... England 1901
Gilmore, Virginia .... El Monte, Cal. 1919
Gish, Dorothy .... Massillon, Ohio 1898
Gish, Lillian .... Springfield, Ohio 1896
Golden, John .... New York 1874
Goodner, Carol .... New York City 1904
Gordon, Ruth .... Wollaston, Mass. 1896

Gough, Lloyd ....New York City 1906
Greaza, Walter ....St. Paul, Minn. 1900
Green, Mitzi ....New York City 1920
Greenstreet, Sydney ....England 1880
Guinness, Alec ....London 1914
Gwenn, Edmund ....Glamorgan, Wales 1875

Hagen, Uta ....Göttingen, Germany 1919
Hammerstein, Oscar, II .....New York City 1895
Hampden, Walter ....Brooklyn, N. Y. 1879
Hannen, Nicholas ....London, England 1881
Hardie, Russell ....Griffin Mills, N. Y. 1906
Hardwicke, Sir Cedric .....Lye, Stourbridge, England 1893
Harris, Julie ....Grosse Point, Mich. 1925
Hart, Moss ....New York City 1904
Hart, Richard ....Providence, R. I. 1915
Havoc, June ....Seattle, Wash. 1916
Haydon, Julie ....Oak Park, Ill. 1910
Hayes, Helen ....Washington, D. C. 1900
Hayward, Leland ....Nebraska City, Neb. 1902
Heflin, Frances ....Oklahoma City, Okla. 1924
Heineman, Eda ....Japan 1891
Helpmann, Robert ....South Australia 1911
Henie, Sonja ....Oslo, Norway 1913
Hepburn, Audrey ....Brussels 1919
Hepburn, Katharine ....Hartford, Conn. 1909
Hiller, Wendy ....Bramhall, England 1912
Holliday, Judy ....New York City 1924
Holm, Celeste ....New York City 1919
Homolka, Oscar ....Vienna 1898
Hull, Josephine ....Newtonville, Mass. 1886
Hull, Henry ....Louisville, Ky. 1890
Hunt, Martita ....Argentine Republic 1900
Hussey, Ruth ....Providence, R. I. 1917

Inescort, Frieda ....Hitchin, Scotland 1901
Ives, Burl ....Hunt Township, Ill. 1909

Johnson, Harold J. (Chic) ...Chicago, Ill. 1891
Joy, Nicholas ....Paris, France 1889

Kane, Whitford ....Larne, Ireland 1882
Kanin, Garson ....Rochester, N. Y. 1912

Karloff, Boris .... Dulwich, England 1887
Kaufman, George S. .... Pittsburgh, Pa. 1889
Kaye, Danny .... New York City 1914
Kazan, Elia .... Constantinople 1909
Keith, Robert .... Fowler, Ind. 1898
Kilbride, Percy .... San Francisco, Cal. 1880
King, Dennis .... Coventry, England 1897
Kingsford, Walter .... England 1881
Kingsley, Sidney .... New York City 1906
Kirkland, Patricia .... New York 1927
Knox, Alexander .... Ontario 1907
Kruger, Otto .... Toledo, Ohio 1885

Lackland, Ben .... Waco, Texas 1901
Lahr, Bert .... New York City 1895
Landis, Jessie Royce .... Chicago, Ill. 1904
Laughton, Charles .... Scarborough, England 1899
Lawrence, Gertrude .... London 1898
LeGallienne, Eva .... London 1899
Leigh, Vivien .... Darjeeling, India 1913
Leighton, Margaret .... Barnt Green, England 1922
Lillie, Beatrice .... Toronto, Canada 1898
Lindsay, Howard .... Waterford, N. Y. 1899
Linn, Bambi .... Brooklyn, N. Y. 1926
Lockhart, Gene .... Ontario 1892
Loeb, Philip .... Philadelphia, Pa. 1892
Lonergan, Lenore .... Toledo, Ohio 1928
Lord, Pauline .... Hanford, Cal. 1890
Lukas, Paul .... Budapest, Hungary 1891
Lunt, Alfred .... Milwaukee, Wis. 1893
Lytell, Bert .... New York City 1885

MacMahon, Aline .... McKeesport, Pa. 1899
Mamoulian, Rouben .... Tiflis 1898
Mantle, Burns .... Watertown, N. Y. 1873
March, Fredric .... Racine, Wis. 1897
Martin, Mary .... Weatherford, Texas 1913
Mason, James .... Huddersfield, England 1909
Massey, Raymond .... Toronto, Canada 1896
Matteson, Ruth .... San Jose, Cal. 1905
McClintic, Guthrie .... Seattle, Wash. 1893
McCormick, Myron .... Albany, Ind. 1907
McCracken, Joan .... Philadelphia, Pa. 1923

McGrath, Paul .... Chicago, Ill. 1900
McGuire, Dorothy .... Omaha, Neb. 1918
Menotti, Gian-Carlo .... Italy 1912
Meredith, Burgess .... Cleveland, Ohio 1908
Merman, Ethel .... Astoria, L. I. 1909
Middleton, Ray .... Chicago, Ill. 1907
Miller, Gilbert .... New York 1884
Mitchell, Thomas .... Elizabeth, N. J. 1892
Moore, Victor .... Hammonton, N. J. 1876
Moorehead, Agnes .... Clinton, Mass. 1906
Morgan, Claudia .... New York 1912
Morley, Robert .... Semley, England 1908
Moss, Arnold .... Brooklyn, N. Y. 1910
Muni, Paul .... Lemberg, Austria 1895

Nagel, Conrad .... Keokuk, Iowa 1897
Natwick, Mildred .... Baltimore 1908
Nesbitt, Cathleen .... Cheshire, England 1889
Nugent, Elliott .... Dover, Ohio 1900

Odets, Clifford .... Philadelphia 1906
Oenslager, Donald .... Harrisburg, Pa. 1902
Olivier, Sir Laurence .... Dorking, Surrey, England 1907
Olsen, John Siguard (Ole) ... Peru, Ind. 1892
O'Malley, Rex .... London, England 1906
O'Neal, Frederick .... Brookville, Miss. 1905
O'Neill, Eugene Gladstone ... New York 1888

Petina, Irra .... Leningrad, Russia 1900
Picon, Molly .... New York City 1898
Pinza, Ezio .... Rome, Italy 1895
Porter, Cole .... Peru, Indiana 1892
Price, Vincent .... St. Louis, Mo. 1914

Raitt, John .... Santa Ana, Cal. 1917
Rathbone, Basil .... Johannesburg 1892
Redman, Joyce .... Newcastle, Ireland 1918
Reed, Florence .... Philadelphia, Pa. 1883
Rennie, James .... Toronto, Canada 1890
Richardson, Sir Ralph ...... Cheltenham, England 1902
Rice, Elmer .... New York City 1892
Roberts, Joan .... New York City 1918
Rodgers, Richard .... New York City 1902

NECROLOGY

June 1, 1951—May 31, 1952

Allen, Kelcey (born Eugene Kuttner), 75, critic. Joined drama department of *Women's Wear Daily* in 1915; attended more than 6,500 first nights. For 20 years prior to joining *Women's Wear* was on staff of the New York *Clipper*. He re-named himself after two players he admired, Herbert Kelcey and Viola Allen. Born Brooklyn; died New York, July 23, 1951.

Banks, Leslie, 61, actor. Made stage début in England in 1911; made New York début in 1914 in "Eliza Comes to Stay"; returned in 1924 as Captain Hook in "Peter Pan"; had a New York success in "Springtime for Henry." Born near Liverpool; died London, April 21, 1952.

Boreo, Emile, 65, actor. Was brought from France by Morris Gest with "Chauve Souris," in which he introduced "The Parade of the Wooden Soldiers"; became a vaudeville and night club star; in 1940 appeared in "The Fifth Column." Born Poland; died New York, July 27, 1951.

Briggs, Harlan, 72, actor. Made stage début as a baby with mother, Clara Miller, in "East Lynne." Began as concert singer, went into operettas and comedies. Had long career as character man in plays and films; was in "The Big Pond," "It's a Wise Child," "Dodsworth" and "Ramshackle Inn." Born Blissfield, Michigan; died Hollywood, January 26, 1952.

Broadhurst, George Howells, 85, playwright. Worked as theatre manager in Milwaukee, Baltimore and San Francisco; wrote "What Happened to Jones," "The American Lord," "The Coward," "A Fool and His Money," "Bought and Paid For" and many other successes. Born Walsall, England; died Santa Barbara, California, January 31, 1952.

Bromberg, J. Edward, 47, actor. Began as silk salesman, candy manufacturer and laundry worker; studied acting under Leo Bulgakov and made début at Provincetown Theatre (N. Y.) in "Princess Turandot"; spent four years in Eva LeGallienne's Civic Repertory Theatre; was a leading actor with the Group Theatre beginning 1931, playing in "The House of Connelly,"

"Men in White," "Awake and Sing" and other dramas; also was in many films. Born Temesvar, Hungary; died London, December 6, 1951.

Christians, Mady, 51, actress. Came to New York in 1912 with her father, who managed a German company at the Irving Place Theatre; studied in Germany under Reinhardt and toured with him five years; was in Maurice Evans' "Hamlet" in 1938, and in "Watch on the Rhine"; had greatest success in "I Remember Mama." Born Vienna; died Norwalk, Connecticut, October 28, 1951.

Cooper, Ashley, 70, actor. Played with the Duncan sisters in "Topsy and Eva" and with William Faversham in "The Squaw Man"; was in "Tobacco Road," "Broadway," "Arsenic and Old Lace" and other plays. Born Australia; died New York, January 3, 1952.

De Basil, Wassily, age unrecorded, ballet impresario. Had distinguished military career in Russian army; became manager of Vladimir Horowitz, pianist; toured Russian Opera Company with Chaliapin as star; fled Bolshevist uprising; organized ballet company in Switzerland in 1920; organized Ballet Russe de Monte Carlo in 1932 and brought it to New York in 1933. Born Russia; died Paris, July 27, 1951.

Emery, Edwin, 78, actor. Began career in 1893; appeared with E. H. Sothern and Maude Adams; was member of the Alcazar Theatre Company in San Francisco. Born Philadelphia; died New York, June 26, 1951.

Epstein, Philip G., 42, screenwriter and playwright. Wrote "And Stars Remain" for the Theatre Guild; with his twin brother, Julius, wrote numerous scenarios, including "Casablanca," "Gift of Gab" and the screen treatments of "The Man Who Came to Dinner" and "Arsenic and Old Lace." Born New York; died Hollywood, February 7, 1952.

Errol, Leon, 70, actor. Made New York début in 1911 in his own musical, "The Lilies"; was in several Ziegfeld "Follies" and "Sally"; made many motion picture comedies. Born Sydney, Australia; died Hollywood, October 12, 1951.

Fischer, Clifford C., 69, producer. Produced a series of "Folies" and "Folies Bergère" in New York, London and elsewhere; as an agent was instrumental in the American careers of Sir Harry Lauder, Maurice Chevalier, Charles Boyer, Charles Chaplin and others. Born Belgium; died Westwood, New Jersey, October 11, 1951.

Fox, Stuart, 57, actor. Began acting career in Cleveland, made New York début with William Gillette in "Secret Service"; played in "Claudia," "Another Love Story" and other plays; was assistant director for John Golden, David Belasco and the Shuberts. Born Cleveland; died New York, June 17, 1951.

Garfield, John (born Jules Garfinkel), 39, actor. As a youth was an amateur boxer; gained stage experience with Eva LeGallienne's Civic Repertory Theatre; made sudden success as the fighter in "Golden Boy" in 1937; thereafter played many tough-guy roles on stage and screen; was in "Waiting for Lefty," "Lost Boy," "Counsellor-at-Law," "Having Wonderful Time" and "Awake and Sing"; last New York appearances were in "Peer Gynt" and a revival of "Golden Boy." Born New York; died New York, May 21, 1952.

Garrett, Oliver H. P., 54, playwright and scenarist. In 1935 wrote one of the first anti-Nazi dramas, "Waltz in Goose Step," which was produced in 1938; with his wife, Charlcie Hedge Garrett, wrote "Sleep, My Pretty One," in 1944; wrote screenplays including "A Farewell to Arms" and "Duel in the Sun." Born New Bedford, Massachusetts; died New York, February 23, 1952.

Gould, Harold, 78, actor. Began as amateur actor with Riverside Comedy Club, which he helped found in 1894; joined Amateur Comedy Club in 1906 and played fifty-seven parts there; professional appearances included "The Perfect Marriage," the Players' revival of "Uncle Tom's Cabin"; "John Brown," "Othello" and "Arsenic and Old Lace." Born New York; died New York, July 17, 1952.

Gow, James, 44, playwright. Beginning in 1928, worked in the drama and motion picture departments of the New York *World;* with Arnaud d'Usseau wrote "Tomorrow the World," "Deep Are the Roots" and "Legend of Sarah." Born Creston, Iowa; died New York, February 11, 1952.

Harvey, Georgette, 69, actress. Began with a singing quartet called the Creole Belles; became a night club star in St. Petersburg and after the revolution fled to and acted in Japan; in New York appeared in "Solid South," "Five Star Final," "Mamba's Daughters" and other plays. Born St. Louis; died New York, February 17, 1952.

Hoffe, Monckton, 70, playwright. Wrote many plays for London and Broadway production, including "The Little Damozel," "The Faithful Heart" and "Many Waters." Born Connemara, Ireland; died London, November 4, 1951.

Hoier, Thomas P., 74, actor. Made début in 1898 with barnstorm-
ing repertory company; played in operetta, vaudeville and the
drama; acted most recently in "Story for Strangers" and "Suds
in Your Eye"; wrote a best-selling song, "Don't Bite the Hand
That's Feeding You." Born Denmark; died New York, December 20, 1951.

Hupfeld, Herman, 57, songwriter. Was accompanist for Irene
Castle; played own songs at Ziegfeld's "Midnight Frolic" on
New Amsterdam Roof; wrote for various editions of "The Little
Show"; his song hits included "As Time Goes By," "When
Yuba Plays the Rumba on His Tuba," "Let's Put Out the
Lights and Go to Sleep" and "Sing Something Simple." Born
Montclair, New Jersey; died Montclair, June 8, 1951.

Irvine, Harry, age unrecorded, actor. Made professional stage début
in London in 1905 with Sir Herbert Beerbohm Tree's company;
was in Max Reinhardt's London production of "The Miracle";
came to America in 1915 with Forbes-Robertson; directed stock
for Jessie Bonstelle; was with Walter Hampden's company four
years; played so many clerical roles became known as the
Bishop of Broadway; recent plays included "Anne of the Thousand Days," "Arsenic and Old Lace," "Life with Father," "Murder in the Cathedral." Born British India; died Nyack, New
York, August 7, 1951.

Jouvet, Louis, 63, actor. One of the leading actors of France; well
known in America through his film roles; in 1951 brought his
Théâtre de l'Athénée company to New York in "L'École des
Femmes." Born Brittany; died Paris, August 16, 1951.

Lee, Canada (real name, Lionel Canegata), 45, actor. Began career
as a child violinist; at 15 became a jockey; then turned to box-
ing and became a successful pro; made stage début in Federal
Theatre Project production, "Brother Mose." Had stage tri-
umphs in "Native Son" and "Othello," and played Caliban in
white-face in "The Tempest." Was in a number of films, including "Cry, the Beloved Country." Born New York; died
New York, May 9, 1952.

Leffler, George, 77, producer and booking manager. Started in box
office of old Casino Theatre; was manager for Della Fox and
booking manager for A. H. Woods and A. L. Erlanger. Born
New York; died New York, August 5, 1951.

Lister, Francis, 52, actor. Son of an actor of the same name; came
to New York in 1923 to support Mrs. Fiske in "Mary, Mary,
Quite Contrary"; returned in 1930 as Katharine Cornell's leading man in "Dishonored Lady"; last New York appearance in

1935 in "Substitute for Murder." Born London; died London, October 28, 1951.

Lynn, William H., 63, actor. Began as a singer and dancer in "Jumping Jupiter," then went into vaudeville doing "character songs and dances"; had his greatest stage success as Erwin in "Three Men on a Horse"; last appeared in a revival of "Twentieth Century." Born Providence, Rhode Island; died New York, January 5, 1952.

Margetson, Arthur, 54, actor. Made New York début in "Passing Show of 1922"; London début in 1917 in "Theodore and Co."; was in "Life with Father" for a year, and in "Clutterbuck." Born London; died London, August 13, 1951.

Martin, Townsend, 55, writer. Wrote "A Most Immoral Lady," a success starring Alice Brady, and film scenarios for Gloria Swanson, Richard Dix, Thomas Meighan and others. Born New York; died New York, November 22, 1951.

Methot, Mayo, 47, actress. Began as child actress with Baker Stock Company in Portland, Ore.; scored New York hit in 1923 with George M. Cohan in "The Song and Dance Man"; had one of her greatest successes in "Torch Song," and another singing "More Than You Know" in Vincent Youmans' "Great Day"; was an ex-wife of Humphrey Bogart. Born Portland; died Portland, June 9, 1951.

Molnar, Ferenc, 74, playwright. His first play, "Der Doktor," was written in 1902; afterward he wrote at least forty-one other plays, among the most successful of which were "The Guardsman," "The Good Fairy," "Liliom" and "The Play's the Thing." Born Budapest; died New York, April 1, 1952.

Oursler, Fulton, 59, playwright, novelist and editor. Was an editor of *Reader's Digest;* wrote "The Greatest Story Ever Told" and other works on religious subjects; for the theatre wrote, in collaboration with others, "The Spider," "Sandalwood," "Behold This Dreamer," "The Walking Gentleman" and other plays. Born Baltimore; died New York, May 24, 1952.

Physioc, Joseph Allen, 86, scenic artist. Designed sets for first Shaw play produced in America, "Arms and the Man," for Richard Mansfield; did sets for "Peg o' My Heart," "Lightnin'," "Bird of Paradise," "Seventh Heaven" and many other plays. Born Richmond, Virginia; died Columbia, South Carolina, August 3, 1951.

Pitoëff, Ludmilla, 51, actress. Noted in Paris for her roles in Ibsen, Chekhov and Shaw; appeared in New York in 1942 in "L'Annonce Faite à Marie" and in 1944 in "The House in Paris." Born Tiflis, Russia; died Paris, September 15, 1951.

Riggs, Ralph, 62, actor and dancer. Made début as baby in "Uncle Tom's Cabin"; appeared in ballet, opera and grand opera; with his father's traveling stock company played "Little Lord Fauntleroy"; was the Chief Justice in "Of Thee I Sing." Birthplace unrecorded; died New York, September 16, 1951.

Robinson-Duff, Frances, 74, actress and dramatic teacher. Her pupils included Mary Garden, Ina Claire, Henry Miller, Katharine Hepburn, Helen Hayes, Norma Shearer, Lillian and Dorothy Gish, Fay Bainter, Clark Gable and Mary Pickford. Born Blue Hill, Maine; died New York, October 30, 1951.

Romberg, Sigmund, 64, composer. Wrote the scores of seventy-eight musicals, including "The Student Prince," "The Desert Song," "New Moon" and "Blossom Time"; was a pioneer in the American Society of Composers, Authors and Publishers, and an authority on music copyrights. Born Nagykanizsa, Hungary; died New York, November 9, 1951.

Rothier, Léon, 76, opera singer and actor. A leading basso with the Metropolitan Opera from 1910 to 1941; made his stage début in 1944 as a priest in "A Bell for Adano"; sang the role of Mephisto in "Faust" more than 500 times. Born Rheims; died New York, December 6, 1951.

Sheahan, John J., 66, actor. Began in a Shakespeare company in San Francisco in 1906; made New York début in 1909 with Chauncey Olcott in "Ragged Robin"; appeared in "Good News," "Follow Thru" and other musicals, and played many comedy roles in films. Born Oakland, California; died Hollywood, February 15, 1952.

Shepley, Ruth, 59, actress. Made stage début in "All for a Girl" in 1908; was in "It Pays to Advertise"; had great success in "The Boomerang"; last New York appearance in 1936 in "Dear Old Darling." Born Providence, Rhode Island; died New York, October 16, 1951.

Simpson, Ivan, 76, actor. Came to New York in 1905; acted for Charles Frohman; won success with George Arliss in "The Green Goddess"; was in "The Male Animal," with Cedric Hardwicke in "Caesar and Cleopatra," and many films. Born Hargate, England; died New York, October 12, 1951.

Sinclair, Arthur, 68, actor. Among the most prominent of Dublin's Abbey Theatre actors; had great success in "Juno and the Paycock"; made New York début in 1911 in "The Rising of the Moon"; followed in "The Playboy of the Western World"; last

New York appearance in "Jumbo" in 1931. Born Dublin; died Belfast, December 14, 1951.

Smith, Robert B., 76, librettist and songwriter. Was brother of the late Harry B. Smith. Wrote "Twirly Whirly" for Weber and Fields in 1902, in which Lillian Russell sang "Come Down, My Evening Star"; collaborated with brother on several Victor Herbert operettas, including "Sweethearts." Born Chicago; died New York, November 6, 1951.

Stevens, Ashton, 78, critic. Began theatre reporting on the San Francisco *News Letter* in 1894; in 1907 joined New York *Evening Journal;* in 1910 went to the Chicago *Examiner;* was on the staff of the Chicago *Herald-American* until he died. Born San Francisco; died Chicago, July 12, 1951.

Tilden, Milano C., 73, actor. Played with Mansfield, Sothern and Marlowe and Guy Bates Post; later acted in "June Moon," "Call Me Ziggy" and other plays. Born Paris; died Grant City, Staten Island, September 30, 1951.

Van Allstyne, E. A., 73, songwriter. Wrote music for more than 700 songs, including "In the Shade of the Old Apple Tree," "Memories," "Pony Boy" and "That Old Girl of Mine." Born Marengo, Illinois; died Chicago, July 9, 1951.

Ward, Fannie, 79, actress. Made début at the Broadway Theatre in 1890 as Cupid in "Pippino"; this was the beginning of a long career in comedy, vaudeville and silent films. Born St. Louis; died New York, January 27, 1952.

Warfield, David, 84, actor. Began as usher in San Francisco; had first speaking role in Napa, California, in 1888 in "The Ticket of Leave Man"; made New York début in 1890 in a monologue at a concert hall; his first big hit was in "The Auctioneer" in 1901; in 1904 came one of his greatest roles in "The Music Master," which he played 1,007 times; in 1911 appeared in "The Return of Peter Grimm"; in 1922 began three years of acting Shylock in "The Merchant of Venice." Born San Francisco; died New York, June 27, 1951.

Weber, Mrs. Joe (Lillian Friedman), 76, actress. Married Joe Weber in 1897 and toured for many years with the team of Weber & Fields. Died New York, November 10, 1951.

Wenrich, Percy, 72, composer. With his wife, Dorothy Connolly, had a vaudeville song-and-dance act for fifteen years; co-authored the musicals "Castle in the Air" and "The Right Girl"; was a founder of ASCAP; his song hits included "Put on Your Old Gray Bonnet" and "When You Wore a Tulip and I Wore a

Big Red Rose." Born Joplin, Missouri; died New York, March 7, 1952.

Wilstach, Paul, 81, dramatist. For nine years beginning in 1898 was play reader for Richard Mansfield; wrote a biography of Mansfield in 1908; wrote "A Capitol Comedy," "The Poor Rich" and several other plays between 1898 and 1914. Born Lafayette, Indiana; died Washington, D. C., February 9, 1952.

THE DECADES' TOLL

(Prominent Theatrical Figures Who Have Died
in Recent Years)

	Born	Died
Arliss, George	1869	1946
Baker, George Pierce	1866	1935
Barrymore, John	1882	1942
Bates, Blanche	1873	1941
Belasco, David	1856	1931
Bennett, Richard	1873	1944
Carroll, Earl	1893	1948
Carte, Rupert D'Oyly	1876	1948
Christians, Mady	1900	1951
Cochran, Charles B.	1872	1951
Cohan, George M.	1878	1942
Collier, Willie	1866	1943
Cowl, Jane	1884	1950
Craven, Frank	1890	1945
Crews, Laura Hope	1880	1942
Crosman, Henrietta	1865	1944
Digges, Dudley	1879	1947
Elliott, Maxine	1871	1940
Errol, Leon	1881	1951
Eltinge, Julian	1883	1941
Faversham, William	1868	1940
Fields, Lew	1867	1941
Fields, W. C.	1879	1946
Fiske, Harrison Grey	1861	1942
Frohman, Daniel	1851	1940
Garfield, John	1913	1952
Gaige, Crosby	1883	1949
Gershwin, George	1898	1937
Gest, Morris	1881	1941
Hart, Lorenz	1895	1943
Hart, William S.	1870	1946
Hooker, Brian	1881	1947
Howard, Willie	1883	1949

	Born	*Died*
Jolson, Al.	1886	1950
Jouvet, Louis	1887	1951
Kern, Jerome D.	1885	1945
Lehar, Franz	1870	1948
Leonard, Eddie	1871	1941
Loftus, Cecilia	1876	1943
Lord, Pauline	1890	1950
Mantle, Burns	1873	1948
Marlowe, Julia	1866	1950
Merivale, Philip	1886	1946
Molnar, Ferenc	1878	1952
Moore, Grace	1901	1947
Morgan, Helen	1900	1941
Nazimova, Alla	1879	1945
Nethersole, Olga	1870	1951
Patterson, Joseph Medill	1879	1946
Perry, Antoinette	1888	1946
Powers, James T.	1862	1943
Reinhardt, Max	1873	1943
Romberg, Sigmund	1887	1951
Royle, Edwin Milton	1862	1941
Selwyn, Edgar	1875	1944
Shaw, G. B.	1856	1950
Sheldon, Edward	1886	1946
Skinner, Otis	1858	1942
Tarkington, Booth	1869	1946
Tauber, Richard	1890	1948
Tyler, George C.	1867	1946
Ward, Fannie	1872	1952
Warfield, David	1866	1951
Weber, Joe	1867	1942
Webster, Ben	1864	1947
Whitty, Dame May	1865	1948
Woods, Al H.	1870	1951
Woollcott, Alexander	1887	1943
Youmans, Vincent	1899	1946

INDICES

INDEX OF AUTHORS

INDEX OF PLAYS AND CASTS

Bold face page numbers refer to pages on which Cast of Characters may be found.

377

INDEX OF PRODUCERS, DIRECTORS AND DESIGNERS

DATE DUE